Primary Source Reader for World History

Volume II: Since 1500

ELSA A. NYSTROM
Kennesaw State University

THOMSON

WADSWORTH

Australia • Canada • Mexico • Brazil • Singapore • Spain
United Kingdom • United States

THOMSON
™
WADSWORTH

Primary Source Reader for World History
Volume II: Since 1500

Elsa A. Nystrom

Publisher: *Clark Baxter*
Assistant Editor: *Paul Massicotte*
Editorial Assistant: *Lucinda Bingham*
Technology Project Manager: *David Lionetti*
Marketing Manager: *Lori Grebe Cook*
Marketing Assistant: *Teresa Jessen*
Project Manager, Editorial Production: *Katy German*
Art Director: *Maria Epes*

Print Buyer: *Lisa Claudeanos*
Permissions Editor: *Sarah Harkrader*
Production Service: *Cadmus*
Copy Editor: *Megan A. Costello*
Cover Designer: *Laurie Anderson*
Cover Image: *Erich Lessing/Art Resource, NY*
Cover Printer: *Transcontinental Printing/Interglobe*
Printer: *Transcontinental Printing/Louiseville*

Printed in Canada
1 2 3 4 5 6 7 09 08 07 06 05

For more information about our products, contact us at:
Thomson Learning Academic Resource Center
1-800-423-0563

For permission to use material from this text or product, submit a request online at
http://www.thomsonrights.com.

Any additional questions about permissions can be submitted by email to
thomsonrights@thomson.com.

Library of Congress Control Number: 2005927657

ISBN 0-495-00610-6

Thomson Higher Education
10 Davis Drive
Belmont, CA 94002-3098
USA

Asia (including India)
Thomson Learning
5 Shenton Way
#01-01 UIC Building
Singapore 068808

Australia/New Zealand
Thomson Learning Australia
102 Dodds Street
Southbank, Victoria 3006
Australia

Canada
Thomson Nelson
1120 Birchmount Road
Toronto, Ontario M1K 5G4
Canada

UK/Europe/Middle East/Africa
Thomson Learning
High Holborn House
50–51 Bedford Row
London WC1R 4LR
United Kingdom

Latin America
Thomson Learning
Seneca, 53
Colonia Polanco
11560 Mexico
D.F. Mexico

Spain (including Portugal)
Thomson Paraninfo
Calle Magallanes, 25
28015 Madrid, Spain

Contents

CHAPTER 16   ARTS AND CULTURE AGE OF CHANGE—1500–1750 CE   361

CHAPTER 17   RELIGION AND PHILOSOPHY—1750–1914 CE   379

CHAPTER 24   SCIENCE, MEDICINE, AND TECHNOLOGY—1914–PRESENT   563

CHAPTER 25   DAILY LIFE IN THE POSTMODERN WORLD—1914–PRESENT   583

**CHAPTER 26   ARTS AND CULTURE IN THE POST
MODERN WORLD—1914–
PRESENT   607**

Introduction

Primary source documents enhance the study of history. A primary document can be as simple as graffiti on a wall in Pompeii or as complex as the discourse of ancient philosophers. What primary documents are not is a synthesis of the past found in all history survey texts. Reading a primary document written or passed down orally through generations gives you an opportunity to determine what motivated its writer so that you can make your own decision regarding the meaning of his or her words. You will be reading the same kind of primary sources historians use when they research materials to write the text books that are used for survey classes and making your own judgments on their meaning.

Many primary documents are interesting and entertaining in their own right. However, in order to gain the most benefit from primary sources, you should learn as much about the origin and purpose of the document as possible.

This book contains a selection of documents that should enhance the study of world civilization and is intended to be used as a companion to a comprehensive world civilization text.

Most of the documents are brief and they are arranged both topically and chronologically to allow you to more easily determine the similarities and differences that have existed between world societies over time. The documents are also divided into three time periods: 1500 to 1750, 1750 to 1914, and 1914–Present, all in the Common Era. Within each time period, the documents are grouped under five headings: Religion and Philosophy; Law, Government, and War; Science, Medicine, and Technology; Daily Life; and Arts and Culture. In the last two time periods, the heading Law, Government, and War is expanded to include documents on Revolution.

Under each heading, the documents are arranged from earliest to latest. Within each section I have tried to select documents that show both the commonality and differences between people over time especially in the area of religious belief, government, and culture. Additionally, in the Daily Life section, I have chosen documents that portray gender roles in a variety of cultures and the interaction of male and female over time. Also included throughout the sections whenever possible are traveler's accounts illustrating their perception of a foreign culture. In the Science, Medicine, and Technology section, besides documents dealing with scientific discoveries, I have included some that show the development of medical theory and practice and how it varied from East to West and changed over time.

HOW TO READ PRIMARY DOCUMENTS

One of the common failings of historians and students alike is their willingness to believe that the people who lived in the past were just like us. When reading these documents, you may well find that in some cases those who are alive today only in the pages of history texts did seem to share seemingly *modern* concerns. Other documents however will give you exactly the opposite feeling. It is then that you will understand that you have to know more before you can make a valid judgment concerning the meaning of an individual document. You must determine what circumstances in that individual's life and society shaped his/her thoughts and values and made the creation of that document possible.

Perhaps the first question to ask when reading a primary document is where did the author get his/her information? It is also important to know who wrote the document and what position the author had in society. Can you tell why the document was written? Is it likely that the author had some bias or was writing with a particular point of view? Was the document a true depiction of the event described? Might the author have altered the reality for a particular purpose? What is the main argument of the document? Does this document agree with your text or other knowledge of the subject?

As you become accustomed to reading and analyzing the contents of primary documents following these simple steps, the process should enrich your understanding of world history and culture.

CHAPTER 12

Religion and Philosophy—
1500–1750 CE

A t the beginning of the sixteenth century, the Catholic Church faced serious problems in Europe. The Church was charged with corruption, and many disillusioned Christians called for return to a simpler, Bible-based faith. Yet this period also produced some of the greatest saints of the Catholic Church.

In Asia, there was conflict between Indian Muslims and Hindus. In Central and Latin America, Spanish conquistadors and priests were both intrigued and appalled by the religious beliefs of the peoples they conquered.

The documents in this section start with the ironic Erasmus, who criticized the Church but did not reject it. Luther and Calvin, on the other hand, took up the cause of Reformation, split with the Catholic Church, and established the Protestant Church. Their counterparts within the Catholic Church were the ex-soldier and founder of the Jesuits, Ignatius of Loyola, and the mystic, Teresa of Avila. What did all these disparate individuals have in common?

These accounts are followed by two strikingly different descriptions by Europeans of Aztec and Maya religious rituals. Why might one be sympathetic toward the conquered Aztecs and Mayans? Another document comes from India under the tolerant Mughal rulers, who tried to reconcile Muslim and Hindu believers. Finally, in the last document, Pascal struggles to reconcile faith and reason. Do you think Luther and Calvin would have been sympathetic to his plight?

103

From *In Praise of Folly* by Desiderius Erasmus—1509

An illegitimate child, the Dutch humanist Erasmus was schooled in a monastery and later became a monk. Because of his intellectual gifts, he was allowed to travel throughout Europe looking for ancient manuscripts and improving his skills as a writer. Although he published an edition of the Greek New Testament *and the* Writings of Saint Jerome, *he is better known for popular works such as the satire* In Praise of Folly. *In this excerpt, Erasmus criticizes both Christians and the Church. Historians consider Erasmus responsible for laying the groundwork for Martin Luther's break from the Catholic Church. In what way is Erasmus' criticism of the Church and its leaders similar to that of Luther? Why did he believe that superstition had degraded the message of the Church?*

The next to be placed among the regiment of fools are such as make a trade of telling or inquiring after incredible stories of miracles and prodigies: never doubting that a lie will choke them, they will muster up a thousand several strange relations of spirits, ghosts, apparitions, raising of the devil, and such like bugbears of superstition, which the farther they are from being probably true, the more greedily they are swallowed, and the more devoutly believed. And these absurdities do not only bring an empty pleasure, and cheap divertisement, but they are a good trade, and procure a comfortable income to such priests and friars as by this craft get their gain. To these again are nearly related such others as attribute strange virtues to the shrines and images of saints and martyrs, and so would make their credulous proselytes believe, that if they pay their devotion to St. Christopher in the morning, they shall be guarded and secured the day following from all dangers and misfortunes: if soldiers, when they first take arms, shall come and mumble over such a set prayer before the picture of St. Barbara, they shall return safe from all engagements: or if any pray to Erasmus on such particular holidays, with the ceremony of wax candles, and other fopperies, he shall in a short time be rewarded with a plentiful increase of wealth and riches.

The next to these are another sort of brainsick fools, who style themselves monks and of religious orders, though they assume both tides very unjustly: for as to the last, they have very little religion in them; and as to the former, the etymology of the word monk implies a solitariness, or being alone; whereas they are so thick abroad that we cannot pass any street or alley without meeting them. Now I cannot imagine what one degree of men would be more

Erasmus, *In Praise of Folly*, London: Reeves & Turner, 1876.

hopelessly wretched, if I did not stand their friend, and buoy them up in that lake of misery, which by the engagements of a holy vow they have voluntarily immerged themselves in. But when this sort of men are so unwelcome to others, as that the very sight of them is thought ominous, I yet make them highly in love with themselves, and fond admirers of their own happiness. The first step whereunto they esteem a profound ignorance, thinking carnal knowledge a great enemy to their spiritual welfare, and seem confident of becoming greater proficients in divine mysteries the less they are poisoned with any human learning. They imagine that they bear a sweet consort with the heavenly choir, when they tone out their daily tally of psalms, which they rehearse only by rote, without permitting their understanding or affections to go along with their voice.

Among these some make a good profitable trade of beggary, going about from house to house, not like the apostles, to break, but to beg, their bread; nay, thrust into all public-houses, come aboard the passage-boats, get into the travelling waggons, and omit no opportunity of time or place for the craving people's charity; doing a great deal of injury to common highway beggars by interloping in their traffic of alms. And when they are thus voluntarily poor, destitute, not provided with two coats, nor with any money in their purse, they have the impudence to pretend that they imitate the first disciples, whom their master expressly sent out in such an equipage.

It is pretty to observe how they regulate all their actions as it were by weight and measure to so exact a proportion, as if the whole loss of their religion depended upon the omission of the least punctilio. Thus they must be very critical in the precise number of knots to the tying on of their sandals: what distinct colours their respective habits, and what stuff made of, how broad and long their girdles: how big, and in what fashion, their hoods; whether their bald crowns be to a hair's-breadth of the right cut; how many hours they must sleep, at what minute rise to prayers, and so on. And these several customs are altered according to the humours of different persons and places. While they are sworn to the superstitious observance of these trifles, they do not only despise all others, but are very inclinable to fall out among themselves; for though they make profession of an apostolic charity, yet they will pick a quarrel, and be implacably passionate for such poor provocations, as the girting on a coat the wrong way, for the wearing of clothes a little too darkish coloured or any such nicety not worth the speaking of.

Some are so obstinately superstitious that they will wear their upper garment of some coarse dog's hair stuff, and that next their skin as soft as silk: but others on the contrary will have linen frocks outermost, and their shirts of wool, or hair. Some again will not touch a piece of money, though they make no scruple of the sin of drunkenness, and the lust of the flesh. All their several orders are mindful of nothing more than of their being distinguished from each other by their different customs and habits. They seem indeed not so careful of becoming like Christ, and of being known to be his disciples, as the being unlike to one another, and distinguishable for followers of their several founders.

Most of them place their greatest stress for salvation on a strict conformity to their foppish ceremonies, and a belief of their legendary traditions; wherein they fancy to have acquitted themselves with so much of supererogation, that one heaven can never be a condign reward for their meritorious life; little thinking that the Judge of all the earth at the last day shall put them off, with a who hath required these things at your hands; and call them to account only for the stewardship of his legacy, which was the precept of love and charity. It will be pretty to hear their pleas before the great tribunal: one will brag how he mortified his carnal appetite by feeding only upon fish: another will urge that he spent most of his time on earth in the divine exercise of singing psalms: a third will tell how many days he fasted, and what severe penance he imposed on himself for the bringing his body into subjection: another shall produce in his own behalf as many ceremonies as would load a fleet of merchant-men: a fifth shall plead that in threescore years he never so much as touched a piece of money, except he fingered it through a thick pair of gloves: a sixth, to testify his former humility, shall bring along with him his sacred hood, so old and nasty, that any seaman had rather stand bare headed on the deck, than put it on to defend his ears in the sharpest storms: the next that comes to answer for himself shall plead, that for fifty years together, he had lived like a sponge upon the same place, and was content never to change his homely habitation: another shall whisper softly, and tell the judge he has lost his voice by a continual singing of holy hymns and anthems: the next shall confess how he fell into a lethargy by a strict, reserved, and sedentary life: and the last shall intimate that he has forgot to speak, by having always kept silence, in obedience to the injunction of taking heed lest he should have offended with his tongue.

Now as to the popes of Rome, who pretend themselves Christ's vicars, if they would but imitate his exemplary life, in the being employed in an unintermitted course of preaching; in the being attended with poverty, nakedness, hunger, and a contempt of this world; if they did but consider the import of the word pope, which signifies a father; or if they did but practice their surname of most holy, what order or degrees of men would be in a worse condition? There would be then no such vigorous making of parties, and buying of votes, in the conclave upon a vacancy of that see: and those who by bribery, or other indirect courses, should get themselves elected, would never secure their sitting firm in the chair by pistol, poison, force, and violence.

How much of their pleasure would be abated if they were but endowed with one dram of wisdom? Wisdom, did I say? Nay, with one grain of that salt which our Saviour bid them not lose the savour of. All their riches, all their honour, their jurisdictions, their Peter's patrimony, their offices, their dispensations, their licenses, their indulgences, their long train and attendants (see in how short a compass I have abbreviated all their marketing of religion); in a word, all their perquisites would be forfeited and lost; and in their room would succeed watchings, fastings, tears, prayers, sermons, hard studies, repenting sighs, and a thousand such like severe penalties: nay, what's yet more deplorable, it would then follow, that all their clerks, amanuenses, notaries, advocates, proctors, secretaries, the offices of grooms, ostlers, serving-men, pimps (and somewhat else, which for modesty's sake I shall not mention); in short, all these troops of attendants, which depend on his holiness, would all lose their several employments. This indeed would be hard, but what yet remains would be more dreadful: the very Head of the Church, the spiritual prince, would then be brought from all his splendour to the poor equipage of a scrip and staff.

But all this is upon the supposition only that they understood what circumstances they are placed in; whereas now, by a wholesome neglect of thinking, they live as well as heart can wish: whatever of toil and drudgery belongs to their office that they assign over to St. Peter, or St. Paul, who have time enough to mind it; but if there be any thing of pleasure and grandeur, that they assume to themselves, as being hereunto called: so that by my influence no sort of people live more to their own ease and content. They think to satisfy that Master they pretend to serve, our Lord and Saviour, with their great state and magnificence, with the ceremonies of instalments, with the titles of reverence and holiness, and with exercising their episcopal function only in blessing and cursing. The working of miracles is old and out-dated; to teach the people is too laborious; to interpret scripture is to invade the prerogative of the schoolmen; to pray is too idle; to shed tears is cowardly and unmanly; to fast is too mean and sordid; to be easy and familiar is beneath the grandeur of him, who, without being sued to and entreated, will scarce give princes the honour of kissing his toe; finally, to die for religion is too self-denying; and to be crucified as their Lord of Life, is base and ignominious.

Their only weapons ought to be those of the Spirit; and of these indeed they are mighty liberal, as of their interdicts, their suspensions, their denunciations, their aggravations, their greater and lesser excommunications, and their roaring bulls, that fright whomever they are thundered against; and these most holy fathers never issue them out more frequently than against those, who, at the instigation of the devil, and not having the fear of God before their eyes, do feloniously and maliciously attempt to lessen and impair St. Peter's patrimony: and though that apostle tells our Saviour in the gospel, in the name of all the other disciples, we have left all, and followed you, yet they challenge as his inheritance, fields, towns, treasures, and large dominions; for the defending whereof, inflamed with a holy zeal, they fight with fire and sword, to the great loss and effusion of Christian blood, thinking they are apostolical maintainers of Christ's spouse, the church, when they have murdered all such as they call her enemies; though indeed the church has no enemies more bloody and tyrannical than such impious popes, who give dispensations for the not preaching of Christ; evacuate the main effect and design of our redemption by their pecuniary bribes and sales; adulterate the gospel by their forced interpretations, and undermining traditions; and lastly, by their lusts and wickedness grieve the Holy Spirit, and make their Saviour's wounds to bleed anew.

104

From *The Freedom of a Christian* by Martin Luther—1520

Martin Luther (1483–1546) was an Augustinian monk who broke away from the Catholic Church, initially because of controversy over the sale of indulgences in the city. More broadly, Luther called for the Church to return to the teachings of the Bible. In trouble with the Pope and the Holy Roman Emperor, he broke away from the Church. Luther was protected by German nobles while he developed what would become the Lutheran religion. In The Freedom of a Christian, *Luther states the key points of his theology. What are they? How important was faith to Martin Luther?*

THE FREEDOM OF A CHRISTIAN

Many people have considered Christian faith an easy thing, and not a few have given it a place among the virtues. They do this because they have not experienced it and have never tasted the great strength there is in faith. It is impossible to write well about it or to understand what has been written about it unless one has at one time or another experienced the courage which faith gives a man when trials oppress him. But he who has had even a faint taste of it can never write, speak, meditate, or hear enough concerning it. It is a living "spring of water welling up to eternal life," as Christ calls it in John 4 [:14].

As for me, although I have no wealth of faith to boast of and know how scant my supply is, I nevertheless hope that I have attained to a little faith, even though I have been assailed by great and various temptations; and I hope that I can discuss it, if not more elegantly, certainly more to the point, than those literalists and subtile disputants have previously done, who have not even understood what they have written.

To make the way smoother for the unlearned—for only them do I serve—I shall set down the following two propositions concerning the freedom and the bondage of the spirit:

A Christian is a perfectly free lord of all, subject to none.

A Christian is a perfectly dutiful servant of all, subject to all.

These two theses seem to contradict each other. If, however, they should be found to fit together they would serve our purpose beautifully. Both are Paul's own statements, who says in I Cor. 9 [:19], "For though I am free from all men,

From "Table Talk" in *Luther's Works*, Vol. 31, trans. and ed. by William Hazlitt (London, George Bell & Sons, 1895).

I have made myself a slave to all," and in Rom. 13 [:8] "Owe no one anything, except to love one another." Love by its very nature is ready to serve and be subject to him who is loved. So Christ, although he was Lord of all, was "born of woman, born under the law" [Gal. 4:4], and therefore was at the same time a free man and a servant, "in the form of god" and "of a servant" [Phil. 2:6–7].

Let us start, however, with something more remote from our subject, but more obvious. Man has a twofold nature, a spiritual and a bodily one. According to the spiritual nature, which men refer to as the soul, he is called a spiritual, inner, or new man. According to the bodily nature, which men refer to as flesh, he is called a carnal, outward, or old man. Because of this diversity of nature the Scriptures assert contradictory things concerning the same man, since these two men in the same man contradict each other, "for the desires of the flesh are against the Spirit, and the desires of the Spirit are against the flesh," according to Gal. 5[:17]

First, let us consider the inner man to see how a righteous, free, and pious Christian, that is, a spiritual, new, and inner man becomes what he is. It is evident that no external thing has any influence in producing Christian righteousness or freedom, or in producing unrighteousness or servitude. A simple argument will furnish the proof of this statement. What can it profit the soul if the body is well, free, and active, and eats, drinks, and does as it pleases? For in these respects even the most godless slaves of vice may prosper. On the other hand, how will poor health or imprisonment or hunger or thirst or any other external misfortune harm the soul?

One thing, and only one thing, is necessary for Christian life, righteousness, and freedom. That one thing is the most holy Word of God, the gospel of Christ, as Christ says, John 11 [:25], "I am the resurrection and the life; he who believes in me, though he die, yet shall he live"; and John 8 [:36], "So if the Son makes you free, you will be free indeed"; and Matt. 4 [:4], "Man shall not live by bread alone, but by every word that proceeds from the mouth of God." Let us then consider it certain and firmly established that the soul can do without anything except the Word of God and that where the Word of God is missing there is no help at all for the soul. If it has the Word of God it is rich and lacks nothing since it is the Word of life, truth, light, peace, righteousness, salvation, joy, liberty, wisdom, power, grace, glory, and of every incalculable blessing.

You may ask, "What then is the Word of God, and how shall it be used, since there are so many words of God?" I answer: The Apostle explains this in Romans 1. The Word is the gospel of God concerning his Son, who was made flesh, suffered, rose from the dead, and was glorified through the Spirit who sanctifies. Faith alone is the saving and efficacious use of the Word of God, according to Rom. 10 [:9]: "If you confess with your lips that Jesus is Lord and believe in your heart that God raised him from the dead, you will be saved." Furthermore, "Christ is the end of the law, that every one who has faith may be justified" [Rom. 10:4]. Again, in Rom. 1 [:17], "He who through faith is righteous shall live." The Word of God cannot be received and cherished by any works whatever but only by faith. Therefore it is clear that, as the soul needs only the Word of God for its life and righteousness, so it is justified by faith alone and not any works; for if it could be justified by anything else, it would not need the Word, and consequently it would not need faith.

Should you ask how it happens that faith alone justifies and offers us such a treasure of great benefits without works in view of the fact that so many works, ceremonies, and laws are prescribed in the Scriptures, I answer: First of all, remember what has been said, namely, that faith alone, without works, justifies, frees, and saves; we shall make this clearer later on. Here we must point out that the entire Scripture of God is divided into two parts: commandments and promises. Although the commandments teach things that are good, the things taught are not done as soon as they are taught, for the commandments show us what we ought to do but do not give us the power to do it. They are intended to teach man to know himself, that through them he may recognize his inability to do good and may despair of his own ability. That is why they are called the Old Testament and constitute the Old Testament. For example, the commandment, "You shall not covet" [Exod. 20:17], is a command which proves us all to be sinners, for no one can avoid coveting no matter how much he may struggle against it. Therefore, in order not to covet and to fulfil the commandment, man is compelled to despair of himself, to seek the help which he does not find in himself elsewhere and from someone else, as stated in Hosea [13:9]: "Destruction is your own, O Israel: your help is only in me." As we fare with respect to one commandment, so we fare with all, for it is equally impossible for us to keep any one of them.

Now when a man has learned through the commandments to recognize his helplessness and is distressed about how he might satisfy the law—since the law must be fulfilled so that not a jot or tittle shall be lost, otherwise man will be condemned without hope—then, being truly humbled and reduced to nothing in his own eyes, he finds in himself nothing whereby he may be justified and saved. Here the second part of Scripture comes to our aid, namely, the promises of God which declare the glory of God, saying, "If you wish to fulfil the law and not covet, as the law demands, come, believe in Christ in whom grace, righteousness, peace, liberty, and all things are promised you. If you believe, you shall have all things; if you do not believe, you shall lack all things."

The following statements are therefore true: "Good works do not make a good man, but a good man does good works: evil works do not make a wicked man, but a wicked man does evil works." Consequently it is always necessary that the substance or person himself be good before there can be any good works, and that good works follow and proceed from the good person, as Christ also says, "A good tree cannot bear evil fruit, nor can a bad tree bear good fruit" [Matt. 7:18]. It is clear that the fruits do not bear the tree and that the tree does not grow the fruits, also that, on the contrary, the trees bear the fruits and the fruits grow on the trees. As it is necessary, therefore, that the trees exist before their fruits and the fruits do not make trees either good or bad, but rather as the trees are, so are the fruits they bear; so a man must first be good or wicked before he does a good or wicked work, and his works do not make him good or wicked, but he himself makes his works either good or wicked.

Illustrations of the same truth can be seen in all trades. A good or bad house does not make a good or a bad builder; but a good or a bad builder makes a good or a bad house. And in general, the work never makes the workman like itself, but the workman makes the work like himself. So it is with the works of man. As the man is, whether believer or unbeliever, so also is his work—good if it was done in faith, wicked if it was done in unbelief. But the converse is not true, that the work makes the man either a believer or an unbeliever. As works do not make a man a believer, so also they do not make him righteous. But as faith makes a man a believer and righteous, so faith does good works. Since, then, works justify no one, and a man must be righteous before he does a good work, it is very evident that it is faith alone which, because of the pure mercy of God through Christ and in his Word, worthily and sufficiently justifies and saves the person. A Christian has no need of any work or law in order to be saved since through faith he is free from every law and does everything out of pure liberty and freely. He seeks neither benefit nor salvation since he already abounds in all things and is saved through the grace of God because in his faith he now seeks only to please God.

So a Christian, like Christ his head, is filled and made rich by faith and should be content with this form of God which he has obtained by faith; only, as I have said, he should increase this faith until it is made perfect. For this faith is his life, his righteousness, and his salvation: it saves him and makes him acceptable, and bestows upon him all things that are Christ's, as has been said above, and as Paul asserts in Gal. 2 [:20] when he says, "And the life I now live in the flesh I live by faith in the Son of God." Although the Christian is thus free from all works, he ought in this liberty to empty himself, take upon himself the form of a servant, be made in the likeness of men, be found in human form, and to serve, help, and in every way deal with his neighbor as he sees that God through Christ has dealt and still deals with him. This he should do freely, having regard for nothing but divine approval.

He ought to think: "Although I am an unworthy and condemned man, my God has given me in Christ all the riches of righteousness and salvation without any merit on my part, out of pure, free mercy, so that from now on I need nothing except faith which believes that this is true. Why should I not therefore freely, joyfully, with all my heart, and with an eager will do all things which I know are pleasing and acceptable to such a Father who has overwhelmed me with his inestimable riches? I will therefore give myself as a Christ to my neighbor, just as Christ offered himself to me; I will do nothing in this life except what I see is necessary, profitable, and salutary to my neighbor, since through faith I have an abundance of all good things in Christ."

Behold, from faith thus flow forth love and joy in the Lord, and from love a joyful, willing, and free mind that serves one's neighbor willingly and takes no account of gratitude or ingratitude, of praise or blame, of gain or loss. For a man does not serve that he may put men under obligations. He does not distinguish between friends and enemies or anticipate their thankfulness or unthankfulness, but he most freely and most willingly spends himself and all that he has, whether he wastes all on the thankless or whether he gains a reward. As his Father does, distributing all things to all men richly and freely, making "his sun rise on the evil and on the good" [Matt. 5:45], so also the son does all things and suffers all things with that freely bestowing joy which is his delight when through Christ he sees it in God, the dispenser of such great benefits.

Therefore, if we recognize the great and precious things which are given us, as Paul says [Rom. 5:5], our hearts will be filled by the Holy Spirit with the love which makes us free, joyful, almighty workers and conquerors over all tribulations, servants of our neighbors, and yet lords of all. For those who do not recognize the gifts bestowed upon them through Christ, however, Christ has been born in vain; they go their way with their works and shall never come to taste or feel those things. Just as our neighbor is in need and lacks that in which we abound, so we were in need before God and lacked his mercy. Hence, as our heavenly Father has in Christ freely come to our aid, we also ought freely to help our neighbor through our body and it works, each one should become as it were a Christ to the other that we may be Christs to one another and Christ may be the same in all, that is, that we may be truly Christians.

105

From *Spiritual Exercises* by Ignatius Loyola—1541

The Jesuit order, or Society of Jesus, was founded by a Spanish soldier named Ignatius of Loyola, who had a spiritual rebirth while recovering from a wound suffered in 1521. Loyola founded the Society of Jesus as a disciplined order of scholar priests and brothers who fought the effects of the Protestant Reformation. Many Catholics had joined the New Protestant Churches. They also traveled to foreign lands such as China to gain new converts through preaching, charity, missions, and education. Jesuits took a special vow of obedience to the Pope and were known for their far-ranging missionary activities. The Spiritual Exercises *was designed to help individuals discover God's will regarding their lives and aid in their salvation. What does Loyola say about predestination, a key element of Calvinistic theology? How does his attitude toward spiritual authority differ from that of Calvin and Luther?*

From *The Spiritual Exercises of St. Ignatius* by Anthony Mottola. Copyright © 1964 by Doubleday, a division of Random House, Inc. Reprinted by permission of Random House, Inc.

In order to have the proper attitude of mind in the Church Militant we should observe the following rules:

1. Putting aside all private judgment, we should keep our minds prepared and ready to obey promptly and in all things the true spouse of Christ our Lord, our Holy Mother, the hierarchical Church.

2. To praise sacramental confession[1] and the reception of the Most Holy Sacrament once a year, and much better once a month, and better still every week, with the requisite and proper dispositions.

3. To praise the frequent hearing of Mass, singing of hymns and psalms, and the recitation of long prayers, both in and out of church; also the hours arranged for fixed times for the whole Divine Office, for prayers of all kinds and for the canonical hours.[2]

4. To praise highly religious life, virginity, and continence; and also matrimony, but not as highly as any of the foregoing.

5. To praise the vows of religion, obedience, poverty, chastity, and other works of perfection.[3] It must be remembered that a vow is made in matters that lead to evangelical perfection. It is therefore improper to make a vow in matters that depart from this perfection; as, for example, to enter business, to get married, and so forth.

6. To praise the relics of the saints by venerating them and by praying to these saints. Also to praise the stations, pilgrimages, indulgences, jubilees, Crusade indulgences, and the lighting of candles in the churches.[4]

7. To praise the precepts concerning fasts and abstinences, such as those of Lent, Ember Days, Vigils, Fridays, and Saturdays; likewise to praise acts of penance, both interior and exterior.

8. To praise the adornments and buildings of churches as well as sacred images, and to venerate them according to what they represent.

9. Finally, to praise all the precepts of the Church, holding ourselves ready at all times to find reasons for their defense, and never offending against them.

10. We should be more inclined to approve and praise the directions and recommendations of our superiors as well as their personal behavior. Although sometimes these may not be or may not have been praiseworthy, to speak against them when preaching in public or in conversation with

---

1 Protestants rejected auricular confession—confessing one's sins to God through a priest, who offers absolution in the name of God.

2 In his *Table Talk*, Martin Luther denies the merit of such "good works" as prayers, veneration of relics, and pilgrimages, claiming that external actions cannot earn God's grace. He argues that grace is a freely given gift that comes only with a God-instilled faith in Jesus and the promise of salvation.

3 Arguing that all believers in Jesus are priests, all Protestant groups rejected a special priesthood of celibate ministers.

4 Many Protestant reformers considered images and decoration in churches a form of idolatry.

people would give rise to murmuring and scandal rather than to edification. As a result, the people would be angry with their superiors, whether temporal or spiritual. Still, while it does harm to our superiors in their absence to speak ill of them in the presence of the people, it might be useful to speak of their bad conduct to those who can apply a remedy. . . .

13. If we wish to be sure that we are right in all things, we should always be ready to accept this principle: I will believe that the white that I see is black, if the hierarchical Church so defines it. For, I believe that between the Bridegroom, Christ our Lord, and the Bride, His Church, there is but one spirit, which governs and directs us for the salvation of our souls, for the same Spirit and Lord, who gave us the Ten Commandments, guides and governs our Holy Mother Church.

14. Although it be true that no one can be saved unless it be predestined and unless he have faith and grace, still we must be very careful of our manner of discussing and speaking of these matters.

15. We should not make predestination[5] an habitual subject of conversation. If it is sometimes mentioned we must speak in such a way that no person will fall into error, as happens on occasion when one will say, "It has already been determined whether I will be saved or lost, and in spite of all the good or evil that I do, this will not be changed." As a result, they become apathetic and neglect the works that are conducive to their salvation and to the spiritual growth of their souls.

16. In like manner, we must be careful lest by speaking too much and with too great emphasis on faith, without any distinction or explanation, we give occasion to the people to become indolent and lazy in the performance of good works, whether it be before or after their faith is founded in charity.

17. Also in our discourse we ought not to emphasize the doctrine that would destroy free will.[6] We may therefore speak of faith and grace to the extent that God enables us to do so, for the greater praise of His Divine Majesty. But, in these dangerous times of ours, it must not be done in such a way that good works or free will suffer any detriment or be considered worthless.

18. Although the generous service of God for motives of pure love should be most highly esteemed, we should praise highly the fear of His Divine Majesty, for filial fear and even servile fear are pious and most holy things. When one cannot attain anything better or more useful, this fear is of great help in rising from mortal sin, and after this first step one easily advances to filial fear which is wholly acceptable and pleasing to God our Lord, since it is inseparable from Divine Love.

---

5 Luther, Calvin, and other reformers argued that because faith is given by God and not earned, persons are predestined to either salvation or damnation.

6 In his treatise of 1525, *On the Bondage of the Will,* Luther argued that on matters of salvation, God's will completely controls the human will, that one is not free to accept or reject His gift of salvation. The Catholic position places the responsibility on the individual Christian to choose freely if he or she wants to live a meritorious life and thus earn salvation.

106

From *Institutes of the Christian Religion* by John Calvin—1534

John Calvin (1509–1564) was the first of the second generation of Christian religious reformers. A Frenchman trained as a lawyer, Calvin eventually established himself in Geneva, Switzerland. There, he developed a new form of church government that made Geneva a Protestant theological center. The key elements of Calvin's theology were predestination—the belief that one's salvation or damnation was decided before birth—and a rejection of anything not mentioned in the Bible. What differences do you see between the reforms of Luther and Calvin? Why were the scriptures so important to Calvin?

KNOWLEDGE OF GOD INVOLVES
TRUST AND REVERENCE

What is God? Men who pose this question are merely toying with idle speculations. It is far better for us to inquire, "What is his nature?" and to know what is consistent with his nature. What good is it to profess with Epicurus some sort of God who has cast aside the care of the world only to amuse himself in idleness? What help is it, in short, to know a God with whom we have nothing to do? Rather, our knowledge should serve first to teach us fear and reverence; secondly, with it as our guide and teacher, we should learn to seek every good from him, and having received it, to credit it to his account. For how can the thought of God penetrate your mind without your realizing immediately that, since you are his handiwork, you have been made over and bound to his command by right of creation, that you owe your life to him?—that whatever you undertake, whatever you do, ought to be ascribed to him? If this be so, it now assuredly follows that your life is wickedly corrupt unless it be disposed to his service, seeing that his will ought for us to be the law by which we live. Again, you cannot behold him clearly unless you acknowledge him to be the fountainhead and source of every good. From this too would arise the desire to cleave to him and trust in him, but for the fact that man's depravity seduces his mind from rightly seeking him.

Because it acknowledges him as Lord and Father, the pious mind also deems it meet and right to observe his authority in all things, reverence his

From John Calvin, *Selections from His Writings*, ed. John Dillenberger (New York: Oxford University Press, 1971).

majesty, take care to advance his glory, and obey his commandments. Because it sees him to be a righteous judge, armed with severity to punish wickedness, it ever holds his judgment seat before its gaze, and through fear of him restrains itself from provoking his anger. And yet it is not so terrified by the awareness of his judgment as to wish to withdraw, even if some way of escape were open. But it embraces him no less as punisher of the wicked than as benefactor of the pious. For the pious mind realizes that the punishment of the impious and wicked and the reward of life eternal for the righteous equally pertain to God's glory. Besides, this mind restrains itself from sinning, not out of dread of punishment alone; but, because it loves and reveres God as Father, it worships and adores him as Lord. Even if there were no hell, it would still shudder at offending him alone.

Here indeed is pure and real religion; faith so joined with an earnest fear of God that this fear also embraces willing reverence, and carries with it such legitimate worship as is prescribed in the law. And we ought to note this fact even more diligently: all men have a vague general veneration for God, but very few really reverence him; and wherever there is great ostentation in ceremonies, sincerity of heart is rare indeed.

SUPERSTITION

Experience teaches that the seed of religion has been divinely planted in all men. But barely one man in a hundred can be found who nourishes in his own heart what he has conceived; and not even one in whom it matures, much less bears fruit in its season (cf. Ps. 1:3). Now some lose themselves in their own superstition, while others of their own evil intention revolt from God, yet all fall away from true knowledge of him. As a result, no real piety remains in the world. But as to my statement that some erroneously slip into superstition, I do not mean by this that their ingenuousness should free them from blame. For the blindness under which they labor is almost always mixed with proud vanity and obstinacy. Indeed, vanity joined with pride can be detected in the fact that, in seeking God, miserable men do not rise above themselves as they should, but measure him by the yardstick of their own carnel stupidity, and neglect sound investigation; thus out of curiosity they fly off into empty speculations. They do not therefore apprehend God as he offers himself, but imagine him as they have fashioned him in their own presumption. When this gulf opens, in whatever direction they move their feet, they cannot but plunge headlong into ruin. Indeed, whatever they afterward attempt by way of worship or service of God, they cannot bring as tribute to him, for they are worshiping not God but a figment and a dream of their own heart. Paul eloquently notes this wickedness: "Striving to be wise, they make fools of themselves" (Rom. 1:22f.). He had said before that "they became futile in their thinking" (Rom. 1:21). In order, however, that no one might excuse their guilt, he adds that they are justly blinded. For not content with sobriety but claiming for themselves more than is right, they wantonly bring darkness upon themselves—in fact, they become fools in their empty and perverse haughtiness. From this it follows that their stupidity is not excusable, since it is caused not only by vain curiosity but by an inordinate desire to know more than is fitting, joined with a false confidence.

THE DIVINE WISDOM DISPLAYED
FOR ALL TO SEE

There are innumerable evidences both in heaven and on earth that declare his wonderful wisdom; not only those more recondite matters for the closer observation of which astronomy, medicine, and all natural science are intended, but also those which thrust themselves upon the sight of even the most untutored and ignorant persons, so that they cannot open their eyes without being compelled to witness them. Indeed, men who have either quaffed or even tasted the liberal arts penetrate with their aid far more deeply into the secrets of the divine wisdom. Yet ignorance of them prevents no one from seeing more than enough of God's workmanship in his creation to lead him to break forth in admiration of the Artificer. To be sure, there is need of art and of more exacting toil in order to investigate the motion of the stars, to determine their assigned stations, to measure their intervals, to note their properties. As God's providence shows itself more explicitly when one observes these, so the mind must rise to a somewhat higher level to look upon his glory. Even the common folk and the most untutored, who have been taught only by the aid of the eyes, cannot be unaware of the excellence of divine art, for it reveals itself in this innumerable and yet distinct and well-ordered variety of the heavenly host. It is, accordingly, clear that there is no one to whom the Lord does not abundantly show his wisdom. Likewise, in regard to the structure of the human body one must have the greatest keenness in order to weigh, with Galen's skill, its articulation, symmetry, beauty, and use. But yet, as all acknowledge, the human body shows itself to be a composition so ingenious that its Artificer is rightly judged a wonder-worker.

MAN AS THE LOFTIEST PROOF
OF DIVINE WISDOM

Certain philosophers, accordingly, long ago not ineptly called a man a microcosm because he is a rare example of God's power, goodness, and wisdom, and contains within himself enough miracles to occupy our minds, if only we are not irked at paying attention to them. Paul, having stated that the blind can find God by feeling after him, immediately adds that he ought not to be sought afar off (Acts 17:27). For each one undoubtedly feels within the heavenly grace that quickens him. Indeed, if there is no need to go outside ourselves to comprehend God, what pardon will the indolence of that man deserve who is loath to descend within himself to find God? For the same reason, David, when he has briefly praised the admirable name and glory of God, which shine everywhere, immediately exclaims: "What is man that thou art mindful of him?" (Ps. 8:4). Likewise, "Out of the mouths of babes and sucklings thou hast established strength" (Ps. 8:2). Indeed, he not only declares that a clear mirror of God's works is in humankind, but that infants, while they nurse at their mother's breasts, have tongues so eloquent to preach his glory that there is no need at all of other orators. Consequently, also, he does not hesitate to bring their infant speech into the debate, as if they were thoroughly instructed, to refute the madness of those who might desire to extinguish God's name in favor of their own devilish pride. Consequently, too, there comes in that which Paul quotes from Aratus, that we are God's offspring (Acts 17:28), because by adorning us with such great excellence he testifies that he is our Father. In the same way the secular poets, out of a common feeling and, as it were, at the dictation of experience, called him "the Father of men." Indeed, no one gives himself freely and willingly to God's service unless, having tasted his fatherly love, he is drawn to love and worship him in return.

GOD BESTOWS THE ACTUAL KNOWLEDGE OF HIMSELF UPON US ONLY IN THE SCRIPTURES

That brightness which is borne in upon the eyes of all men both in heaven and on earth is more than enough to withdraw all support from men's ingratitude—just as God, to involve the human race in the same guilt, sets forth to all without exception his presence portrayed in his creatures. Despite this, it is needful that another and better help be added to direct us aright to the very Creator of the universe. It was not in vain, then, that he added the light of his Word by which to become known unto salvation; and he regarded as worthy of this privilege those whom he pleased to gather more closely and intimately to himself. For because he saw the minds of all men tossed and agitated, after he chose the Jews as his very own flock, he fenced them about that they might not sink into oblivion as others had. With good reason he holds us by the same means in the pure knowledge of himself, since otherwise even those who seem to stand firm before all others would soon melt away. Just as old or bleary-eyed men and those with weak vision, if you thrust before them a most beautiful volume, even if they recognize it to be some sort of writing, yet can scarcely construe two words, but with the aid of spectacles will begin to read distinctly; so Scripture, gathering up the otherwise confused knowledge of God in our minds, having dispersed our dullness, clearly shows us the true God.

THE WORD OF GOD AS HOLY SCRIPTURE

But whether God became known to the patriarchs through oracles and visions or by the work and ministry of men, he put into their minds what they should then hand down to their posterity. At any rate, there is no doubt that firm certainty of doctrine was engraved in their hearts, so that they were convinced and understood that what they had learned proceeded from God. For by his Word, God rendered faith unambiguous forever, a faith that should be superior to all opinion. Finally, in order that truth might abide forever in the world with a continuing succession of teaching and survive through all ages, the same oracles he had given to the patriarchs it was his pleasure to have recorded, as it were, on public tablets. With this intent the law was published, and the prophets afterward added as its interpreters. For even though the use of the law was manifold, as will be seen more clearly in its place, it was especially committed to Moses and all the prophets to teach the way of reconcilation between God and men, whence also Paul calls "Christ the end of the law" (Rom. 10:4). Yet I repeat once more: besides the specific doctrine of faith and repentance that sets forth Christ as Mediator, Scripture adorns with unmistakable marks and tokens the one true God, in that he has created and governs the universe, in order that he may not be mixed up with the throng of false gods. Therefore, however fitting it may be for man seriously to turn his eyes to contemplate God's works, since he has been placed in this most glorious theater to be a spectator of them, it is fitting that he prick up his ears to the Word, the better to profit. And it is therefore no wonder that those who were born in darkness become more and more hardened in their insensibility; for there are very few who, to contain themselves within bounds, apply themselves teachably to God's Word, but they rather exult in their own vanity. Now, in order that true religion may shine upon us, we ought to hold that it must take its beginning from heavenly doctrine and that no one can get even the slightest taste of right and sound doctrine unless he be a pupil of Scripture. Hence, there also emerges the beginning of true understanding when we reverently embrace what it pleases God there to witness of himself. But not only faith, perfect and in every way complete, but all right knowledge of God is born of obedience. And surely in this respect God has, by his singular providence, taken thought for mortals through all ages.

FAITH RESTS UPON GOD'S WORD

This, then, is the true knowledge of Christ, if we receive him as he is offered by the Father: namely, clothed with his gospel. For just as he has been appointed as the goal of our faith, so we cannot take the right road to him unless the gospel goes before us. And there, surely, the treasures of grace are opened to us; for if they had been closed, Christ would have benefited us little. Thus Paul yokes faith to teaching, as an inseparable companion, with these words: "You did not so learn Christ if indeed you were taught what is the truth in Christ" (Eph. 4:20–21 p.)

Yet I do not so restrict faith to the gospel without confessing that what sufficed for building it up had been handed down by Moses and the prophets. But because a fuller manifestation of Christ has been revealed in the gospel, Paul justly calls it the "doctrine of faith" (cf. I Tim. 4:6). For this reason, he says in another passage that by the coming of faith the law was abolished (Rom. 10:4; cf. Gal. 3:25). He understands by this term the new and extraordinary kind of teaching by which Christ, after he became our teacher, has more clearly set forth the mercy of the Father, and has more surely testified to our salvation.

Yet it will be an easier and more suitable method if we descend by degrees from general to particular. First, we must be reminded that there is a permanent relationship between faith and the Word. He could not separate one from the other any more than we could separate the rays from the sun from which they come. For this reason, God exclaims in The Book of Isaiah: "Hear me and your soul shall live" (ch 55:3). And John shows this same wellspring of faith in these words: "These things have been written that you may believe" (John 20:31). The prophet, also, desiring to exhort the people to faith, says: "Today if you will hear his voice" (Ps. 95:7; 94:8, Vg.). "To hear" is generally understood as meaning to believe. In short, it is not without reason that in The Book of Isaiah, God distinguishes the children of the church from outsiders by this mark: he will teach all his children (Isa. 54:13; John 6:45) that they may learn of him (cf. John 6:45). For if benefits were indiscriminately given, why would he have directed his Word to a few? To this corresponds the fact that the Evangelists commonly use the words "believers" and "disciples" as synonyms. This is especially Luke's usage in The Acts of the Apostles: indeed he extends this title even to a woman in Acts 9:36.

Therefore if faith turns away even in the slightest degree from this goal toward which it should aim, it does not keep its own nature, but becomes uncertain credulity and vague error of mind. The same Word is the basis whereby faith is supported and sustained; if it turns away from the Word, it falls. Therefore, take away the Word and no faith will then remain.

We are not here discussing whether a human ministry is necessary for the sowing of God's Word, from which faith may be conceived. This we shall discuss in another place. But we say that the Word itself, however it be imparted to us, is like a mirror in which faith may contemplate God. Whether, therefore, God makes use of man's help in this or works by his own power alone, he always represents himself through his Word to those whom he wills to draw to himself. And for this reason, Paul defines faith as that obedience which is given to the gospel (Rom. 1:5), and elsewhere praises allegiance to faith in Philippians (Phil. 1:3–5; cf. I Thess. 2:13). In understanding faith it is not merely a question of knowing that God exists, but also—and this especially—of knowing what is his will toward us. For it is not so much our concern to know who he is in himself, as what he wills to be toward us.

Now, therefore, we hold faith to be a knowledge of God's will toward us, perceived from his Word. But the foundation of this is a preconceived conviction of God's truth. As for its certainty, so long as your mind is at war with itself, the Word will be of doubtful and weak authority, or rather of none. And it is not even enough to believe that God is trustworthy (cf. Rom. 3:3), who can neither deceive nor lie (cf. Titus 1:2), unless you hold to be beyond doubt that whatever proceeds from him is sacred and inviolable truth.

107

From *Royal Commentaries of the Inca* by Garcilaso de la Vega—1609

The author of this document was the son of a Spanish conquistador and an Incan princess who was a Catholic convert. As a result, de la Vega received a classic Spanish education but also learned about his Incan ancestors from his mother's relatives. The Royal Commentaries *is important because de la Vega used knowledge gained from his Incan relatives as well as personal observation and information from missionaries and other historians to write this account. Because Spanish missionaries had destroyed much of the Incas' writings, de la Vega's book is considered to be the most authoritative early history of the Incas. In this excerpt, the author describes Incan religious festivals. Was the Incan religion ethical? How does it compare with what you have learned about other religions of the time?*

The word *Raymi* is equivalent to our word Easter. Among the four festivals which the Inca kings celebrated . . . the most solemn was that in honor of the Sun, during the month of June. It was called the "Solemn Feast of the Sun" . . ., and look place in the June solstice.

They celebrated this festival of the Sun in acknowledgment that they held and adored Him as the sole and universal God who, by his light and power, creates and sustains all things on earth; and that He was the natural father of first Inca[1] Manco Ccapac and of his wife Mama[2] Odlo Huaco, and of all their descendants, who were sent to this earth for the benefit of all people. For these reasons, as they themselves say, this was their most solemn feast. . . .

All prepared themselves for the *Raymi* of the Sun by a rigorous fast; for, in three days they ate nothing but a little unripe maize, and a few herbs, with plain water. During this time no fire was lighted throughout the city, and all men abstained from sleeping with their wives.

From Inca Garcilaso de Vega, *Royal Commentaries of the Incas*, Vol. 2, trans. by Clements R. Markham (London: Hakluyt Society, 1809–1871).

1 Inca means "sovereign lord," and in its strictest sense should be used only to refer to this civilization's god-kings. De la Vega at times uses the term loosely to refer to anyone who shared royal blood, himself included. The tribe from which the Incas came was the Quechua.

2 Mother. The queen was the divine mother of her people. As eldest sister and wife of the Inca, she was *Mama-quilla*, or mother moon.

After the fast, in the evening before the festival, the Inca sacrificial Priests prepared the sheep and lambs for sacrifice, and got ready the other offerings of food and drink that were to be offered to the Sun. All these offerings had been provided by the people who came to the feast. . . .

The women of the Sun[3] were engaged, during the night, in preparing an immense quantity of maize pudding called *Canca*. This was made up into small round cakes, about the size of an apple. . . .

The flour for this bread, especially for what was intended for the Inca and those of the blood royal, was ground by the chosen virgins of the Sun, who cooked all the other food for this feast; that it might appear to be given rather by the Sun to his children than by his sons to him; and it was therefore prepared by the virgins, as women of the Sun. . . .

The necessary preparations having been made, the Inca came forth at dawn, on the day of the festival, accompanied by all his relations marching according to their age and dignity. They proceeded to the great square. . . . Here they waited for sunrise, all of them being barefooted, and all watching the east with great attention. As soon as the sun appeared, they all bent down, resting on their elbows (which, among these Indians, is the same as going down on the knees), with the arms apart and the hands raised. Thus they worshiped, and kissed the air . . . and they adored with much fervor and devotion, looking upon the Sun as their god and natural father. . . .

Presently the King rose to his feet, the rest being still prostrate, and took two great cups of gold, full of the beverage that they drink. He performed this ceremony as the first-born, in the name of his father, the Sun, and, with the cup in his right hand, invited all his relations to drink. . . .

Having given the invitation to drink, the Inca emptied the vase in his right hand, which was dedicated to the Sun, into a jar of gold, whence the liquor flowed down a stone conduit of very beautiful masonry from the great square to the temple of the Sun, thus being looked upon as drunk by the Deity. . . .

THE ROYAL PROCESSION THEN ENTERED
THE TEMPLE OF THE SUN

The Inca offered to the Sun the golden vases with which he had performed the ceremony, and the other members of his family gave their cups to the Inca priests, who were set apart for that office; for persons who were not priests, even if they were of the royal blood, were not allowed to perform the priestly office. . . .

As soon as the offerings were made. . . the priests came out with many lambs, ewes, and rams of all colors, for the native sheep of that country are of

---

3 Virgins of royal blood who spent their lives in perpetual seclusion, serving the Sun, to
  whom they were symbolically married.

different colors, like the horses in Spain. All this flock was the property of the Sun. They took a black lamb, for among the Indians this color was preferred for the sacrifices, as more sacred. For they said that a black beast was black all over, while a white one, though its body might be white, always had a black nose, which was a defect, and caused it to be less perfect than a black beast. For this reason also, the Kings generally dressed in black. . . .

This first sacrifice of a black lamb was made to predict the omens of the festival. For they almost always sacrificed a lamb before undertaking any act either of peace or war, in order to see, by examining the heart and lungs, whether it was acceptable to the Sun, that is to say, whether it would be successful or the reverse. In order to seek an omen to tell them whether a harvest would be good; for some crops they used a lamb, for others a ram, for others a sterile ewe; but they never killed a fruitful sheep even to eat, until it was past bearing.

They took the lamb or sheep, and placed it with the head towards the east. They did not tie its feet, but three or four Indians held it, and it was cut open on the left side while still alive. They then forced their hands in, and pulled out the heart with the lungs and gullet up to the mouth, and the whole had to be taken out entire, without being cut. . . .

If the sacrifice of the lamb did not furnish good auguries, they made another sacrifice of a sheep, and if this was also unpropitious they offered up another. But, even if the third sacrifice was unlucky, they did not desist from celebrating the festival, though they did so with inward sorrow and misgiving, believing that their father, the Sun, was enraged against them for some fault or negligence that they must have unintentionally committed against his service. . . .

After the sacrifice of the lamb, they brought a great quantity of lambs and sheep for a general sacrifice, and they did not cut these open while they were alive, but beheaded them first. The blood and hearts of all these, as well as of the first lamb, were preserved and offered to the Sun, and the bodies were burnt until they were converted to ashes.

It was necessary that the fire for the sacrifice should be new, and given by the hand of the Sun, as they expressed it. For this purpose they took a large bracelet. . . . This was held by the high priest. It was larger than usual, and had on it a highly polished concave plate, about the diameter of an orange. They put this towards the Sun, at an angle, so that the reflected rays might concentrate on one point, where they had placed a little cotton wool well pulled out, for they did not know how to make tinder; but the cotton was soon lighted in the natural way. With this fire, thus obtained from the hands of the Sun, they consumed the sacrifice, and roasted all the meat on that day. Portions of the fire were then conveyed to the temple of the Sun, and to the convent of virgins, where they were kept in all the year, and it was an evil omen if they were allowed to go out.

108

From *Relation of the Things of Yucatan* by Bishop Diego de Landa—16th century

Both savior and destroyer of Mayan history, Bishop Diego de Landa (1524–1579) burned 27 rolls of Mayan hieroglyphics as "works of the devil." Yet he also left the main source of information available today about the Maya: Relation of the Things of Yucatan. *In the following excerpt on Mayan religious ritual, de Landa describes both the learning of the Mayan priests and their participation in ritual human sacrifice. Did de Landa have some admiration for the Maya? Why might he have destroyed their written works? How do you explain the contrast between this account of a Mayan ritual and the description of an Incan religious ceremony?*

The natives of Yucatan were as attentive to the matters of religion as to those of government, and they had a high priest. . . . In him was the key of their learning and it was to these matters that they dedicated themselves mostly; and they gave advice to the lords and replies to their questions. . . .

They taught the sons of the other priests and the second sons of the lords who brought them for this purpose from their infancy, if they saw that they had an inclination for this profession.

The sciences which they taught were the computation of the years, months and days, the festivals and ceremonies, the administration of the sacraments, the fateful days and seasons, their methods of divination and their prophecies, events and the cures for diseases, and their antiquities and how to read and write with the letters and characters, with which they wrote, and drawings which illustrate the meaning of the writings.

Their books were written on a large sheet doubled in folds, which was enclosed entirely between two boards which they decorated, and they wrote on both sides in columns following the order of the folds. And they made this paper of the roots of a tree and gave it a white gloss upon which it was easy to write. . . .

From Alfred M. Tozzer, "Landa's Relacion de las cosas de Yucatan," in *Papers of the Peabody Museum of American Archaeology and Ethnology*, Harvard University, Vol. 18 (Cambridge, Mass.: Harvard University Press, 1941).

Besides the festivals in which they sacrificed persons in accordance with their solemnity, the priest or *Chilan*, on account of some misfortune or necessity, ordered them to sacrifice human beings, and everyone contributed to this, that slaves should be bought, or some in their devotion gave their little children, who were made much of, and feasted up to the day. . . .

If the heart of the victim was to be taken out, they led him with a great show and company of people of the temple, and having smeared him with blue and put on a *coroza*, they brought him up to the round altar, which was the place of sacrifice, and after the priest and his officials had anointed the stone with a blue color, and by purifying the temple drove out the evil spirit, the *Chacs* seized the poor victim, and placed him very quickly on his back upon that stone, and all four held him by the legs and arms, so that they divided him in the middle. At this came the executioner, the *Nacom*, with a knife of stone, and struck him with great skill and cruelty a blow between the ribs of his left side under the nipple, and he at once plunged his hand in there and seized the heart like a raging tiger and snatched it out alive and, having placed it upon a plate, he gave it to the priest, who went very quickly and anointed the faces of the idols with that fresh blood. Sometimes they made this sacrifice on the stone and high altar of the temple, and then they threw the body, now dead, rolling down the steps. The officials below took it and flayed it whole, taking off all the skin with the exception of the feet and hands, and the priest, all bare, covered himself, stripped naked as he was, with that skin, and the others danced with him. And this was considered as a thing of great solemnity amongst them. The custom was usually to bury in the court of the temple those whom they had sacrified, or else they ate them.

A Muslim Explains the Hindu Religion by Abul Fazl Akbarnama—16th century

The Muslim Mughal emperors gradually accepted the religion of their Hindu subjects in order to gain their political support. The reign of Akbar in India (1556–1605) brought toleration of the Hindu religion to its highest point. Akbar not only included Hindus in his government, but he also allowed them to openly practice religious observance at court. He also took a Hindu woman as his chief mistress. Many orthodox Muslims were shocked by their emperor's acceptance of people they considered to be unbelievers. As a result, Akbar's chief minister, Abul Fazl, wrote the following document in the hope of assuaging Muslim concerns about Hinduism. How does Abu Fazl attempt to make Hinduism acceptable to Muslims? How does he answer the charge that Hindus are idol worshippers?

They one and all believe in the unity of God, and as to the reverence they pay to images of stone and wood and the like, which simpletons regard as idolatry, it is not so. The writer of these pages has exhaustively discussed the subject with many enlightened and upright men, and it became evident that these images . . . are fashioned as aids to fix the mind and keep the thoughts from wandering, while the worship of God alone is required as indispensable. In all their ceremonial observances and usage they ever implore the favor of the world-illumining sun and regard the pure essence of the Supreme Being as transcending the idea of power in operation.

Brahma. . . they hold to be the Creator; Vishnu, the Nourisher and Preserver; and Rudra,[1] called also Mahadeva, the Destroyer. Some maintain that God who is without equal, manifested himself under these three divine forms, without thereby sullying the garment of His inviolate sanctity, as the Nazarenes hold of the Messiah.[2] Others assert that these were human creatures exalted to these dignities through perfectness of worship, probity of thought

---

From Abul Fazl, *The Ain-i-Akbari*, trans. by H.S. Jarrett, 3 vols. (Calcutta: Baptist Mission Press, 1868–1894).

1 Also known as Shiva.

2 Abul Fazi draws two comparisons here. He compares this Hindu trinity with both the Christian (Nazarene) Holy Trinity (three divine and fully separate persons in one God) and with the incarnation of Jesus Christ (the Messiah), the Second Person of the Holy Trinity. His Muslim audience would have known basic Christian beliefs.

and righteousness of deed. The godliness and self-discipline of this people is such as is rarely to be found in other lands.

They hold that the world had a beginning, and some are of opinion that it will have an end. . . . They allow of no existence external to God. The world is a delusive appearance, and as a man in sleep sees fanciful shapes, and is affected by a thousand joys and sorrows, so are its seeming realities. . . .

Brahman is the Supreme Being; and is essential existence and wisdom and also bliss. . . .

Since according to their belief, the Supreme Deity can assume an elemental form without defiling the skirt of the robe of omnipotence, they first make various idols of gold and other substances to represent this ideal and gradually withdrawing the mind from this material worship, they become meditatively absorbed in the ocean of His mysterious Being. . . .

They believe that the Supreme Being in the wisdom of His counsel, assumes an elementary form of a special character[3] for the good of the creation, and many of the wisest of the Hindus accept this doctrine. . . .

TORTOISE-INCARNATION

In the *Satya Yuga* in the light half of the month of *Karttika* (Oct.–Nov.), on the twelfth lunar day, the Creator manifested himself in the shape of a tortoise. They relate that the deities wished to obtain the water of immortality after the manner of butter by churning the ocean of milk. Instead of a churning-stick, they used the largest of the mountains, *Mandara.* From its excessive weight the mountain sunk into the ocean, and great were their difficulties. The Deity assumed this shape and bore up the mountain on his back and the gods obtained their desire.

By this miraculous act, fourteen priceless objects were brought up from the sea:—(1). *Lakshmi,* the goddess of fortune, appeared as a bride and thus a source of happiness to all creatures was obtained. (2). *Kaustubha-mani* or the wonderful jewel *Kaustubha,* of extraordinary luster and in value beyond price. (3). *Parijataka-vriksha,* the miraculous tree *Parijataka* whose flowers never fade and whose fragrance fills the universe. Some say that it grants all desires. It is called also *Kalpavriksha.* (4). *Sura,* (the goddess of) wine. (5). *Dhanvantari,* the physician (of the gods) who could heal the sick and raise the dead to life. In his right hand, he held a leech and in his left (a branch of) the myrobalan tree. His Majesty considers that these two should be regarded separately and the number of treasures be accounted sixteen. (6). *Ohandra-mani,* the (moon-gem or) world-illumining moon. (7). *Kama-dhenu,* the miraculous cow which gave forth from her udders the gratification of every wish. (8). *Airavata,* the white elephant (of Indra) with four tusks. (9). *Sankha,* the white conch-shell of wondrous

---

3 That is, the Hindu Supreme Being assumes various bodies. These incarnations are
   known as *avatara.*

sound that bestowed victory on whomsoever possessed it. (10). *Visha,* deadly poison. (11). *Amrita,* the water of life. (12) *Rambha*, the nymph, beautiful and sweet-dispositioned. (13) *Asea*, the horse with eight heads. (14). *Sarangadhanus,* or the bow *Saranga* of which the unerring arrow carried to any distance.

After producing these inestimable treasures, the tortoise descended into the earth and is believed still to exist.

INCARNATION AS KRISHNA[4]

More than four thousand years ago, Ugrasena of the Yadu race bore away in his capital of Mathura. His son Kansa rebelled and dethroning his father ruled with a persecuting hand, while at the same time Jarasandha, Sisupala and other princes of the Daityas exorcised unbounded tyranny. The afflicted earth assuming the form of a cow, hastened with Brahma to Vishnu and implored their destruction. The prayer was granted and the divine commission was entrusted to Krishna. They say that the astrologers foretold to Kansa that a child would shortly be born and that his reign would be at an end. He there-upon ordered the slaughter of all infants and thus each year the blood of many innocent children was shed until his sister Devaki married Vasudeva of the Yadu race. Now Kansa heard a report that Devaki's eighth son would be the cause of his death. He therefore confined them both in prison and put to death every son that was born to them. In the beginning of the *Kali Yuga*, on the eighth lunar day of the dark half of the month of *Bhadrapada* (Aug.–Sept.), in the city of Mathura near the metropolis of Agra, the child was born while the guards were negligent. The fetters fell off and the doors were opened and the child spoke thus. "On the other side of the Jamuna, a girl has even now been born in the house of the cowherd Nanda, and the family are asleep. Take and leave me there and bring the girl hither." As Vasudeva set out to fulfil this injunction, the river became fordable and the command was obeyed. Krishna in his ninth year killed Kansa, released Ugrasena from prison and seated him on the throne. He also engaged the other tyrants and overthrew them.

He lived one hundred and twenty-five years and had 16,108 wives, each of whom gave birth to ten sons and one daughter, and each wife thought that she alone shared her husband's bed. . . .

CASTE

The Hindu philosophers reckon four states of auspiciousness which they term *varna*. 1. *Brahman*. 2. *Kshatriya*. 3. *Vaisya*. 4. *Sudra*. Other than these are termed

---

4 Krishna, an avatar of Vishnu the Preserver, is the most popular of all Hindu divine
  incarnations.

Mlechchha.[5] At the creation of the world the first of these classes was produced from the mouth of Brahma, a brief account of whom has already been given: the second, from his arms; the third, from his thigh and the fourth from his feet; the fifth from the cow *Kamadhenu*, the name of Mlechchha being employed to designate them.

The *Brahmans* have six recognized duties. 1. The study of the Vedas[6] and other sciences. 2. The instruction of others (in the sacred texts). 3. The performance of the *Jag*, that is oblation of money and kind to the Devatas.[7] 4. Inciting others to the same. 5. Giving presents. 6. Receiving presents.

Of these six the *Kshatriya* must perform three. 1. Perusing the holy texts. 2. The performance of the Jag. 3. Giving presents. Further they must, 1. Minister to Brahmans. 2. Control the administration of worldly government and receive the reward thereof. 3. Protect religion. 4. Exact fines for delinquency and observe adequate measure therein. 5. Punish in proportion to the offense. 6. Amass wealth and duly expend it. 7. Supervise the management of elephants, horses, and cattle and the functions of ministerial subordinates. 8. Levy war on due occasion. 9. Never ask an alms. 10. Favor the meritorious and the like.

The *Vaisya* also must perform the same three duties of the Brahman, and in addition must occupy himself in: 1. Service. 2. Agriculture. 3. Trade. 4. The care of cattle. 5. The carrying of loads. . . .

The Sudra is incapable of any other privilege than to serve these three castes, wear their cast-off garments and eat their leavings. He may be a painter, goldsmith, blacksmith, carpenter, and trade in salt, honey, milk, butter-milk, clarified butter and grain.

Those of the fifth class, are reckoned as beyond the pale of religion, like infidels, Jews and the like.[8] By the inter-marriages of these, sixteen other classes are formed. The son of Brahman parents is acknowledged as a Brahman. If the mother be a Kshatriya, (the father being a Brahman) the progeny is called *Murdhavasikta*. If the mother be a Vaisya, the son is named *Ambastha,* and if a Sudra girl, *Nishada*. If the father and mother are both Kshatriya, the progeny is Kshatriya. If the mother be a Brahman, (and the father a Kshatriya) the son is called *Suta*. If the mother be a Vaisya, the son is *Mahisya*. If the mother be a Sudra, the progeny is *Ugra*. If both parents be Vaisya, the progeny is Vaisya. If the mother be a Brahman, (which is illicit) the progeny is *Vaideha* but if she be a Kshatriya, which also is regarded as improper, he is *Magadha*. From the Vaisya by a Sudra mother is produced a *Karana*. When both parents are Sudra, the progeny is Sudra. If the mother be a Brahman, the progeny is *Chandala*. If she

---

5 The "outcastes" of Hindu society.

6 The four collections of ancient poetry that are essential sacred texts among Hindus.

7 Hindu deities.

8 Abul Fazl is drawing an analogy for his Muslim readers. Just as Muslims consider all nonbelievers to be outside the community of God, so Hindus regard the Mlechchha as outside the community.

be a Kshatriya, it is called *Chatta*. From a Sudra by a Vaisya girl is produced the *Ayogava*.

In the same away still further ramifications are formed, each with different customs and modes of worship and each with infinite distinctions of habitation, profession, and rank of ancestry that defy computation. . . .

KARMA

Or the ripening of actions. This is a system of knowledge of an amazing and extraordinary character, in which the learned of Hindustan concur without dissenting opinion. It reveals the particular class of actions performed in a former birth which have occasioned the events that befall men in this present life, and prescribes the special expiation of each sin, one by one. It is of four kinds.

The first kind discloses the particular action which has brought a man into existence in one of the five classes into which mankind is divided, and the action which occasions the assumption of a male or female form. A *Kshatriya* who lives continently, will, in his next birth, be born a *Brahman*. A *Vaisya* who hazards his transient life to protect a Brahman, will become a *Kshatriya*. A *Sudra* who lends money without interest and does not defile his tongue by demanding repayment, will be born a *Vaisya*. A *Mlechchha* who serves a *Brahman* and eats food from his house till his death, will become a *Sudra*. A *Brahman* who undertakes the profession of a *Kshatriya* will become a *Kshatriya*, and thus a *Kshatriya* will become a *Vaisya*, and a *Vaisya* a *Sudra*, and a *Sudra* a *Mlechchha*. Whosoever accepts in alms . . . the bed on which a man has died[9] . . . will, in the next birth, from a man become a woman. Any woman or *Mlechchha*, who in the temple . . . sees the form of *Narayana*,[10] and worships him with certain incantations, will in the next birth, if a woman, become a man, and if a *Mlechchha*, a *Brahman*. . . .

The second kind shows the strange effects of actions on health of body and in the production of manifold diseases.

Madness is the punishment of disobedience to father and mother. . . .

Pain in the eyes arises from having looked upon another's wife. . . .

Dumbness is the consequence of killing a sister. . . .

Colic results from having eaten with an impious person or a liar. . . .

Consumption is the punishment of killing a *Brahman*. . . .

The third kind indicates the class of actions which have caused sterility and names suitable remedies. . . .

A woman who does not menstruate, in a former existence . . . roughly drove away the children of her neighbors who had come as usual to play at her house. . . .

A woman who gives birth to only daughters is thus punished for having contemptuously regarded her husband from pride. . . .

---

9 An "unclean" object.

10 The personification of solar and cosmic energy underlying creation.

A woman who has given birth to a son that dies and to a daughter that lives, has, in her former existence, taken animal life. Some say that she had killed goats. . . .

The fourth kind treats of riches and poverty, and the like. Whoever distributes alms at auspicious times, as during eclipses of the moon and sun, will become rich and bountiful (in his next existence). Whoso at these times, visits any place of pilgrimage . . . and there dies, will possess great wealth, but will be avaricious and of a surly disposition. Whosoever when hungry and with food before him, hears the supplication of a poor man and bestows it all upon him, will be rich and liberal. But whosoever has been deprived of these three opportunities, will be empty-handed and poor in his present life.

110

From *The Life of St. Teresa—*1611

Both mystic and spiritual leader, Teresa de Cepeda (1515–1582) was born at Avila, Spain. Her family was prosperous and initially discouraged her from joining a convent. However, Teresa believed that the convent was the best choice for her life. At the age of 21, she joined the Carmelite order and almost immediately became seriously ill. She had health problems for the rest of her life, but they did not stop her from rigorous spiritual exercises and devotion. Neither did they keep her from founding new monasteries and convents, despite the initial disapproval of her superiors. Teresa was canonized a saint in 1622, only 40 years after her death. Her autobiography was published posthumously. In it, she discusses her personal and mystical relationship with God. Do you see any similarities or differences between Teresa of Avila's writing and that of her contemporaries Calvin, Luther, and Erasmus, or even Ignatius of Loyola? What kind of relationship did Teresa have with God?

I was one day in prayer, when I found myself in a moment, without knowing how, plunged apparently into hell. I understood that it was our Lord's will I should see the place which the devils kept in readiness for me, and which I had deserved by my sins. It was but a moment, but it seems to me impossible I should ever forget it even if I were to live many years.

From *The Life of St. Teresa of Avila* by St. Teresa of Avila, trans. from the Spanish by Davis Lewis. Reprinted by permission of Tan Books.

The entrance seemed to be by a long and narrow pass, like a furnace, very low, dark, and close. The ground seemed to be saturated with water, mere mud, exceedingly foul, sending forth pestilential odours, and covered with loathsome vermin. At the end was a hollow place in the wall, like a closet, and in that I saw myself confined. All this was even pleasant to behold in comparison with what I felt there. There is no exaggeration in what I am saying.

But as to what I then felt, I do not know where to begin, if I were to describe it; it is utterly inexplicable. I felt a fire in my soul. I cannot see how it is possible to describe it. My bodily sufferings were unendurable. I have undergone most painful sufferings in this life, and, as the physicians say, the greatest that can be borne, such as the contraction of my sinews when I was paralysed, without speaking of others of different kinds, yea, even those of which I have also spoken, inflicted on me by Satan; yet all these were as nothing in comparison with what I felt then, especially when I saw that there would be no intermission, nor any end to them.

These sufferings were nothing in comparison with the anguish of my soul, a sense of oppression, of stifling, and of pain so keen, accompanied by so hopeless and cruel an infliction, that I know not how to speak of it. If I said that the soul is continually being torn from the body, it would be nothing, for that implies the destruction of life by the hands of another; but here it is the soul itself that is tearing itself in pieces. I cannot describe that inward fire or that despair, surpassing all torments and all pain. I did not see who it was that tormented me, but I felt myself on fire, and torn to pieces, as it seemed to me; and, I repeat it, this inward fire and despair are the greatest torments of all.

Left in that pestilential place, and utterly without the power to hope for comfort, I could neither sit nor lie down; there was no room. I was placed as it were in a hole in the wall; and those walls, terrible to look on of themselves, hemmed me in on every side. I could not breathe. There was no light, but all was thick darkness. I do not understand how it is; though there was no light, yet everything that can give pain by being seen was visible.

I know not how it was, but I understood distinctly that it was a great mercy that our Lord would have me see with mine own eyes the very place from which His compassion saved me. I have listened to people speaking of these things, and I have at other times dwelt on the various torments of hell, though not often, because my soul made no progress by the way of fear; and I have read of the divers tortures, and how the devils tear the flesh with red-hot pincers. But all is as nothing before this; it is a wholly different matter. In short, the one is a reality, the other a picture; and all burning here in this life is as nothing in comparison with the fire that is there.

Ever since that time, as I was saying, everything seems endurable in comparison with one instant of sufferings such as those I had then to bear in hell. I am filled with fear when I see that, after frequently reading books which describe in some manner the pains of hell, I was not afraid of them, nor made any account of them. Where was I? How could I possibly take any pleasure in those things which led me directly to so dreadful a place? Blessed forever be Thou, O my God! and oh, how manifest is it that Thou didst love me much more than I did love Thee! How, often, O Lord, didst Thou save me from that fearful prison! and how I used to get back to it contrary to Thy will!

It was that vision that filled me with the very great distress which I feel at the sight of so many lost souls, especially of the Lutherans—for they were once members of the Church by baptism—and also gave me the most vehement desires for the salvation of souls; for certainly I believe that, to save even one from those overwhelming torments, I would most willingly endure many deaths. If here on earth we see one whom we specially love in great trouble or pain, our very nature seems to bid us compassionate him; and if those pains be great, we are troubled ourselves. What, then, must it be to see a soul in danger of pain, the most grievous of all pains, forever? Who can endure it? It is a thought no heart can bear without great anguish. Here we know that pain ends with life at last, and that there are limits to it; yet the sight of it moves our compassion so greatly. That other pain has no ending; and I know not how we can be calm, when we see Satan carry so many souls daily away.

The Effects of the Divine Graces in the Soul—The Inestimable Greatness of One Degree of Glory

It is painful to me to recount more of the graces which our Lord gave me than these already spoken of; and they are so many, that nobody can believe they were ever given to one so wicked: but in obedience to our Lord, who has commanded me to do it, and you, my fathers, I will speak of some of them to His glory. May it please His Majesty it may be to the profit of some soul! For if our Lord has been thus gracious to so miserable a thing as myself, what will He be to those who shall serve Him truly? Let all people resolve to please His Majesty, seeing that He gives such pledges as these even in this life.

My love of, and trust in, our Lord, after I had seen Him in a vision, began to grow, for my converse with Him was so continual. I saw that, though He was God, He was man also; that He is not surprised at the frailties of men; that He understands our miserable nature, liable to fall continually, because of the first sin, for the reparation of which He had come. I could speak to Him as a friend, though He is my Lord, because I do not consider Him as one of our earthly lords, who affect a power they do not possess, who give audience at fixed hours, and to whom only certain persons may speak. If a poor man have any business with these, it will cost him many goings and comings, and currying favour with others, together with much pain and labour before he can speak to them. Ah, if such a one has business with a king! Poor people, not of gentle blood, cannot approach him, for they must apply to those who are his friends; and certainly these are not persons who tread the world under their feet; for they who do this speak the truth, fear nothing, and ought to fear nothing; they are not courtiers, because it is not the custom of a court, where they must be silent about those things they dislike, must not even dare to think about them, lest they should fall into disgrace.

O my Lord! O my King! who can describe Thy Majesty? It is impossible not to see that Thou art Thyself the great Ruler of all, that the beholding of Thy Majesty fills men with awe. But I am filled with greater awe, O my Lord, when I consider Thy humility, and the love Thou hast for such as I am. We can converse and speak with Thee about everything whenever we will; and when we lose our first fear and awe at the vision of Thy Majesty, we have a greater dread of offending Thee—not arising out of the fear of punishment, O my Lord, for that is as nothing in comparison with the loss of Thee!

I am not yet fifty, and yet I have seen so many changes during my life, that I do not know how to live. What will they do who are only just born, and who may live many years? Certainly I am sorry for those spiritual people who, for certain holy purposes, are obliged to live in the world; the cross they have to carry is a dreadful one.

Certain Heavenly Secrets, Visions, and Revelations

One night I was so unwell that I thought I might be excused making my prayer; so I took my rosary, that I might employ myself in vocal prayer, trying not to be recollected in my understanding, though outwardly I was recollected, being in my oratory. These little precautions are of no use when our Lord will have it otherwise. I remained there but a few moments thus, when I was rapt in spirit with such violence that I could make no resistance whatever. It seemed to me that I was taken up to heaven; and the first persons I saw there were my father and my mother. I saw other things also; but the time was no longer than that in which the *Ave Maria* might be said, and I was amazed at it, looking on it all as too great a grace for me. But as to the shortness of the time, it might have been longer, only it was all done in a very short space.

It happened, also, as time went on, and it happens now from time to time, that our Lord showed me still greater secrets. The soul, even if it would, has neither the means nor the power to see more than what He shows it; and so, each time, I saw nothing more than what our Lord was pleased to let me see. But such was the vision, that the least part of it was enough to make my soul amazed, and to raise it so high that it esteems and counts as nothing all the things of this life. I wish I could describe in some measure, the smallest portion of what I saw; but when I think of doing it, I find it impossible; for the mere difference alone between the light we have here below, and that which is seen in a vision—both being light—is so great, that there is no comparison between them; the brightness of the sun itself seems to be something exceedingly loathsome. In a word, the imagination, however strong it may be, can neither conceive nor picture to itself this light, nor any one of the things which our Lord showed me in a joy so supreme that it cannot be described; for then all the senses exult so deeply and so sweetly, that no description is possible.

I was in this state once for more than an hour, our Lord showing me wonderful things. He seemed as if He would not leave me. He said to me: "See, My daughter, what they lose who are against Me; do not fail to tell them of it." Ah, my Lord, how little good my words will do them, who are made blind by their own conduct, if Thy Majesty will not give them light! Some, to whom Thou hast given it, there are, who have profited by the knowledge of Thy greatness; but as they see it revealed to one so wicked and base as I am, I look upon it as a great thing if there should be any found to believe me. Blessed be Thy name, and blessed be Thy compassion; for I can trace, at least in my own soul, a visible improvement. Afterwards I wished I had continued in that trance for ever, and that I had not returned to consciousness.

111

"On the Necessity of the Wager" From *Pensees* by Blaise Pascal— 1660

A mathematician and physicist, Blaise Pascal (1623–1662) accomplished much during his brief life. Born to a French middle-class family, his mathematical talents were obvious by the time he was 15 years old. Although of a pragmatic and rational disposition, Pascal was also concerned with the mysterious relationship between God and man, which troubled many Enlightenment thinkers. In this selection from his Pensees *("Thoughts"), Pascal speculates about the nature of this relationship. What wager did Pascal think one should make? Why?*

184. A letter to incite to the search after God.

And then to make people seek Him among the philosophers, sceptics, and dogmatists, who disquiet him who inquires of them.

185. The conduct of God, who disposes all things kindly, is to put religion into the mind by reason, and into the heart by grace. But to will to put it into the mind and heart by force and treats is not to put religion there, but terror; *terorrem potius quam religionem.*[22]

"I know not who put me into the world, nor what the world is, nor what I myself am. I am in terrible ignorance of everything. I know not what my body is, nor my senses, nor my soul, not even that part of me which thinks what I

From *Pensees* by Blaise Pascal, trans. by W.F. Trotter. The Harvard Classics (New York: P.F. Collier & Son, 1909–14).

say, which reflects on all and on itself, and knows itself no more than the rest. I see those frightful spaces of the universe which surround me, and I find myself tied to one corner of this vast expanse, without knowing why I am put in this place rather than in another, nor why the short time which is given me to live is assigned to me at this point rather than at another of the whole eternity which was before me or which shall come after me. I see nothing but infinites on all sides, which surround me as an atom and as a shadow which endures only for an instant and returns no more. All I know is that I must soon die, but what I know least is this very death which I cannot escape.

"As I know not whence I come, so I know not whither I go. I know only that, in leaving this world, I fall for ever either into annihilation or into the hands of an angry God, without knowing to which of these two states I shall be for ever assigned. Such is my state, full of weakness and uncertainty. And from all this I conclude that I ought to spend all the days of my life without caring to inquire into what must happen to me. Perhaps I might find some solution to my doubts, but I will not take the trouble, nor take a step to seek it; and after treating with scorn those who are concerned with this care, I will go without foresight and without fear to try the great event, and let myself be led carelessly to death, uncertain of the eternity of my future state."

Who would desire to have for a friend a man who talks in this fashion? Who would choose him out from others to tell him of his affairs? Who would have recourse to him in affliction? And indeed to what use in life could one put him?

In truth, it is the glory of religion to have for enemies men so unreasonable; and their opposition to it is so little dangerous that it serves, on the contrary, to establish its truths. For the Christian faith goes mainly to establish these two facts: the corruption of nature, and redemption by Jesus Christ. Now I contend that, if these men do not serve to prove the truth of the redemption by the holiness of their behaviour, they at least serve admirably to show the corruption of nature by sentiments so unnatural.

Nothing is so important to man as his own state, nothing is so formidable to him as eternity; and thus it is not natural that there should be men indifferent to the loss of their existence, and to the perils of everlasting suffering. They are quite different with regard to all other things. They are afraid of mere trifles; they foresee them; they feel them. And this same man who spends so many days and nights in rage and despair for the loss of office, or for some imaginary insult to his honour, is the very one who knows without anxiety and without emotion that he will lose all by death. It is a monstrous thing to see in the same heart and at the same time this sensibility to trifles and this strange insensibility to the greatest objects. It is an incomprehensible enchantment, and a supernatural slumber, which indicates as its cause an all–powerful force.

There must be a strange confusion in the nature of man, that he should boast of being in that state in which it seems incredible that a single individual should be. However, experience has shown me so great a number of such persons that the fact would be surprising, if we did not know that the greater part of those who trouble themselves about the matter are disingenuous and not, in fact, what they say. They are people who have heard it said that it is the fashion to be thus daring. It is what they call "shaking off the yoke," and they try to imitate this. But it would not be difficult to make them understand how greatly they deceive themselves in thus seeking esteem. This is not the way to gain it, even I say among those men of the world who take a healthy view of things and who know that the only way to succeed in this life is to make ourselves appear honourable, faithful, judicious, and capable of useful service to a friend; because naturally men love only what may be useful to them. Now, what do we gain by hearing it said of a man that he has now thrown off the yoke, that he does not believe there is a God who watches our actions, that he considers himself the sole master of his conduct, and that he thinks he is accountable for it only to himself.? Does he think that he has thus brought us to have hence-forth complete confidence in him and to look to him for consolation, advice, and help in every need of life? Do they profess to have delighted us by telling us that they hold our soul to be only a little wind and smoke, especially by telling us this in a haughty and self-satisfied tone of voice? Is this a thing to say gaily? Is it not, on the contrary, a thing to say sadly, as the saddest thing in the world?

Who then will blame Christians for not being able to give a reason for their belief, since they profess a religion for which they cannot give a reason? They declare, in expounding it to the world, that it is a foolishness, and then you complain that they do not prove it! If they proved it, they would not keep their word; it is in lacking proofs that they are not lacking in sense. "Yes, but although this excuses those who offer it as such and takes away from them the blame of putting it forward without reason, it does not excuse those who receive it." Let us then examine this point, and say, "God is, or He is not." But to which side shall we incline? Reason can decide nothing here. There is an infinite chaos which separated us. A game is being played at the extremity of this infinite distance where heads or tails will turn up. What will you wager? According to reason, you can do neither the one thing nor the other; according to reason, you can defend neither of the propositions.

Do not, then, reprove for error those who have made a choice; for you know nothing about it. "No, but I blame them for having made, not this choice, but a choice; for again both he who chooses heads and he who chooses tails are equally at fault, they are both in the wrong. The true course is not to wager at all."

Yes; but you must wager. It is not optional. You are embarked. Which will you choose then? Let us see. Since you must choose, let us see which interests you least. You have two things to lose, the true and the good; and two things to stake, your reason and your will, your knowledge and your happiness; and your nature has two things to shun, error and misery. Your reason is no more shocked in choosing one rather than the other, since you must of necessity choose. This is one point settled. But your happiness? Let us weigh the gain and the loss in wagering that God is. Let us estimate these two chances. If you gain, you gain all; if you lose, you lose nothing. Wager, then, without hesitation that He is. "That is very fine. Yes, I must wager, but I may perhaps wager too much." Let us see. Since there is an equal risk of gain and of loss, if you had only to gain two lives, instead of one, you might still wager. But if there were three lives to gain, you would have to play (since you are under the necessity of playing), and you would be imprudent, when you are forced to play, not to chance your life to gain three at a game where there is an equal risk of loss and gain. But there is an eternity of life and happiness. And this being so, if there were an infinity of chances, of which one only would be for you, you would still be right in wagering one to win two, and you would act stupidly, being obliged to play, by refusing to stake one life against three at a game in which out of an infinity of chances there is one for you, if there were an infinity of an infinitely happy life to gain. But there is here an infinity of an infinitely happy life to gain, a chance of gain against a finite number of chances of loss, and what you stake is finite. It is all divided; where-ever the infinite is and there is not an infinity of chances of loss against that of gain, there is no time to hesitate, you must give all. And thus, when one is forced to play, he must renounce reason to preserve his life, rather than risk it for infinite gain, as likely to happen as the loss of nothingness.

CHAPTER 13

Law, Government, and War—1500–1750 CE

I n 1500, Europe was beginning its move toward world domination. At this time, the Ottoman Empire was at the peak of its power, and Japan was about to close its borders to outsiders. The samurai dominated the feudal government in Japan, while peasants worked the land and struggled to make a living. The same was true in Russia, where increasing numbers of peasants were reduced to serfdom. In Europe, however, the feudal system was being challenged by the growth of urban communities. China was still a vast, sophisticated, and powerful empire administered along Confucian lines. Religious tolerance was on its way out in India under the last of the Mughal rulers, the devout Aurangzeb.

This section starts with Machiavelli's very modern advice to his Prince and continues with a document praising the rule and organization of the Ottoman court. Would Suleiman have heeded or needed Machiavelli's advice?

The documents on Japan and Russia show that feudal society was still strong in these areas, whereas the last two provide insight into the Chinese and Mughal empires. Do you see any similarity between the styles of government in the Ottoman, Mughal, and Chinese empires?

From *The Prince* by Niccolo Machiavelli—1513

A diplomat in the service of the Republic of Florence, Niccolo Machiavelli (1469–1527) wrote The Prince *after he was forced into exile by the fall of the Republic. This work is considered to be one of the classics of modern political science. Influenced by his experiences in government, Machiavelli wrote this tract in the hope that it would help him regain favor and a job. What is Machiavelli's view of human nature? How does it compare with that of John Calvin? What is "modern" about Machiavelli's ideas?*

That Which Concerns a Prince on the Subject of the Art of War

The Prince ought to have no other aim or thought, nor select anything else for his study, than war and its rules and discipline; for this is the sole art that belongs to him who rules, and it is of such force that it not only upholds those who are born princes, but it often enables men to rise from a private station to that rank. And, on the contrary, it is seen that when princes have thought more of ease than of arms they have lost their states. And the first cause of your losing it is to neglect this art; and what enables you to acquire a state is to be master of the art. Francesco Sforza, though being martial, from a private person became Duke of Milan; and the sons, through avoiding the hardships and troubles of arms, from dukes became private persons. For among other evils which being unarmed brings you, it causes you to be despised, and this is one of those ignominies against which a prince ought to guard himself, as is shown later on.

Concerning Things for Which Men, and Especially Princes, are Blamed

It remains now to see what ought to be the rules of conduct for a prince toward subject and friends. And as I know that many have written on this point, I expect I shall be considered presumptuous in mentioning it again, especially as in discussing it I shall depart from the methods of other people. But it being my intention to write a thing which shall be useful to him to apprehends it, it appears to me more appropriate to follow up the real truth of a matter than the imagination of it; for many have pictured republics and principalities which in fact have never been known or seen, because how one lives is so far distant from how one ought to live, that he who neglects what is done

From Niccolo Machiavelli, *The Prince*, ed. W.K. Marriott (London: J.M. Dent and Sons, 1908).

for what ought to be done, sooner effects his ruin than his preservation; for a man who wishes to act entirely up to his professions of virtue soon meets with what destroys him among so much that is evil.

Hence, it is necessary for a prince wishing to hold his own to know how to do wrong, and to make use of it or not according to necessity. Therefore, putting on one side imaginary things concerning a prince, and discussing those which are real, I say that all men when they are spoken of, and chiefly princes for being more highly placed, are remarkable for some of those qualities which bring them either blame or praise; and thus it is that one is reputed liberal, another miserly . . .; one is reputed generous, one rapacious; one cruel, one compassionate; one faithless, another faithful. . . . And I know that every one will confess that it would be most praiseworthy in a prince to exhibit all the above qualities that are considered good; but because they can neither be entirely possessed nor observed, for human conditions do not permit it, it is necessary for him to be sufficiently prudent that he may know how to avoid the reproach of those vices which would lose him his state . . .

Concerning Cruelty and Clemency, and Whether it is Better to be Loved than Feared

Upon this a question arises: whether it is better to be loved than feared or feared than loved? It may be answered that one should wish to be both, but, because it is difficult to unite them in one person, it is much safer to be feared than loved, when, of the two, either must be dispensed with. Because this is to be asserted in general of men, that they are ungrateful, fickle, false, cowardly, covetous, and as long as you succeed they are yours entirely; they will offer you their blood, property, life, and children, as is said above, when the need is far distant; but when it approaches they turn against you. And that prince who, relying entirely on their promises, has neglected other precautions, is ruined; because friendships that are obtained by payments, and not by nobility or greatness of mind, may indeed be earned, but they are not secured, and in time of need cannot be relied upon; and men have less scruple in offending one who is beloved than one who is feared, for love is preserved by the link of obligation which, owing to the baseness of men, is broken at every opportunity for their advantage; but fear preserved you by a dread of punishment which never fails.

Nevertheless a prince ought to inspire fear in such a way that, if he does not win love, he avoids hatred; because he can endure very well being feared whilst he is not hated, which will always be as long as he abstains from the property of his citizens and subjects and from their women.

113

From *Turkish Letters* by
Ogier Ghiselin de Busbecq—1589

Born in Flanders, Ogier Ghiselin de Busbecq (1522–1592) served as an ambassador for the Hapsburgs and the Holy Roman Emperor. He was sent to the Ottoman Empire at the height of its power under Suleiman the Magnificent. He wrote four letters to his friend Nicholas Michault about his impressions of Turkey. Busbecq was also responsible for importing tulips into Europe and starting tulip mania. The following excerpt deals with Suleiman and his court. What impressed Bubecq about Suleiman and his court? What did he think was the main difference between the Turkish and European armies?

On our arrival . . . we were taken to call on Achmet Pasha (the chief Vizier) and the other pashas[1]—for the Sultan himself was not then in the town—and commenced our negotiations with them touching the business entrusted to us by King Ferdinand. The pashas . . . did not offer any strong opposition to the views we expressed, and told us that the whole matter depended on the Sultan's pleasure. On his arrival we were admitted to an audience; but the manner and spirit in which he [the Sultan] listened to our address, our arguments, and our message, was by no means favorable.

The Sultan was seated on a very low ottoman, not more than a foot from the ground, which was covered with a quantity of costly rugs and cushions of exquisite workmanship; near him lay his bow and arrows. His air, as I said, was by no means gracious, and his face wore a stern, though dignified, expression.

On entering we were separately conducted into the royal presence by the chamberlains,[2] who grasped our arms. . . . After having gone through a pretence of kissing his hand, we were conducted backwards to the wall opposite his seat, care being taken that we should never turn our backs on him. The Sultan then listened to what I had to say; but the language I used was not at all to his taste, for the demands of his Majesty breathed a spirit of independence and dignity, which was by no means acceptable to one who deemed that his wish was law; and so he made no answer beyond saying in an impatient way, "Giusel, giusel," i.e. well, well. After this we were dismissed to our quarters.

From C.T. Foster and F.H. blackburne Daniell, eds., *The Life and Letters of Ogier Ghiselin de Busbecq*, 2 vols. (London: Hakluyt Society, 1881).

1 Pasha was an honorary title for a high-ranking military or government official; a vizier served the sultan as an adviser or provincial governor.

2 An official of the royal court involved in matters connected with the king's household.

The Sultan's hall was crowded with people, among whom were several officers of high rank. Besides these there were all the troopers of the Imperial guard,[3] and a large force of Janissaries;[4] but there was not in all that great assembly a single man who owed his position to anything save his valor and his merit. No distinction is attached to birth among the Turks; the respect to be paid to a man is measured by the position he holds in the public service. There is no fighting for precedence; a man's place is marked out by the duties he discharges. . . . It is by merit that men rise in the service, a system which ensures that posts should only be assigned to the competent. Each man in Turkey carries in his own hand his ancestry and his position in life, which he may make or mar as he will. Those who receive the highest offices from the Sultan are for the most part the sons of shepherds or herdsmen, and so far from being ashamed of their parentage, they actually glory in it, and consider it a matter of boasting that they owe nothing to the accident of birth; for they do not believe that high qualities are either natural or hereditary, nor do they think that they can be handed down from father to son, but that they are partly the gift of God, and partly the result of good training, great industry, and unwearied zeal; arguing that high qualities do not descend from a father to his son or heir, any more than a talent for music, mathematics, or the like. . . . Among the Turks, therefore, honors, high posts, and judgeships are the rewards of great ability and good service. If a man is dishonest, or lazy, or careless, he remains at the bottom of the ladder, an object of contempt; for such qualities there are no honors in Turkey!

This is the reason that they are successful in their undertakings, that they lord it over others, and are daily extending the bounds of their empire. These are not our ideas, with us there is no opening left for merit; birth is the standard for everything; the prestige of birth is the sole key to advancement in the public service. . . .

The Turkish monarch going to war takes with him over 40,000 camels and nearly as many baggage mules, of which a great part, when he is invading Persia,[5] are loaded with rice and other kinds of grain. These mules and camels also serve to carry tents and armor, and likewise tools and munitions for the campaign. The territories, which bear the name of Persia . . . are less fertile than our country, and even such crops as they bear are laid waste by the inhabitants in time of invasion in hopes of starving out the enemy, so that it is very dangerous for an army to invade Persia, if it is not furnished with abundant supplies. The invading army carefully abstains from encroaching on its supplies

---

3 The Imperial Guard under Suleiman consisted of approximately 4,000 men who camped around his tent at night and served as his personal bodyguard in battle.

4 An elite military force in the service of the sultan, whose ranks originally were filled by young sons of Christian families who were converted to Islam and given over completely to military training. Ideally, they lived according to a strict code of absolute obedience, abstinence from luxury, religious observance, celibacy, and confinement to barracks.

5 The Shi'ite empire of Persia was the bitter enemy of the Ottoman sultans throughout the sixteenth century.

at the outset, as they are well aware that, when the season for campaigning draws to a close, they will have to retreat over districts wasted by the enemy, or scraped as bare by countless hordes of men and droves of baggage animals, as if they had been devastated by locusts; accordingly they reserve their stores as much as possible for this emergency. . . .

From this you will see that it is the patience, self-denial, and thrift of the Turkish soldier that enable him to face the most trying circumstances, and come safely out of the dangers that surround him. What a contrast to our men! . . .

. . . For each man is his own worst enemy, and has no foe more deadly than his own intemperance, which is sure to kill him, if the enemy be not quick. It makes me shudder to think of what the result of a struggle between such different systems must be; one of us must prevail and the other be destroyed, at any rate we cannot both exist in safety. On their side is the vast wealth of their empire, unimpaired resources, experience and practice in arms, a veteran soldiery, an uninterrupted series of victories, readiness to endure hardships, union, order, discipline, thrift, and watchfulness. On ours are found an empty exchequer, luxurious habits, exhausted resources, broken spirits, a raw and insubordinate soldiery, and greedy generals; there is no regard for discipline, license runs riot, the men indulge in drunkenness and debauchery, and, worst of all, the enemy are accustomed to victory, we, to defeat. Can we doubt what the result must be?

114

Rules for Peasant Life in Japan—1619

After centuries of warfare, the Tokugawa Shoguns and leading nobles (daimyo) of Japan were determined to maintain a stable society by restricting peasant life to productive work. Peasants were forbidden to fight in war because this was the traditional occupation of the samurai. The following document was written by Naoe Kanetaugu, a Japanese official in the service of the daimyo of Aizu. Japanese society and culture was strongly influenced by China. Can you see any Confucian influence in this selection? What was the role of peasant women in rural Japan during this period?

From *Sources of Japanese History*, ed. and trans. by David John Lu (New York: McGraw-Hill, 1974), Vol. 2, p. 216–218.

1. Consider the Lord of your domain, the sun and the moon. Respect your fief holder[1] or magistrate as the patron deity of your place. Treat your village head[2] as if he were your own father.

2. During the first five days of the new year, pay respect to those around you in accordance with your position. Within the first fifteen days, make more than enough ropes needed to perform your major and minor public services (corvée labor[3] for the year). After the first fifteen days, when mountains and fields are covered with snow, accumulate all the firewood needed for the year. Use a sleigh to pull nightsoil on the fields. At night make sandals for horses. Daughters and wives must sew and weave China-grass[4] to make clothing for their menfolk. If there is a housewife who makes an excessive amount of tea to entertain others, visits around in the absence of menfolk and gossips, then she must have a hidden lover. Even if a man has a child with her, that kind of woman must be sent away. . . .

5. During the fourth month, men must work in the fields from dawn to dusk and make furrows as deep as the hoe can penetrate. Wives and daughters must make meals three times, put on red headbands and take the meals to the fields. Old and young alike must put the meals in front of the men who are soiled from their work. By seeing the wives attired in red, men, old and young alike, can be so encouraged . . . to the extent of forgetting their fatigue. Once men are home after dusk, give them bath water, and let them wash their feet. Sisters-in-law and female cousins must put the chapped feet of the man on the stomach of his wife and massage them. Let him forget the toil of the day.

Near the end of the fourth month, put a harrow on the horse and rake the fields. Cut miscanthus grass from the nearby mountains and put them on the China-grass field. If the field is located near a house, always check how the wind is blowing before burning the miscanthus grass. If time is appropriate, sow millet, barley and wheat seeds.

13. During the twelfth month, if there is a notification from the fief holder or magistrate about a tax overdue, quickly make the payment. For this favor he renders you, send a bowl of loach[5] fish soup accompanied by a dish of fried sardines. Although, according to the regulations, all that is expected of a farmer on such an occasion is a bowl of soup and a dish of vegetables, the ones just suggested are more appropriate. If no tax is paid after the due notice, you can have your precious wife taken away from you as security. Do not forget that in your master's house there are many young minor officials and

---

1 Landowner.

2 The head of village government was drawn from local landowning families.

3 Corvée labor refers to unpaid labor required of peasants on the lord's lands or on various public works projects.

4 China-grass and miscanthus grass, mentioned later in the document, were both plants grown for their fiber.

5 A species of carp.

middlemen who may steal your wife. To make sure that kind of thing never happens to you, pay all your taxes before the end of the eleventh month. Take heed that this advice is adhered to. You are known as a man of lowly origin. But even so, you do not wish to see your precious wife exposed to wild winds (misfortunes), being taken away from you and stolen by younger men. In this fashion you may lose the support of the way of heaven, come to the end of the rope, be scorned by your lowly peer groups, and regret the incident forever. Always remember that such a misfortune can befall you, and be diligent in delivering your annual tax rice and in doing work for the magistrate. Once all the annual taxes are paid, prepare for the coming of the new year. Make the remaining rice into rice cake (*mochi*), brew some *sake*, buy some salted fish, and add another year to your life happily. New Year is the time you must be able to chant along with others: I set sail on this journey of longevity. May the moon also accompany me!.

115

Laws Governing the Military Households by Tokugawa Hidetada—1615

The founder of the powerful Tokugawa dynasty, Tokugawa Ieyasu became shogun in 1603. Although he gave the office of Shogun to his son Hidetada in 1606, Ieyasu dominated the government for many years. He decided to have a committee of scholars draw up a code of behavior for the samurai, Japan's feudal aristocracy. The following document contains the system of laws regulating their behavior that was proclaimed in 1615. How did Ieyasu try to maintain control over his nobles through these laws? What elements of Chinese influence do you detect?

1. The study of literature and the practice of the military arts, archery and horsemanship, must be cultivated diligently. . . .

From Ryusaku Tsunoda, et al., *Sources of Japanese Tradition*, p. 335–338. Copyright © 1958 by Columbia University Press. Reprinted by permission.

From of old the rule has been to practice "the arts of peace on the left hand, and the arts of war on the right"; both must be mastered. Archery and horsemanship are indispensable to military men. Though arms are called instruments of evil, there are times when they must be resorted to. In peacetime we should not be oblivious to the danger of war. Should we not, then, prepare ourselves for it?

2. Drinking parties and wanton revelry should be avoided.

In the codes that have come down to us this kind of dissipation has been severely proscribed. Sexual indulgence and habitual gambling lead to the downfall of a state.

3. Offenders against the law should not be harbored or hidden in any domain.

Law is the basis of social order. Reason may be violated in the name of the law, but law may not be violated in the name of reason. Those who break the law deserve heavy punishment.

4. Great lords (daimyo), the lesser lords, and officials should immediately expel from their domains any among their retainers or henchmen who have been charged with treason or murder.

Wild and wicked men may become weapons for overturning the state and destroying the people. How can they be allowed to go free?

5. Henceforth no outsider, none but the inhabitants of a particular domain, shall be permitted to reside in that domain.

Each domain has its own ways. If a man discloses the secrets of one's own country to another domain or if the secrets of the other domain are disclosed to one's own, that will sow the seeds of deceit and sycophancy.

6. Whenever it is intended to make repairs on a castle of one of the feudal domains, the (shogunate) should be notified. The construction of any new castles is to be halted and stringently prohibited.

"Big castles are a danger to the state."[1] Walls and moats are the cause of great disorders.

7. Immediate report should be made of innovations which are being planned or of factional conspiracies being formed in neighboring domains.

"Men all incline toward partisanship; few are wise and impartial. There are some who refuse to obey their masters, and others who feud with their neighbors."[2] Why, instead of abiding by the established order, do they wantonly embark upon new schemes?

8. Do not enter into marriage privately (i.e., without notifying the shogunate authorities).

---

1 The quotation is a paraphrase from one of the Confucian Classics, "The Tradition of Tso," originally a commentary on one of the other Classics, "The Spring and Autumn Annals."

2 From the Seventeen Article Constitution of Prince Shotuku (573–621). While serving as regent for his aunt, Empress Suiko, the prince drew up seventeen principles of government designed to strengthen central authority and end disorder. He drew heavily on Confucian principles.

Marriage follows the principle of harmony between yin and yang,[3] and must not be entered into lightly. In the *Book of Changes*[4], . . . it says, "Marriage should not be contracted out of enmity (against another). Marriages intended to effect an alliance with enemies (of the state) will turn out badly." The Peach Blossom ode in *The Book of Poetry* also says that "When men and women are proper in their relationships and marriage is arranged at the correct time; then throughout the land there will be no loose women." To form an alliance by marriage is the root of treason.

9. Visits of the *daimyo* to the capital are to be in accordance with regulations.

The *Chronicles of Japan, Continued*[5] contains a regulation that "Clansmen should not gather together whenever they please, but only when they have to conduct some public business; and also that the number of horsemen serving as an escort in the capital should be limited to twenty. . . ." Daimyo should not be accompanied by a large number of soldiers. Twenty horsemen shall be the maximum escort for daimyo with an income of from one million to two hundred thousand *koku* of rice.[6] For those with an income of one hundred thousand *koku* or less, the escort should be proportionate to their income. On official missions, however, they may be accompanied by an escort proportionate to their rank.

10. Restrictions on the type and quality of dress to be worn should not be transgressed.

Lord and vassal, superior and inferior, should observe what is proper to their station in life. (Then follows an injunction against the wearing of fine white damask or purple silk by retainers without authorization.)

11. Persons without rank shall not ride in palanquins.[7]

From of old there have been certain families entitled to ride in palanquins without special permission, and others who have received such permission. Recently, however, even the ordinary retainers and henchmen of some families have taken to riding about in palanquins, which is truly the worst sort of presumption. Henceforth permission shall be granted only to the lords of the

---

3 Yin and yang are the two fundamental forces, tendencies, or elements in Chinese philosophy that since ancient times have been used to explain change in natural processes of all sorts. Yin suggests qualities that are female, weak, dark, cold, and connected with the moon; Yang suggests qualities that are male, strong, warm, bright, and connected with the sun.

4 *The Book of Changes*, a treatise on divination, and *The Book of Poetry*, a collection of songs, are among the oldest of the Confucian Classics.

5 *Nihon shoki, The Chronicle of Japan*, written in A.D. 720, is the oldest official history of Japan, covering the mythical age of the gods up to the time of the Empress Jito, who reigned from A.D. 686 to 697. This quote comes from a sequel to *The Chronicle*, written in 697, called the *Shoku nihongi*.

6 One koku equaled about five bushels; a person's rank was determined by the amount of rice his lands produced.

7 Enclosed carriages, or litters, usually for one person, borne on the shoulders of several men by means of poles.

various domains, their close relatives and ranking officials, medical men and astrologers, those over sixty years of age, and those ill or infirm. In the cases of ordinary household retainers or henchmen who willfully ride in palanquins, their masters shall be held accountable.

Exceptions to this law are the court families, Buddhist prelates, and the clergy in general.

12. The samurai of the various domains shall lead a frugal and simple life.

When the rich make a display of their wealth, the poor are humiliated and envious. Nothing engenders corruption so much as this, and therefore it must be strictly curbed.

13. The lords of the domains should select officials with a capacity for public administration.

Good government depends on getting the right men. Due attention should be given to their merits and faults; rewards and punishments must be properly meted out. If a domain has able men, it flourishes; if it lacks able men it is doomed to perish. This is the clear admonition of the wise men of old.

The purport of the foregoing should be conscientiously observed.

116

Russian Law Code—1649

The following legal code was drawn up by Tsar Alexis I (1645–1676) after discussion with the national assembly. The code was extensive; laws relating to blasphemers and heretics as well as illegal taverns were contained among its 25 chapters. This excerpt deals with laws that affected many Russians, that is, the process by which free peasants became serfs permanently bound to a noble's estate. By the end of the seventeenth century, large numbers of peasants had been reduced to serfdom and could be bought and sold by their lords. Serfdom differed from slavery only in that a family of serfs had a small plot of land where they could grow their own crops. According to this legal code, who controlled the rights of marriage in peasant society? What rights did the wives and children of serfs have?

From *Readings in Russian Civilization*, ed. by Thomas Rhia, Vol. I, p. 155–162. Copyright © 1969 by University of Chicago Press. Reprinted by permission.

CHAPTER XI. PROCEDURE CONCERNING THE PEASANTS

1. All peasants who have fled from lands belonging to the Tsar[1] and are now living on lands belonging to church officials, hereditary landowners and service landowners[2] are to be returned to the Tsar's lands according to the land cadastres of 1627–31[3] regardless of the fifteen-year limit.[4] These peasants are to be returned with their wives, children, and all movable property.

2. The same applies to peasants who have fled from hereditary landowners and service landowners to other hereditary landowners and service landowners, or to the towns, to the army, or to lands belonging to the Tsar.

3. Fugitive peasants must be returned with their wives, children, and movable property, plus their standing grain and threshed grain. But the possessions which the fugitive peasants owned in the years prior to this code are not to be claimed. If a fugitive peasant gave his daughter, sister, or niece in marriage to a local peasant, do not break up the marriage. Leave the girl with the local peasant. It was not a crime in the past to receive fugitive peasants—there was only a time limit for recovering them. Therefore the lord of the local peasant should not be deprived of his labor, especially as lands have changed hands frequently so that the present lord may not have been the person who received the fugitives anyway.

4. All hereditary landowners, service landowners, and officials managing the Tsar's lands must have proper documents identifying their peasants in case of dispute. Such documents must be written by public scribes. . . . Illiterate landholders must have their documents signed by impartial, trustworthy persons. . . .

7. A hereditary landowner who buys an estate has a right to all the peasants who were inscribed in the land cadastres of 1627–31. If all such peasants are not on the estate as listed in the purchase documents, the purchaser may take from the seller's other estates replacement peasants with all their movable property, their standing grain, and their threshed grain. . . .

10. Henceforth a person who harbors another's peasants must pay the rightful lord ten rubles[5] per year for each fugitive to compensate the

---

1 Villages and agricultural land owned by the tsar, the income from which supported the imperial court and other government activities.

2 As the two terms imply, hereditary landowners held their land as private property and could pass it on to their heirs. Service landowners received their land from the tsar in return for serving in the tsar's administration or army. The land was returned to the tsar when the landowner left government service or died.

3 Books that recorded the general census after the Moscow fire of 1626 destroyed earlier records.

4 In the previous century, the number of years in which a landlord could seek out and force the return of fugitive slaves had been raised to fifteen years. Now the limit was lifted altogether.

5 The ruble is a unit of Russian money; to give some idea of its value at the time, a contract between a landlord and a peasant in 1636 reveals that five rubles would buy a horse, two rubles would buy a cow, and one ruble would buy a hog; a document from 1672 states that fifty rubles were needed to set up a peasant with seed, animals, farm implements, and household goods.

plaintiff[6] for his lost income and the taxes he paid while the peasant was absent and must surrender the fugitive peasants to him. . . .

12. If a girl flees after the promulgation of this code and marries another landholder's peasant, then her husband and children will be returned with her to her former landholder. The movable property of her husband, however, will not be returned with them.

13. When a widower marries a fugitive peasant girl, any children he had by a previous marriage will not be surrendered with him to the lord of his new wife, but will remain with the lord of his first wife. . . .

15. If a widowed peasant remarries in flight, then both she and her husband will be returned to the lord of her first husband, provided her first husband was registered with a landholder.

16. If the peasant widow's first husband was not registered with a landholder, then she must live on the premises belonging to the lord of the peasant she married.

17. If a peasant in flight marries off his daughter, then his son-in-law will be returned to the landholder of his wife. . . .

18. A peasant women in flight who marries will be returned with her husband to her former landholder.

19. Peasant women who are permitted to marry another landholder's peasant must be given release documents in which they are precisely described.

20. When peasants arrive in a hereditary estate or in a service estate and say that they are free people and wish to live with the landholder as peasants, the landholder must ascertain the truth of their claim. Within a year such people must be brought to Moscow or another large city for certification.

21. The lord who did not check carefully whether such people were free must pay the plaintiff to whom the peasants rightfully belong ten rubles per year per fugitive to compensate the plaintiff for his lost income and the taxes he paid while the peasant was absent.

22. Peasant children who deny their parents must be tortured.

23. Those people of any rank who give loans to another lord's peasant to entice them to their lands will lose the loans when the peasants are returned to their rightful lords. . . .

26. If the defendant[7] admits that he has the fugitive peasants but denies that the peasants came to him with any property; and if the plaintiff lists the property in his suit and then wins the case by an oath, award him five rubles for the movable property of each peasant and return the peasants to him.

27. If someone denies during a trial that he has someone's peasant and takes an oath on this, and later the peasant turns up on his estate, return the peasant to the plaintiff with all the movable property listed in the suit. Beat the false oath taker with the knout[8] for three days in the market place as an

---

6 A person who brings a grievance against a defendant in a court of law; in this case, a landowner demanding the return of fugitive serfs.

7 The landowner accused of harboring fugitive serfs.

8 A leather whip used to flog criminals.

example to others and then jail him for a year. Henceforth do not believe him in any matter and do not grant him a trial against anyone for anything.

28. The children of peasants who are taken from a defendant and surrendered to a plaintiff by a court order must be surrendered even though they were not inscribed in the land cadastres of 1627–31—provided they are living with their parents and not separately. . . .

32. Peasants may voluntarily hire themselves out to work for people of all ranks, but the latter may not hire them on condition of servitude or bondage. When the hirelings finish their work, they must be discharged without any hindrance.

33. Bondmen and peasants who flee abroad and then return to Russia cannot claim that they are free men, but must be returned to their former hereditary landowners and service landowners.

34. When fugitive peasants of different landowners marry abroad, and then return to Russia, the landholders will cast lots for the couple. The winning service landowner gets the couple and must pay five rubles to the landholder who lost because both of the peasants were in flight abroad.

117

From *Self-Portrait of a Chinese Emperor* by K'ang Hsi—1654–1722

One of the most successful emperors of the Ch'ing dynasty, K'ang Hsi left behind a collection of writings that revealed much about his thoughts. He inherited the throne in 1661 and ruled wisely for 61 years. In the following document, K'ang Hsi discusses the problems faced by an emperor in administering justice as well as difficulties with the Chinese civil service examination. How does the emperor feel about the use of capital punishment? What does he feel were some of the abuses of the examination system? How could they be eliminated?

From Jonathan D. Spence, *Emperor of China: Self-Portrait of K'ang-Hsi* (New York: Alfred A. Knopf, 1974), p. 29–34, 40–41, 50–51. Copyright © 1973 by Jonathan D. Spence. Reprinted by permission of Alfred A. Knopf, a division of Random House, Inc.

Giving life to people and killing people—those are the powers that the emperor has. He knows that administrative errors in government bureaus can be rectified, but that a criminal who has been executed cannot be brought back to life any more than a chopped string can be joined together again. He knows, too, that sometimes people have to be persuaded into morality by the example of an execution. In 1683, after Taiwan had been captured, the court lecturers and I discussed the image of the fifty-sixth hexagram in the *Book of Changes,*[1] "Fire on the Mountain": the calm of the mountain signifies the care that must be used in imposing penalties; the fire moves rapidly on, burning up the grass, like lawsuits that should be settled speedily. My reading of this was that the ruler needs both clarity and care in punishing: his intent must be to punish in order to avoid the need for further punishing.

Hu Chien-ching was a subdirector of the Court of Sacrificial Worship whose family terrorized their native area in Kiangsu, seizing people's lands and wives and daughters, and murdering people after falsely accusing them of being thieves. When a commoner finally managed to impeach him, the Governor was slow to hear the case, and the Board of Punishments recommended that Hu be dismissed and sent into exile for three years. I ordered instead that he be executed with his family and in his native place, so that all the local gentry might learn how I regarded such behavior. Corporal Yambu was sentenced to death for gross corruption in the shipyards. I not only agreed to the penalty but sent guards officer Uge to supervise the beheading, and ordered that all shipyard personnel from generals down to private soldiers kneel down in full armor and listen to my warning that execution would be their fate as well unless they ended their evil ways. . . .

The final penalty of lingering death[2] must be given in cases of treason, as the Legal Code requires. . . . I awarded the same punishment to the rebel Wang Shihyüan, who had claimed to be Chu San Tái-tzu, the surviving Ming claimant to the throne, so that the Ming prince's name should be invoked no more as a rallying point for rebels, as had been done too many times before. When Ilaguksan Khutuktu, who had had his spies in the lamas' residences so that they would welcome Galdan's[3] army into China, and had plotted with Galdan and encouraged him in his rebellion, was finally caught, I had him brought to Peking and cut to death in the Yellow Temple, in the presence of all the Manchu and Mongol princes, and the senior officials, both civil and military. All that was left of Galdan were the ashes, but these we exposed to the public outside the Forbidden City. . . .

But apart from such treason cases, when there are men who have to be executed immediately . . . or when one is dealing with men like those who

---

1 Also known as the *I ching,* or *Classic of Changes,* this is one of the Confucian Classics; it is a handbook for telling the future based on the study of eight trigrams (figures made up of three lines) and sixty-four hexagrams (figures made up of six lines).

2 A slow, painful, and humiliating punishment in which a person died from the administration of numerous cuts on the body.

3 A lama was a Buddhist priest, or monk, in Tibet, Mongolia, and western China. Galdan was a leader of a Western Mongol tribe who in the late seventeenth century conquered much of Chinese Turkestan and Outer Mongolia; when he threatened Peking (modern Beijing), Emperor K'ang-hsi raised an army and crushed him in 1696.

plotted against me in the Heir-Apparent crisis[4] and had to be killed immediately and secretly without trial, I have been merciful where possible. For the ruler must always check carefully before executions, and leave room for the hope that men will get better if they are given the time. In the hunt one can kill all the animals caught inside the circle, but one can't always bear to shoot them as they stand there, trapped and exhausted. . . .

Of all the things that I find distasteful, none is more so than giving a final verdict on the death sentences that are sent to me for ratification. . . . Though naturally I could not go through every case in detail, I nevertheless got in the habit of reading through the lists in the palace each year, checking the name and registration and status of each man condemned to death, and the reason for which the death penalty had been given. Then I would check through the list again with the Grand Secretaries and their staff in the audience hall, and we would decide who might be spared. . . .

Each year we went through the lists, sparing sixteen out of sixty-three at one session, eighteen out of fifty-seven at another, thirty-three out of eighty-three at another. For example, it was clear to me that the three cases of husbands killing wives that came up . . . were all quite different. The husband who hit his wife with an ax because she nagged at him for drinking, and then murdered her after another domestic quarrel—how could any extenuating circumstances be found? But Pao-erh, who killed his wife for swearing at his parents; and Meng, whose wife failed to serve him properly and used foul language so that he killed her—they could have their sentences reduced. . . . At other times what looked like a lighter crime proved to be serious: thus Liu-ta had killed Ma-erh with a stone, but as the Grand Secretaries explained, the victim had been struck twelve times in all, and his brains had burst out onto the ground. Liu-ta was obviously an experienced killer and should be executed. . . .

It's a good principle to look for the good points in a person, and to ignore the bad. If you are always suspicious of people they will suspect you too; that was why, when Dantsila was brought to my tent, although he was Galdan's nephew and had been fleeing to Tibet with the ashes of Galdan's body before he despaired and surrendered, I showed my trust by having him sit near me, and offered him a knife with which to cut his meat. Later I gave him a prince's title, and he served me faithfully. Though the Russians had been killing our people on the northern frontier, I ordered that the Russian prisoners should be given new suits of clothes and be released just as we began the siege of Albazin, and after the second siege in 1687 I ordered that the sick Russians be treated personally by my own doctors and sent home. So thirty years later the Uriang-hai people submitted to us without a battle, because they remembered our clemency to the Russians long before.

. . .

---

4 One of several plots designed to bring the Ming back to power in China.

There are too many men who claim to be pure scholars and yet are stupid and arrogant; we'd be better off with less talk of moral principle and more practice of it. Even in those who have been the best officials in my reign there are obvious failings. . . . P'eng P'eng was always honest and courageous—when robbers were in his district he simply put on his armor, rode out, and routed them—but when angry he was wild and vulgar in his speech, and showed real disrespect. Chao Shen-ch'iao was completely honest, traveled with only thirteen servants and no personal secretaries at all, but was too fond of litigation and was constantly getting the common people involved in complex cases. Shih Shih-lun was an official of complete integrity, but he swung too much in favor of the poor—in any lawsuit when a commoner was involved with a junior degree holder he'd favor the commoner, and when a junior degree holder was involved with a member of the upper gentry he'd favor the junior degree holder. . . . And Chang P'eng-ko, whom I praised so often and kept in the highest offices, could write a memorial so stupid that I ordered it printed up and posted in major cities so that everyone could read it—for he claimed that the drop in the river's level was due to a miracle performed by the spirit of the waters, when the real reason was that no rain had fallen for six months in the upper reaches of the Yellow River. . . .

This is one of the worst habits of the great officials, that if they are not recommending their teachers or their friends for high office then they recommend their relations. This evil practice used to be restricted to the Chinese: they've always formed cliques and then used their recommendations to advance the other members of the clique. Now the practice has spread to the Chinese Bannermen[5] like Yü Ch'eng-lung; and even the Manchus, who used to be so loyal, recommend men from their own Banners, knowing them to have a foul reputation, and will refuse to help the Chinese. . . .

In 1694 I noted that we were losing talent because of the ways the exams were being conducted: even in the military exams most of the successful candidates were from Chekiang and Chiangnan, while there was only one from Honan and one from Shansi.[6] The successful ones had often done no more than memorize old examination answer books, whereas the best *should* be selected on the basis of riding and archery. Yet it is always the strong men from the western provinces who are eager to serve in the army, while not only are troops from Chekiang and Chiangnan among the weakest, they also pass on their posts to their relatives who are also weak.

Even among the examiners there are those who are corrupt, those who do not understand basic works, those who ask detailed questions about practical matters of which they know nothing, those who insist entirely on memorization of the *Classics*[7] and refuse to set essays, those who put candidates from

---

5 Minor members of the noble class, usually provided with land and a small stipend by the government.

6 Chekiang and Chiangnan were southeast coastal regions of China; Honan and Shansi were north-central provinces with no seacoast.

7 A clearly specified set of books associated with China's Confucian tradition.

their own geographical area at the top of the list, or those who make false claims about their abilities to select the impoverished and deserving. . . . As to the candidates, not only are there few in the Hanlin Academy who can write a proper eulogy, there are many whose calligraphy is bad and who can't even punctuate the basic history books. . . . Other candidates hire people to sit the exams for them, or else pretend to be from a province that has a more liberal quota than their own. It's usually easy enough to check the latter, since I've learnt to recognize the accents from thirteen provinces, and if you watch the person and study his voice you can tell where he is really from. As to the other problems, one can overcome some of them by holding the exams under rigorous armed supervision and then reading the exam papers oneself.

118

The Ideal Muslim Prince, Aurangzeb—1658–1707

The Indian Mughal Empire was blessed with a series of talented rulers, beginning with its founding in 1526 and extending to the middle of the seventeenth century. These rulers made the court at the imperial city of Agra and later at Delhi a great cultural center of the world. Under Akbar, for example, there was increasing religious tolerance and discussion between Muslims, Hindus, and Christians. This process continued under his son and grandson, Jahangir and Shah Jehan, respectively. Aurangzeb, the last Mughal emperor, who ruled from 1658 to 1707, reversed this trend because of his character and personal beliefs. The following excerpt comes from the History of the World, *written by the Persian Bahkhtawar Khan, an admirer of Aurangzeb. Why does the author believe that Aurangzeb was the perfect Muslim prince? What does Aurangzeb believe is the purpose of literature and poetry?*

Be it known to the readers of this work that this humble slave of the Almighty is going to describe in a correct manner the excellent character, the worthy habits and the refined morals of this most virtuous monarch, Aurangzeb, according as he has witnessed them with his own eyes. The Emperor, a great worshiper of God by natural propensity, is remarkable for his

From Henry M. Elliot and John Dawson, eds., *The History of India as Told by Its Own Historians*, 8 vols. (London: Truebner, 1867–1877), vol. 7, p. 156–162.

rigid attachment to religion. . . . Having made his ablutions, he always occupies a great part of his time in adoration of the Deity, and says the usual prayers, first in the mosque and then at home, both in congregation and in private, with the most heartfelt devotion. He keeps the appointed fasts on Fridays and other sacred days, and he reads the Friday prayers in *Jami* mosque[1] with the common people of the Muslim faith. He keeps vigils during the whole of the sacred nights, and with the light of the favor of God illumines the lamps of religion and prosperity. From his great piety, he passes whole nights in the mosque which is in his palace, and keeps company with men of devotion. In privacy he never sits on a throne. He gave away in alms before his accession a portion of his allowance of lawful food and clothing, and now devotes to the same purpose the income of a few villages in the district of Delhi, and the proceeds of two or three salt-producing tracts, which are appropriated to his private purse. . . . During the whole month of Ramadan he keeps fast, says the prayers appointed for that month, and reads the holy Qur'an in the assembly of religious and learned men, with whom he sits for that purpose during six, and sometimes nine hours of the night. During the last ten days of the month, he performs worship in the mosque, and although, on account of several obstacles, he is unable to proceed on a pilgrimage to Mecca,[2] yet the care which he takes to promote facilities for pilgrims to that holy place may be considered equivalent to the pilgrimage. . . .

Though he has collected at the foot of his throne those who inspire ravishment in joyous assemblies of pleasure, in the shape of singers who possess lovely voices and clever instrumental performers, and in the commencement of his reign sometimes used to hear them sing and play, and though he himself understands music well, yet now for several years past, on account of his great restraint and self-denial . . . he entirely abstains from this amusement. If any of the singers and musicians becomes ashamed of his calling, he makes an allowance for him or grants him land for his maintenance. . . .

In consideration of their rank and merit, he shows much honor and respect to the saints and learned men, and through his cordial and liberal exertions, the sublime doctrines of our pure religion have obtained such prevalence throughout the wide territories of Hindustan as they never had in the reign of any former king.

Hindu writers have been entirely excluded from holding public offices, and all the worshipping places of the infidels[3] and the great temples of these infamous people have been thrown down and destroyed in a manner which excites astonishment at the successful completion of so difficult a task. . . .

---

1 The *Jami* mosque, usually the largest mosque in a city or village, is the cite of the congregational prayers said by Muslims on Friday.

2 Along with the creed (by which one affirms belief in God and the prophecy of Muhammad), daily prayer, alms-giving, and fasting during the holy month of Ramadan, making a pilgrimage to Mecca, the city of Muhammad's birth, was considered an act that every Muslim should strive to perform.

3 Hindus; although on Aurangzeb's orders many Hindu temples were destroyed, the author wildly exaggerates when he claims that all Hindu edifices were destroyed.

As it is a great object with this Emperor that all Muslims should follow the principles of the religion . . . and as there was no book which embodied them all, and as until many books had been collected and a man had obtained sufficient leisure, means and knowledge of theological subjects, he could not satisfy his inquiries on any disputed point, therefore His Majesty, the protector of the faith, determined that a body of eminently learned and able men of Hindustan should take up the voluminous and most trustworthy works which were collected in the royal library, and having made a digest of them, compose a book which might form a standard canon of the law,[4] and afford to all an easy and available means of ascertaining the proper and authoritative interpretation. The chief conductor of this difficult undertaking was the most learned man of the time, Shaikh Nizam, and all the members of the society were very handsomely and liberally paid, so that up to the present time a sum of about two hundred thousand rupees[5] has been expended in this valuable compilation, which contains more than one hundred thousand lines. When the work, with God's pleasure, is completed, it will be for all the world the standard exposition of the law. . . .

The Emperor is perfectly acquainted with the commentaries, traditions and law. . . . One of the greatest excellences of this virtuous monarch is, that he has learned the Qur'an by heart. Though in his early youth he had committed to memory some chapters of that sacred book, yet he learned the whole by heart after ascending the throne. He took great pains and showed much perseverance in impressing it upon his mind. He writes in a very elegant . . . hand, and has acquired perfection in this art. He has written two copies of the holy book with his own hand, and having finished and adorned them with ornaments and marginal lines, at the expense of seven thousand rupees, he sent them to the holy cities of Mecca and Medina. . . . He is a very elegant writer in prose, and has acquired proficiency in versification, but agreeably to the words of God, "Poets deal in falsehoods," he abstains from practicing it. He does not like to hear verses except those which contain a moral. "To please Almighty God he never turned his eye towards a flatterer, nor gave his ear to a poet."

The Emperor has given a very liberal education to his fortunate and noble children, who, by virtue of his attention and care, have reached to the summit of perfection, and made great advances in rectitude, devotion, and piety, and in learning the manners and customs of princes and great men. Through his instruction they have learned the Book of God[6] by heart, obtained proficiency in the sciences and polite literature, writing the various hands, and in learning the Turkish and the Persian languages.

---

4 Islamic law.

5 A unit of Indian money. By comparison, Shah Jahan is reputed to have spent 40,000,000 rupees on the Taj Mahal.

6 The Qur'an.

In like manner, the ladies of the household also, according to his orders, have learned the fundamental and necessary tenets of religion, and all devote their time to the adoration and worship of the Deity, to reading the sacred Qur'an, and performing virtuous and pious acts. The excellence of character and the purity of morals of this holy monarch are beyond all expression. As long as nature nourishes the tree of existence, and keeps the garden of the world fresh, may the plant of the prosperity of this preserver of the garden of dignity and honor continue fruitful!

CHAPTER 14

Science, Medicine, and Technology— 1500–1750 CE

Startling discoveries regarding planetary motion and physics by Galileo and Newton were at the core of the scientific revolution of the sixteenth and seventeenth centuries, despite the efforts of Christian churches to suppress these new discoveries. How might their own religious beliefs have affected the work of Galileo and Newton? Why might both the Protestant and Catholic Churches have been alarmed by these new discoveries?

China was still the most technically advanced country in the world in 1500. In one of the documents in this section, the Jesuit missionary Matteo Ricci marvels at the sophistication of Chinese technology. What did Ricci feel was superior about Chinese printing?

The study of medicine still lagged behind the other sciences, although some advances were made during this period. Treatment of gunshot wounds posed new problems for surgeons such as Pare, whereas Vesalius struggled against the long-held belief of the medical community in the error-filled work of Galen. What methods did Pare and Vesalius use to develop new medical practices? The prescription written by William Harvey, one of the leading Western scientists of the day, shows that medical practice during this period was not much different than that of the ancient Egyptians. Is there anything scientific about the remedies Harvey prescribed?

From *The Two New Sciences* by Galileo Galilei—1638

Galileo Galilei (1564–1642 CE) was born in Florence and educated in Padua, Italy. Building on the theory of the Polish astronomer Copernicus that the Earth revolved around the Sun, Galileo developed the first telescope. With it, he identified the moons of Jupiter. When he wrote a dialogue comparing the Copernican system with the Aristotelian system accepted by the Catholic Church, Galileo was arrested by the Inquisition and charged with heresy. Forced to recant his belief in the Copernican system, he remained under house arrest but had Two New Sciences *smuggled out of Italy to the Netherlands, where it was published. The following excerpt discusses the theory of inertia, one of the most important discoveries of the new scientists. What kind of reasoning does Galileo use to make his point? According to Galileo, why are some people unwilling to accept new scientific theories?*

SAGREDO. I have always considered it to be an idle notion of the common people that in these and similar frameworks one cannot reason from the small to the large, because many mechanical devices succeed on a small scale that cannot exist in great size. Now, all reasonings about mechanics have their foundations in geometry, in which I do not see that largeness and smallness make large circles, triangles, cylinders, cones, or any other figures [or] solids subject to properties different from those of small ones; hence if the large scaffolding is built with every member proportional to its counterpart in the smaller one, and if the smaller is sound and stable under the use for which it is designed, I fail to see why the larger should not also be proof against adverse and destructive shocks that it may encounter.

SALVATI. Here you must note how conclusions that are true may seem improbable at a first glance, and yet when only some small thing is pointed out, they cast off their concealing cloaks and, thus naked and simple, gladly show off their secrets. For who does not see that a horse falling from a height of three or four braccia will break its bones, while a dog falling from the same height, or a cat from eight or ten, or even more, will suffer no harm? Thus a cricket might fall without damage from a tower, or an ant from the moon. Small children remain unhurt in falls that would break the legs, or the heads, of their elders. And just as smaller animals are proportionately stronger or more robust than larger ones, so smaller plants will sustain themselves better. I think you both know that if an oak were two hundred feet high, it could not support branches spread out similarly to those of an oak of average size. Only by a miracle could nature form a horse the size of twenty horses, or a giant ten times the height of a man—unless she greatly altered the proportions of the members, especially those of the skeleton, thickening the bones far beyond their ordinary symmetry.

Similarly, to believe that in artificial machines the large and small are equally practicable and durable is a manifest error. Thus, for example, small spires, little columns, and other solid shapes can be safely extended or heightened without risk of breaking them, whereas very large ones will go to pieces at any adverse accident, or for no more cause than that of their own weight.

I say that that motion is equably or uniformly accelerated which,
abandoning rest, adds on to itself equal momenta of swiftness in equal times.

SAGREDO. Just as it would be unreasonable for me to oppose this, or any other definition whatever assigned by any author, all [definitions] being arbitrary, so I may, without offence, doubt whether this definition, conceived and assumed in the abstract, is adapted to, suitable for, and verified in the kind of accelerated motion that heavy bodies in fact employ in falling naturally. And since it seems that the Author promises us that what he has defined is the natural motion of heavy bodies, I should like to hear you remove certain doubts that disturb my mind, so that I can then apply myself with better attention to the propositions that are expected, and their demonstrations.

SALVATI. It will be good for you and Simplicio to propound the difficulties, which I imagine will be the same ones that occurred to me when I first saw this treatise, and that our Author himself put to rest for me in our discussions, or that I removed for myself by thinking them out.

SAGREDO. I picture to myself a heavy body falling. It leaves from rest; that is, from the deprivation of any speed whatever, and enters into motion in which it goes accelerating according to the ratio of increase of time from its first instant of motion. It will have obtained, for example, eight degrees of speed in eight pulse-beats, of which at the fourth beat it will have gained four; at the second [beat], two; and at the first, one. Now, time being infinitely divisible, what follows from this? The speed being always diminished in this ratio, there will be no degree of speed, however small (or we might say, "no degree of slowness, however great"), such that the moveable will not be found to have this [at some time] after its departure from infinite slowness, that is, from rest. Thus if the degree of speed that it had at four beats of time were such that, maintaining this uniformly, it would run two miles in one hour, while with the degree of speed that it had at the second beat it would have made one mile an hour, it must be said that in instants of time closer and closer to the first [instant] of its moving from rest, it would be found to be so slow that, continuing to move with this slowness, it would not pass a mile in an hour, nor in a day, nor in a year, nor in a thousand [years], and it would not pass even one span in some still longer time. Such events

I find very hard to accommodate in my imagination, when our senses show us that a heavy body in falling arrives immediately at a very great speed.

SALVATI. This is one of the difficulties that gave me pause at the outset; but not long afterward I removed it, and its removal was effected by the same experience that presently sustains it for you.

You say that it appears to you that experience shows the heavy body, having hardly left from rest, entering into a very considerable speed; and I say that this same experience makes it clear to us that the first impetuses of the falling body, however heavy it may be, are very slow indeed. Place a heavy body on some yielding material, and leave it until it has pressed as much as it can with its mere weight. It is obvious that if you now raise it one or two braccia, and then let it fall on the same material, it will make a new pressure on impact, greater than it made by its weight alone. This effect will be caused by the falling moveable in conjunction with the speed gained in fall, and will be greater and greater according as the height is greater from which the impact is made; that is, according as the speed of the striking body is greater. The amount of speed of a falling body, then, we can estimate without error from the quality and quantity of its impact.

But tell me, gentlemen: if you let a sledge fall on a pole from a height of four braccia, and it drives this, say, four inches into the ground, and will drive it much less from a height of two braccia, and still less from a height of one, and less yet from a span only; if finally it is raised but a single inch, how much more will it accomplish than if it were placed on top [of the pole] without striking it at all? Certainly very little. And its effect would be quite imperceptible if it were lifted only the thickness of a leaf. Now, since the effect of impact is governed by the speed of a given percussent, who can doubt that its motion is very slow and minimal when its action is imperceptible? You now see how great is the force of truth, when the same experience that seemed to prove one thing at first glance assures us of the contrary when it is better considered.

But without restricting ourselves to this experience, though no doubt it is quite conclusive, it seems to me not difficult to penetrate this truth by simple reasoning. We have a heavy stone, held in the air at rest. It is freed from support and set at liberty; being heavier than air, it goes falling downward, not with uniform motion, but slowly at first and continually accelerated thereafter. Now, since speed may be increased or diminished *in infinitum,* what argument can persuade me that this moveable, departing from infinite slowness (which is rest), enters immediately into a speed of ten degrees rather than into one of four, or into the latter before a speed of two, or one, or one-half, or one one-hundredth? Or, in short, into all the lesser [degrees] *in infinitum?*

Please hear me out. I believe you would not hesitate to grant me that the acquisition of degrees of speed by the stone falling from the state of rest may occur in the same order as the diminution and loss of those same degrees when, driven by impelling force, the stone is hurled upward to the same height. But if that is so, I do not see how it can be supposed that in the diminution of speed in the ascending stone, consuming the whole speed, the stone can arrive at rest before passing through every degree of slowness.

SIMPLICIO. But if the degrees of greater and greater tardity are infinite, it will never consume them all, and this rising heavy body will never come to rest, but will move forever while always slowing down—something that is not seen to happen.

SALVATI. This would be so, Simplicio, if the moveable were to hold itself for any time in each degree; but it merely passes there, without remaining beyond an instant. And since in any finite time [*temp quanta*], however small, there are infinitely many instants, there are enough to correspond to the infinitely many degrees of diminished speed. It is obvious that this rising heavy body does not persist for any finite time in any one degree of speed, for if any finite time is assigned, and if the moveable had the same degree of speed at the first instant of that time and also at the last, then it could likewise be driven upward with this latter degree [of speed] through as much space [again], just as it was carried from the first [instant] to the second; and at the same rate it would pass from the second to a third, and finally, it would continue its uniform motion *in infinitum*.

SIMPLICIO. Truly, I should be one of those who concede that the falling heavy body *vires acquirat eundo* [acquires force in going], the speed increasing in the ratio of the space, while the momentum of the same percussent is doubled when it comes from double height, appear to me as propositions to be granted without repugnance or controversy.

SALVATI. And yet they are as false and impossible as [it is] that motion should be made instantaneously, and here is a very clear proof of it. When speeds have the same ratio as the spaces passed or to be passed, those spaces come to be passed in equal times, if therefore the speeds with which the falling body passed the space of four braccia were the doubles of the speeds with which it passed the first two braccia, as one space is double the other space, then the times of those passages are equal; but for the same moveable to pass the four braccia and the two in the same time cannot take place except in instantaneous motion. But we see that the falling heavy body makes its motion in time, and passes the two braccia in less [time] than the four; therefore it is false that its speed increases as the space.

The other proposition is shown to be false with the same clarity. For that which strikes being the same body, the difference and momenta of the impacts must be determined only by the difference of the speeds; if therefore the percussent coming from a double height delivers a blow of double momentum, it must strike with double speed; but double speed passes the double space in the same time, and we see the time of descent to be longer from the greater height.

SAGREDO. Too evident and too easy is this [reasoning] with which you make hidden conclusions manifest. This great facility renders the conclusions less prized than when they were under seeming contradiction. I think that people generally will little esteem ideas gained with so little trouble, in comparison with those over which long and unresolvable altercations are waged.

SALVATI. Things would not be so bad if men who show with great brevity and clarity the fallacies of propositions that have commonly been held to be true by people in general received only such bearable injury as scorn in place of thanks. What is truly unpleasant and annoying is a certain other attitude that some people habitually take. Claiming, in the same studies, at least parity with anyone that exists, these men see that the conclusions they have been putting forth as true are later exposed by someone else, and shown to be false by short and easy reasoning. I shall not call their reaction envy, which then usually transforms itself into rage and hatred against those who reveal such fallacies, but I do say that they are goaded by a desire to maintain inveterate errors rather than to permit newly discovered truths to be accepted. This desire sometimes induces them to write in contradiction to those truths of which they themselves are only too aware in their own hearts, merely to keep down the reputations of other men in the estimation of the common herd of little understanding. I have heard from our Academician not a few such false conclusions, accepted as true and [yet] easy to refute; and I have kept a record of some of these.

120

"Problems of Medical Research" From *De Humani Corporis Fabrica* by Andreas Vesalius—1543

The Belgian anatomist and physician Andreas Vesalius (1514–1564) helped to correct medical misconceptions that had prevailed since ancient times by writing about his experience in dissecting human bodies. Born in Brussels, he attended the University of Louvain and the University of Paris, where he studied medicine and developed his interest in anatomy. He was able to prove through his own research that the teachings of Galen were based on the anatomy of animals, even though they were meant as guides to the human body.

Vesalius' seven volumes on the structure of the human body, De Humani Corporis Fabrica, *were illustrated with fine engravings based on his own drawings. His books were the most complete works on human anatomy available at the time. In the following excerpt from* Fabrica, *Vesalius writes about the problems physicians faced during this period.*

From *Andreas Vesalius of Brussels, 1514–1564* by C.D. O'Malley (Berkeley, University of California Press, 1965).

According to Vesalius, what hinders discoveries in medical science? Why were physicians of his era often scorned? Why does he criticize those who followed Galen's teachings?

TRANSLATIONS FROM THE
FABRICA (1543)

Various things, most gracious Emperor Charles, very seriously hinder those investigating the scientific arts so that they are not accurately or fully learned, and I believe furthermore that no little loss occurs through the too-great separation that has taken place between those disciplines that complement one another for the fullest comprehension of a single art; even much more the very capricious division by practitioners of an art into separate specialties so that those who set the limits of the art for themselves tenaciously grasp one part of it while other things which are in fact very closely related are cast aside. Consequently they never demonstrate excellence and never attain their proposed end but constantly fall away from the true foundation of that art.

Passing over the other arts in silence, I shall speak briefly of that which concerns the health of mankind; indeed, of all the arts the genius of man has discovered it is by far the most beneficial and of prime necessity, although difficult and laborious. Nothing was able to plague it more than when at one time, and especially after the Gothic invasions and the reign of Mansor, King of Persia—under whom the Arabs lived, as was proper, on terms of familiarity with the Greeks—medicine began to be maimed by the neglect of that primary instrument, the hand, so that [the manual aspects of medicine] were relegated to ordinary persons wholly untrained in the disciplines subserving the art of medicine. Once there were three medical sects, that is, Dogmatic, Empirical, and Methodical, but their members consulted the whole art as the means of preserving health and driving away sicknesses. All the thoughts of each sect were directed toward this goal and three methods were employed: The first was a regimen of diet, the second the use of drugs, and the third the use of the hands. Except for this last, the other methods clearly indicate that medicine is the addition of things lacking and the withdrawal of superfluities; as often as we resort to medicine it displays its usefulness in the treatment of sickness, as time and experience teach, and its great benefit to mankind. This triple method of treatment was equally familiar to the physicians of each sect, and those using their own hands according to the nature of the sickness used no less effort in training them than in establishing a theory of diet or in understanding and compounding drugs.

In addition to the other books so perfectly composed by the divine Hippocrates, this is very clearly demonstrated in those *On the function of the physician, On fractures of bones,* and *On dislocations of joints and similar ailments.* Furthermore, Galen, after Hippocrates the prince of medicine, in addition to his occasional boast that the care of the gladiators of Pergamum was entrusted solely to him, and that although age was already weighing him down it did not please him that the monkeys he was to dissect should be skinned by slaves, frequently assures us of his pleasure in the employment of his hands, and how zealously, like other Asiatic physicians, he used them. Indeed, none of the other ancients was so concerned that the treatment made with the hands, as well as that performed by diet and drugs, be handed down to posterity.

Especially after the devastation of the Goths when all the sciences, formerly so flourishing and fittingly practised, had decayed, the more fashionable physicians, first in Italy in imitation of the old Romans, despising the use of the hands, began to relegate to their slaves those things which had to be done manually for their patients and to stand over them like architects. Then when, by degrees, others who practised true medicine also declined those unpleasant duties—not, however, reducing their fees or dignity—they promptly degenerated from the earlier physicians, leaving the method of cooking and all the preparation of the patients' diet to nurses, the composition of drugs to apothecaries, and the use of the hands to barbers. And so in the course of time the art of treatment has been so miserably distorted that certain doctors assuming the name of physicians have arrogated to themselves the prescription of drugs and diet for obscure diseases, and have relegated the rest of medicine to those whom they call surgeons but consider scarcely as slaves. They have shamefully rid themselves of what is the chief and most venerable branch of medicine, that which based itself principally upon the investigation of nature—as if there were any other; even today [this branch of medicine] is exercised among the Indians, especially by the kings, and in Persia by law of inheritance it is handed down to the children as once the whole art was by the Asclepiads. The Thracians, with many other nations, cultivate and honor it very highly almost to the neglect of that other part of the art, the prescription of drugs. This the Romans once proscribed from the state considering it delusive and destructive of mankind, and of no benefit to nature since, although seeking to aid nature while it is wholly concerned in an attempt the throw off the sickness, drugs frequently make matters worse and distract nature from its proper function.

Hence it is that so many jibes are frequently cast at physicians and this very holy art is mocked, although part of it, which those trained in the liberal arts shamefully permit to be torn away from them, could readily adorn it forever with special lustre. When Homer, that source of genius, declared that a physician is more distinguished than a host of other men, and, with all the poets of Greece, celebrated Podalirius and Machaon, those divine sons of Aesculapius were praised not so much because they dispelled a little fever or something else of slight consequences, which nature alone could cure more readily without the aid of a physician than with it, nor because they yielded to the summons of men in obscure and desperate affections, but because they devoted themselves especially to the treatment of luxations, fractures, wounds, and other solutions of continuity and fluxions of blood, and because they freed Agamemnon's noble warriors of javelins, darts, and other evils of that sort which are the peculiar accompaniment of wars, and which always require the careful attention of the physician.

However, most august Emperor Charles, I certainly do not propose to give preference to one instrument of medicine over the others, since the aforesaid triple method of treatment can in no way be disunited and the whole of it belongs to the one practitioner; and that he may employ it properly all parts of medicine have been equally established so that the successful use of a single part depends upon the degree to which they are all combined, for how rare is the sickness that does not immediately require the three instruments of treatment. Hence a proper scheme of diet must be determined, and something must be done with drugs, and finally with the hands, so that the tyros of this art ought—if it please the gods—to be urged in every way, like the Greeks, to scorn the whisperings of those physicians and, as nature teaches, to employ their hands in treatment, lest they convert the mangled rationale of treatment into a calamity for the life of mankind. They ought to be urged the more strongly to this since we see learned physicians abstain from the use of the hands as from a plague lest the rabbins of medicine decry them before the ignorant mass as barbers and they acquire less wealth and honor than those [who are] scarcely half-physicians, and stand in less estimation before the uncomprehending mass of the people. Indeed, it is especially this detestable, vulgar opinion that prevents us, even in our age, from taking up the art of treatment as a whole, limiting us to the treatment of only internal diseases, to the great harm of mankind, and—if I may speak frankly—we strive to be physicians only in part.

When first the whole composition of drugs was relegated to the apothecaries, then the physicians promptly lost the necessary knowledge of simple medicines, and they were responsible for the apothecaries' shops becoming filled with barbarous names, and even false remedies, and for so many admirable compositions of the ancients being lost to us, several of which are still missing. Furthermore, they prepared an unending labor for learned men not only of our age but also for those who preceded it by some years, who have devoted themselves untiringly to the study of simple medicines and are seen to have contributed much through their effort to restore that knowledge to its former brilliance; Gerard van Veltwyck, secretary to your Majesty and rare example of this age, is representative of the many celebrated men engaged in this matter. Endowed with wide erudition in many disciplines and tongues he is the most skilled of our people in the knowledge of plants.

Furthermore, this very perverse distribution of the instruments of treatment among a variety of practitioners caused a very baleful disaster and a far more cruel blow to that chief branch of natural philosophy which, since it includes the description of man, ought rightfully to be considered the very beginning and solid foundation of the whole art of medicine. Hippocrates and Plato attributed so much to it that they did not hesitate to award it first place among the parts of medicine, and although at first it was especially cultivated by physicians, who strained every nerve to acquire it, finally it began miserably to collapse when they, resigning manual operations to others, destroyed anatomy. For when the physicians assumed that only the treatment of internal complaints concerned them, believing furthermore that knowledge of only the viscera was sufficient, they neglected the structure of the bones, muscles, nerves, and of the veins and arteries which creep through those bones and muscles, as of no concern to them. In addition, when the use of the hands was wholly entrusted to the barbers, not only was true knowledge of the viscera lost to the physicians, but also the practice of dissection soon died away, because they did not undertake it, and those to whom the manual skills had been entrusted were so unlearned that they did not understand the writings of the professors of dissection.

Thus it was impossible that so very difficult and abstruse an art, acquired mechanically by this latter type of men, could be preserved for us, for the deplorable division of the art of treatment introduced into the schools that detestable procedure by which usually some conduct the dissection of the human body and others present the account of its parts, the latter like jackdaws aloft in their high chair, with egregious arrogance croaking things they have never investigated but merely committed to memory from the books of others, or reading what has already been described. The former are so ignorant of languages that they are unable to explain their dissections to the spectators and muddle what ought to be displayed according to the instructions of the physician who, since he has never applied his hand to the dissection of the body, haughtily governs the ship from a manual. Thus everything is wrongly taught in the schools, and days are wasted in ridiculous questions so that in such confusion less is presented to the spectators than a butcher in his stall could teach a physician. I omit mention of several schools where scarcely ever is even consideration given to the presentation of human anatomy, so far has ancient medicine declined from its former glory.

In the great felicity of this age—which the gods desire to be controlled by your sagacious Majesty—with all studies greatly revitalized, anatomy has begun to raise its head from profound gloom, so that it may be said without contradiction that it seems almost to have recovered its ancient brilliance in some universities; and with nothing more urgently desired than that knowledge of the parts of the human body be recovered, I, aroused by the example of so many distinguished men, decided to give what assistance I could and by those means at my command. And lest all others should successfully accomplish something for the sake of our common studies while I alone remain idle, and lest I achieve less than my ancestors, I decided that this branch of natural philosophy ought to be recalled from the region of the dead. If it does not attain a fuller development among us than ever before or elsewhere among the early professors of dissection, at least it may reach such a point that one can assert without shame that the presence science of anatomy is comparable to that of the ancients and that in our age nothing has been so degraded and then wholly restored as anatomy.

My intention could by no means have been fulfilled if, when I was studying medicine in Paris, I had not put my own hand to the matter but had accepted without question the several casual and superficial demonstrations of a few organs presented to me and to my fellow students in one or two public dissections by unskilled barbers. So perfunctory was the presentation of anatomy there where we first saw medicine reborn that I, experienced by several dissections of brutes under the direction of the never-to-be-sufficiently-praised Jacobus Sylvius, at the third dissection at which I was ever present and at the urging of my fellow students and the teachers, conducted it publicly and more completely than was usually the case. When I conducted it a second time—the barbers having been waved aside—I attempted to display the muscles of the arms as well as to make a more-accurate dissection of the viscera, for, except for eight abdominal muscles shamefully mangled and in the wrong order, no other muscle or any bone, and much less an accurate series of nerves, veins, or arteries was ever demonstrated to me by anyone. Later at Louvain, whither I had to return because of the outbreak of war, and where for eighteen years the physicians had not even dreamed of anatomy, in order to assist the students of that university and to acquire greater skill in a subject still obscure but of the first importance for medicine, I dissected with somewhat greater accuracy than at Paris and lectured on the entire structure of the human body. As a result, the younger professors of that university now seem to be seriously engaged in gaining a knowledge of the parts of man, fully appreciating what valuable philosophical material is to be acquired from this knowledge. At Padua, in that most famous university of the whole world, in order not to dissociate myself from the rest of medicine and induced by the salary offered by the very illustrious Venetian Senate, by far the most liberal to professional studies, I gave the lectures on surgical medicine, and because anatomy is related to this, I devoted myself to the investigation of man's structure. Thus I have already conducted anatomy very often here and in Bologna, and, discarding the ridiculous fashion of the schools, I demonstrated and taught in such a way that there was nothing in my procedure that varied from the tradition of the ancients, and the construction of no part met with remained unstudied.

However, the slothfulness of physicians has prevented the preservation for us of the writings of Eudemus, Herophilus, Marinus, Andreas, Lycus, and other distinguished anatomists, since not even a fragment of any page remains of those illustrious authors, more than twenty in number, whom Galen mentions in his second commentary on Hippocrates's book *The nature of man,* and indeed of Galen's anatomical books scarcely a half have been saved from destruction. But if any of those who followed him, among whom I mention Oribasius, Theophilus, and the Arabs, and if our own writers whom I have thus far read—and I ask their pardon—handed on anything worthy of being read, they borrowed it from Galen; and, by Jove, to one earnestly concerned with dissection there is nothing in which they seem to have had less interest than in the dissection of the human body. They are so firmly dependent upon I-know-not-what-quality in the writing of their leader that, coupled with the failure of others to dissect, they have shamefully reduced Galen into brief compendia and never depart from him—if ever they understood his meaning—by the breadth of a nail. Indeed, in the prefaces of their books they announce that their writings are wholly pieced together from Galen's conclusions and that all that is theirs is his, adding that if anyone by chance were to criticize their writings they would consider that Galen also had been criticized. So completely have all yielded to him that there is no physician who would declare that even the slightest error had ever been found, much less can now be found, in Galen's anatomical books, although—except that Galen often corrects himself, frequently alluding to his negligence in earlier books and often teaching the opposite in later ones after he became more experienced—it is now clear to me from the reborn art of dissection, from diligent reading of Galen's books and their restoration in several places—for which we need feel no shame—that he never dissected a human body; but deceived by his monkeys—although he did have access to two dried human cadavers—he frequently and improperly opposed the ancient physicians trained in human dissection. Nay, more, how many incorrect observations you will find in Galen, even regarding his monkeys, not to mention that it is very astonishing that Galen noticed none of the many and infinite differences between the organs of the human body and of the monkey except in the fingers and the bend of the knee, which undoubtedly he would have overlooked with the others except that they were obvious to him without human dissection.

121

On the Treatment of Gunshot Wounds by Ambroise Pare—1575

During the sixteenth century, the proliferation of the cannon and other new weapons that used shot and gunpowder meant army surgeons had to treat different kinds of wounds. In this document, army surgeon Ambroise Pare (1510–1590) discusses the treatment he developed for wounds caused by "fiery engines." Pare first gained fame for learning how to control a hemorrhage, one of the major problems facing surgeons even today. He later had a long and useful career as a doctor and wrote many books on surgery. What treatment was initially used on gunshot wounds? What did Pare find to be the best way to treat this type of wound?

From Les Oevers de M. Ambroïsé Pare, 1575. Trans. by Thomas Johnson, "The Works of that famous Chirurgion Ambrose Parey, translated out of the Latine and compared with the French," 1634.

OF VVOUNDS MADE BY GVNSHOT, OTHER FIERIE ENGENINES, AND ALL SORTS OF VVEAPONS

I have thought good here to premise my opinion of the originall, encrease, and hurt of fiery Engines, for that I hope it will be an ornament and grace to this my whole treatise; as also to intice my Reader, as it were with these junckets, to our following Banquet so much savouring of Gunpouder. For thus it shall bee knowne to all whence Guns had their originall, and how many habits and shapes they have acquired from poore and obscure beginnings; and lastly how hurtfull to mankind the use of them is.

Polydore Virgill writes that a Germane of obscure birth and condition was the inventor of this new engine which we terme a Gun, being induced thereto by this occasion. He kept in a mortar covered with a tyle, or slate, for some other certaine uses a pouder (which since that time for its chiefe and new knowne faculty, is named Gunpouder.) Now it chanced as hee strucke fire with a steele and flint, a sparke thereof by accident fell into the mortar, where-upon the pouder suddainly catching fire, casts the stone or tyle which covered the mortar, up on high; he stood amazed at the novelty and strange effect of the thing, and withall observed the formerly unknowne faculty of the pouder; so that he thought good to make experiment thereof in a small Iron trunke framed for the purpose according to the intention of his minde.

When all things were correspondent to his expectation, he first shewed the use of his engine to the Venetians, when they warred with the Genovese at Fosse Clodiana, now called Chiozzia, in the yeare of our Lord 1380. Yet in the opinion of Peter Messias, their invention must have beene of greater antiquity; for it is read in the Chronicles of Alphonsus the eleaventh King of Castile, who subdued the isles Argezires, that when he beseiged the cheefe Towne in the yeare of our Lord 1343, the beseiged Moores shot as it were thunder against the assailants, out of iron mortars. But we have read in the Chronicles written by Peter Bishop, of Leons, of that Alphonsus who conquered Toledo, that in a certain sea fight fought by the King of Tunis, against the Moorish King of Sivill, whose part King Alphonsus favoured, the Tunetans cast light-ning out of certaine hollow Engines or Trunkes with much noise, which could be no other, than our Guns, though not attained to that perfection of art and execution which they now have.

I think the deviser of this deadly Engine hath this for his recompence, that his name should be hidden by the darkenesse of perpetuall ignorance, as not meriting for this his most pernicious invention, any mention from posterity. Yet Andrew Thevet in his Cosmography published some few years agone, when hee comes to treate of the Suevi, the inhabitants of Germany, brings upon the authority and credite of a certaine old Manuscript, that the Germane the inventor of this warlike Engine was by profession a monke and Philosopher or Alchymist, borne at Friburge, and named Constantine Ancken. Howsoever it was, this kind of Engine was called Bombarda, i.e. a Gun, from that noise it makes, which the Greekes and Latines according to the sound call Bombus; then in the following ages, time, art, and mans maliciousnesse added much to this rude and unpolisht invention. For first for the matter, Brasse and Copper, mettalls farre more tractable, fusible and lesse subject to rust, came as supplies to Iron. Then for the forme, that rude and undigested barrell, or mortar-like-basse, hath undergone many formes and fashions, even so farre as it is gotten upon wheeles, that so it might run not onely from the higher ground, but also with more rapide violence to the ruine of mankinde; when as the first and rude mortars seemed not to be so nimbly traversed, nor sufficiently cruell for our destruction by the onely casting forth of Iron and fire.

Hence sprung these horrible monsters of Canons, double Canons, Bastards, Musquits, feild peices; hence these cruell and furious beasts, Culverines, Serpentines, Basilisques, Sackers, Falcons, Falconets, and divers other names not only drawne from their figure and making, but also from the effects of their cruelty. Wherefore certainly I cannot sufficiently admire the wisedome of our Ancestors, who have so rightly accommodated them with names agreeable to their natures; as those who have not onely taken them from the swiftest birds of prey, as Falcons; but also from things most harme-full and hatefull to mankinde, such as Serpents, Snakes, and Basilisks. That so wee might clearly discerne, that these engines were made for no other purpose, nor with other intent, but onely to be imployed for the speedy and cruell slaughter of men; and that by onely hearing them named we might detest and abhorre them, as pernicious enemies of our lives. I let passe other engines of this ofspring, being for their quantitie small, but so much the more pernicious and harmfull, for that they nearer assaile our lives, and may trayterously and forthwith seaze upon us not thinking nor fearing any such thing, so that we can scarse have any means of escape; such are Pistolls and other small hand guns, which for shortnesse you may carry in your pocket, and so privily and suddainly taking them forth oppresse the carelesse and secure.

THE FIRST DISCOVRSE

Vvherein Vvounds Made by Gvnshot Are Freed From Being Bvrnt, or Cavterized According to Vigoes Methode

Fowling pieces which men usually carry upon their shoulders, are of the middle ranke of these engines, as also Muskets and Caleevers, which you cannot well discharge unlesse lying upon a Rest, which therefore may be called Breast-guns for that they are not laid to the cheeke, but against the Breast by

---

* Les Oevers de M. Ambroïse Paré, 1575. Translation by Thomas Johnson, "The Works of that famous Chirurgion Ambrose Parey, translated out of the Latine and compared with the French," 1634.

reason of their weight and shortness; All which have beene invented for the commodity of footemen, and light horsemen. This middle sort of engine we call in Latine by a generall name Sclopus, in imitation of the sound, and the Italians who terme it Sclopetere; the French call it Harquebuse, a word likewise borrowed from the Italians, by reason of the touch-hole by which you give fire to the peice, for the Italians call a hole Buzio.

In the year of our Lord 1536, Francis the French King, for his acts in warre and peace stiled the Great, sent a puissant Army beyond the Alpes, under the Government and leading of Annas of Mommorancie high Constable of France, both that he might releeve Turin with victualls, souldiers, and all things needefull, as also to recover the Citties of that Province taken by the Marquis du Guast, Generall of the Emperours forces. I was in the Kings Army the Chirurgion of Monsieur of Montejan, Generall of the foote. The Imperialists had taken the straits of Suze, the Castle of Villane, and all the other passages, so that the Kings army was not able to drive them from their fortifications but by fight. In this conflict there were many wounded on both sides with all sorts of weapons but cheefely with bullets. I will tell the truth, I was not very expert at that time in matters of Chirurgery; neither was I used to dresse wounds made by gunshot. Now, I had read in Iohn de Vigo that wounds made by Gunshot were venerate or poisoned, and that by reason of the Gunpouder; Wherefore for their cure, it was expedient to burne or cauterize them with oyle of Elders scalding hot, with a little Treacle mixed therewith.

But for that I gave no great credite neither to the author, nor remedy, because I knew that caustickes could not be powred into wounds, without excessive paine; I, before I would runne a hazard, determined to see whether the Chirurgions, who went with me in the army, used any other manner of dressing to these wounds. I observed and saw that all of them used that Method of dressing which Vigo prescribes; and that they filled as full as they could, the wounds made by Gunshot with Tents and pledgets dipped in the scalding Oyle, at the first dressings; which encouraged me to doe the like to those, who came to be dressed of me.

It chanced on a time, that by reason of the multitude that were hurt, I wanted this Oyle. Now because there were some few left to be dressed, I was forced, that I might seeme to want nothing, and that I might not leave them undrest, to apply a digestive made of the yolke of an egg, oyle of Roses, and Turpentine. I could not sleep all that night, for I was troubled in minde, and the dressing of the precedent day, (which I judged unfit) troubled my thoughts; and I feared that the next day I should finde them dead, or at the point of death by the poyson of the wound, whom I had not dressed with the scalding oyle. Therefore I rose early in the morning. I visited my patients and beyond expectation, I found such as I had dressed with a digestive onely, free from vehemencie of paine to have had good rest, and that their wounds were not inflamed, nor tumifyed; but on the contrary the others that were burnt with the scalding oyle were feaverish, tormented with much paine, and the parts about their wounds were swolne. When I had many times tryed this in divers others I thought this much, that neither I nor any other should ever cauterize any wounded with Gun-shot.

122

The Art of Printing in China by Matteo Ricci—16th century

Matteo Ricci was born in Italy and later joined the Jesuit order against his father's wishes. He was sent to the China mission, where he embraced Chinese culture and provided the Chinese with access to Western works in mathematics and cartography. Ricci is still honored in China today; his tomb is in the Beijing suburbs. In the following document, Ricci discusses the advanced development of printing in China. What does he seem to admire most about Chinese printing technology?

The art of printing was practiced in China at a date somewhat earlier than that assigned to the beginning to printing in Europe, which was about 1405. It is quite certain that the Chinese knew the art of printing at least five centuries ago, and some of them assert that printing was known to their people before the beginning of the Christian era, about 50 BCE. Their method of printing differs widely from that employed in Europe, and our method would be quite impracticable for them because of the exceedingly large number of Chinese characters and symbols. At present they cut their characters in a reverse position and in a simplified form, on a comparatively' small tablet made for the most part from the wood of the pear tree or the apple tree, although at times the wood of the jujube tree is also used for this purpose.

Their method of making printed books is quite ingenious. The text is written in ink, with a brush made of very fine hair, on a sheet of paper which is inverted and pasted on a wooden tablet. When the paper has become thoroughly dry, its surface is scraped off quickly and with great skill, until nothing but a fine tissue bearing the characters remains on the wooden tablet. Then, with a steel graver, the workman cuts away the surface following the outlines of the characters until these alone stand out in low relief. From such a block a skilled printer can make copies with incredible speed, turning out as many as fifteen hundred copies in a single day. Chinese printers are so skilled in engraving these blocks, that no more time is consumed in making one of them than would be required by one of our printers in setting up a form of type and making the necessary corrections. This scheme of engraving wooden blocks is well adapted for the large and complex nature of the Chinese characters, but I

From *The Diary of Matthew Ricci*, in Matthew Ricci, *China in the Sixteenth Century*, trans. by Louis Gallagher (New York: Random House, 1943, 1970).

do nor. think it would lend itself very aptly to our European type which could hardly be engraved upon wood because of its small dimensions.

Their method of printing has one decided advantage, namely, that once these tablets are made, they can be preserved and used for making changes in the text as often as one wishes. Additions and subtractions can also be made as the tablets can be readily patched. Again, with this method, the printer and the author are not obliged to produce herc and now an excessively large edition of a book, but are able to print a book in smaller or larger lots sufficient to meet the demand at the time, We have derived great benefit from this method of Chinese printing, as we employ the domestic help in our homes to strike off copies of the books on religious and scientific subjects which we translate into Chinese from the languages in which they were written originally, In truth, the whole method is so simple that one is tempted to try it for himself after once having watched the process. The simplicity of Chinese printing is what accounts for the exceedingly large numbers of books in circulation here and the ridiculously low prices at which they are sold. Such facts as these would scarcely be believed by one who had not witnessed them.

They have another odd method of reproducing reliefs which have been cut into marble or wood, An epitaph, for example, or a picture set out in low relief on marble or on wood, is covered with a piece of moist paper which in turn is overlayed with several pieces of cloth. Then the entire surface is beaten with a small mallet until all the lineaments of the relief are impressed upon the paper. When the paper dries, ink or some other coloring substance is applied with a light touch, after which only the impression of the relief stands out on the original whiteness of the paper. This method cannot be employed when the relief is shallow; or traced in delicate lines.

123

Prescriptions for Mrs. Lucia Troute by William Harvey—1652

One of the leading scientists and doctors of his age, William Harvey (1578–1657) discovered the way blood circulated through the heart and veins. He was also the first to determine that humans and other mammals reproduced through fertilization of an egg by sperm, although it would take two centuries before a mammalian egg was actually observed. Harvey was the oldest of seven children and received an excellent education, earning a Bachelor of Arts degree at Cambridge University and later studying medicine at the University of Padua. Despite his intelligence and groundbreaking discoveries, Harvey often used medical remedies that were not much different from those of the ancient Egyptians. The following document contains several prescriptions written by Harvey for one of his patients. What kind of ingredients did physicians use during the seventeenth century? Do you think these remedies had a beneficial effect?

II. PRESCRIPTIONS FOR MRS. LUCIA TROUTE (AET. 14), 1652

Dr Harvey's direction for a dyett drinke for Mistress Lucia Troute February 1652, for the Kings Evill, not the malignant Evil but the white Evill.

Take the wood of Guiacum 3 oz. infuse it for 24 howers in 6 pints of springe water afterwards boyle it to the consumpcion of halfe addinge to it of the leaves of Bittany 3 handfulls, Tamaris one handfull, Coriander seeds 2 scruples, the leaves of Scenna 4 oz., Rhubarb one oz., sweete fennell seeds one oz. Lett it be boyled to the halfe addinge to it the fruite of Tamarinds 1/2 an oz., the best manna 3 oz. and of clarified honey 3 oz. Then straine it and take 3 or 4 oz. at a tyme for a dose every morninge. If for a child then the halfe quantity to be made.

After The Dr directed the swellinge to be opened by a Chirurgion in the nature of an issue and a pease to be put therein and a plaster to kepe the same in it, but the soare beinge ripe, which . . .[1] broake it selfe next day, but the directions was followed.

Aprill 53. after the soare was broke and had rune, then in Apr.[2] 56. direct the dyet drinke followinge:

From *Life of William Harvey* by Geoffrey Keynes (Oxford: Clarendon Press, 1966).

1 Three more words here above the line inserted over a caret are illegible.
2 The reading seems to be right, but the meaning is not clear.

1 Take a handfull of Bugle and a handfull of Bittany and a sprigg of tyme, boyle these in water and whitwyne and lett her drinke morninge and in the afternoone at 4 of the clocke.

2 This plaister to be applyed to the soare:

Take a handfull of Redd sage, boyle it in a pinte of Smithes water to halfe a pint then straine the liquor and add it to that underwritten which the Appothecary makes and then wett soe much lint therein as will cover the soare and soe apply it and cover it with a plaister to make it sticke.

That which the Dr appointed the Appothecary to make and was to be mingled with the smiths water was as followeth:

3 Take burn't vitriol, verdigrease, burn't Allum, of each 2 drams, fine bolalminacke[3] one drame, soe mingle it with an oz. of honey of roses and keep it for your use.

The plaister wich covered the lynt and soare was spred with cerat diachilon simple.

Febr. 1653. Dr. Harvey prescribed Mistress Lucia Troute she beinge weake this followinge Electuary:

℞ fol. sennae pulv.,[4]
   radicum rusci, sarsaparillae,
   radicum scrophulariae, ana ℥ j.
   radicis jalappae ℨ j.
   trochisci de viperis optimi[5] ℥ ij.
   electuarii lenitivi[6] q.s.
   cum conserva rosarum damascenarum.[7]
   Elect. cap. singulo mane q.[8] nucis moschatae vel juglantis . . .[9]

The plaister for the soare, for after one was healed it brake out in another place:

℞ diachyl. simpl. ℥ iij.
   matanstur[10] cum pinguedine hominis q.s. et
   unguento à floribus Aurantiorum ℥ j.
   Fiat ceratum pro summit.

After the child have a could and cough and a swellinge under her Arme the Dr prescribed as followeth, first for a broth she being in a consumpcion speene[1] and the scurvey:

To a pint of water infuse 1 oz. of china thyn sliced. After 12 howers infusion maker broth thereof and put in scabious, mayden haire and folefoote,

---

3 So written, but not understood.
4 *Pharmacopoeia Londinensis,* 1638, p. 70.
5 Ibid., p. 115.
6 Ibid., p. 93.
7 Ibid., p. 53.
8 Seems to be a *q*; but *cum* would have been expected. Perhaps this *q* stands for *quum*?
9 The last two words uncertain; it should be the amount of nutmeg and walnut.
10 This seems to be what is written. Probably a mistake for *miscetur.*

fresh water cresses which byte the tongue and a sprige of winter savery and French barley first scalded in other water, raisins stoned, currants and one slice of Spanish liquorice scraped.

1 July 1655. Dr Harvey prescribed another Electuary:

[The receipt is not given and the remainder of the folio is blank except for a note written across the bottom which reads:
I shall endeavour to supply you with the Recipes here intended as soone as I finde them which at present are mislayde.]

Another Electuary of Dr Harvey's for Mistress Lucia Troute the 20 of March 1655 when the greate soare under her chynn brake:

Take of diaphaenicon one ounce, of the trochiske of vipers 2 drams, of sarsaparilla and of China rootes in powder and of scena of each 2 drams, of Rubarb and Agaricke of each one dram, of Jalop 2 scruples, of Cassia newly drawne 3 drams, of the species of diacodion abbatis and of the trochiske of Alkakengi[11] in powder of each one scruple. Make this according to Arte with the forme of an Electuary whereof take every newe and full moone the quantity of a Chesnutt at a tyme. If it worke not well and answerable to desire the next tyme Augment the quantity of as much more. (*In the margin*: After this directe her to drinke swete wyne.)
13 March 1659 (Dr Harvey then dead) Dr Pruieans prescription for Mistress Lucy Troute (14 ans) he seeinge some of Dr Harveys Recipes. Take etc.

[British Museum, MS. Sloane 206A, f. 139]

---

11 See *Pharmacopoeia Londinensis*, p. 116.

124

From *Opticks* by
Sir Isaac Newton—1704

A leading figure of the Enlightenment, Isaac Newton (1642–1727) was born in the year Galileo died. He was likely the world's most influential scientist because his discoveries in mathematics, optics, and physics revolutionized the field of science. Educated at Trinity College, Cambridge, he lived there until 1696, when he was appointed the Master of the Royal Mint and moved to London. Newton provides an orderly explanation for the workings of the universe in his two books, Opticks *and* Principia. *In this excerpt, Newton, who was deeply religious in a nontraditional way, develops his atomic theory. Does Newton use inductive or deductive reasoning to develop this theory? Does he recognize God as the first cause?*

ATOMIC THEORY

All these things being considered, it seems probable to me, that God in the beginning formed, Matter in solid, massy, hard, impenetrable, moveable particles, of such sizes and figures, and with such other properties, and in such proportion to space, as most conduced to the end for which he formed them; and that these primitive particles, being solids, are incomparably harder than any porous bodies compounded of them; even so very hard, as never to wear or break in pieces; no ordinary power being able to divide what God himself made one in the first creation. While the particles continue entire, they may compose bodies of one and the same nature and texture in all ages: But should they wear away, or break in pieces, the nature of things depending on them would be changed. Water and earth, composed of old worn particles and fragments of particles would not be of the same nature and texture now, with water and earth composed of entire particles in the beginning. And therefore, that nature may be lasting, the changes of corporeal things are to be placed only in the various separations and new associations and motions of these permanent particles; compound bodies being apt to break, not in the midst of solid particles, but where those particles are laid together, and only touch in a few points.

It seems to me farther, that those particles have not only a force of inertia accompanied with such passive laws of motion as naturally result from that

From Isaac Newton, *Optics, or, a Treatise of the Reflections, Refractions, IrMlections and Colours of Light*, 4th ed. (London, 1730).

force, but also that they are moved by certain active principles, such as is that of gravity, and that which causes fermentation, and the cohesion of bodies. These principles I consider, not as occult qualities, supposed to result from the specific forms of things, but as general laws of nature, by which the things themselves are formed; their truth appearing to us by phenomena, though their causes be not yet discovered. For these are manifest qualities, and their causes only are occult. And the *Aristotelians* gave the name of occult qualities, not to manifest qualities, but to such qualities only as they supposed to lie hid in bodies, and to be the unknown causes of manifest effects: Such as would be the causes of gravity, and of magnetic and electric attractions, and of fermentations, if we should suppose that these forces or actions arose from qualities unknown to us, and uncapable of being discovered and made manifest. Such occult qualities put a stop to the improvement of natural philosophy, and therefore of late years have been rejected. To tell us that every species of things is endowed with an occult specific quality by which it acts and produces manifest effects, is to tell us nothing: But to derive two or three general principles of motion from phenomena, and afterwards to tell us how the properties and actions of all corporeal things follow from those manifest principles, would be a very great step in philosophy, though the causes of those principles were not yet discovered: And therefore I scruple not to propose the principles of motion abovementioned, they being of very general extent, and leave their causes to be found out.

Now by the help of these principles, all material things seem to have been composed of the hard and solid particles abovementioned, variously associated in the first creation by the counsel of an intelligent agent. For it became him who created them to set them in order. And if he did so, it's unphilosophical to seek for any other origin of the world, or to pretend that it might arise out of a chaos by the mere laws of nature; though being once formed, it may continue by those laws for many ages. For while comets move in very eccentric orbs in all manner of positions, blind fate could never make all the planets move one and the same way in orbs concentric, some inconsiderable irregularities excepted, which may have risen from the mutual actions of comets and planets upon one another, and which will be apt to increase, till this System wants a reformation. Such a wonderful uniformity in the planetary system must be allowed the effect of choice. And so much the uniformity in the bodies of animals, they having generally a right and a left side shaped alike, and on either side of their bodies two legs behind, and either two arms, or two legs, or two wings before their shoulders, a neck running down into a backbone, and a head upon it; and in the head two ears, two eyes, a nose, a mouth, and a tongue, alike situated. Also the first contrivance of those very artificial parts of animals, the eyes, ears, brain, muscles, heart, lungs, midriff, glands, larynx, hands, wings, swimming bladders, natural spectacles, and other organs of sense and motion; and the instinct of brutes and insects, can be the effect of nothing else than the wisdom and skill of a powerful everliving agent, who being in all places, is more able by his will to move the bodies within his boundless uniform sensorium, and thereby to form and reform the parts of the universe, than we are by our will to move the parts of our bodies. And yet we are not to consider the world as the body of God, or the several parts thereof, as the parts of God. He is a uniform being, void of organs, members or parts, and they are his creatures subordinate to him, and subservient to his will; and he is no more the soul of them, than the soul of man is the soul of the species of things carried through the organs of sense into the place of its sensation, where it perceives them by means of its immediate presence, without the intervention of any third thing. The organs of sense are not for enabling the soul to perceive the species of things in its sensorium, but only for conveying them thither; and God has no need of such organs, he being everywhere present to the things themselves. And since space is divisible *in infinitum* and matter is not necessarily in all places, it may be also allowed that God is able to create particles of matter of several sizes and figures, and in several proportions to space, and perhaps of different densities and forces, and thereby to vary the laws of nature, and make worlds of several sorts in several parts of the universe. At least, I see nothing of contradiction in all this.

INDUCTION

As in mathematics, so in natural philosophy, the investigation of difficult things by the method of analysis, ought ever to precede the method of composition. This analysis consists in making experiments and observations, and in drawing general conclusions from them by induction and admitting of no objections against the conclusions, but such as are taken from experiments, or other certain truths. For hypotheses are not to be regarded in experimental philosophy. And although the arguing from experiments and observations by induction be no demonstration of general conclusions; yet it is the best way of arguing which the nature of things admits of, and may be looked upon as so much the stronger, by how much the induction is more general. And if no exception occur from phenomena, the conclusion may be pronounced generally. But if at any time afterwards any exception shall occur from experiments, it may then begin to be pronounced with such exceptions as occur. By this way of analysis we may proceed from compounds to ingredients, and from motions to the forces producing them; and in general, from effects to their causes, and from particular causes to more general ones, till the argument ends in the most general. This is the method of analysis: And the synthesis consists in assuming the causes discovered, and established as principles, and by them explaining the phenomena proceeding from them, and proving the explanations.

CHAPTER 15

Daily Life in the Age of Change—1500–1750 CE

One of the ongoing themes of this reader is the role and status of women in different societies through the ages. Unfortunately, in the Age of Change women made few advances, and most women in the world had few rights. In which of the societies described in this section's documents did women appear to have the most freedom? Why?

During the sixteenth and seventeenth centuries, Europeans traveled extensively for purposes of business, diplomacy, and conquest; books relating their experiences in foreign lands were in great demand. Do you see any similarities between visitors' accounts of Africa and India?

Martin Luther is best known as the founder of the Lutheran Church, but he also had strong views on the role of women. His beliefs had great influence on women's status in Western society. How did his ideas compare with the established customs in Russia, Africa, and Turkey in the sixteenth and seventeenth centuries?

125

From *A General and Natural History of the Indies* by Gonzalo Fernandez de Oviedo y Valdes— 1535–1537

Gonzalo Fernandez de Oviedo y Valdes was a contemporary of Cortes and Pizarro who served as an administrator in what is now Mexico, Panama, and Columbia. A careful observer of the conquered Aztecs, he wrote a 20-volume history of the Aztecs upon his return to Spain. How was Aztec society divided? How were the peasants controlled by their lords? Is this description similar to what you have learned about sixteenth-century European life?

The Indians of New Spain . . . are the poorest of the many nations that live in the Indies at the present time. In their homes they have no furnishings or clothing other than the poor garments which they wear on their persons, one or two stones for grinding maize, some pots in which to cook the maize, and a sleeping mat. Their meals consist chiefly of vegetables cooked with chili, and bread. They eat little—not that they would not eat more if they could get it, for the soil is very fertile and yields bountiful harvests, but the common people and plebeians suffer under the tyranny of their Indian lords, who tax away the greater part of their produce in a manner that I shall describe. Only the lords and their relatives, and some principal men and merchants, have estates and lands of their own; they sell and gamble with their lands as they please, and they sow and harvest them but pay no tribute.[1] Nor is any tribute paid by artisans, such as masons, carpenters, feather-workers, or silversmiths, or by singers and kettle-drummers (for every Indian lord has musicians in his house-hold, each according to his station). But such persons render personal service[2] when it is required, and none of them is paid for his labor.

Each Indian lord assigns to the common folk who come from other parts of the country to settle on his land (and to those who are already settled there) specific fields, that each may know the land that he is to sow. And the majority

From *Readings in Latin American Civilization*, ed. and trans. by Benjamin Keen (Boston: Houghton Mifflin, 1955), p. 17–18. Reprinted by permission of the author.

1 That is, they make no payments to the king or priesthood.

2 Farm labor, work on maintenance of buildings, roads, and temples.

of them have their homes on their land; and between twenty and thirty, or forty and fifty houses have over them an Indian head who is called *tiquitlato*, which in the Castilian[3] tongue means "the finder (or seeker) of tribute." At harvest time this *tiquitlato* inspects the cornfield and observes what each one reaps, and when the reaping is done they show him the harvest, and he counts the ears of corn that each has reaped, and the number of wives and children that each of the vassals in his charge possesses. And with the harvest before him he calculates how many ears of corn each person in that household will require till the next harvest, and these he gives to the Indian head of that house; and he does the same with the other produce, namely kidney beans, which are a kind of small beans, and chili, which is their pepper; and *chia*, which is as fine as mustard seed, and which in warm weather they drink, ground and made into a solution in water and use for medicine, roasted and ground; and cocoa, which is a kind of almond that they use as money, and which they grind, make into a solution, and drink; and cotton, in those places where it is raised . . .; and pulque,[4] which is their wine; and all the various products obtained from the maguey[5] plant, from which they obtain food and drink and footwear and clothing. . . . Of all these and other products they leave the vassal only enough to sustain him for a year. And in addition the vassal must earn enough to pay the tribute of mantles, gold, silver, honey, wax, lime, wood, or whatever products it is customary to pay as tribute in that country. They pay this tribute every forty, sixty, seventy, or ninety days, according to the terms of the agreement. This tribute also the *tiquitlato* receives and carries to his Indian lord.

Ten days before the close of the sixty or hundred days, or whatever is the period appointed for the payment of tribute, they take to the house of the Indian lord the produce brought by the *tiquitlatos*; and if some poor Indian should prove unable to pay his share of tribute, whether for reasons of health or poverty, or lack of work, the *tiquitlato* tells the lord that such-and-such will not pay the proportion of the tribute that had been assigned to him; then the lord tells the *tiquitlato* to take the recalcitrant vassal to a *tianguez* or market, which they hold every five days in all the towns of the land, and there sell him into slavery, applying the proceeds of the sale to the payment of his tribute. . . .

All the towns have their own lands, long ago assigned for the provision of the . . . temples where they kept their idols; and these lands were and are the best of all. And they have this custom: At seeding time all would go forth at the summons of the town council to sow these fields, and to weed them at the proper time, and to cultivate the grain and harvest it and carry it to a house in which lived the pope and the *teupisques, pioches, exputhles* and *piltoutles* (or, as we would say, the bishops, archbishops, and canons and prebendaries, and even choristers, for each major temple had these five classes of officials).[6] And they

---

3 The language of Castile, the largest province in Spain.

4 A fermented drink, made from the juice of the agave, a desert plant.

5 A fiber-yielding plant with fleshy leaves, grown in Mexico and the southwestern United States.

6 Fernández is drawing an analogy between the Aztec priesthood and the hierarchy of the Roman Catholic Church.

supported themselves from this harvest, and the Indians also raised chickens for them to eat.

In all the towns Montezuma[7] had his designated lands, which they sowed for him in the same way as the temple lands; and if no garrison was stationed in their towns, they would carry the crops on their backs to the great city of Tenochtitlan;[8] but in the garrison towns the grain was eaten by Montezuma's soldiers, and if the town did not sow the land, it had to supply the garrison with food, and also give them chickens and all other needful provisions.

---

7 The Aztec empeor.

8 The Aztec capital, the site of modern Mexico City.

126

"Marriage Customs in 16th Century Russia" From *Notes on Russia* by Sigismund von Herberstein—1549

The following document, an excerpt from Notes on Russia, *was published in 1549. Herberstein was an Austrian nobleman and diplomat who served in Russia between 1516 and 1518. This brief document deals with the role of women in Russian society. Does there seem to have been much difference between the status of upper-class women and peasant women in Russia during this period? How does this document compare with others on the status of women during the early modern era?*

I t is held to be dishonorable and a disgrace for a young man to address a girl, in order that he may obtain her hand in marriage. It is the part of the father to communicate with the young man upon the subject of his marrying his daughter. It is generally the custom for them to use such words as the following: "As I have a daughter, I should wish to have you for a son-in-law." To which the young man replies: "If you desire to have me for a

---

From *Notes upon Russi*, by Sigismund von Herberstein, ed. by R.H. Majo (London: Hakluyt Society, 1851), Vol. I, p. 91–94.

son-in-law, I will, if you think fit, have a meeting with my parents, and confer with them upon the subject." Then, if his parents and nearest relatives agree, a meeting is held to treat of the sum which the girl's father is willing to give by way of dowry. After the dowry is settled, a day is appointed for the wedding. Meanwhile, the young man is forbidden the house of his betrothed; so strictly indeed, that if he should happen to try to get a sight of her, the parents usually reply: "Learn what she is from others who have known her." Certainly, unless the espousals have been first confirmed with very heavy penalties, so that the young man who is betrothed could not, if he would, repudiate her without a heavy punishment, no access is permitted to him. Horses, dresses, weapons, cattle, servants, and the like, are generally given as dowry. . . .

They do not call it adultery unless one have the wife of another. Love between those that are married is for the most part lukewarm, especially among the nobles and princes, because they marry girls whom they have never seen before; and being engaged in the service of the prince, they are compelled to desert them, and become corrupted with disgraceful connections with others.

The condition of the women is most miserable; for they consider no woman virtuous unless she live shut up at home, and be so closely guarded, that she go out nowhere. They give a woman, I say, little credit for modesty, if she be seen by strangers or people out of doors. But shut up at home they do nothing but spin and sew, and have literally no authority or influence in the house. All the domestic work is done by the servants. Whatever is strangled by the hands of a woman, whether it be a fowl, or any other kind of animal, they abominate as unclean. The wives, however, of the poorer classes do the household work and cook. But if their husbands and the men-servants happen to be away, and they wish to strangle a fowl, they stand at the door holding the fowl, or whatever other animal it may be, and a knife, and generally beg the men that pass by to kill it. They are very seldom admitted into the churches . . . unless they be very old and free from all suspicion. On certain holidays, however, men allow their wives and daughters, as a special gratification, to meet in very pleasant meadows, where they seat themselves on a sort of wheel of fortune, and are moved alternately up and down, or they fasten a rope somewhere, with a seat to it, in which they sit, and are swung backwards and forwards; or they otherwise make merry with clapping their hands and singing songs, but they have no dances whatever.

From *History and Description of Africa* by Leo Africanus—1550

Born in Granada to a prominent Moorish family, Leo Africanus (1485–1554) moved to Morocco in 1492 after the Moors were expelled from Spain. (His Arabic name was Al-Hassan ibn Muhammed el Wazzan.) He was educated by Arab scholars and eventually became a merchant, traveling throughout Northern Africa and the Middle East. On one of his trading voyages, Africanus was captured by pirates and eventually presented to Pope Leo X, who instructed him in both Christianity and Latin. Africanus introduced Europeans to Arabic culture, science, and philosophy, but he is best known for his History and Description of Africa, *which was the principal source of information about North Africa available to Europeans. He wrote the book first in Arabic and then translated it into Italian. After reading this brief excerpt, do you think Leo Africanus was writing for an Arab or European audience? Why does he spend so much time describing the dress of Arab women?*

Their women (according to the guise of that country) go very gorgeously attired: they wear linen gowns dyed black, with exceeding wide sleeves, over which sometimes they cast a mantle of the same colour or of blue, the corners of which mantle are very artificially fastened about their shoulders with a fine silver clasp. Likewise they have rings hanging at their ears, which for the most part are made of silver; they wear many rings also upon their fingers. Moreover they usually wear about their thighs and ankles certain scarfs and rings, after the fashion of the Africans. They cover their faces with certain masks having only two holes for the eyes to peep out at. If any man chance to meet with them, they presently hide their faces, passing by him with silence, except it be some of their allies or kinsfolks; for unto them they always discover their faces, neither is there any use of the said mask so long as they be in presence. These Arabians when they travel any journey (as they oftentimes do) they set their women upon certain saddles made handsomely of wicker for the same purpose, and fastened to their camel backs, neither be they anything too wide, but fit only for a woman to sit in. When they go to the wars each man carries his wife with him, to the end that she may cheer up her good man, and give him encouragement. Their damsels which are unmarried do

---

From *The History and Description of Africa, and of the notable things therein* by Leo Africanus (New York: Burt Franklin), p. 158–159.

usually paint their faces, breasts, arms, hands, and fingers with a kind of counterfeit colour: which is accounted a most decent custom among them.

128

Turkish Women, Turkish Letters by Ogier Ghiselin de Busbecq— 1555–1561

In an earlier document, Ogier Ghiselin de Busbecq, the ambassador of Ferdinand I to the Court of the Ottoman Empire at Constantinople, discussed the court of Suleiman the Magnificent. Busbecq was an acute observer interested in every aspect of life in sixteenth-century Turkey. In the following excerpt, he discusses Turkish women's status and marriage customs. What conclusions can you draw about the legal status of married women and concubines in Turkey during this period? How did their position compare with that of women in other parts of the world at this time?

The Turks are the most careful people in the world of the modesty of their wives, and therefore keep them shut up at home and hide them away, so that they scarce see the light of day. But if they have to go into the streets, they are sent out so covered and wrapt up in veils that they seem to those who meet them mere gliding ghosts. They have the means of seeing men through their linen or silken veils, while no part of their own body is exposed to men's view. For it is a received opinion among them, that no woman who is distinguished in the very smallest degree by her figure or youth, can be seen by a man without his desiring her, and therefore without her receiving some contamination; and so it is the universal practice to confine the women to the harem. Their brothers are allowed to see them, but not their brothers-in-law. Men of the richer classes, or of higher rank, make it a condition when they marry, that their wives shall never set foot outside the threshold, and that no man or woman shall be admitted to see them for any reason whatever, not even their nearest relations, except

From C.T. Foster and F.H. Blackburne Daniell, eds., *The Life and Letters of Ogier Ghiselin de Busbecq*, 2 vols. (London: Hakluyt Society, 1881).

their fathers and mothers, who are allowed to pay a visit to their daughters at the Turkish Easter.[1]

On the other hand, if the wife has a father of high rank, or has brought a larger dowry than usual, the husband promises on his part that he will take no concubine, but will keep to her alone. Otherwise, the Turks are not forbidden by any law to have as many concubines as they please in addition to their lawful wives. Between the children of wives and those of concubines there is no distinction, and they are considered to have equal rights. As for concubines they either buy them for themselves or win them in war; when they are tired of them there is nothing to prevent their bringing them to market and selling them; but they are entitled to their freedom if they have borne children to their master. This privilege Roxolana, Suleiman's wife, turned to her own advantage, when she had borne him a son while still a slave. Having thus obtained her freedom, and become her own mistress, she refused to submit any longer to his will, unless, contrary to the custom of the Ottoman Sultans, she was made his lawful wife. The only distinction between the lawful wife and the concubine is, that the former has a dowry, while the slaves have none. A wife who has a portion settled on her is mistress of her husband's house, and all the other women have to obey her orders. The husband, however, may choose which of them shall spend the night with him. He makes known his wishes to the wife, and she sends to him the slave he has selected. . . . Only Friday night, which is their Sabbath,[2] is supposed to belong to the wife; and she grumbles if her husband deprives her of it. On all the other nights he may do so as he pleases.

Divorces are granted among them for many reasons which it is easy for the husbands to invent. The divorced wife receives back her dowry, unless the divorce has been caused by some fault on her part. There is more difficulty in a woman's getting a divorce from her husband.

Among the reasons which are considered sufficient for granting a divorce are the deprivation of the necessaries of life by the husband, and certain kinds of ill treatment. In the latter case the woman goes before the judge, and makes a declaration that she is unable to remain any longer with her husband; when the judge asks the reason, she gives no answer, but takes off one of her shoes and turns it upside down. This the judge accepts as sufficient evidence that her husband has treated her improperly.

---

1 Busbecq apparently is referring to the festival of Bairam, which follows Ramadan, the Muslim month of fasting from sunup to sundown. He equated Ramadan with the Christian practice of Lent, so the identification of Bairam with Easter is logical but lacking in theological merit.

2 Like Sundays in Christian lands, Fridays (actually beginning at sunset on Thursday) in the Muslim world were days of rest, given over to religious acts and rituals.

129

On Marriage by Martin Luther— 1566

Martin Luther (1483–1546), the founder of the Lutheran religion, initiated many reforms in his new version of Christianity. One of these was allowing clergy to marry. Later in life, Luther married a former nun, Katherine von Bora. Luther's views on marriage were collected by his followers after his death and published in Table Talk. *What reasons does Luther give for why clergymen should be allowed to marry? How does he define women's role in marriage?*

OF MARRIAGE AND CELIBACY

DCCXV

A preacher of the gospel, being regularly called, ought, above all things, first, to purify himself before he teaches others. Is he able, with a good conscience, to remain unmarried? Let him so remain; but if he cannot abstain living chastely, then let him take a wife; God has made that plaster for that sore.

DCCXVI

It is written in the first book of Moses, concerning matrimony: God created a man and woman and blessed them. Now, although this sentence was chiefly spoken of human creatures, yet we may apply it to all the creatures of the world—to the fowls of the air, the fish in the waters, and the beasts of the field, wherein we find a male and a female consorting together, engendering and increasing. In all these, God has placed before our eyes the state of matrimony. We have its image, also, even in the trees and earth.

DCCXVII

Between husband and wife there should be no question as to *meum* and *tuum*. All things should be in common between them, without any distinction or means of distinguishing.

From "Table Talk" by Martin Luther, *Luther's Works*, Vol. 31, trans. and ed. by William Hazlitt. (London: George Bell & Sons, 1895).

DCCXVIII

St. Augustine said, finely: A marriage without children is the world without the sun.

DCCXIX

Maternity is a glorious thing, since all mankind have been conceived, born, and nourished of women. All human laws should encourage the multiplication of families.

DCCXX

The world regards not, nor comprehends the works of God. Who can sufficiently admire the state of conjugal union, which God has instituted and founded, and whence all human creatures, yea, all states proceed. Where were we, if it existed not? But neither God's ordinance, nor the gracious presence of children, the fruit of matrimony, moves the ungodly world, which beholds only the temporal difficulties and troubles of matrimony, but sees not the great treasure that is hid therein. We were all born of women—emperors, kings, princes, yea, Christ himself, the Son of God, did not disdain to be born of a virgin. Let the contemners and rejecters of matrimony go hang, the Anabaptists and Adamites, who recognise not marriage, but live all together like animals, and the papists, who reject married life, and yet have strumpets; if they must needs contemn matrimony, let them be consistent and keep no concubines.

DCCXXI

The state of matrimony is the chief in the world after religion: but people shun it because of its inconveniences, like one who, running out of the rain, falls into the river. We ought herein to have more regard to God's command and ordinance, for the sake of the generation, and the bringing up of children, than to our untoward humours and cogitations; and further, we should consider that it is a physic against sin and unchastity. None indeed, should be compelled to marry; the matter should be left to each man's conscience, for bride-love may not be forced. God has said, "It is not good that the man should be alone;" and St. Paul compares the church to a spouse, or bride and a bridegroom. But let us ever take heed that, in marrying, we esteem neither money nor wealth, great descent, nobility, nor lasciviousness.

DCCXXII

The Lord has never changed the rules he imposed on marriage, but in the case of the conception of his Son Jesus Christ. The Turks, however, are of opinion that 'tis no uncommon thing for a virgin to bear a child. I would by no means introduce this belief into my family.

DCCXXV

Men have broad and large chests, and small narrow hips, and more understanding than the women, who have but small and narrow breasts, and broad hips, to the end they should remain at home, sit still, keep house, and bear and bring up children.

DCCXXVI

Marrying cannot be without women, nor can the world subsist without them. To marry is physic against incontinence. A woman is, or at least should be, a friendly, courteous, and merry companion in life, whence they are named, by the Holy Ghost, house-honours, the honour and ornament of the house, and inclined to tenderness, for thereunto are they chiefly created, to bear children, and be the pleasure, joy, and solace of their husbands.

DCCXXVII

Dr. Luther said one day to his wife: You make me do what you will; you have full sovereignty here, and I award you, with all my heart, the command in all household matters, reserving my rights in other points. Never any good came out of female domination. God created Adam master and lord of living creatures, but Eve spoilt all, when she persuaded him to set himself above God's will. 'Tis you women, with your tricks and artifices, that lead men into error.

130

African Women in 17th Century Benin by Samuel Blommaart—1688

Although it is a second-hand source, the following account is considered to be reliable by modern experts. This document contains information related by Samuel Blommaart to Olfert Dapper, a Dutch physician and historian who wrote about African society, although he never traveled there himself. Blommaart, a Dutch merchant, lived and worked in Africa for several years. What seems to have been the status of women in

From *Nigerian Perspectives* by Thomas Hodgkin (London Oxford University Press, 1974), p. 162–164, 170. Reprinted by permission of Oxford University Press.

Benin at this time? How does it compare with women's status in other societies during the seventeenth century?

When a woman has had a son by her deceased husband she becomes the servant of the son and may not be given in marriage to another person without his permission, but must wait upon the son as a slave. Should it happen that any man desires such a widow he asks the son for permission to marry her and promises to provide a young woman as a wife instead who must then serve as a slave for as long as he requires. The man may not sell the old mother without the king's permission unless the son agrees.

A daughter is not given in marriage by her father until she is twelve or fourteen years old, after which time she is no longer his concern.

After a man dies all the wives with whom he has had sexual relations become the King's and are given again in marriage by him; but those with whom he has not slept go to the son who may keep them or remarry them to others. . . .

After a man's wife has been in childbed he has no sexual relations with her until the child is one-and-a-half years old and can walk. But if he comes to know that his wife has meanwhile been making shift with another he makes a complaint to the Fiadors.[1] . . .

In matters of inheritance they proceed in this way: the man takes all the goods which the wife leaves behind without letting the children keep anything unless the mother gave it to them during her lifetime. But the wife in contrast, after her husband's death, cannot touch the least of his goods, since everything—wives and slaves as well as other things—goes to the King. If there are sons the King often makes the eldest the only heir to his father's slaves and property, and also to any wives with whom the father has not slept, because those with whom he has slept are given as wives to others.

The King has a great number of wives; the number would be well over a thousand, because with his father's death he inherits all the wives with whom his father has not slept. The others may by no means marry again, but are locked up together in a cloister and guarded by eunuchs. Should one of these women try to escape with someone and be caught she must die directly with all her belongings.

---

1 Judges in Benin society.

From *The Book of the Samurai (Hagakure)* by Tsunetomo Yamamoto—1716

Influenced by Zen Buddism and Confucianism, Yamamoto Tsunetomo (1659–1720) incorporated their precepts into the ideals of the samurai cult contained in the Book of the Samurai. *Yamamoto's work relates the collected wisdom of three generations of the Nabeshima family at a time when the role of the warrior class in Japanese society was changing. After Japan's long civil war ended, samurai no longer fought in battle and pursued literary rather than martial goals. However, the samurai tradition was essential to their lives and defined their role in Japanese society. What was the right way for a samurai to die? Why do you think there is so much emphasis on correct behavior in this book?*

Although it stands to reason that a samurai should be mindful of the Way of the Samurai, it would seem that we are all negligent. Consequently, if someone were to ask, "What is the true meaning of the Way of the Samurai?" the person who would be able to answer promptly is rare. This is because it has not been established in one's mind beforehand. From this, one's unmindfulness of the Way can be known

Negligence is an extreme thing.

The Way of the Samurai is found in death. When it comes to either/or, there is only the quick choice of death. It is not particularly difficult. Be determined and advance. To say that dying without reaching one's aim is to die a dog's death is the frivolous way of sophisticates. When pressed with the choice of life or death, it is not necessary to gain one's aim.

We all want to live. And in large part we make our logic according to what we like. But not having attained our aim and continuing to live is cowardice. This is a thin dangerous line. To die without gaining one's aim is a dog's death and fanaticism. But there is no shame in this. This is the substance of the Way of the Samurai. If by setting one's heart right every morning and evening, one is able to live as though his body were already dead, he gains freedom in the Way. His whole life will be without blame, and he will succeed in his calling.

A man is a good retainer to the extent that he earnestly places importance in his master. This is the highest sort of retainer. If one is born into a prominent family that goes back for generations, it is sufficient to deeply consider the matter of obligation to one's ancestors, to lay down one's body and mind, and to earnestly esteem one's master. It is further good fortune if, more than this, one has wisdom and talent and can use them appropriately. But even a person who is good for nothing and exceedingly clumsy will be a reliable retainer if only he has the determination to think earnestly of his master. Having only wisdom and talent is the lowest tier of usefulness.

According to their nature, there are both people who have quick intelligence, and those who must withdraw and take time to think things over. Looking into this thoroughly, if one thinks selflessly and adheres to the four vows of the Nabeshima samurai, surprising wisdom will occur regardless of the high or low points of one's nature.

People think that they can clear up profound matters if they consider them deeply, but they exercise perverse thoughts and come to no good because they do their reflecting with only self-interest at the center.

It is difficult for a fool's habits to change to selflessness. In confronting a matter, however, if at first you leave it alone, fix the four vows in your heart, exclude self-interest, and make an effort, you will not go far from your mark.

Because we do most things relying only on our own sagacity we become self-interested, turn our backs on reason, and things do not turn out well. As seen by other people this is sordid, weak, narrow and inefficient. When one is not capable of true intelligence, it is good to consult with someone of good sense. An advisor will fulfill the Way when he makes a decision by selfless and frank intelligence because he is not personally involved. This way of doing things will certainly be seen by others as being strongly rooted. It is, for example, like a large tree with many roots. One man's intelligence is like a tree that has been simply stuck in the ground.

Being a retainer is nothing other than being a supporter of one's lord, entrusting matters of good and evil to him, and renouncing self-interest. If there are but two or three men of this type, the fief will be secure.

If one looks at the world when affairs are going smoothly, there are many who go about putting in their appearance, being useful by their wisdom, discrimination and artfulness. However, if the lord should retire or go into seclusion, there are many who will quickly turn their backs on him and ingratiate themselves to the man of the day. Such a thing is unpleasant even to think about. Men of high position, low position, deep wisdom and artfulness all feel that *they* are the ones who are working righteously, but when it comes to the point of throwing away one's life for his lord, all get weak in the knees. This is rather disgraceful. The fact that a useless person often becomes a matchless warrior at such times is because he has already given up his life and has become one with his lord. . . .

Loyalty is said to be important in the pledge between lord and retainer. Though it may seem unobtainable, it is right before your eyes. If you once set yourself to it, you will become a superb retainer at that very moment.

To give a person one's opinion and correct his faults is an important thing. It is compassionate and comes first in matters of service. But the way of doing this is extremely difficult. To discover the good and bad points of a person is an easy thing, and to give an opinion concerning them is easy, too. For the most part, people think that they are being kind by saying the things that others find distasteful or difficult to say. But if it is not received well, they think that there is nothing more to be done. This is completely worthless. It is the same as bringing shame to a person by slandering him. It is nothing more than getting it off one's chest.

To give a person an opinion one must first judge well whether that person is of the disposition to receive it or not. One must become close with him and make sure that he continually trusts one's word. Approaching subjects that are dear to him, seek the best way to speak and to be well understood. Judge the occasion, and determine whether it is better by letter or at the time of leave-taking. Praise his good points and use every device to encourage him, perhaps by talking about one's own faults without touching on his, but so that they will occur to him. Have him receive this in the way that a man would drink water when his throat is dry, and it will be an opinion that will correct faults.

This is extremely difficult. If a person's fault is a habit of some years prior, by and large it won't be remedied. I have had this experience myself. To be intimate with all one's comrades, correcting each other's faults, and being of one mind to be of use to the master is the great compassion of a retainer. By bringing shame to a person, how could one expect to make him a better man?

It is bad taste to yawn in front of people. When one unexpectedly has to yawn, if he rubs his forehead in an upward direction, the sensation will stop. If that does not work, he can lick his lips while keeping his mouth closed, or simply hide it with his hand or his sleeve in such a way that no one will know what he is doing. It is the same with sneezing. One will appear foolish There are other things besides these about which a person should use care and training.

Every morning one should first do reverence to his master and parents and then to his patron deities and guardian Buddhas. If he will only make his master first in importance, his parents will rejoice and the gods and Buddhas will give their assent. For a warrior there is nothing other than thinking of his master. If one creates this resolution within himself, he will always be mindful of the master's person and will not depart from him even for a moment.

Moreover, a woman should consider her husband first, just as he considers his master first.

There are two things that will blemish a retainer, and these are riches and honor. If one but remains in strained circumstances, he will not be marred.

Once there was a certain man who was very clever, but it was his character to always see the negative points of his jobs. In such a way, one will be useless. If one does not get it into his head from the very beginning that the world is full of unseemly situations, for the most part his demeanor will be poor and he will not be believed by others. And if one is not believed by others, no matter how good a person he may be, he will not have the essence of a good person. This can also be considered as a blemish.

There was a man who said, "Such and such a person has a violent disposition, but this is what I said right to his face. . . ." This was an unbecoming thing to say, and it was said simply because he wanted to be known as a rough fellow. It was rather low, and it can be seen that he was still rather immature. It is because a samurai has correct manners that he is admired. Speaking of other people in this way is no different from an exchange between low class spearmen. It is vulgar.

CHAPTER 16

Arts and Culture Age of Change—1500–1750 CE

The sixteenth and seventeenth centuries witnessed a vast outpouring of European literature in the vernacular as a result of the Renaissance. Two of the documents in this section come from men who were celebrated in other fields. Michelangelo was probably the greatest sculptor and painter of the day. Giordano Bruno was a noted scientist. Michelangelo provides some insight into the mind of an artist; Bruno seems to advocate space travel in his short poem.

In the oft-quoted segment from *Hamlet,* Shakespeare captures the essence of the humanist spirit of the age, hinted at by Michelangelo and Bruno. At the same time, however, the metaphysical poet John Donne expressed anguish regarding faith in life after death was replaced by fears of death and decay. How can you reconcile the optimism of Bruno with the near despair of Donne?

Travel writing remained a popular literary form throughout the world. How does the sample from Turkey compare with accounts in the preceding section?

By the beginning of the eighteenth century, European writers had begun to use satire to castigate governments and push them toward reform. Swift's brief essay is a shocking and powerful example of this form. How do you think the British government reacted to his essay?

Four Poems by Michelangelo Buonarroti—16th century

Michelangelo (1475–1564) was a sculptor, painter, architect, poet, and perhaps the greatest artist of all time. He was one of the few whose genius was recognized during his lifetime. Yet, despite his great talent and fame, Michelangelo was caught up in the power struggle between the Florentine Medici family and the Popes in Rome. The following four poems express his views about art and life. Was Michelangelo a humanist? How was his thinking influenced by the Renaissance Neo-Platonic movement? How important was art to Michelangelo?

I

La forza d'un bel volto al ciel mi sprona

The pow'r of one fair face spurs me to heaven—
    For such delight the world can nowhere show—
    And I rise, living, and with angels go,
    A gift to man still mortal rarely given.
So with its maker does the work accord
    That my conceptions high become divine
    And they inspire each thought and word of mine
    While burning in the love such beings afford.

If then from those two eyes I cannot turn
    My own regard, I find in them the light
    Which shows the way to God that I employ,
And if, in kindling at their fire I burn,
    In my proud flame there gloweth sweet and bright
    The heavens' laughter of eternal joy.

Translated by W. C. GREENE*

From *The Age of Adventure: The Renaissance Philosophers* (The Great Ages of Western Philosophy), ed. by Giorgio De Santillana, (Freeport, NY: Books for Libraries Press, 1970).

* As we had to discard Wordsworth's version as painfully ornate and bowdlerized, we had recourse to the courtesy of Prof. William C. Greene of M.I.T., and he gave us the above, as well as the next version, which are remarkably faithful to the original.

II

Non ha l'ottimo artista alcun concetto

No concept that the artist apprehends
  But marble in itself will circumscribe
  With its excess; and thereto may arrive
  Alone the hand that intellect attends.
The evil that I flee, what good portends
  In you, fair lady, proud and heavenly,
  Are likewise hid; but bringing death to me
  My art goes counter to its wished-for ends.
Love bears not then—nor does your beauty's grace
  Your great disdain nor your severity—
  Blame for my pain, nor chance nor fortune's breath,
If in your heart both death and pity's place
  At one I find and my poor talent free,
  In burning, from that marble only death.

      Translated by W. C. GREENE

III

Sì amico al freddo sasso è il fuoco acerbo*

So friendly is the fire to flinty stone,
  That, struck therefrom and kindled to a blaze,
  It burns the stone, and from the ash doth raise,
  What lives thenceforward binding stones in one;
Kiln-hardened this resists both frost and sun,
  Acquiring higher worth for endless days—
  As the purged soul from hell returns with praise,
  Amid the heavenly host to take her throne.
E'en so the fire struck from my soul, that lay
  Close-hidden in my heart, may temper me,
  Till burned and slaked to better life I rise.
If made mere smoke and dust I live today,
  Fire-hardened I shall live eternally;
  Such gold, not iron, my spirit strikes and tries.

---

* This and the following sonnet are from Michelangelo, *op. cit.*

VI

Carico d'anni e di peccati pieno

Burdened with years and full of sinfulness,
    With evil custom grown inveterate,
    Both deaths I dread that close before me wait,
    Yet feed my heart on poisonous thoughts no less.
No strength I find in mine own feebleness
    To change or life or love or use or fate,
    Unless thy heavenly guidance come, though late,
    Which only helps and stays our nothingness.
'Tis not enough, dear Lord, to make me yearn
    [For heaven, if you need to have my soul
    Made out again, as erst it was, of nought]
Nay, ere though strip her mortal vestment, turn
    My steps toward the steep ascent, that whole
    And pure before thy face she may be brought.

133

From *L'Envoi* by Giordano Bruno—16th century

Italian renaissance poet, physicist, and philosopher Giordano Bruno (1548-1600) fled from the Dominican monastery he had entered at the age of 16 because of his unorthodox beliefs. An admirer of Copernicus, his own speculations about the universe were much more radical. Bruno believed not only that the universe was infinite in size but also that each star in the firmament was the center of its own solar system and contained planets inhabited by intelligent beings. When he returned to Italy, Bruno was arrested and imprisoned for 8 years, but unlike Galileo, he did not recant. Because he refused to confess the error of his beliefs, Bruno was burnt at the stake at Campo di Fiori on February 19, 1600. In L'Envoi, Bruno uses literature to convey his beliefs. What is his view of the universe? Why might his ideas have upset the establishment? How does Bruno

From *The Age of Adventure: The Renaissance Philosophers* (The Great Ages of Western Philosophy), ed. by Giorgio De Santillana, (Freeport, NY: Books for Libraries Press, 1970).

feel about the new discoveries of his age? How does his attitude compare with that of John Donne, a near contemporary?

L'ENVOI

(From Bruno's *de l'Infinito, Universo e Mondi*)

Who gives me wings and who removes my fears
Of death and fortune? Who inflames my heart?
Who breaks the chains and makes the portals start
Whence but a rare one, freed at last, appears?

Time's Children and his weapons, ages, years,
Months, days, and hours, all that host whose art
Makes even adamant and iron part
Have now secured me from his fury's spears.

Wherefore I spread my wings upon the air
No crystal spheres I find nor other bar
But flying to the immense I cleave the skies
And while from my small globe I speed elsewhere
And through the ethereal ranges further rise
I leave behind what there is seen from far.

Translated by W. C. GREENE

134

From *Hamlet* by William Shakespeare—ca. 1600

One of the world's greatest writers, William Shakespeare (1564–1616) captured the essence of the human condition in both comedy and tragedy. Because of the power and breadth of his work, many people over the centuries have claimed that he was not the author of his plays or that they were written by several people. However, because there is considerable historical evidence regarding his life, most historians believe Shakespeare was the author of the plays that bear his name. The following excerpt is from one of the most

From *Hamlet*, by William Shakespeare.

famous speeches from Hamlet. *How can you tell that Hamlet was a humanist influenced by the Renaissance movement? How does he seem to regard the state of being human?*

HAMLET

To be, or not to be, that is the question:
Whether 'tis nobler in the mind to suffer
The slings and arrows of outrageous fortune,
Or to take arms against a sea of troubles
And by opposing end them. To die, to sleep—
No more—and by a sleep to say we end
The heartache and the thousand natural shocks
That flesh is heir to. 'Tis a consummation
Devoutly to be wished. To die, to sleep;
To sleep, perchance to dream. Ay, there's the rub,
For in that sleep of death what dreams may come,
When we have shuffled off this mortal coil,
Must give us pause. There's the respect
That makes calamity of so long life.
For who would bear the whips and scorns of time,
Th' oppressor's wrong, the proud man's contumely,
The pangs of disprized love, the law's delay,
The insolence of office, and the spurns
That patient merit of th' unworthy takes,
When he himself might his quietus make
With a bare bodkin? Who would fardels bear,
To grunt and sweat under a weary life,
But that the dread of something after death,
The undiscovered country from whose bourn
No traveler returns, puzzles the will,
And makes us rather bear those ills we have
Than fly to others that we know not of?
Thus conscience does make cowards of us all;
And thus the native hue of resolution
Is sicklied o'er with the pale cast of thought,
And enterprises of great pitch and moment
With this regard their currents turn awry
And lose the name of action.—Soft you now,
The fair Ophelia. Nymph, in thy orisons
Be all my sins remembered.

What a piece of work is a man! How noble in reason, how infinite in faculties, in form and moving how express and admirable, in action how like an angel, in apprehension how like a god! The beauty of the world, the paragon of animals! And yet, to me, what is this quintessence of dust? Man delights not me—

From "The Anatomy of the World" by John Donne—1611

John Donne (1572–1630), perhaps the greatest English metaphysical poet, was raised a Catholic during the Reformation. He later converted to Anglicanism and was ordained a minister. Much of his poetry deals with matters of life and death. The following excerpt comes from a long poem dealing with a gloomy subject—the frailty and decay of the world. What seems to have concerned Donne about the new scientific discoveries of his age? Was he a conservative by nature? How did he feel about the Enlightenment?

Thou knowest how poor a trifling thing man is,
And learn'st thus much by our anatomy,
The heart being perish'd, no part can be free,
And that except thou feed (not banquet) on
The supernatural food, religion,
Thy better growth grows withered, and scant;
Be more than man, or thou'rt less than an ant.
Then, as mankind, so is the world's whole frame
Quite out of joint, almost created lame,
For, before God had made up all the rest,
Corruption ent'red, and deprav'd the best;
It seiz'd the angels, and then first of all
The world did in her cradle take a fall,
And turn'd her brains, and took a general maim,
Wronging each joint of th'universal frame.
The noblest part, man, felt it first; and then
Both beasts and plants, curs'd in the curse of man.
So did the world from the first hour decay,
That evening was beginning of the day,
And now the springs and summers which we see,
Like sons of women after fifty be.
And new philosophy calls all in doubt,
The element of fire is quite put out,
The sun is lost, and th'earth, and no man's wit
Can well direct him where to look for it.
And freely men confess that this world's spent,

From "An anatomy of the world" by John Donne, 1611.

When in the planets and the firmament
They seek so many new; they see that this
Is crumbled out again to his atomies.
'Tis all in pieces, all coherence gone,
All just supply, and all relation;
Prince, subject, father, son, are things forgot,
For every man alone thinks he hath got
To be a phoenix, and that then can be
None of that kind, of which he is, but he.
This is the world's condition now, and now
She that should all parts to reunion bow,
She that had all magnetic force alone,
To draw, and fasten sund'red parts in one;
She whom wise nature had invented then
When she observ'd that every sort of men
Did in their voyage in this world's sea stray,
And needed a new compass for their way;
She that was best and first original
Of all fair copies, and the general
Steward to fate; she whose rich eyes and breast
Gilt the West Indies, and perfum'd the East;
Whose having breath'd in this world, did bestow
Spice on those Isles, and bade them still smell so,
And that rich India which doth gold inter,
Is but as single money, coin'd from her;
She to whom this world must it self refer,
As suburbs or the microcosm of her,
She, she is dead; she's dead: when thou know'st this.
Thou know'st how lame a cripple this world is

136

From *Book of Travels*
by Evliya Celebi—17th century

Travel literature has always been popular and since ancient times has provided an excellent source of information about a variety of societies and cultures. Evliya Celebi (1611–1684) was born in Istanbul to a wealthy man with estates in several countries. Thus, Celebi could afford to travel, which he much enjoyed. He was educated in the palace school, where he learned music, Arabic grammar, and calligraphy, among other subjects. He worked for the government and often traveled in an official capacity. The following excerpt describes his adventures in Boudonitza, a small city on the island of Morea in southern Greece. Who were the "infidels" Celebi refers to in this narrative? Why did the infidel fleet attack the city?

THE CITY OF BOUDONÍTZA

Description of the powerful Towers and Mighty
Walls of the strong castle of Boudonítza[1]

The castle is less than two hours distance westward from the seashore. It is a strongly built circular castle, with four subdivisions, on a high place in the mountains, and it is altogether four thousand paces round in circumference. The two lower divisions of the castle, however, were destroyed after the conquest, and since that event the walls have stood in ruins in several places. But it would be an easy matter, if there were money and interest enough, to restore them. As for the third subdivision and the inner keep, they are very strong indeed.

By the will of the Lord, before arriving at this castle, your poor servant heard the noise of cannonfire and musketry on the road in front of us. Since we also heard the shouting of the Muhammadan war-cry,[2] however, we were not frightened off, but as we came up, slowly slowly, towards the city, we encountered several thousand of Muhammad's people, together with their entire households, who had fled from the place, with rags bound around their heads and feet. It appeared that the infidel[3] fleet had disembarked an army which came up from

---

From *The Book of Travels* by Evliya Celebi, trans. by Pierre A. MacKay.

1 A small city on the coast of the island of Morea in southern Greece.

2 Probably the phrase *Allahu akbar!* (God is great!).

3 Christian.

the sea-shore into the residential section of the castle. Together with a certain infidel named Captain Giorgio,[4] who had come from the landward side, they attacked the city; sacked and plundered it; and after throwing everything into confusion, set fire to it and departed with two hundred prisoners, thousands of groats[5] worth of commercial goods and supplies, and the chief judge himself, whom they had taken prisoner along with his entire household.

Cause of the Assault on the Castle
of Boudonítza

The judge is alleged to have been a tyrant so manifestly oppressive in his infringement of the rights of both the tributary and the exempt populace that the tributary subjects,[6] because of the judge's oppression, went off in boats to Captain Giorgio, whom they found cruising near the Venetian island of Tenos. When they got there, they complained of the judge, saying, "He has taken all our property from us so, in the name of our Lord Jesus, restore our rights to us." So saying, they gave this Captain Giorgio the pretext by which he came by land and sea, and for the sake of a single oppressive judge, the infidels destroyed and devastated this charming city, looted it, and took all those many prisoners.

We made so bold as to come into the city in the midst of this turmoil, and saw that the infidels were still busy binding and chaining their captives, poor creatures of the Lord, and sending them off. Those of Muhammad's people who were shut up in the castle opened the castle gate as soon as they saw us, and cried out to us, "Hey Heroes, what shall we do, when so many of our families, our wives and our children, are taken prisoner, and now, see, they are taking them away."

Then, making up a party together with my servants and the men of the town, we extinguished such fires as we could in some of the neighborhoods, and while we were doing so, we saw the warlike hero warriors from Zitúni,[7] horse and foot, coming to help. Then all the people of the city gathered together and attacked the low-born infidels where they had assembled their forces near the sea-shore, and rescued much wealth and property and many prisoners, elderly men and women of Muhammad's people. There were also forty-five infidels whose strength was exhausted from running and from carrying their heavy load of loot. These remained behind, and thanks be to the Lord, we took them prisoner. But as we went further on and arrived close to the infidels' boats at the sea-shore, the accursed infidels let loose at us from their galleons and six gunnery barges, with their large cannon, and we were forced to take all our prisoners and retire once again. Having liberated so many of Muhammad's people, and repossessed so much material and heavy baggage,

---

4 A known pirate of the region.

5 An English silver coin widely used in commerce.

6 Christians. *Exempt populace:* Muslims

7 A town just to the north of Boudonítza.

we made them very happy when we went back to the city with our infidel prisoners and in keeping with our exploits they gave your humble servant one of the infidel prisoners. Praise be to God, we found ourselves thus in a purely fortuitous battle, but what good was there in it, since all those people of Muhammad had been taken captive? There came news too that there were infidels lying in ambush in the mountains, so all the men from Boudonítza, from Zitúni and from Molo[8] came in,several thousands of them, and gathering together they patrolled through the hills and valleys around the city, and remained on watch there.

Concluding Description of the City

One ruinous old mosque in the lower residential quarter escaped the fire, and one inn. One dirty bath, ten shops, a hundred Muslim houses and a hundred and fifty infidel houses remained, all with tile roofs, and gardens and orchards. The rest were all set afire and burned.

Later on, the warriors from Boudonítza and Zitúni who had gone out into the mountains and valleys came back with the news that there was no trace or sign of infidels to be found, but we were still too fearful to sleep in the outer city, and so went into the middle redoubt,[9] where we were hospitably entertained. It is indeed a castle which rises level with the very sky, but the hills along the road that leads to Molo give artillery command over it. In the inner redoubt there are fifty dwellings for the poor wretches of garrison personnel, supplies of produce, and stores and depositories for weapons. But the arsenal is a small one, containing only five long brass falconets.[10] There is only the one small mosque, and no other public edifices. Here and there outside the castle there are gardens and orchards.

Description of Places of Pilgrimage to the Great Saints of God in the Castle of Boudonítza

Outside the city, in the high lands to the east, there is an elevated parkland of cypresses and tall trees. Here, in a meadow from which the entire world may be observed, under a huge lead-roofed cupola, is buried that source of sacred knowledge, who is sprung from an illustrious stock, the seed of Musa Reza, the venerated offspring of Kâzim, who is buried in the heavenly paradise of Baghdad, that recourse of the righteous, entranced by the uniqueness of God, and annihilated in his power, that guide through the stations of sanctity and mirror of illustrious generosity, that son of the noblest of princes, the chosen servant of God, the Sheyh[11] Sultan Veliüllah, son of the Imam Ali Musa Reza,

---

8 A coastal village to the north of Boudonítza.

9 Fortification

10 Small cannons.

11 Or sheikh.

son of the Imam Kâzim, son of the Imam Ja'fer Sadik, son of the Imam Bâkir, son of the Imam Zeyn al-Abidin, son of the Imam Hüseyin, son of the Imam Ali Murteza and his wife, the glorious Lady Fatima, daughter of the excellent Muhammad, who is Ahmed, Mahmud, and Mustafa, may God exalt him, and be pleased with all of them.[12]

This excellent Sultan Veliüllah, being of such an illustrious line, found a final repose in this city of Boudonítza, and lies here in tranquility, buried with all his dependents, children and friends in a brilliant shrine beneath a luminous dome.

---

12 This somewhat eccentric genealogy traces the descent of the Shiite Imam from Muhammad. *Ahmed* (most praiseworthy), *Mahmud* (praised), and *Mustafa* (chosen [by God]) are attributes of *Muhammad* (praised).

137

A Modest Proposal
by Jonathan Swift—1729

Born to an Anglo-Irish family, Jonathan Swift (1667–1745) was a writer and satirist. After attending Trinity College in Dublin, he held a variety of positions that introduced him to the world of politics; eventually, he was ordained a clergyman. By the end of the seventeenth century, Swift had begun to write the satirical works for which he later gained fame. Much of his voluminous output was devoted to the struggle for Irish home rule. The most famous of his books is Gulliver's Travels, *which satirizes a number of society's failings. The following excerpt is probably his most savage essay. What does Swift suggest to alleviate hunger in Ireland? How do you think this essay was received? Who was it directed toward?*

It is a melancholy object to those who walk through this great town or travel in the country, when they see the streets, the roads, and cabin doors, crowded with beggars of the female sex, followed by three, four, or six children, all in rags and importuning every passenger for an alms. These mothers, instead of

---

"A Modest Proposal for preventing the children of poor people in Ireland from being a burden to their parents or country, and for making them beneficial to the public" by Jonathan Swift, 1729.

being able to work for their honest livelihood, are forced to employ all their time in strolling to beg sustenance for their helpless infants: who as they grow up either turn thieves for want of work, or leave their dear native country to fight for the Pretender in Spain, or sell themselves to the Barbadoes.

I think it is agreed by all parties that this prodigious number of children in the arms, or on the backs, or at the heels of their mothers, and frequently of their fathers, is in the present deplorable state of the kingdom a very great additional grievance; and, therefore, whoever could find out a fair, cheap, and easy method of making these children sound, useful members of the commonwealth, would deserve so well of the public as to have his statue set up for a preserver of the nation.

But my intention is very far from being confined to provide only for the children of professed beggars; it is of a much greater extent, and shall take in the whole number of infants at a certain age who are born of parents in effect as little able to support them as those who demand our charity in the streets.

As to my own part, having turned my thoughts for many years upon this important subject, and maturely weighed the several schemes of other projectors, I have always found them grossly mistaken in the computation. It is true, a child just dropped from its dam may be supported by her milk for a solar year, with little other nourishment; at most not above the value of 2s., which the mother may certainly get, or the value in scraps, by her lawful occupation of begging; and it is exactly at one year old that I propose to provide for them in such a manner as instead of being a charge upon their parents or the parish, or wanting food and raiment for the rest of their lives, they shall on the contrary contribute to the feeding, and partly to the clothing, of many thousands.

There is likewise another great advantage in my scheme, that it will prevent those voluntary abortions, and that horrid practice of women murdering their bastard children, alas! too frequent among us! sacrificing the poor innocent babes I doubt more to avoid the expense than the shame, which would move tears and pity in the most savage and inhuman breast.

The number of souls in this kingdom being usually reckoned one million and a half, of these I calculate there may be about two hundred thousand couple whose wives are breeders; from which number I subtract thirty thousand couples who are able to maintain their own children, although I apprehend there cannot be so many, under the present distresses of the kingdom; but this being granted, there will remain an hundred and seventy thousand breeders. I again subtract fifty thousand for those women who miscarry, or whose children die by accident or disease within the year. There only remains one hundred and twenty thousand children of poor parents annually born. The question therefore is, how this number shall be reared and provided for, which, as I have already said, under the present situation of affairs, is utterly impossible by all the methods hitherto proposed. For we can neither employ them in handicraft or agriculture; we neither build houses (I mean in the country) nor cultivate land: they can very seldom pick up a livelihood by stealing, till they arrive at six years old, except where they are of towardly parts, although I confess they learn the rudiments much earlier, during which time, they can however be properly looked upon only as probationers, as I have been informed by a principal gentleman in the county of Cavan, who protested to me that he never knew above one or two instances under the age of six, even in a part of the kingdom so renowned for the quickest proficiency in that art.

I am assured by our merchants, that a boy or a girl before twelve years old is no salable commodity; and even when they come to this age they will not yield above three pounds, or three pounds and half-a-crown at most on the exchange; which cannot turn to account either to the parents or kingdom, the charge of nutriment and rags having been at least four times that value.

I shall now therefore humbly propose my own thoughts, which I hope will not be liable to the least objection.

I have been assured by a very knowing American of my acquaintance in London, that a young healthy child well nursed is at a year old a most delicious, nourishing, and wholesome food, whether stewed, roasted, baked, or boiled; and I make no doubt that it will equally serve in a fricassee or a ragout.

I do therefore humbly offer it to public consideration that of the hundred and twenty thousand children already computed, twenty thousand may be reserved for breed, whereof only one-fourth part to be males; which is more than we allow to sheep, black cattle or swine; and my reason is, that these children are seldom the fruits of marriage, a circumstance not much regarded by our savages, therefore one male will be sufficient to serve four females. That the remaining hundred thousand may, at a year old, be offered in the sale to the persons of quality and fortune through the kingdom; always advising the mother to let them suck plentifully in the last month, so as to render them plump and fat for a good table. A child will make two dishes at an entertainment for friends; and when the family dines alone, the fore or hind quarter will make a reasonable dish, and seasoned with a little pepper or salt will be very good boiled on the fourth day, especially in winter.

I have reckoned upon a medium that a child just born will weigh 12 pounds, and in a solar year, if tolerably nursed, increaseth to 28 pounds.

I grant this food will be somewhat dear, and therefore very proper for landlords, who, as they have already devoured most of the parents, seem to have the best title to the children.

Infant's flesh will be in season throughout the year, but more plentiful in March, and a little before and after; for we are told by a grave author, an eminent French physician, that fish being a prolific diet, there are more children born in Roman Catholic countries about nine months after Lent than at any other season; therefore, reckoning a year after Lent, the markets will be more glutted than usual, because the number of popish infants is at least three to one in this kingdom: and therefore it will have one other collateral advantage, by lessening the number of papists among us.

I have already computed the charge of nursing a beggar's child (in which list I reckon all cottagers, laborers, and four-fifths of the farmers) to be about two shillings per annum, rags included; and I believe no gentleman would repine to give ten shillings for the carcass of a good fat child, which, as I have said, will make four dishes of excellent nutritive meat, when he hath only some particular friend or his own family to dine with him. Thus the squire will learn to be a good landlord, and grow popular among his tenants; the mother will have eight shillings net profit, and be fit for work till she produces another child.

Those who are more thrifty (as I must confess the times require) may flay the carcass; the skin of which artificially dressed will make admirable gloves for ladies, and summer boots for fine gentlemen.

As to our city of Dublin, shambles may be appointed for this purpose in the most convenient parts of it, and butchers we may be assured will not be wanting; although I rather recommend buying the children alive, and dressing them hot from the knife, as we do roasting pigs.

A very worthy person, a true lover of his country, and whose virtues I highly esteem, was lately pleased in discoursing on this matter to offer a refinement upon my scheme. He said that many gentlemen of this kingdom, having of late destroyed their deer, he conceived that the want of venison might be well supplied by the bodies of young lads and maidens, not exceeding fourteen years of age nor under twelve; so great a number of both sexes in every country being now ready to starve for want of work and service; and these to be disposed of by their parents, if alive, or otherwise by their nearest relations. But with due deference to so excellent a friend and so deserving a patriot, I cannot be altogether in his sentiments; for as to the males, my American acquaintance assured me, from frequent experience, that their flesh was generally tough and lean, like that of our schoolboys by continual exercise, and their taste disagreeable; and to fatten them would not answer the charge. Then as to the females, it would, I think, with humble submission be a loss to the public, because they soon would become breeders themselves; and besides, it is not improbable that some scrupulous people might be apt to censure such a practice (although indeed very unjustly), as a little bordering upon cruelty; which, I confess, hath always been with me the strongest objection against any project, however so well intended.

But in order to justify my friend, he confessed that this expedient was put into his head by the famous Psalmanazar, a native of the island Formosa, who came from thence to London above twenty years ago, and in conversation told my friend, that in his country when any young person happened to be put to death, the executioner sold the carcass to persons of quality as a prime dainty; and that in his time the body of a plump girl of fifteen, who was crucified for an attempt to poison the emperor, was sold to his imperial majesty's prime minister of state, and other great mandarins of the court, in joints from the gibbet, at four hundred crowns. Neither indeed can I deny, that if the same use were made of several plump young girls in this town, who without one single groat to their fortunes cannot stir abroad without a chair, and appear at playhouse and assemblies in foreign fineries which they never will pay for, the kingdom would not be the worse.

Some persons of a desponding spirit are in great concern about that vast number of poor people, who are aged, diseased, or maimed, and I have been desired to employ my thoughts what course may be taken to ease the nation of so grievous an encumbrance. But I am not in the least pain upon that matter, because it is very well known that they are every day dying and rotting by cold and famine, and filth and vermin, as fast as can be reasonably expected. And as to the young laborers, they are now in as hopeful a condition; they cannot get work, and consequently pine away for want of nourishment, to a degree that if at any time they are accidentally hired to common labor, they have not strength to perform it; and thus the country and themselves are happily delivered from the evils to come.

I have too long digressed, and therefore shall return to my subject. I think the advantages by the proposal which I have made are obvious and many, as well as of the highest importance.

For first, as I have already observed, it would greatly lessen the number of papists, with whom we are yearly overrun, being the principal breeders of the nation as well as our most dangerous enemies; and who stay at home on purpose with a design to deliver the kingdom to the Pretender, hoping to take their advantage by the absence of so many good protestants, who have chosen rather to leave their country than stay at home and pay tithes against their conscience to an episcopal curate.

Secondly, The poorer tenants will have something valuable of their own, which by law may be made liable to distress and help to pay their landlord's rent, their corn and cattle being already seized, and money a thing unknown.

Thirdly, Whereas the maintenance of an hundred thousand children, from two years old and upward, cannot be computed at less than ten shillings a-piece per annum, the nation's stock will be thereby increased fifty thousand pounds per annum, beside the profit of a new dish introduced to the tables of all gentlemen of fortune in the kingdom who have any refinement in taste. And the money will circulate among ourselves, the goods being entirely of our own growth and manufacture.

Fourthly, The constant breeders, beside the gain of eight shillings sterling per annum by the sale of their children, will be rid of the charge of maintaining them after the first year.

Fifthly, This food would likewise bring great custom to taverns; where the vintners will certainly be so prudent as to procure the best receipts for dressing it to perfection, and consequently have their houses frequented by all the fine gentlemen, who justly value themselves upon their knowledge in good eating: and a skilful cook, who understands how to oblige his guests, will contrive to make it as expensive as they please.

Sixthly, This would be a great inducement to marriage, which all wise nations have either encouraged by rewards or enforced by laws and penalties. It would increase the care and tenderness of mothers toward their children, when they were sure of a settlement for life to the poor babes, provided in some sort by the public, to their annual profit instead of expense. We should see an honest emulation among the married women, which of them could bring the fattest child to the market. Men would become as fond of their wives during the time of their pregnancy as they are now of their mares in foal, their cows in calf, their sows when they are ready to farrow; nor offer to beat or kick them (as is too frequent a practice) for fear of a miscarriage.

Many other advantages might be enumerated. For instance, the addition of some thousand carcasses in our exportation of barreled beef, the propagation of swine's flesh, and improvement in the art of making good bacon, so much wanted among us by the great destruction of pigs, too frequent at our tables; which are no way comparable in taste or magnificence to a well-grown, fat, yearling child, which roasted whole will make a considerable figure at a lord mayor's feast or any other public entertainment. But this and many others I omit, being studious of brevity.

After all, I am not so violently bent upon my own opinion as to reject any offer proposed by wise men, which shall be found equally innocent, cheap, easy, and effectual. But before something of that kind shall be advanced in contradiction to my scheme, and offering a better, I desire the author or authors will be pleased maturely to consider two points. First, as things now stand, how they will be able to find food and raiment for an hundred thousand useless mouths and backs. And secondly, there being a round million of creatures in human figure throughout this kingdom, whose whole subsistence put into a common stock would leave them in debt two millions of pounds sterling, adding those who are beggars by profession to the bulk of farmers, cottagers, and laborers, with their wives and children who are beggars in effect: I desire those politicians who dislike my overture, and may perhaps be so bold as to attempt an answer, that they will first ask the parents of these mortals, whether they would not at this day think it a great happiness to have been sold for food, at a year old in the manner I prescribe, and thereby have avoided such a perpetual scene of misfortunes as they have since gone through by the oppression of landlords, the impossibility of paying rent without money or trade, the want of common sustenance, with neither house nor clothes to cover them from the inclemencies of the weather, and the most inevitable prospect of entailing the like or greater miseries upon their breed for ever.

I profess, in the sincerity of my heart, that I have not the least personal interest in endeavoring to promote this necessary work, having no other motive than the public good of my country, by advancing our trade, providing for infants, relieving the poor, and giving some pleasure to the rich. I have no children by which I can propose to get a single penny; the youngest being nine years old, and my wife past child-bearing.

CHAPTER 17

Religion and Philosophy— 1750–1914 CE

B y the end of the eighteenth century, the emphasis on reform of the Catholic Church in the West had shifted towards reform of society and government. Philosophers rather than theologians were the prophets of the day. Rousseau, Voltaire, and Beccaria all wanted to reform society, but each took a different approach. Which of these philosophers seems most in line with modern thought? Why?

Both Hegel and Marx were concerned with the importance of history and its relation to social change. Do you think that Marx was influenced by Hegel? In what way? Adam Smith explores the foundation of modern market capitalism, and Greg discusses the problems it created. How do these two documents relate to each other?

138

From *The Social Contract* by Jean Jacques Rousseau—1762

Jean Jacques Rousseau (1712–1778) was born to Protestant parents in Geneva, Switzerland. He ran away at the age of 16 and settled in Paris, where he attempted to earn a living as a writer. Although Rousseau had relatively little formal education, his keen intelligence helped him to develop into a philosopher of note. The Social Contract is probably his best-known work and strongly influenced the course of the French Revolution. The following excerpt deals with Rousseau's views on slavery and the Social Contract. Why does he argue that slavery is wrong? According to Rousseau, why is society necessary for individuals to reach their full potential?

CHAPTER II THE FIRST SOCIETIES

The most ancient of all societies, and the only one that is natural, is the family: and even so the children remain attached to the father only so long as they need him for their preservation. As soon as this need ceases, the natural bond is dissolved. The children, released from the obedience they owed to the father, and the father, released from the care he owed his children, return equally to independence. If they remain united, they continue so no longer naturally, but voluntarily; and the family itself is then maintained only by convention.

This common liberty results from the nature of man. His first law is to provide for his own preservation, his first cares are those which he owes to himself; and, as soon as he reaches years of discretion, he is the sole judge of the proper means of preserving himself, and consequently becomes his own master.

The family then may be called the first model of political societies: the ruler corresponds to the father, and the people to the children; and all, being born free and equal, alienate their liberty only for their own advantage. The whole difference is that, in the family, the love of the father for his children repays him for the care he takes of them, while, in the State, the pleasure of commanding takes the place of the love which the chief cannot have for the peoples under him. . . .

From Jean-Jacques Rousseau, *The Social Contract and Discourses*, trans. by G.D.H. Cole (New York: Dutton, 1973). Reprinted by permission.

CHAPTER IV SLAVERY

If an individual, says Grotius, can alienate his liberty and make himself the slave of a master, why could not a whole people do the same and make itself subject to a king? There are in this passage plenty of ambiguous words which would need explaining; but let us confine ourselves to the word *alienate*. To alienate is to give or to sell. Now, a man who becomes the slave of another does not give himself; he sells himself, at the least for his subsistence: but for what does a people sell itself? A king is so far from furnishing his subjects with their subsistence that he gets his own only from them; and, according to Rabelais, kings do not live on nothing. Do subjects then give their persons on condition that the king takes their goods also? I fail to see what they have left to preserve.

It will be said that the despot assures his subjects civil tranquility. Granted; but what do they gain, if the wars his ambition brings down upon them, his insatiable avidity, and the vexatious conduct of his ministers press harder on them than their own dissensions would have done? What do they gain, if the very tranquility they enjoy is one of their miseries? Tranquility is found also in dungeons; but is that enough to make them desirable places to live in? The Greeks imprisoned in the cave of the Cyclops lived there very tranquilly, while they were awaiting their turn to be devoured.

To say that a man gives himself gratuitously, is to say what is absurd and inconceivable; such an act is null and illegitimate, from the mere fact that he who does it is out of his mind. To say the same of a whole people is to suppose a people of madmen; and madness creates no right.

Even if each man could alienate himself, he could not alienate his children: they are born men and free; their liberty belongs to them, and no one but they has the right to dispose of it. Before they come to years of discretion, the father can, in their name, lay down conditions for their preservation and well-being, but he cannot give them irrevocably and without conditions: such a gift is contrary to the ends of nature, and exceeds the rights of paternity. It would therefore be necessary, in order to legitimize an arbitrary government, that in every generation the people should be in a position to accept or reject it; but, were this true, the government would be no longer arbitrary.

To renounce liberty is to renounce being a man, to surrender the rights of humanity and even its duties. For him who renounces everything no indemnity is possible. Such a renunciation is incompatible with man's nature; to remove all liberty from his will is to remove all morality from his acts. Finally, it is an empty and contradictory convention that sets up, on the one side, absolute authority, and, on the other, unlimited obedience. Is it not clear that we can be under no obligation to a person from whom we have the right to exact everything? Does not this condition alone, in the absence of equivalence or exchange, in itself involve the nullity of the act? For what right can my slave have against me, when all that he has belongs to me, and, his right being mine, this right of mine against myself is a phrase devoid of meaning?

Grotius and the rest find in war another origin for the so-called right of slavery. The victor having, as they hold, the right of killing the vanquished, the latter can buy back his life at the price of his liberty; and this convention is the more legitimate because it is to the advantage of both parties.

But it is clear that this supposed right to kill the conquered is by no means deducible from the state of war. Men, from the mere fact that, while they are living in their primitive independence, they have no mutual relations stable enough to constitute either the state of peace or the state of war, cannot be naturally enemies. War is constituted by a relation between things, and not between persons; and, as the state of war cannot arise out of simple personal relations, but only out of real relations, private war, or war of man with man, can exist neither in the state of nature, where there is no constant property, nor in the social state, where everything is under the authority of the laws. . . .

War then is a relation, not between man and man, but between State and State, and individuals are enemies only accidentally, not as men, nor even as citizens, but as soldiers; not as members of their country, but as its defenders. Finally, each State can have for enemies only other States, and not men; for between things disparate in nature there can be no real relation. . . .

The object of the war being the destruction of the hostile State, the other side has a right to kill its defenders, while they are bearing arms; but as soon as they lay them down and surrender, they cease to be enemies or instruments of the enemy, and become once more merely men, whose life no one has any right to take. Sometimes it is possible to kill the State without killing a single one of its members; and war gives no right which is not necessary to the gaining of its object. These principles are not those of Grotius; they are not based on the authority of poets, but derived from the nature of reality and based on reason. . . .

So, from whatever aspect we regard the question, the right of slavery is null and void, not only as being illegitimate, but also because it is absurd and meaningless. The words *slave* and *right* contradict each other, and are mutually exclusive. It will always be equally foolish for a man to say to a man or to a people: "I make with you a convention wholly at your expense and wholly to my advantage; I shall keep it as long as I like, and you will keep it as long as I like." . . .

CHAPTER VI   THE SOCIAL COMPACT

I suppose men to have reached the point at which the obstacles in the way of their preservation in the state of nature show their power of resistance to be greater than the resources at the disposal of each individual for his maintenance in that state. That primitive condition can then subsist no longer; and the human race would perish unless it changed its manner of existence.

But, as men cannot engender new forces, but only unite and direct existing ones, they have no other means of preserving themselves than the formation, by aggregation, of a sum of forces great enough to overcome the resistance. These they have to bring into play by means of a single motive power, and cause to act in concert.

This sum of forces can arise only where several persons come together; but, as the force and liberty of each man are the chief instruments of his self-preservation, how can he pledge them without harming his own interests, and neglecting the care he owes to himself? This difficulty, in its bearing on my present subject, may be stated in the following terms:

The problem is to find a form of association which will defend and protect with the whole common force the person and goods of each associate, and in which each, while uniting himself with all, may still obey himself alone, and remain as free as before. This is the fundamental problem of which the social contract provides the solution.

The clauses of this contract are so determined by the nature of the act that the slightest modification would make them vain and ineffective; so that, although they have perhaps never been formally set forth, they are everywhere the same and everywhere tacitly admitted and recognized, until, on the violation of the social compact, each regains his original rights and resumes his natural liberty, while losing the conventional liberty in favour of which he renounced it.

The clauses, properly understood, may be reduced to one—the total alienation of each associate, together with all his rights, to the whole community; for, in the first place, as each gives himself absolutely, the conditions are the same for all; and, this being so, no one has any interest in making them burdensome to others.

Moreover, the alienation being without reserve, the union is as perfect as it can be, and no associate has anything more to demand: for, if the individuals retained certain rights, as there would be no common superior to decide between them and the public, each, being on one point his own judge, would ask to be so on all; the state of nature would thus continue, and the association would necessarily become inoperative or tyrannical.

Finally, each man, in giving himself to all, gives himself to nobody; and as there is no associate over which he does not acquire the same right as he yields others over himself, he gains an equivalent for everything he loses, and an increase of force for the preservation of what he has.

If then we discard from the social compact what is not of its essence, we shall find that it reduces itself to the following terms:

Each of us puts his person and all his power in common under the supreme direction of the general will, and, in our corporate capacity, we receive each member as an indivisible part of the whole.

139

Treatise on Toleration by
Voltaire—1763

Francois-Marie Arouet (1694–1778) is best known by his pen name, Voltaire. He was one of the leading figures of the French Enlightenment, a writer who used wit and elegance to promote its ideals. Born into a middle-class Parisian family, Voltaire wrote literally thousands of works of fiction, satire, history, poetry, and journalism. Because he was not only clever and insightful but also extremely prolific, Voltaire had a powerful influence on eighteenth-century Europe. Voltaire was especially concerned with universal tolerance and the freedom of thought and speech. He believed organized religion was responsible for much of the suffering and cruelty in the world. According to Voltaire, what makes a person truly religious? Was he an atheist? What was his relation with God, if any?

OF UNIVERSAL TOLERANCE

No great art or studied eloquence is needed to prove that Christians should tolerate one another. I go even further and declare that we must look upon all men as our brothers. But the Turk, my brother? the Chinese, the Jew, the Siamese? Yes, of course; are we not all the children of one father and creatures of the same God?

But these people despise us; they call us idolators! Then I'll tell them they are quite wrong. I think I could at least shock the proud obstinacy of an imam,[1] if I said to them something like this:

This little globe, nothing more than a point, rolls in space like so many other globes; we are lost in this immensity. Man, some five feet tall, is surely a very small part of the universe. One of these imperceptible beings says to some of his neighbors in Arabia or Africa: "Listen to me, for the God of all these worlds has enlightened me: there are nine hundred million little ants like us on the earth, but only my anthill is beloved of God; He will hold all others in horror through all eternity; only mine will be blessed, the others will be eternally wretched."

At that, they would cut me short and ask what fool made that stupid remark. I would be obliged to reply, "You yourselves." Then I would try to mollify them; but that would not be easy.

From *Les Philosophes*, ed. by Norman L. Torrey. Reprinted by permission of Penguin Group (USA), Inc.

1 For Sunni Muslims, an imam is a prayer leader at a mosque; for Shiites, he is one of the twelve successors of Muhammad. Voltaire is using the word in the former sense.

I would speak now to the Christians and dare say, for example, to a Dominican Inquisitor: "My brother, you know that every province in Italy has its dialect, and people in Venice and Bergamo speak differently from those in Florence. The Academy della Crusca[2] has standardized the language; its dictionary is an inescapable authority, and Buonmattei's[3] grammar is an absolute and infallible guide; but do you believe that the head of the Academy and in his absence, Buonmattei, would have been able in all good conscience to cut out the tongues of all those from Venice and Bergamo who persisted in using their own dialect?"

The Inquisitor replies: "There is a great difference; here it's a question of your salvation. It's for your own good the Director of the Inquisition orders that you be seized on the testimony of a single person, no matter how infamous or criminal he may be; that you have no lawyer to defend you; that the very name of your accuser be unknown to you; that the Inquisitor promise you grace and then condemn you; that you undergo five different degrees of torture and then be whipped or sent to the galleys, or ceremoniously burned at the stake. . . ."

I would take the liberty of replying: "My brother, perhaps you are right: I am convinced that you wish me well, but couldn't I be saved without all that?"

To be sure, these horrible absurdities do not soil the face of the earth everyday, but they are frequent enough, and a whole volume could easily be written about them much longer than the Gospels which condemn them. Not only is it very cruel to persecute in this brief existence of ours those who differ from us in opinion, but I am afraid it is being bold indeed to pronounce their eternal damnation. It hardly seems fitting for us atoms of the moment, for that is all we are, to presume to know in advance the decrees of our own Creator. . . .

Oh, sectarians of a merciful God, if you had a cruel heart, if, while adoring Him whose only law consists in the words: "Love God and thy neighbor as thyself (Luke X, 27)," you had overloaded this pure and holy law with sophisms and incomprehensible disputations; if you had lighted the torch of discord either over a new word or a single letter of the alphabet; if you had made eternal punishment the penalty for the omission of a few words or ceremonies which other nations could not know about, I would say to you, as I wept in compassion for mankind: "Transport yourselves with me to the day when all men will be judged and when God will do unto each man according to his works."

"I see all the dead of all centuries, past and present, appear before His presence. Are you quite sure that our Creator and Father will say to the wise and virtuous Confucius, to Solon the law-giver, to Pythagoras, Zaleucus, Socrates, and Plato, to the divine Antoninus, good Trajan, and Titus, the flowering of mankind, to Epictetus and so many other model men:[4] "Go, you monsters; go

---

2 Florentine Academy of Letters, founded in 1582.

3 Seventeenth-century Italian grammarian.

4 These were all men famous for their writings on ethics and morality who lived before
   Christianity.

and suffer punishment, limitless in time and intensity, eternal as I am eternal. And you, my beloved, Jean Chatel, Ravaillac, Damiens, Cartouche, etc.,[5] who died according to the prescribed formulas, share forever at my right hand my empire and my felicity."

You draw back in horror from these words, and since they escaped me, I have no more to say.

PRAYER TO GOD

I no longer address myself to men, but to thee, God of all beings, all worlds, and all ages. If indeed it is allowable for feeble creatures, lost in immensity and imperceptible to the rest of the universe, to dare ask anything of Thee who hast given all things, whose decrees are as immutable as they are eternal, deign to look with compassion upon the failings inherent in our nature, and grant that these failings lead us not into calamity.

Thou didst not give us hearts that we should hate each other or hands that we should cut each other's throats. Grant that we may help each other bear the burden of our painful and brief lives; that the slight difference in the clothing with which we cover our puny bodies, in our inadequate tongues, in all our ridiculous customs, in all our imperfect laws, in all our insensate opinions, in all our stations in life so disproportionate in our eyes but so equal in Thy sight, that all these little variations that differentiate the atoms called *man,* may not be the signals for hatred and persecution. . . .

May all men remember that they are brothers; may they hold in horror tyranny that is exercised over souls, just as they hold in execration the brigandage that snatches away by force the fruits of labor and peaceful industry. If the scourge of war is inevitable, let us not hate each other, let us not tear each other apart in the lap of peace; but let us use the brief moment of our existence in blessing in a thousand different tongues, from Siam to California, Thy goodness which has bestowed this moment upon us.

---

5 Four notorious criminals, including murderers and highway robbers.

140

On Crimes and Punishment by Cesare Beccaria—1764

The Enlightenment of eighteenth-century Europe produced a number of intellectuals who were dedicated to improving society in a variety of ways. Cesare Beccaria (1738–1794) was born into an aristocratic family in northern Italy and earned a degree in law. He was inspired by reform-minded intellectual peers to try to improve the legal system in Italy. His ideas brought him fame throughout Europe, and he gained an important position in Milan. The issue of capital punishment is much discussed today. How did Beccaria feel about capital punishment? Did he believe it acts as a deterrent? How do his views agree with current thought on this subject?

If we glance at the pages of history, we will find that laws, which surely are, or ought to be, compacts of free men, have been, for the most part, a mere tool of the passions of some, or have arisen from an accidental and temporary need. Never have they been dictated by a dispassionate student of human nature who might, by bringing the actions of a multitude of men into focus, consider them from this single point of view; the *greatest happiness shared by the greatest number.* Happy are those few nations that have not waited for the slow succession of coincidence and human vicissitude to force some little turn for the better after the limit of evil has been reached, but have facilitated the intermediate progress by means of good laws.

IMPRISONMENT

An error no less common that it is contrary to the purpose of association—which is assurance of personal security—is that of allowing a magistrate charged with administering the laws to be free to imprison a citizen at his own pleasure, to deprive an enemy of liberty on frivolous pretexts, and to leave a friend unpunished notwithstanding the clearest evidences of his guilt. Detention in prison is a punishment which, unlike every other, must of necessity precede conviction for crime, but this distinctive character does not remove the other which is essential—namely, that only the law determines the cases in which a man is to suffer punishment. It pertains to the law, therefore,

From *On Crimes and Punishments* by Beccaria, trans. by H. Paolucci. Copyright © 1963.
Reprinted by permission of Pearson Education, Upper Saddle River, NJ.

to indicate what evidences of crime justify detention of the accused, his sub-jection to investigation and punishment. A man's notoriety, his flight, his non-judicial confession, the confession of an accomplice, threats and the constant enmity of the injured person, the manifest fact of the crime, and similar evi-dences, are proofs sufficient to justify imprisonment of a citizen. But these proofs must be determined by the law, not by judges, whose decrees are always contrary to political liberty when they are not particular applications of a gen-eral maxim included in the public code. When punishments have become more moderate, when squalor and hunger have been removed from prisons, when pity and mercy have forced a way through barred doors, overmastering the inexorable and obdurate ministers of justice, then may the laws be content with slighter evidences as grounds for imprisonment.

A man accused of a crime, who has been imprisoned and acquitted, ought not to be branded with infamy. How many Romans accused of very great crimes, and then found innocent, were revered by the populace and honored with public offices! For what reason, then, is the fate of an inno-cent person so apt to be different in our time? It seems to be because, in the present system of criminal law, the idea of power and arrogance prevails over that of justice, because accused and convicted are thrown indiscrimi-nately into the same cell, because imprisonment is rather the torment than the confinement of the accused, and because the internal power that pro-tects the laws and the external power that defends the throne and nation are separated when they ought to be united. By means of the common sanction of the laws, the former [internal power] would be combined with judicial authority, without, however, passing directly under its sway; the glory that attends the pomp and ceremony of a military corps would remove infamy, which, like all popular sentiments, is more attached to the manner than to the thing itself, as is proved by the fact that military prisons are, according to the common opinion, less disgraceful than the civil. Still discernible in our people, in their customs and laws, which always lag several ages behind the actual enlightened thought of a nation—still discernible are the barbaric impressions and savage notions of those people of the North who hunted down our forefathers.

THE DEATH PENALTY

This useless prodigality of torments, which has never made men better, has prompted me to examine whether death is really useful and just in a well-organized government.

What manner of right can men attribute to themselves to slaughter their fellow beings? Certainly not that from which sovereignty and the laws derive. These are nothing but the sum of the least portions of the private liberty of each person; they represent the general will, which is the aggregate of particu-lar wills. Was there ever a man who can have wished to leave to other men the choice of killing him? Is it conceivable that the least sacrifice of each person's liberty should include sacrifice of the greatest of all goods, life? And if that were the case, how could such a principle be reconciled with the other, that man is not entitled to take his own life? He must be, if he can surrender that right to others or to society as a whole.

The punishment of death, therefore, is not a right, for I have demonstrated that it cannot be such; but it is the war of a nation against a citizen whose destruction it judges to be necessary or useful. If, then, I can show that death is neither useful nor necessary I shall have gained the cause of humanity.

There are only two possible motives for believing that the death of a citizen is necessary. The first: when it is evident that even if deprived of liberty he still has connections and power such as endanger the security of the nation—when, that is, his existence can produce a dangerous revolution in the established form of government. The death of a citizen thus becomes necessary when a nation is recovering or losing its liberty or, in time of anarchy, when disorders themselves take the place of laws. But while the laws reign tranquilly, in a form of government enjoying the consent of the entire nation, well defended externally and internally by force, and by opinion, which is perhaps even more efficacious than force, where executive power is lodged with the true sovereign alone, where riches purchase pleasures and not authority. I see no necessity for destroying a citizen, except if his death were the only real way of restraining others from committing crimes; this is the second motive for believing that the death penalty may be just and necessary.

It is not the intensity of punishment that has the greatest effect on the human spirit, but its duration, for our sensibility is more easily and more permanently affected by slight but repeated impressions than by á powerful but momentary action. The sway of habit is universal over every sentient being; as man speaks and walks and satisfies his needs by its aid, so the ideas of morality come to be stamped upon the mind only by long and repeated impressions. It is not the terrible yet momentary spectacle of the death of a wretch, but the long and painful example of a man deprived of liberty, who, having become a beast of burden, recompenses with his labors the society he has offended, which is the strongest curb against crimes. That efficacious idea—efficacious, because very often repeated to ourselves—"I myself shall be reduced to so long and miserable a condition if I commit a similar misdeed" is far more potent than the idea of death, which men envision always at an obsure distance.

The death penalty becomes for the majority a spectacle and for some others an object of compassion mixed with disdain; these two sentiments rather than the salutary fear which the laws pretend to inspire occupy the spirits of the spectators. But in moderate and prolonged punishments the dominant sentiment is the latter, because it is the only one. The limit which the legislator ought to fix on the rigor of punishments would seem to be determined by the sentiment of compassion itself, when it begins to prevail over every other in the hearts of those who are the witnesses of punishment, inflicted for their sake rather than for the criminal's.

For a punishment to be just it should consist of only such gradations of intensity as suffice to deter men from committing crimes. Now, the person does not exist who, reflecting upon it, could choose for himself total and perpetual loss of personal liberty, no matter how advantageous a crime might seem to be. Thus the intensity of the punishment of a life sentence of servitude, in place of the death penalty, has in it what suffices to deter any determined spirit. It has, let me add, even more. Many men are able to took calmly and with firmness upon death—some from fanaticism, some from vanity, which almost always accompanies man even beyond the tomb, some from a final and desperate attempt either to live no longer or to escape their misery. But neither fanaticism nor vanity can subsist among fetters or chains, under the rod, under the yoke, in a cage of iron, where the desperate wretch does not end his woes but merely begins them. Our spirit resists violence and extreme but momentary pains more easily than it does time and incessant weariness, for it can, so to speak, collect itself for a moment to repel the first, but the vigor of its elasticity does not suffice to resist the long and repeated action of the second.

If one were to cite against me the example of all the ages and of almost all the nations that have applied the death penalty to certain crimes, my reply would be that the example reduced itself to nothing in the face of truth, against which there is no prescription; that the history of men leaves us with the impression of a vast sea of errors, among which, at great intervals, some rare and hardly intelligible truths appear to float on the surface. Human sacrifices were once common to almost all nations, yet who will dare to defend them? That only a few societies, and for a short time only, have abstained from applying the death penalty, stands in my favor rather than against me, for that conforms with the usual lot of great truths; which are about as long-lasting as a lightning flash in comparison with the long dark night that envelops mankind. The happy time has not yet arrived in which truth shall be the portion of the greatest number, as error has heretofore been. And from this universal law those truths only have been exempted which Infinite Wisdom has chosen to distinguish from others by revealing them.

From *The Wealth of Nations* by Adam Smith—1776

An outstanding figure of the Scottish Enlightenment of the eighteenth century, Adam Smith (1723–1790) is the father of Western economic theory. Although he came from a relatively modest middle-class background, Smith desired and achieved a university career. He was later appointed to the chair of moral philosophy at Glasgow University when it was one of the leading European schools. While there, Smith began to develop the principles of economic theory detailed in his greatest work, The Wealth of Nations. *Smith was the first to show the importance of a free marketplace and self-interest to successful economic exchange. His ideas still form the core of modern capitalist doctrine. According to Smith, how does supply and demand regulate the marketplace? How does Smith feel about government regulation of markets?*

OF THE NATURAL AND MARKET PRICE
OF COMMODITIES

There is in every society or neighbourhood an ordinary or average rate both of wages and profit in every different employment of labour and stock. This rate is naturally regulated, as I shall show hereafter, partly by the general circumstances of the society, their riches or poverty, their advancing, stationary, or declining condition; and partly by the particular nature of each employment.

There is likewise in every society or neighbourhood an ordinary or average rate of *rent,* which is regulated too, as I shall show hereafter, partly by the general circumstances of the society or neighbourhood in which the land is situated, and partly by the natural or improved fertility of the land.

These ordinary or average rates may be called the natural rates of wages, profit, and rent, at the time and place in which they commonly prevail.

When the price of any commodity is neither more nor less than what is sufficient to pay the rent of the land, the wages of the labour, and the profits of the stock employed in raising, preparing, and bringing to market, according to their natural rates, the commodity is then sold for what may be called its natural price.

The commodity is then sold precisely for what it is worth, or for what it really costs the person who brings it to market; for though in common language what is called the prime cost of any commodity does not comprehend

From *The Wealth of Nations* by Adam Smith, 1776.

the profit of the person who is to sell it again, yet if he sells it at a price which does not allow him the ordinary rate of profit in his neighbourhood, he is evidently a loser by the trade; since by employing his stock in some other way he might have made that profit. His profit, besides, is his revenue, the proper fund of his subsistence. As, while he is preparing and bringing the goods to market, he advances to his workmen their wages, or their subsistence; so he advances to himself, in the same manner, his own subsistence, which is generally suitable to the profit which he may reasonably expect from the sale of his goods. Unless they yield him this profit, therefore, they do not repay him what they may very properly be said to have really cost him.

Though the price, therefore, which leaves him this profit is not always the lowest at which a dealer may sometimes sell his goods, it is the lowest at which he is likely to sell them for any considerable time; at least where there is perfect liberty, or where he may change his trade as often as he pleases.

The actual price at which any commodity is commonly sold is called its market price. It may either be above, or below, or exactly the same with its natural price.

The market price of every particular commodity is regulated by the proportion between the quantity which is actually brought to market, and the demand of those who are willing to pay the natural price of the commodity, or the whole value of the rent, labour, and profit which must be paid in order to bring it thither. Such people may be called the effectual demanders, and their demand the effectual demand; since it may be sufficient to effectuate the bringing of the commodity to market. It is different from the absolute demand. A very poor man may be said in some sense to have a demand for a coach and six; he might like to have it; but his demand is not an effectual demand, as the commodity can never be brought to market in order to satisfy it.

When the quantity of any commodity which is brought to market falls short of the effectual demand, all those who are willing to pay the whole value of the rent, wages, and profit which must be paid in order to bring it thither, cannot be supplied with the quantity which they want. Rather than want it altogether, some of them will be willing to give more. A competition will immediately begin among them, and the market price will rise more or less above the natural price, according as either the greatness of the deficiency, or the wealth and wanton luxury of the competitors, happen to animate more or less the eagerness of the competition. Among competitors of equal wealth and luxury the same deficiency will generally occasion a more or less eager competition, according as the acquisition of the commodity happens to be of more or less importance to them. Hence the exorbitant price of the necessaries of life during the blockade of a town or in a famine.

When the quantity brought to market exceeds the effectual demand, it cannot be all sold to those who are willing to pay the whole value of the rent, wages, and profit which must be paid in order to bring it thither. Some part must be sold to those who are willing to pay less, and the low price which they give for it must reduce the price of the whole. The market price will sink more or less below the natural price, according as the greatness of the excess increases more or less the competition of the sellers, or according as it happens to be more or less important to them to get immediately rid of the commodity. The same excess in the importation of perishable, will occasion a much greater competition than in that of durable commodities; in the importation of oranges, for example, than in that of old iron.

When the quantity brought to market is just sufficient to supply the effectual demand and no more, the market price naturally comes to be either exactly, or as nearly as can be judged of, the same with the natural price. The whole quantity upon land can be disposed of for this price, and cannot be disposed of for more. The competition of the different dealers obliges them all to accept of this price, but does not oblige them to accept of less.

The quantity of every commodity brought to market naturally suits itself to the effectual demand. It is the interest of all those who employ their land, labour, or stock in bringing any commodity to market, that the quantity never should exceed the effectual demand; and it is the interest of all other people that it never should fall short of that demand.

If at any time it exceeds the effectual demand, some of the component parts of its price must be paid below their natural rate. If it is rent, the interest of the landlords will immediately prompt them to withdraw a part of their land; and if it is wages or profit, the interest of the labourers in the one case, and of their employers in the other, will prompt them to withdraw a part of their labour or stock from this employment. The quantity brought to market will soon be no more than sufficient to supply the effectual demand. All the different parts of its price will rise to their natural rate, and the whole price to its natural price.

If, on the contrary, the quantity brought to market should at any time fall short of the effectual demand, some of the component parts of its price must rise above their natural rate. If it is rent, the interest of all other landlords will naturally prompt them to prepare more land for the raising of this commodity; if it is wages or profit, the interest of all other labourers and dealers will soon prompt them to employ more labour and stock in preparing and bringing it to market. The quantity brought thither will soon be sufficient to supply the effectual demand. All the different parts of its price will soon sink to their natural rate, and the whole price to its natural price.

But in some employments the same quantity of industry will in different years produce very different quantities of commodities; while in others it will produce always the same, or very nearly the same. The same number of labourers in husbandry will, in different years, produce very different quantities of corn, wine, oil, hops, &c. But the same number of spinners and weavers will every year produce the same or very nearly the same quantity of linen and woollen cloth. It is only the average produce of the one species of industry which can be suited in any respect to the effectual demand; and as its actual produce is frequently much greater and frequently much less than its average produce, the quantity of the commodities brought to market will sometimes exceed a good deal, and sometimes fall short a good deal, of the effectual demand. Even though that demand therefore should continue always the same, their market price will be liable to great fluctuations, will sometimes fall a good deal below, and sometimes rise a good deal above their natural price. In the other species of industry, the produce of equal quantities of labour being always the same or very nearly the same, it can be more exactly suited to the effectual demand. While that demand continues the same, therefore, the market price of the commodities is likely to do so too, and to be either altogether, or as nearly as can be judged of, the same with the natural price. That the price of linen and woollen cloth is liable neither to such frequent nor to such great variations as the price of corn, every man's experience will inform him. The price of the one species of commodities varies only with the variations in the demand: that of the other varies, not only with the variations in the demand, but with the much greater and more frequent variations in the quantity of what is brought to market in order to supply that demand.

But though the market price of every particular commodity is in this manner continually gravitating, if one may say so, towards the natural price, yet sometimes particular accidents, sometimes natural causes, and sometimes particular regulations of policy, may, in many commodities, keep up the market price for a long time together a good deal above the natural price.

When by an increase in the effectual demand the market price of some particular commodity happens to rise a good deal above the natural price, those who employ their stocks in supplying that market are generally careful to conceal this change. If it was commonly known, their great profit would tempt so many new rivals to employ their stocks in the same way, that, the effectual demand being fully supplied, the market price would soon be reduced to the natural price, and perhaps for some time even below it. If the market is at a great distance from the residence of those who supply it, they may sometimes be able to keep the secret for several years together, and may so long enjoy their extraordinary profits without any new rivals. Secrets of this kind, however, it must be acknowledged, can seldom be long kept; and the extraordinary profit can last very little longer than they are kept.

A monopoly granted either to an individual or to a trading company has the same effect as a secret in trade or manufactures. The monopolists, by keeping the market constantly understocked, by never fully supplying the effectual demand, sell their commodities much above the natural price, and raise their emoluments, whether they consist in wages or profit, greatly above their natural rate.

The price of monopoly is upon every occasion the highest which can be got. The natural price, or the price of free competition, on the contrary, is the lowest which can be taken, not upon every occasion, indeed, but for any considerable time together. The one is upon every occasion the highest which can be squeezed out of the buyers, or which, it is supposed, they will consent to give: the other is the lowest which the sellers can commonly afford to take and at the same time continue their business.

The exclusive privileges of corporations, statutes of apprenticeship, and all those laws which restrain in particular employments the competition to a smaller number than might otherwise go into them, have the same tendency, though in a less degree. They are a sort of enlarged monopolies, and may frequently, for ages together, and in whole classes of employments, keep up the market price of particular commodities above the natural price, and maintain both the wages of the labour and the profits of the stock employed about them somewhat above their natural rate.

Such enhancements of the market price may last as long as the regulations of policy which give occasion to them.

The market price of any particular commodity, though it may continue long above, can seldom continue long below its natural price. Whatever part of it was paid below the natural rate, the persons whose interest it affected would immediately feel the loss, and would immediately withdraw either so much land, or so much labour, or so much stock, from being employed about it, that the quantity brought to market would soon be no more than sufficient to supply the effectual demand. Its market price, therefore, would soon rise to the natural price. This at least would be the case where there was perfect liberty.

142

From *The Philosophy of History* by Georg Wilhelm Friedrich Hegel—1832

Born in Stuttgart, Germany, Georg Wilhelm Friedrich Hegel devoted his entire life to scholarly pursuits, teaching at the universities of Jena, Nuremberg, Heidelberg, and Berlin. Hegel hoped to develop a comprehensive worldview based on dialectical reasoning, the only method of progress in human thought. Hegelian philosophy has always been controversial, but no one can deny its influence on twentieth-century thought. In this brief excerpt, Hegel discusses the importance of reason to history. According to Hegel, what is reason's position in the world? How might he have influenced twentieth-century political thought?

III. The third kind of history—the *Philosophical.* No explanation was needed of the two previous classes; their nature was self-evident. It is otherwise with

From *The Philosophy of History* by G.W.F. Hegel, trans. by J. Sibree (New York: Wiley, 1944), p. 8–26. Reprinted by permission.

this last, which certainly seems to require an exposition or justification. The most general definition that can be given, is, that the Philosophy of History means nothing but the *thoughtful consideration of it.* Thought is, indeed, essential to humanity. It is this that distinguishes us from the brutes. In sensation, cognition, and intellection; in our instincts and volitions, as far as they are truly human, Thought is an invariable element. To insist upon Thought in this connection with history may, however, appear unsatisfactory. In this science it would seem as if Thought must be subordinate to what is given, to the realities of fact; that this is its basis and guide: while Philosophy dwells in the region of self-produced ideas, without reference to actuality. Approaching history thus prepossessed, Speculation might be expected to treat it as a mere passive material; and, so far from leaving it in its native truth, to force it into conformity with a tyrannous idea, and to construe it, as the phrase is, *"à priori."* But as it is the business of history simply to adopt into its records what is and has been, actual occurrences and transactions; and since it remains true to its character in proportion as it strictly adheres to its data, we seem to have in Philosophy a process diametrically opposed to that of the historiographer. This contradiction, and the charge consequently brought against Speculation, shall be explained and confuted. We do not, however, propose to correct the innumerable special misrepresentations, trite or novel, that are current respecting the aims, the interests, and the modes of treating history, and its relation to Philosophy.

The only Thought which Philosophy brings with it to the contemplation of History, is the simple conception of *Reason;* that Reason is the Sovereign of the World; that the history of the world, therefore, presents us with a rational process. This conviction and intuition is a hypothesis in the domain of history as such. In that of Philosophy it is no hypothesis. It is there proved by speculative cognition, that Reason—and this term may here suffice us, without investigating the relation sustained by the Universe to the Divine Being—is *Substance,* as well as *Infinite Power;* its own *Infinite Material* underlying all the natural and spiritual life which it originates, as also the *Infinite Form*—that which sets this Material in motion. On the one hand, Reason is the *substance* of the Universe; viz., that by which and in which all reality has its being and subsistence. On the other hand, it is the *Infinite Energy* of the Universe; since Reason is not so powerless as to be incapable of producing anything but a mere ideal, a mere intention—having its place outside reality, nobody knows where; something separate and abstract, in the heads of certain human beings. It is *the infinite complex of things,* their entire Essence and Truth. It is its own material which it commits to its own Active Energy to work up; not needing, as finite action does, the condition of an external material of given means from which it may obtain its support, and the objects of its activity. It supplies its own nourishment, and is the object of its own operations. While it is exclusively its own basis of existence, and absolute final aim, it is also the energizing power realizing this aim; developing it not only in the phenomena of the Natural, but also of the Spiritual Universe—the History of the World. That this "Idea" or "Reason" is the *True,* the *Eternal,* the absolutely *powerful* essence; that it reveals itself in the World, and that in that World nothing else is revealed but this and its honor and glory—is the thesis which, as we have said, has been proved in Philosophy, and is here regarded as demonstrated.

* * *

I will only mention two phases and points of view that concern the generally diffused conviction that Reason has ruled, and is still ruling the world, and consequently the world's history; because they give us, at the same time, an opportunity for more closely investigating the question that presents the greatest difficulty, and for indicating a branch of the subject, which will have to be enlarged on in the sequel.

I. One of these points is, that passage in history, which informs us that the Greek Anaxagoras was the first to enunciate the doctrine that *νοῦς,* Understanding generally, or Reason, governs the world. It is not intelligence as self-conscious Reason—not a Spirit as such that is meant; and we must clearly distinguish these from each other. The movement of the solar system takes place according to unchangeable laws. These laws are Reason, implicit in the phenomena in question. But neither the sun nor the planets, which revolve around it according to these laws, can be said to have any consciousness of them.

* * *

We have next to notice the rise of this idea—that Reason directs the World—in connection with a further application of it, well known to us—in the form, viz., of the *religious truth,* that the world is not abandoned to chance and external contingent causes, but that a *Providence* controls it. I stated above that I would not make a demand on your faith, in regard to the principle announced. Yet I might appeal to your belief in it, *in this religious aspect,* if, as a general rule, the nature of philosophical science allowed it to attach authority to presuppositions. To put it in another shape—this appeal is forbidden, because the science of which we have to treat, proposes itself to furnish the proof (not indeed of the abstract *Truth* of the doctrine, but) of its correctness as compared with facts. The truth, then, that a Providence (that of God) presides over the events of the World—consorts with the proposition in question; for *Divine* Providence is Wisdom, endowed with an infinite Power, which realizes its aim, viz., the absolute rational design of the world. Reason is Thought conditioning itself with perfect freedom. But a difference—rather a contradiction—will manifest itself, between this belief and our principle . . . For that belief is similarly indefinite; it is what is called a belief in a general Providence, and is not followed out into definite application, or displayed in its bearing on the grand total—the entire course of human history. But to *explain* History is to depict the passions of mankind, the genius, the active powers, that play their part on the great stage; and the providentially determined process which these exhibit, constitutes what is generally called the "plan" of Providence. Yet it is this very plan which is supposed to be concealed from our view: which it is deemed presumption, even to wish to recognize.

* * *

But in the history of the World, the *Individuals* we have to do with are *Peoples;* Totalities that are States. We cannot, therefore, be satisfied with what we may call this "peddling" view of Providence, to which the belief alluded to limits itself. Equally unsatisfactory is the merely abstract, undefined belief in a Providence, when that belief is not brought to bear upon the details of the process which it conducts. On the contrary our earnest endeavor must be directed to the recognition of the ways of Providence, the means it uses, and the historical phenomena in which it manifests itself; and we must show their connection with the general principle above mentioned. But in noticing the recognition of the plan of Divine Providence generally, I have implicitly touched upon a prominent question of the day; viz., that of the possibility of knowing God: or rather—since public opinion has ceased to allow it to be a matter of *question*—the *doctrine* that it is impossible to know God. In direct contravention of what is commanded in holy Scripture as the highest duty— that we should not merely love, but *know* God—the prevalent dogma involves the denial of what is there said; viz., that it is the Spirit [*der Geist*] that leads into Truth, knows all things, penetrates even into the deep things of the Godhead. While the Divine Being is thus placed beyond our knowledge, and outside the limit of all human things, we have the convenient license of wandering as far as we list, in the direction of our own fancies. We are freed from the obligation to refer our knowledge to the Divine and True. On the other hand, the vanity and egotism which characterize it, find, in this false position, ample justification; and the pious modesty which puts far from it the knowledge of God, can well estimate how much furtherance thereby accrues to its own wayward and vain strivings. I have been unwilling to leave out of sight the connection between our thesis—that Reason governs and has governed the World—and the question of the possibility of a knowledge of God, chiefly that I might not lose the opportunity of mentioning the imputation against Philosophy of being shy of noticing religious truths, or of having occasion to be so; in which is insinuated the suspicion that it has anything but a clear conscience in the presence of these truths. So far from this being the case, the fact is, that in recent times Philosophy has been obliged to defend the domain of religion against the attacks of several theological systems. In the Christian religion God has revealed Himself—that is, he has given us to understand what He is; so that He is no longer a concealed or secret existence. And this possibility of knowing Him, thus afforded us, renders such knowledge a duty. God wishes no narrow-hearted souls or empty heads for his children; but those whose spirit is of itself indeed, poor, but rich in the knowledge of Him; and who regard this knowledge of God as the only valuable possession. That development of the thinking spirit, which has resulted from the revelation of the Divine Being as its original basis, must ultimately advance to the *intellectual* comprehension of what was presented in the first instance, to *feeling* and *imagination*. The time must eventually come for understanding that rich product of active Reason, which the History of the World offers to us. It was for awhile the fashion to profess admiration for the wisdom of God, as displayed in animals, plants, and isolated occurrences. But, if it be allowed that Providence manifests itself in such objects and forms of existence, why not also in Universal History? This is deemed too great a matter to be thus regarded. But Divine Wisdom, i.e., Reason, is one and the same in the great as in the little; and we must not imagine God to be too weak to exercise his wisdom on the grand scale. Our intellectual striving aims at realizing the conviction that what was *intended* by eternal wisdom, is actually *accomplished* in the domain of existent, active Spirit, as well as in that of mere Nature. Our mode of treating the subject is, in this aspect, a Theodicæa—a justification of the ways of God— which Leibnitz attempted metaphysically, in his method, i.e., in indefinite abstract categories—so that the ill that is found in the World may be comprehended, and the thinking Spirit reconciled with the fact of the existence of evil. Indeed, nowhere is such a harmonizing view more pressingly demanded than in Universal History; and it can be attained only by recognizing the *positive* existence, in which that negative element is a subordinate, and vanquished nullity. On the one hand, the ultimate design of the World must be perceived; and, on the other hand, the fact that this design has been actually realized in it, and that evil has not been able permanently to assert a competing position. . . .

143

From *The Communist Manifesto* by Karl Marx and Friedrich Engels—1848

Both a statement of ideology and a call to action, The Communist Manifesto *provided the basis for the socialist and communist revolutions that broke out all over the world during the nineteenth and twentieth centuries. Born in Prussia, Marx (1818–1883) was a lawyer's son and received a doctorate in philosophy in 1841. He became a reporter and wrote for a variety of radical papers in Europe while channeling his ideas on social reform into his three-volume analysis of the capitalist system,* Das Kapital. *Engels (1820–1895) was the eldest son of a wealthy German manufacturer. When sent to England to manage his father's cotton factory in Manchester, Engels was horrified by the poverty of the workers. He began writing for radical journals and met Marx in the*

From *Communist Manifesto* by Karl Marx and Friedrich Engels. Reprinted by permission of International Publishers.

1840s. Because they shared similar views about capitalism and the plight of workers, they decided to work together for reform. They wrote the manifesto as a platform for the Communist League, an international worker's organization they had joined a year earlier. What is the Communist view of history? According to Marx and Engels, what is the goal of the Communist party?

BOURGEOIS AND PROLETARIANS

The history of all hitherto existing society is the history of class struggles.

Freeman and slave, patrician and plebeian, lord and serf, guildmaster and journeyman, in a word, oppressor and oppressed, stood in constant opposition to one another, carried on an uninterrupted, now hidden, now open fight, a fight that each time ended, either in a revolutionary reconstitution of society at large, or in the common ruin of the contending classes.

In the earlier epochs of history, we find almost everywhere a complicated arrangement of society into various orders, a manifold gradation of social rank. In ancient Rome we have patricians, knights, plebeians, slaves; in the Middle Ages, feudal lords, vassals, guildmasters, journeyman, apprentices, serfs; in almost all of these classes, again, subordinate gradations.

The modern bourgeois society that has sprouted from the ruins of feudal society, has not done away with class antagonisms. It has but established new classes, new conditions of oppression, new forms of struggle in place of the old ones.

Our epoch, the epoch of the bourgeoisie, possesses, however, this distinctive feature: It has simplified the class antagonisms. Society as a whole is more and more splitting up into two great hostile camps into two great classes directly facing each other—bourgeoisie and proletariat.

PROLETARIANS AND COMMUNISTS

The immediate aim of the Communists is the same as that of all the other proletarian parties; formation of the proletariat into a class, overthrow of bourgeois supremacy, conquest of political power by the proletariat.

The distinguishing feature of Communism is not the abolition of property generally, but the abolition of bourgeois property. But modern bourgeois private property is the final and most complete expression of the system of producing and appropriating products that is based on class antagonisms, on the exploitation of the many by the few.

In this sense, the theory of the Communists may be summed up in the single sentence: abolition of private property.

We Communists have been reproached with the desire of abolishing the right of personally acquiring property as the fruit of man's own labour, which property is alleged to be the groundwork of all personal freedom, activity and independence.

Hard-won, self-acquired, self-earned property! Do you mean the property of the petty artisan and of the small peasant, a form of property that preceded the bourgeois form? There is no need to abolish that; the development of industry has to a great extent already destroyed it, and is still destroying it daily.

Or do you mean modern bourgeois private property?

But does wage-labour create any property for the labourer? Not a bit. It creates capital, *i.e.,* that kind of property which exploits wage-labour, and which cannot increase except upon condition of begetting a new supply of wage-labour for fresh exploitation. Property, in its present form, is based on the antagonism of capital and wage-labour. Let us examine both sides of this antagonism.

To be a capitalist, is to have not only a purely personal, but a social *status* in production. Capital is a collective product, and only by the united action of many members, nay, in the last resort, only by the united action of all members of society, can it be set in motion.

Capital is therefore not a personal, it is a social, power.

When, therefore, capital is converted into common property, into the property of all members of society, personal property is not thereby transformed into social property. It is only the social character of the property that is changed. It loses its class character.

Let us now take wage-labour.

The average price of wage-labour is the minimum wage, *i.e.,* that quantum of the means of subsistence which is absolutely requisite to keep the labourer in bare existence as a labourer. What, therefore, the wage-labourer appropriates by means of his labour, merely suffices to prolong and reproduce a bare existence. We by no means intend to abolish this personal appropriation of the products of labour, an appropriation that is made for the maintenance and reproduction of human life, and that leaves no surplus wherewith to command the labour of others. All that we want to do away with is the miserable character of this appropriation, under which the labourer lives merely to increase capital, and is allowed to live only insofar as the interest of the ruling class requires it.

In bourgeois society, living labour is but a means to increase accumulated labour. In Communist society, accumulated labour is but a means to widen, to enrich, to promote the existence of the labourer.

In bourgeois society, therefore, the past dominates the present; in Communist society, the present dominates the past. In bourgeois society capital is independent and has individuality, while the living person is dependent and has no individuality.

And the abolition of this state of things is called by the bourgeois, abolition of individuality and freedom! And rightly so. The abolition of bourgeois individuality, bourgeois independence, and bourgeois freedom is undoubtedly aimed at.

By freedom is meant, under the present bourgeois conditions of production, free trade, free selling and buying.

But if selling and buying disappears, free selling and buying disappears also. This talk about free selling and buying, and all the other "brave words" of our bourgeois about freedom in general, have a meaning, if any, only in contrast with restricted selling and buying, with the fettered traders of the Middle Ages, but have no meaning when opposed to the Communist abolition of buying and selling, of the bourgeois conditions of production, and of the bourgeoisie itself.

You are horrified at our intending to do away with private property. But in your existing society, private property is already done away with for nine-tenths of the population; its existence for the few is solely due to its non-existence in the hands of those nine-tenths. You reproach us, therefore, with intending to do away with a form of property, the necessary condition for whose existence is the non-existence of any property for the immense majority of society.

In a word, you reproach us with intending to do away with your property. Precisely so; that is just what we intend.

From the moment when labour can no longer be converted into capital, money, or rent, into a social power capable of being monopolised, i.e., from the moment when individual property can no longer be transformed into bourgeois property, into capital, from that moment, you say, individuality vanishes.

You must, therefore, confess that by "individual" you mean no other person than the bourgeois, than the middle class owner of property. This person must, indeed, be swept out of the way, and made impossible.

But you Communists would introduce community of women, screams the whole bourgeoisie in chorus.

The bourgeois sees his wife as a mere instrument of production. He hears that the instruments of production are to be exploited in common, and, naturally, can come to no other conclusion that the lot of being common to all will likewise fall to the woman.

He has not even a suspicion that the real point aimed at is to do away with the status of women as mere instruments of production.

For the rest, nothing is more ridiculous than the virtuous indignation of our bourgeois at the community of women which, they pretend, is to be openly and officially established by the Communists. The Communists have no need to introduce community of women; it has existed almost from time immemorial.

Our bourgeois, not content with having the wives and daughters of their proletarians at their disposal, not to speak of common prostitutes, take the greatest pleasure in seducing each other's wives.

Bourgeois marriage is in reality a system of wives in common and thus, at the most, what the Communists might possibly be reproached with is that they desire to introduce, in substitution for a hypocritically concealed, an openly legalised community of women. For the rest, it is self-evident, that the abolition of the present system of production must bring with it the abolition of the community of women springing from that system, i.e., of prostitution both public and private.

The Communists are further reproached with desiring to abolish countries and nationality.

The workingmen have no country. We cannot take from them what they have not got. Since the proletariat must first of all acquire political supremacy, must rise to be the leading class of the nation, must constitute itself *the* nation, it is, so far, itself national, though not in the bourgeois sense of the word.

National differences and antagonisms between peoples are vanishing gradually from day to day, owing to the development of the bourgeoisie, to freedom of commerce, to the world market, to uniformity in the mode of production and in the conditions of life corresponding thereto.

The supremacy of the proletariat will cause them to vanish still faster. United action, of the leading civilised countries at least, is one of the first conditions for the emancipation of the proletariat.

In proportion as the exploitation of one individual by another is put an end to, the exploitation of one nation by another will also be put an end to. In proportion as the antagonism between classes within the nation vanishes, the hostility of one nation to another will come to an end.

"Undoubtedly," it will be said, "religion, moral, philosophical and juridical ideas have been modified in the course of historical development. But religion, morality, philosophy, political science, and law, constantly survived this change."

"There are, besides, eternal truths, such as Freedom, Justice, etc., that are common to all states of society. But Communism abolishes eternal truths, it abolishes all religion, and all morality, instead of constituting them on a new basis; it therefore acts in contradiction to all past historical experience."

What does this accusation reduce itself to? The history of all past society has consisted in the development of class antagonisms, antagonisms that assumed different forms at different epochs.

But whatever form they may have taken, one fact is common to all past ages, viz., the exploitation of one part of society by the other. No wonder, then, that the social consciousness of past ages, despite all the multiplicity and variety it displays, moves within certain common forms, or general ideas, which cannot completely vanish except with the total disappearance of class antagonisms.

The Communist revolution is the most radical rupture with traditional property relations; no wonder that its development involves the most radical rupture with traditional ideas.

The Communists disdain to conceal their views and aims. They openly declare that their ends can be attained only by the forcible overthrow of all existing social conditions. Let the ruling classes tremble at a Communist revolution. The proletarians have nothing to lose but their chains. They have a world to win.

Workingmen of all countries, unite!

144

Life at High Pressure by
W.R. Greg—1875

*British essayist W.R. Greg (1809–1881) was born in Manchester, England, into a
mill-owning family. By the age of 19, he was managing one of his father's mills; he had
his own business by the age of 23. However, Greg preferred writing and reflection to
running a business. By 1842, his business had begun to fail. Eight years later, he gave it
up and began to publish commentary on the philosophy of the business world. The following document is surprisingly modern in its description of the pressures of business.
According to Greg, what are the characteristics of life in the 1870s? Why is he critical of
the French? What does he think will be the problems faced by the next generation?*

I am only too conscious that I can offer little fitted to occupy the time, or to
command the interest of an audience accustomed to be fed on the cream of
experimental science, and the inexhaustible wonders of the organic world,—
equally conscious that I have nothing original or remarkable to say, even on
the subject I propose to treat;—still it may afford something of the refreshment
of variety at least to look for a while upon a few of the more peculiar features
of the life we are ourselves leading in this age of stir and change; upon some of
the probable issues of that hurried and high-pressure existence, and upon the
question, not less momentous than individually interesting, how far its actuality corresponds, or could be made to correspond, with the ideal we, many of
us, in our higher moments are prone to picture.

It is well in all careers to get occasionally outside of ourselves, to take stock
of our acquisitions and their inherent value; to pause in the race, not only to
measure our progress, but carefully to scrutinize our direction; and the more
breathless the race, the more essential, as assuredly the more difficult and perhaps the more unwelcome, does this scrutiny become.

I

Beyond doubt, the most salient characteristic of life in this latter portion of the
19th century is its SPEED,—what we may call its hurry, the rate at which we
move, the high-pressure at which we work;—and the question to be considered is, first, whether this rapid rate is in itself a good; and, next, whether it is

From "Life at High Pressure" by W.R. Greg, *Contemporary Review* XXV (1875), p. 623–35.

worth the price we pay for it—a price rarely reckoned up, and not very easy thoroughly to ascertain. Unquestionably, life seems fuller and longer for this speed—is it truly *richer* and more effective? No doubt we can do more in our seventy years for the pace at which we travel; but are the extra things we do always worth doing? No doubt, we can *do* more; but is "doing" everything, and "being" nothing?

The first point to notice is, that we have got into a habit of valuing speed *as* speed, with little reference to the objects sought by rapid locomotion, or the use to which we put the time so gained. We are growing feverishly impatient in *temperament*. There is nothing to wonder at in this, however much there may be to regret, when we reflect that all the improvement in the rate of travelling achieved by the human race in its orthodox 6,000 years of existence[2] has been achieved in our own lifetime—that is, in the last 50 years. . . .

> When our fathers wanted to send a message to their nephews, they could do no better, and go no quicker. When we were young, if we wished to travel from London to Edinburgh, we thought ourselves lucky if we could average eight miles an hour,—just as Robert Bruce might have done. Now, in our old age, we feel ourselves aggrieved if we do not average thirty miles. . . . [3]

Our love of and our pride in rapidity of movement, therefore, are under the circumstances natural enough, but they are not rational sentiments; nor are they healthy symptoms, for they grow daily with what they feed on; and national competition, especially transatlantic competition, stimulates them year by year. Mr. [Matthew] Arnold writes:—

> Your middle-class man thinks it the highest pitch of development and civilization when his letters are carried twelve times a day from Islington to Camberwell and from Camberwell to Islington, and if railway trains run to and fro between them every quarter of an hour. He thinks it nothing that the trains only carry him from a dismal illiberal life at Islington to a dismal illiberal life at Camberwell; and that the letters only tell him that such is the life there.

It is impossible to state more tersely (or more tartly) our indictment against the spirit of the age. . . .

The rapidity of railway travelling, I believe observant physicians tell us, produces a kind of chronic disturbance in the nervous system of those who use it much—a disturbance often obviously mischievous in the more sensitive organizations, distinctly perceptible even in hardier frames. The anxiety to be in time, the hurrying pace—often the running to catch trains (which are punctual in starting, whatever they may be in arriving)—cause a daily wear and tear, as well as accelerated action of the heart, of which, in a few months or

---

2 Greg is referring to the belief once widely held by religious people that the world and man were created in 4004 B.C.

3 Greg is quoting "Realisable Ideals," an essay in his *Engimas of Life* (1872), which he cites.

years, most of us become unpleasantly conscious, and which, as we all know, sometimes have a fatal and sudden termination (I know three such instances in my own small acquaintance). And the proportion of the population who habitually travel by rail is already large, and is increasing year by year. . . .

The moral effects of this hurried pace cannot well be separated from those arising from the high-pressure style of life generally, but in combination with this are undeniable, if not easy to be specified. A life without leisure and without pause—a life of *haste*—above all a life of excitement, such as haste inevitably involves—a life filled so full, even if it be full of interest and toil, that we have no time to reflect where we have been and whither we intend to go; what we have done and what we plan to do, still less what is the value, and the purpose, and the *price* of what we have seen, and done, and visited—can scarcely be deemed an adequate or worthy life. . . .

We are, perhaps, most of us, conscious at some moments of our course of the need to be quiet, to be in repose, to be *alone;* but I believe few of us have ever estimated adequately the degree in which an *atmosphere of excitement,* especially when we enter it young and continue in it habitually, is fatal to the higher and deeper life: the subtle poison which it disseminates through the whole character; how it saps solidity and strength of mind; how it daily becomes more necessary and in increasing measure; with what "inexorable logic" it at once enfeebles and renders abnormally sensitive the subtle organization of the brain; and how far, by slow and sure gradations, it carries us on towards a mental and moral condition which may justly be pronounced unsound. The scenes witnessed in a neighbouring country during the distressing years of 1870-71 brought out very forcibly these considerations. I may venture to quote a few paragraphs in illustration, written at the time.[4]

> Among civilised European peoples, the French excitability of to-day seems peculiar in kind as well as excessive in degree. . . .
>
> The explanation, I believe, must be sought in physiological considerations. The wonder would be, looking at the past, if something of the kind had not resulted. For three generations Frenchmen have been "born in bitterness, and nurtured in convulsion." . . . First, the unprecedented catastrophe of 1789. . . .
>
> Then followed another period of excitement of a different order, during which the generation born between 1789 and 1793 had its adolescence and its nurture. The delirium of triumph succeeded the delirium of revolution. Every day brought tidings of a fresh victory; every year saw the celebration of a new conquest. For twenty years the whole nation lived upon continuous stimulants of the most intoxicating sort. The Frenchmen born while society was being convulsed, and bred while Europe was being subdued, became the progenitors of the Frenchmen who witnessed or caused the revolutions of 1830 and 1848; and these in their turn gave birth to those—still punier and still more demoralised and distempered by

---

4 *Suum cuique.* Fraser's Magazine, July, 1871, pp. 124–126. [Greg's note.]

the perpetual dram-drinking which public life in France had been—who now stand before the judgment-seat of Europe as the men and women of 1871. For more than ninety years France has scarcely been sane and sober for an hour; ceaseless emotion has grown into chronic hysteria; and defects, vices, and propensities, mental and moral once, have become constitutional and physical at last.

II

But our "life at high-pressure" is shown even more in our style of work than in our rate of movement. The world is growing more exacting in its demands from all labourers except merely manual ones; and life in one way or other is becoming severer and severer to nearly all. The great prizes of social existence—success in professional, public, and commercial life—demand more strenuous and exhausting toil, a greater strain upon both bodily and mental powers, a sterner concentration of effort and of aim, and a more harsh and rigid sacrifice of the relaxations and amenities which time offers to the easy-going and unambitious, than was formerly the case. The eminent lawyer, the physician in full practice, the minister, and the politician who aspires to be a minister—even the literary workman, or the eager man of science—are one and all condemned to an amount and continued severity of exertion of which our grandfathers knew little, and which forces one after another of them to break off (or to break down) in mid-career, shattered, paralysed, reduced to premature inaction or senility. In every line of life we see almost daily examples; for what actual toil does for the learned professions, perpetual anxiety does for the merchant and the manufacturer. The barrister tells us that he must make hay while the sun shines, because for him it generally shines so late; and his career is so often divided into two equal portions—waiting wearily for work, and being absorbed in it—groaning or sinking under its excess. The physician cannot in middle life refuse or select among the crowding patients whom he has looked and longed for through the years of youth, even though his strength is consciously giving way under the burdensome and urgent calls; while the statesman or the member of Parliament in office has constantly to undergo a degree of prolonged pressure which it is astonishing that so many can endure, and perhaps more astonishing still that so many are found passionately struggling to reach. We all of us remember the description given of this career by one of its most eminent votaries: "There is little reason in my opinion," said Macaulay, "to envy a pursuit in which the most its devotees can expect is that, by relinquishing liberal studies and social comfort, by passing nights without sleep, and summers without one glimpse of the beauties of nature, they may attain that laborious, that invidious, that closely-watched slavery which is mocked with the name of power." . . .

People maintain that this excess of toil is unavoidable, that you must keep the pace, or fall behind and be trampled down by competitors who are more ambitious, more concentrated, or less inclined to measure and appraise the objects and the worth of life; and that in a civilization like ours moderation is forbidden to those who would succeed at all, or not actually fail. It may be so, though I am not quite convinced it is so; and at least, if men must work *over hard*, they need not work *over long;* they might yield the vacant place to younger and needier aspirants. But if it be thus—that it *is* thus is precisely my indictment against the spirit of the age. Excess is enforced; moderation—that which to the wiser Greeks seemed the essence of wisdom—is forbidden, or appears to be so.

But even this is not the extreme limit of the evil to be signalised. Another point seldom enough noticed is that this high-pressure, this ceaselessness and severity of toil, leaves the work of life, and assigns its prizes, more and more to men of *exceptional physique*—the peculiarly healthy, the specially strong, the abnormally tough,—those whose rare frames and constitutions are fitted to endure the unnatural and injurious strain under which the average man succumbs. . . . In short, the race of life is so rapid, the struggle of life so stern, the work of life so hard, that *exceptional organizations* seem to be essential everywhere to great achievement or even ordinary fruits; the moderately-endowed, the steady fair average man, the *medium* in all things—in wealth, in brains, in health and strength—is "nowhere" in the strife. . . .

III

It would seem, again, that the future, in England at least, is not to be for the moderately-wealthy, any more than for the moderately industrious or the moderately clever. There is danger of this in every rapidly progressive country, and the symptoms of it in England have become very manifest of late years. Several operations have combined to produce this result. The aggregate wealth of the country has enormously increased. The profits of *enterprise,* if not of ordinary plodding trade, have been almost unprecedentedly great. More *vast* fortunes have been heaped up, and heaped up in a shorter time, than probably at any former epoch. At the same time the wages of labour, most notably of skilled labour, have increased in many instances 15, 25, even 50 per cent.;—have so increased that if the artisan and mining classes had been prudent, steady, saving, and forecasting, they might, as a rule, have been capitalists as well as labourers now; might have been more at ease in their circumstances, and have had a larger *margin* in their expenditure, than numbers of the educated classes. There is no question as to these facts, and I need not trouble you with statistical details. At the same time, the value of fixed property, of houses and lands, has risen rapidly and largely as a consequence of the general prosperity: more persons are seeking property of this sort, and more purchasers are able and willing to pay a high price for it. In all this, you will say, there is much to rejoice at and nothing to regret. I am not about to controvert this proposition. But let us look for a moment at one or two of the secondary consequences of this state of things.

It is a universal complaint, the substantial truth of which cannot be denied, that life to a vast proportion of the middle classes is becoming more difficult and more costly. . . Probably, on the whole, we are within the mark if we say that, among average middle-class families, the actual cost of living is 25 per cent, higher than it was twenty-five years ago.

But this is only half the story. Owing to the increasing wealth of the wealthy, and the increasing numbers who every year step into the wealthier class, the *style of living,* as well as the cost of the necessaries and comforts of which "living" consists, [have] advanced in an extraordinary ratio; and however frugal, however unostentatious, however rational we may be, however resolute to live as we think we ought, and not as others do around us, it is, as we all find, simply *impossible* not to be influenced by their example and to fall into their ways, unless we are content either to live in remote districts or in an iso-lated fashion. The result is that we need many things that our fathers did not, and that for each of those many things we must pay more. Even where prices are lower, quantities are increased. Locomotion is cheaper; but every middle-class family travels far more than formerly. . . . England is a country in which it is easier to make much than to live upon little; and in which, therefore, the moderate, contented, unstriving natures—those who desire to pass their life neither in making money nor in spending it, who wish to use existence wisely and enjoy it worthily—are in danger of being crushed out of being between the upper and the nether millstones of a prosperous and well-paid labouring class and the lavish expenditure of the noble or ignoble opulent.

Now, I confess this does seem to me a matter for regret, inasmuch as these people are, or, at least, used to be, a valuable and estimable element in the national life. I should grieve to see England consist *only* of the toiling, grind-ing labourer, however highly paid—of the striving, pushing, racing man of enterprise, however successful—and of the plutocrat or aristocrat, however mag-nificent or stately in his affluence. It may be useless to repine at the menaced operation, and I see but one mode by which it can be effectually counteracted. As wealth increases, and as fortunes grow more and more colossal, as year by year successful enterprise places riches within the reach of many, and as the disposition of every class to imitate and emulate the style of living of the classes above it in the social scale remains about the most inveterate of our national characteristics, there would seem to be small hope of attaining a standard of life truly dignified and worthy, except through such a regeneration in the tastes and sentiments of the opulent and noble—the leaders of fashion, the acknowl-edged chiefs and stars of society—as should cause simplicity to become "good style," and luxury beyond a certain point, and ostentation at any point, to be voted vulgar. The seeds of this moral revulsion from our actual excesses are already in existence, and a few bright and resolute examples among the well-placed, the eminent, and the universally admired, might, I am convinced, make them germinate with a rapidity that would amaze us; for there are thousands among our upper ranks to whom all the indulgences and splendour round them bring no true enjoyment, but rather the intense sadness of satiety, and not a little self-reproach, and some dim and fruitless yearning after a course of

days that shall be more really happy while it lasts, and shall leave more reward-
ing memories behind it. . . .

Now, I am not given to preaching; I never knew much good come of sermons, and certainly I am not going so far to abuse your patience as to turn this
desk into a pulpit. But we may philosophise for a moment, and yet steer clear
of moralising. I never had the faintest respect for ASCETICISM, which, indeed, in
every shape, I have always regarded as a mistake, arising out of utter misconceptions, both intellectual and moral. I have not even a word to say (now, at
least,) in favour of self-denial; that noble virtue has its time and place, but it is
out of our province here, where we are dealing with what is rational, not with
what is right—not with what duty would ordain, but with what sagacity and
enlightened selfishness suggest. We need not ask the affluent and the high in
rank to forego any one of the advantages or enjoyments which their vast possessions place within their reach; all that is required is, that they make the most
of those advantages, and make those possessions yield them the maximum of
real pleasure. . . .

CHAPTER 18

Law, Government, Revolution, and War— 1750–1914 CE

The new emphasis on social reform brought revolution and change to many parts of the world. Some of the revolutions succeeded, whereas others failed. At the same time, there was more legal emphasis on human rights and dignity. Nationalism also played a role during this era, causing a new series of revolutions when native populations sought to free their lands from colonial powers such as Britain and Spain. Some governments tried to respond to demands for social reform, but often their responses came too late. Japan, rejecting both tradition and isolation, adopted a new constitution as a framework for modernization.

The documents in this section are far-ranging. From France to Latin America to Russia, they show the development of political thought regarding human rights. What impact do you think the freeing of serfs had on Russian society? Which of the revolutionary plans seems more radical—Lenin's or Zapata's? Why were the Zionists attracted to Palestine despite the problems it might cause?

145

The Declaration of the Rights of Man—1789

Perhaps the most important political document of the French Revolution, the Declaration of the Rights of Man was issued by the National Assembly shortly after it wrested control of the country from the king in 1789. Its members wanted to secure the support of the French people by this declaration of rights. The declaration was influenced by the English Bill of Rights as well as the bills of rights that were part of every state constitution in the new American republic. There had been a keen interest among members of the French National Assembly in the political documents created by the United States. What rights did the citizens gain? Does the Rights of Man share some similarities with the U.S. Bill of Rights?

DECLARATION OF THE RIGHTS OF MAN AND OF THE CITIZEN

The representatives of the French people, organized as a National Assembly, believing that the ignorance, neglect, or contempt of the rights of man are the sole cause of public calamities and of the corruption of governments, have determined to set forth in a solemn declaration the natural, inalienable, and sacred rights of man, in order that this declaration, being constantly before all the members of the social body, shall remind them continually of their rights and duties; in order that the acts of the legislative power, as well as those of the executive power, may be compared at any moment with the objects and purposes of all political institutions and may thus be more respected; and, lastly, in order that the grievances of the citizens, based hereafter upon simple and incontestable principles, shall tend to the maintenance of the constitution and redound to the hapiness of all. Therefore the National Assembly recognizes and proclaims, in the presence and under the auspices of the Supreme Being, the following rights of man and of the citizen:

1. Men are born and remain free and equal in rights. Social distinctions may be founded only upon the general good.

2. The aim of all political association is the preservation of the natural and imprescriptible rights of man. These rights are liberty, property, security, and resistance to oppression.

Declaration of the Rights of Man, 1789.

3. The principle of all sovereignty resides essentially in the nation. No body nor individual may exercise any authority which does not proceed directly from the nation.

4. Liberty consists in the freedom to do everything which injures no one else; hence the exercise of the natural rights of each man has no limits except those which assure to the other members of the society the enjoyment of the same rights. These limits can only be determined by law.

5. Law can only prohibit such actions as are hurtful to society. Nothing may be prevented which is not forbidden by law, and no one may be forced to do anything not provided for by law.

6. Law is the expression of the general will. Every citizen has a right to participate personally, or through his representative, in its formation. It must be the same for all, whether it protects or punishes. All citizens, being equal in the eyes of the law, are equally eligible to all dignities and to all public positions and occupations, according to their abilities, and without distinction except that of their virtues and talents.

7. No person shall be accused, arrested, or imprisoned except in the cases and according to the forms prescribed by law. Any one soliciting, transmitting, executing, or causing to be executed, any arbitrary order, shall be punished. But any citizen summoned or arrested in virtue of the law shall submit without delay, as resistance constitutes an offense.

8. The law shall provide for such punishments only as are strictly and obviously necessary, and no one shall suffer punishment except it be legally inflicted in virtue of a law passed and promulgated before the commission of the offense.

9. As all persons are held innocent until they shall have been declared guilty, if arrest shall be deemed indispensable, all harshness not essential to the securing of the prisoner's person shall be severely repressed by law.

10. No one shall be disquieted on account of his opinions, including his religious views, provided their manifestation does not disturb the public order established by law.

11. The free communication of ideas and opinions is one of the most precious of the rights of man. Every citizen may, accordingly, speak, write, and print with freedom, but shall be responsible for such abuses of this freedom as shall be defined by law.

12. The security of the rights of man and of the citizen requires public military forces. These forces are, therefore, established for the good of all and not for the personal advantage of those to whom they shall be intrusted.

13. A common contribution is essential for the maintenance of the public forces and for the cost of administration. This should be equitably distributed among all the citizens in proportion to their means.

14. All the citizens have a right to decide, either personally or by their representatives, as to the necessity of the public contribution; to grant this freely; to know to what uses it is put; and to fix the proportion, the mode of assessment and of collection and the duration of the taxes.

15. Society has the right to require of every public agent an account of his administration.

16. A society in which the observance of the law is not assured, nor the separation of powers defined, has no constitution at all.

17. Since property is an inviolable and sacred right, no one shall be deprived thereof except where public necessity, legally determined, shall clearly demand it, and then only on condition that the owner shall have been preciously and equitably indemnified.

146

The Declaration of the Rights of Women by Olympe de Gouges—1791

Women were drawn into the intellectual ferment of the French Revolution from its beginning, and some felt they were not adequately protected by the Rights of Man. Olympe de Gouges (1745–1793), the daughter of a butcher and a washerwoman, married a wealthy older man. After his death, she traveled to Paris and worked as a writer. Although she was not well educated and her writing was poor, Olympe de Gouges was a dedicated feminist. Unhappy with the position that women occupied in Revolutionary France, she wrote a groundbreaking feminist manifesto addressed to Queen Marie Antoinette. She was ridiculed because of her feminist stance and her opposition to the execution of the King and his family. Though a supporter of the Revolution, she became a victim of the Terror. Considered a reactionary Royalist by the Jacobins, Olympe de Gouges was guillotined in 1793. What does Olympe de Gouges say women should realize had happened as a result of the Revolution? What rights does she feel women should have? Were these provided by the Rights of Man?

Declaration of the Rights of Woman, 1791.

DECLARATION OF THE RIGHTS
OF WOMAN AND THE FEMALE CITIZEN

Man, are you capable of being just? It is a woman who poses the question; you will not deprive her of that right at least. Tell me, what gives you sovereign empire to oppress my sex? Your strength? Your talents? Observe the Creator in his wisdom; survey in all her grandeur that nature with whom you seem to want to be in harmony, and give me, if you dare, an example of this tyrannical empire. Go back to animals, consult the elements, study plants, finally glance at all the modifications of organic matter, and surrender to the evidence when I offer you the means; search, probe, and distinguish, if you can, the sexes in the administration of nature. Everywhere you will find them mingled; everywhere they cooperate in harmonious togetherness in this immortal masterpiece.

Man alone has raised his exceptional circumstances to a principle. Bizarre, blind, bloated with science and degenerated—in a century of enlightenment and wisdom—into the crassest ignorance, he wants to command as a despot a sex which is in full possession of its intellectual faculties; he pretends to enjoy the Revolution and to claim his rights to equality in order to say nothing more about it.

Declaration of the Rights of Woman and the Female Citizen.

For the National Assembly to decree in its last sessions, or in those of the next legislature:

Preamble

Mothers, daughters, sisters [and] representatives of the nation demand to be constituted into a national assembly. Believing that ignorance, omission, or scorn for the rights of woman are the only causes of public misfortunes and of the corruption of governments, [the women] have resolved to set forth in a solemn declaration the natural, inalienable, and sacred rights of woman in order that this declaration, constantly exposed before all the members of the society, will ceaselessly remind them of their rights and duties; in order that the authoritative acts of women and the authoritative acts of men may be at any moment compared with and respectful of the purpose of all political institutions; and in order that citizens' demands, henceforth based on simple and incontestable principles, will always support the constitution, good morals, and the happiness of all.

Consequently, the sex that is as superior in beauty as it is in courage during the sufferings of maternity recognizes and declares in the presence and under the auspices of the Supreme Being, the following Rights of Woman and of Female Citizens.

Article I

Woman is born free and lives equal to man in her rights. Social distinctions can be based only on the common utility.

Article II

The purpose of any political association is the conservation of the natural and imprescriptible rights of woman and man; these rights are liberty, property, security, and especially resistance to oppression.

Article III

The principle of all sovereignty rests essentially with the nation, which is nothing but the union of woman and man; no body and no individual can exercise any authority which does not come expressly from it [the nation].

Article IV

Liberty and justice consist of restoring all that belongs to others; thus, the only limits on the exercise of the natural rights of woman are perpetual male tyranny; these limits are to be reformed by the laws of nature and reason.

Article V

Laws of nature and reason proscribe all acts harmful to society; everything which is not prohibited by these wise and divine laws cannot be prevented, and no one can be constrained to do what they do not command.

Article VI

The law must be the expression of the general will; all female and male citizens must contribute either personally or through their representatives to its formation; it must be the same for all: male and female citizens, being equal in the eyes of the law, must be equally admitted to all honors, positions, and public employment according to their capacity and without other distinctions besides those of their virtues and talents.

Article VII

No woman is an exception; she is accused, arrested, and detained in cases determined by law. Women, like men, obey this rigorous law.

Article VIII

The law must establish only those penalties that are strictly and obviously necessary, and no one can be punished except by virtue of a law established and promulgated prior to the crime and legally applicable to women.

Article IX

Once any woman is declared guilty, complete rigor is [to be] exercised by the law.

Article X

No one is to be disquieted for his very basic opinions; woman has the right to mount the scaffold; she must equally have the right to mount the rostrum, provided that her demonstrations do not disturb the legally established public order.

Article XI

The free communication of thoughts and opinions is one of the most precious rights of woman, since that liberty assures the recognition of children by their fathers. Any female citizen thus may say freely, I am the mother of a child which belongs to you, without being forced by a barbarous prejudice to hide the truth; [an exception may be made] to respond to the abuse of this liberty in cases determined by the law.

Article XII

The guarantee of the rights of woman and the female citizen implies a major benefit; this guarantee must be instituted for the advantage of all, and not for the particular benefit of those to whom it is entrusted.

Article XIII

For the support of the public force and the expenses of administration, the contributions of woman and man are equal; she shares all the duties [*corvées*] and all the painful tasks; therefore, she must have the same share in the distribution of positions, employment, offices, honors and jobs [*industrie*].

Article XIV

Female and male citizens have the right to verify, either by themselves or through their representatives, the necessity of the public contribution. This can only apply to women if they are granted an equal share, not only of wealth, but also of public administration, and in the determination of the proportion, the base, the collection, and the duration of the tax.

Article XV

The collectivity of women, joined for tax purposes to the aggregate of men, has the right to demand an accounting of his administration from any public agent.

Article XVI

No society has a constitution without the guarantee of rights and the separation of powers; the constitution is null if the majority of individuals comprising the nation have not cooperated in drafting it.

Article XVII

Property belongs to both sexes whether united or separate; for each it is an inviolable and sacred right; no one can be deprived of it, since it is the true patrimony of nature, unless the legally determined public need obviously dictates it, and then only with a just and prior indemnity.

Postscript

Woman, wake up; the tocsin of reason is being heard throughout the whole universe; discover your rights. The powerful empire of nature is no longer surrounded by prejudice, fanaticism, superstition, and lies. The flame of truth has dispersed all the clouds of folly and usurpation. Enslaved man has multiplied his strength and needs recourse to yours to break his chains. Having become free, he has become unjust to his companion. Oh, women, women! When will you cease to be blind? What advantage have you received from the Revolution? A more pronounced scorn, a more marked disdain. In the centuries of corruption you ruled only over the weakness of men. The reclamation of your patrimony, based on the wise decrees of nature—what have you to dread from such a fine undertaking?

147

Jamaican Letter by Simon Bolivar—1815

Latin America's most famous hero, Simon Bolivar (1783–1830), is known simply as El Libertador ("The Liberator"). The son of a Venezuelan nobleman and born into great wealth, Bolivar was educated in Spain, where he was sent to find a suitable bride. Because Napoleon's conquest of Spain had weakened Spain's hold on Venezuela and other Latin American colonies, they soon began to agitate for self-government. In 1811, Venezuela declared its independence from Spain; Bolivar was the leader of the revolutionary army. The Latin American war for independence was a long and bloody struggle that lasted until 1825. Upper Peru, the last territory freed from Spanish rule, was named Bolivia in Bolivar's honor. The following letter was written during a low point in

From *Selected Writings of Bolivar, Volume One*, compiled by Vicente Lecuna, edited by Harold A. Bierck, Jr., trans. by Lewis Bertrand.

the war against Spain; Bolívar, unable to gain funds for the revolution in Europe, was in Jamaica looking for support. To whom did Bolívar address this letter? Why did he ask for support against Spain? What type of government did he hope to establish?

I t is difficult to foresee the future fate of the New World, to set down its political principles, or to prophesy what manner of government it will adopt. Every conjecture relative to America's future is, I feel, pure speculation. When mankind was in its infancy, steeped in uncertainty, ignorance, and error, was it possible to foresee what system it would adopt for its preservation? Who could venture to say that a certain nation would be a republic or a monarchy; this nation great, that nation small? To my way of thinking, such is our own situation. We are a young people. We inhabit a world apart, separated by broad seas. We are young in the ways of almost all the arts and sciences, although, in a certain manner, we are old in the ways of civilized society. I look upon the present state of America as similar to that of Rome after its fall. Each part of Rome adopted a political system conforming to its interest and situation or was led by the individual ambitions of certain chiefs, dynasties, or associations. But this important difference exists: those dispersed parts later reestablished their ancient nations, subject to the changes imposed by circumstances or events. But we scarcely retain a vestige of what once was; we are, moreover, neither Indian nor European, but a species midway between the legitimate proprietors of this country and the Spanish usurpers. In short, though Americans by birth we derive our rights from Europe, and we have to assert these rights against the rights of the natives, and at the same time we must defend ourselves against the invaders. This places us in a most extraordinary and involved situation. Notwithstanding that it is a type of divination to predict the result of the political course which America is pursuing, I shall venture some conjectures which, of course, are colored by my enthusiasm and dictated by rational desires rather than by reasoned calculations.

The rôle of the inhabitants of the American hemisphere has for centuries been purely passive. Politically they were non-existent. We are still in a position lower than slavery, and therefore it is more difficult for us to rise to the enjoyment of freedom. Permit me these transgressions in order to establish the issue. States are slaves because of either the nature or the misuse of their constitutions; a people is therefore enslaved when the government, by its nature or its vices, infringes on and usurps the rights of the citizen or subject. Applying these principles, we find that America was denied not only its freedom but even an active and effective tyranny. Let me explain. Under absolutism there are no recognized limits to the exercise of governmental powers. The will of the great sultan, khan, bey, and other despotic rulers is the supreme law, carried out more or less arbitrarily by the lesser pashas, khans, and satraps of Turkey and Persia, who have an organized system of oppression in which inferiors participate according to the authority vested in them. To them is entrusted the administration of civil, military, political, religious, and tax matters. But, after all is said and done, the rulers of Ispahan are Persians; the viziers of the Grand Turk are Turks; and the sultans of Tartary are Tartars. China does not bring its military leaders and scholars from the land of Genghis Khan, her conqueror, notwithstanding that the Chinese of today are the lineal descendants of those who were reduced to subjection by the ancestors of the present-day Tartars.

How different is our situation! We have been harassed by a conduct which has not only deprived us of our rights but has kept us in a sort of permanent infancy with regard to public affairs. If we could at least have managed our domestic affairs and our internal administration, we could have acquainted ourselves with the processes and mechanics of public affairs. We should also have enjoyed a personal consideration, thereby commanding a certain unconscious respect from the people, which is so necessary to preserve amidst revolutions. That is why I say we have even been deprived of an active tyranny, since we have not been permitted to exercise its functions.

Americans today, and perhaps to a greater extent than ever before, who live within the Spanish system occupy a position in society no better than that of serfs destined for labor, or at best they have no more status than that of mere consumers. Yet even this status is surrounded with galling restrictions, such as being forbidden to grow European crops, or to store products which are royal monopolies, or to establish factories of a type the Peninsula itself does not possess. To this add the exclusive trading privileges, even in articles of prime necessity, and the barriers between American provinces, designed to prevent all exchange of trade, traffic, and understanding. In short, do you wish to know what our future held?—simply the cultivation of the fields of indigo, grain, coffee, sugar cane, cacao, and cotton; cattle raising on the broad plains; hunting wild game in the jungles; digging in the earth to mine its gold—but even these limitations could never satisfy the greed of Spain.

So negative was our existence that I can find nothing comparable in any other civilized society, examine as I may the entire history of time and the politics of all nations. Is it not an outrage and a violation of human rights to expect a land so splendidly endowed, so vast, rich, and populous, to remain merely passive?

As I have just explained, we were cut off and, as it were, removed from the world in relation to the science of government and administration of the state. We were never viceroys or governors, save in the rarest of instances; seldom archbishops and bishops; diplomats never; as military men, only subordinates; as nobles, without royal privileges. In brief, we were neither magistrates nor financiers and seldom merchants—all in flagrant contradiction to our institutions.

It is harder, Montesquieu has written, to release a nation from servitude than to enslave a free nation. This truth is proven by the annals of all times, which reveal that most free nations have been put under the yoke, but very few enslaved nations have recovered their liberty. Despite the convictions of history, South Americans have made efforts to obtain liberal, even perfect, institutions, doubtless out of that instinct to aspire to the greatest possible happiness, which, common to all men, is bound to follow in civil societies founded on the principles of justice, liberty, and equality. But are we capable of maintaining in proper balance the difficult charge of a republic? Is it conceivable that a newly emancipated people can soar to the heights of liberty, and, unlike Icarus, neither have its wings melt nor fall into an abyss? Such a marvel is inconceivable and without precedent. There is no reasonable probability to bolster our hopes.

More than anyone, I desire to see America fashioned into the greatest nation in the world, greatest not so much by virtue of her area and wealth as by her freedom and glory. Although I seek perfection for the government of my country, I cannot persuade myself that the New World can, at the moment, be organized as a great republic. Since it is impossible, I dare not desire it; yet much less do I desire to have all America a monarchy because this plan is not only impracticable but also impossible. Wrongs now existing could not be righted, and our emancipation would be fruitless. The American states need the care of paternal governments to heal the sores and wounds of despotism and war. The parent country, for example, might be Mexico, the only country fitted for the position by her intrinsic strength, and without such power there can be no parent country. Let us assume it were to be the Isthmus of Panamá, the most central point of this vast continent. Would not all parts continue in their lethargy and even in their present disorder? For a single government to infuse life into the New World; to put into use all the resources for public prosperity; to improve, educate, and perfect the New World, that government would have to possess the authority of a god, much less the knowledge and virtues of mankind.

From the foregoing, we can draw these conclusions: The American provinces are fighting for their freedom, and they will ultimately succeed. Some provinces as a matter of course will form federal and some central republics; the larger areas will inevitably establish monarchies, some of which will fare so badly that they will disintegrate in either present or future revolutions. To consolidate a great monarchy will be no easy task, but it will be utterly impossible to consolidate a great republic.

It is a grandiose idea to think of consolidating the New World into a single nation, united by pacts into a single bond. It is reasoned that, as these parts have a common origin, language, customs, and religion, they ought to have a single government to permit the newly formed states to unite in a confederation. But this is not possible. Actually, America is separated by climatic differences, geographic diversity, conflicting interests, and dissimilar characteristics. How beautiful it would be if the Isthmus of Panamá could be for us what the Isthmus of Corinth was for the Greeks! Would to God that some day we may have the good fortune to convene there an august assembly of representatives of republics, kingdoms, and empires to deliberate upon the high interests of peace and war with the nations of the other three-quarters of the globe. This type of organization may come to pass in some happier period of our regeneration. But any other plan, such as that of Abbé St. Pierre, who in laudable delirium conceived the idea of assembling a European congress to decide the fate and interests of those nations, would be meaningless.

Among the popular and representative systems, I do not favor the federal system. It is overperfect, and it demands political virtues and talents far superior to our own. For the same reason I reject a monarchy that is part aristocracy and part democracy, although with such a government England has achieved much fortune and splendor. Since it is not possible for us to select the most perfect and complete form of government, let us avoid falling into demagogic anarchy or monocratic tyranny. These opposite extremes would only wreck us on similar reefs of misfortune and dishonor; hence, we must seek a mean between them. I say: Do not adopt the best system of government, but the one that is most likely to succeed.

148

Account of the Emancipation of the Serfs by Prince Kropotkin—1861–1862

A young noble, Prince Peter Kropotkin (1842–1921) was an eyewitness to the reaction of the Russian people to this momentous event. Kropotkin would later become a famous revolutionary and anarchist, but at the time he was a 19-year-old student in a school for the sons of aristocracy. In the following excerpt from his memoirs, Kropotkin describes what took place in Moscow and on his country estate. Was he sympathetic to the peasants on his estate? How did the peasants react to their new status? What did many aristocrats fear would happen?

KROPOTKIN'S MEMOIR

We went to the parade; and when all the military performances were over, Alexander II, remaining on horseback, loudly called out, "The officers to me!" They gathered round him, and he began, in a loud voice, a speech about the great event of the day.

From "Emancipation of the Serfs" in Kropotkin's Memoir, 1861–62.

"The officers . . . the representatives of the nobility in the army"—these scraps of sentences reached our ears—"an end has been put to centuries of injustice . . . I expect sacrifices from the nobility . . . the loyal nobility will gather round the throne" . . . and so on. Enthusiastic hurrahs resounded amongst the officers as he ended.

We ran rather than marched back on our way to the corps, hurrying to be in time for the Italian opera, of which the last performance in the season was to be given that afternoon; some manifestation was sure to take place then. Our military attire was flung off with great haste, and several of us dashed, lightfooted, to the sixth story gallery. The house was crowded.

During the first entr'acte the smoking-room of the opera filled with excited young men, who all talked to one another, whether acquainted or not. We planned at once to return to the hall, and to sing, with the whole public in a mass choir, the hymn "God Save the Tsar."

However, sounds of music reached our ears, and we all hurried back to the hall. The band of the opera was already playing the hymn, which was drowned immediately in enthusiastic hurrahs coming from all parts of the hall. I saw Bavéri, the conductor of the band, waving his stick, but not a sound could be heard from the powerful band. Then Bavéri stopped, but the hurrahs continued. I saw the stick waved again in the air; I saw the fiddle-bows moving, and musicians blowing the brass instruments, but again the sound of voices overwhelmed the band. Bavéri began conducting the hymn once more, and it was only by the end of that third repetition that isolated sounds of brass instruments pierced through the clamor of human voices.

The same enthusiasm was in the streets. Crowds of peasants and educated men stood in front of the palace, shouting hurrahs, and the Tsar could not appear without being followed by demonstrative crowds running after his carriage. Herzen was right when, two years later, as Alexander was drowning the Polish insurrection in blood, and "Muravioff the Hanger" was strangling it on the scaffold, he wrote, "Alexander Nikolaevich, why did you not die on that day? Your name would have been transmitted in history as that of a hero."

Where were the uprisings which had been predicted by the champions of slavery? Conditions more indefinite than those which had been created by the Polozhenie (the emancipation law) could not have been invented. If anything could have provoked revolts, it was precisely the perplexing vagueness of the conditions created by the new law. And yet, except in two places where there were insurrections, and a very few other spots where small disturbances entirely due to misunderstandings and immediately appeased took place, Russia remained quiet—more quiet than ever. With their usual good sense, the peasants had understood that serfdom was done away with, that "freedom had come," and they accepted the conditions imposed upon them, although these conditions were very heavy.

I was in Nikolskoye [a Kropotkin estate in the Kaluga *guberniia*] in August 1861, and again in the summer of 1862, and I was struck with the quiet, intelligent way in which the peasants had accepted the new conditions.

They knew perfectly well how difficult it would be to pay the redemption tax for the land, which was in reality an indemnity to the nobles in lieu of the obligations of serfdom. But they so much valued the abolition of their personal enslavement that they accepted the ruinous charges—not without murmuring, but as a hard necessity—the moment that personal freedom was obtained.

When I saw our Nikolskoye peasants, fifteen months after the liberation, I could not but admire them. Their inborn good nature and softness remained with them, but all traces of servility had disappeared. They talked to their masters as equals talk to equals, as if they never had stood in different relations. Besides, such men came out from among them as could make a stand for their rights.

149

The Meiji Constitution—1889

In 1868, a group of reformers determined to set in motion the process of modernizing Japan. Ministers went to the West to study European political institutions and economic systems and returned with new ideas and knowledge. They helped transform Japan into a modern military, industrial, and commercial power. Decentralized rule ended in 1868 with the restoration of imperial power. In 1881, prime minister Ito Hirobumi was charged with the production of a new written constitution. He much admired the rise of Prussia and, as a result, the new Japanese constitution of 1889 was modeled after the Prussian one. How much power did the Meiji Emperor have? How did it compare with the power of the Tsar? What rights did the constitution give to the Japanese people? How does it compare to the Declaration of the Rights of Man?

CHAPTER I: THE EMPEROR

Article I

The Empire of Japan shall be reigned over and governed by a line of Emperors unbroken for ages eternal.

Article II

The Imperial Throne shall be succeeded to by Imperial male descendants, according to the provisions of the Imperial House Law.

Article III

The Emperor is sacred and inviolable.

Article IV

The Emperor is the head of the Empire, combining in Himself the rights of sovereignty, and exercises them, according to the provisions of the present Constitution.

Article V

The Emperor exercises the legislative power with the consent of the Imperial Diet.

Article VI

The Emperor gives sanction to laws and orders them to be promulgated and executed.

Article VII

The Emperor convokes the Imperial Diet, opens, closes, and prorogues it, and dissolves the House of Representatives.

Article VIII

The Emperor, in consequence of an urgent necessity to maintain public safety or to avert public calamities, issues, when the Imperial Diet is not sitting, Imperial Ordinances in the place of law.

Such Imperial Ordinances are to be laid before the Imperial Diet at its next session, and when the Diet does not approve the said Ordinances, the Government shall declare them to be invalid for the future.

Article X

The Emperor determines the organization of the different branches of the administration, and salaries of all civil and military officers, and appoints and dismisses the same. Exceptions especially provided for in the present Constitution or in other laws, shall be in accordance with the respective provisions (bearing thereon).

Article XI

The Emperor has the supreme command of the Army and Navy.

Article XII

The Emperor determines the organization and peace standing of the Army and Navy.

Article XIII

The Emperor declares war, makes peace, and concludes treaties.

Article XIV

The Emperor declares a state of siege. The conditions and effects of a state of siege shall be determined by law.

Article XV

The Emperor confers titles of nobility, rank, orders and other marks of honor.

Article XVI

The Emperor orders amnesty, pardon, commutation of punishments and rehabilitation.

CHAPTER II: RIGHTS AND DUTIES OF SUBJECTS

Article XVIII

The conditions necessary for being a Japanese subject shall be determined by law.

Article XIX

Japanese subjects may, according to qualifications determined in laws or Ordinances, be appointed to civil or military or any other public offices equally.

Article XX

Japanese subjects are amenable to service in the Army or Navy, according to the provisions of law.

Article XXI

Japanese subjects are amenable to the duty of paying taxes, according to the provisions of law.

Article XXII

Japanese subjects shall have the liberty of abode and of changing the same within the limits of the law.

Article XXIII

No Japanese subject shall be arrested, detained, tried or punished, unless according to law.

Article XXIV

No Japanese subject shall be deprived of his right of being tried by the judges determined by law.

Article XXV

Except in the cases provided for in the law, the house of no Japanese subject shall be entered or searched without his consent.

Article XXVI

Except in the cases mentioned in the law, the secrecy of the letters of every Japanese subject shall remain inviolate.

Article XXVII

The right of property of every Japanese subject shall remain inviolate.
    Measures necessary to be taken for the public benefit shall be provided for by law.

Article XXVIII

Japanese subjects shall, within limits not prejudicial to peace and order, and not antagonistic to their duties as subjects, enjoy freedom of religious belief.

Article XXIX

Japanese subjects shall, within the limits of law, enjoy the liberty of speech, writing, publication, public meetings and associations.

Article XXX

Japanese subjects may present petitions, by observing the proper forms of respect, and by complying with the rules specially provided for the same.

Article XXXI

The provisions contained in the present Chapter shall not affect the exercises of the powers appertaining to the Emperor, in times of war or in cases of a national emergency.

CHAPTER III: THE IMPERIAL DIET

Article XXXIII

The Imperial Diet shall consist of two Houses, a House of Peers and a House of Representatives.

Article XXXIV

The House of Peers shall, in accordance with the Ordinance concerning the House of Peers, be composed of the members of the Imperial Family, of the orders of nobility, and of those who have been nominated thereto by the Emperor.

Article XXXV

The House of Representatives shall be composed of Members elected by the people, according to the provisions of the Law of Election.

Article XXXVI

No one can at one and the same time be a Member of both Houses.

Article XXXVII

Every law requires the consent of the Imperial Diet.

Article XXXVIII

Both Houses shall vote upon projects of law submitted to it by the Government, and may respectively initiate projects of law.

Article XL

Both Houses can make representations to the Government, as to laws or upon any other subject. When, however, such representations are not accepted, they cannot be made a second time during the same session.

Article XLI

The Imperial Diet shall be convoked every year.

Article XLII

A session of the Imperial Diet shall last during three months. In case of necessity, the duration of a session may be prolonged by the Imperial Order.

Article XLIII

When urgent necessity arises, an extraordinary session may be convoked in addition to the ordinary one. The duration of an extraordinary session shall be determined by Imperial Order.

Article XLV

When the House of Representatives has been ordered to dissolve, Members shall be caused by Imperial Order to be newly elected, and the new House shall be convoked within five months from the day of dissolution.

Article XLVII

Votes shall be taken in both Houses by absolute majority. In the case of a tie vote, the President shall have the casting vote.

Article XLVIII

The deliberations of both Houses shall be held in public. The deliberations may, however, upon demand of the Government or by resolution of the House, be held in secret sitting.

Article XLIX

Both Houses of the Imperial Diet may respectively present addresses to the Emperor.

Article LII

No Member of either House shall be held responsible outside the respective Houses, for any opinion uttered or for any vote given in the House. When, however, a Member himself has given publicity to his opinions by public speech, by documents in print or in writing, or by any other similar means, he shall, in the matter, be amenable to the general law.

Article LIII

The Members of both Houses shall, during the session, be free from arrest, unless with the consent of the House, except in cases of flagrant delicts, or of offenses connected with a state of internal commotion or with a foreign trouble.

Article LIV

The Ministers of State and the Delegates of the Government may, at any time, take seats and speak in either House.

CHAPTER VI: FINANCE

Article LXII

The imposition of a new tax or the modification of the rates (of an existing one) shall be determined by law.

   However, all such administrative fees or other revenue having the nature of compensation shall not fall within the category of the above clause.

   The raising of national loans and the contracting of other liabilities to the charge of the National Treasury, except those that are provided in the Budget, shall require the consent of the Imperial Diet.

Article LXIII

The taxes levied at present shall, in so far as they are not remodelled by a new law, be collected according to the old system.

Article LXIV

The expenditure and revenue of the State require the consent of the Imperial Diet by means of an annual Budget.

Any and all expenditures overpassing the appropriations set forth in the Titles and Paragraphs of the Budget, or that are not provided for in the Budget, shall subsequently require the approbation of the Imperial Diet.

Article LXV

The Budget shall be first laid before the House of Representatives.

Article LXVI

The expenditures of the Imperial House shall be defrayed every year out of the National Treasury, according to the present fixed amount for the same, and shall not require the consent thereto of the Imperial Diet, except in case an increase thereof is found necessary.

Article LXVII

Those already fixed expenditures based by the Constitution upon the powers appertaining to the Emperor, and such expenditures as may have arisen by the effect of law, or that appertain to the legal obligations of the Government, shall be neither rejected nor reduced by the Imperial Diet, without the concurrence of the Government.

Article LXXI

When the Imperial Diet has not voted on the Budget, or when the Budget has not been brought into actual existence, the Government shall carry out the Budget of the preceding year.

150

On the Russian Revolution by Vladimir Ilyich Lenin—1899–1917

The untiring leader of the Bolsheviks, Vladimir Ilyich Lenin (1870–1924 CE) was crucial to the success of the Russian revolution. Of mixed ancestry and born to a middle-class family of civil servants, Vladimir Ilyich Lenin (Ulanov) was radicalized by the execution of his brother for treason. He changed the people's democracy of Marx into an authoritarian state that became a model for many twentieth-century revolutionaries. The four brief excerpts that follow show Lenin's changing ideas about his role in the revolution. What did Lenin think was his role in the revolution? What did he think was the role of the peasants/proletariat? How did he rationalize authoritarian rule?

OUR PROGRAMME (1899)

We take our stand entirely on the Marxist theoretical position: Marxism was the first to transform socialism from a utopia into a science, to lay a firm foundation for this science, and to indicate the path that must be followed in further developing and elaborating it in all its parts. It disclosed the nature of modern capitalist economy by explaining how the hire of the labourer, the purchase of labour power, conceals the enslavement of millions of propertyless people by a handful of capitalists, the owners of the land, factories, mines, and so forth. It showed that all modern capitalist development displays the tendency of large-scale production to eliminate petty production and creates conditions that make a socialist system of society possible and necessary. It taught us how to discern, beneath the pall of rooted customs, political intrigues, abstruse laws, and intricate doctrines—the *class struggle,* the struggle between the propertied classes in all their variety and the propertyless mass, the *proletariat,* which is at the head of all the propertyless. It made clear the real task of a revolutionary socialist party: not to draw up plans for refashioning society, not to preach to the capitalists and their hangers-on about improving the lot of the workers, not to hatch conspiracies, *but to organise the class struggle of the proletariat and to lead this struggle, the ultimate aim of which is the conquest of political power by the proletariat and the organisation of a socialist society.* . . .

From V.I. Lenin, *Selected Works* (New York: International Publishers, 1971).

LEADING A REVOLUTIONARY
MOVEMENT (1902)

I assert that it is far more difficult to unearth a dozen wise men than a hundred fools. This position I will defend, no matter how much you instigate the masses against me for my "anti-democratic" views, etc. As I have stated repeatedly, by "wise men," in connection with organisation, I mean *professional revolutionaries*, irrespective of whether they have developed from among students or working men. I assert: (1) that no revolutionary movement can endure without a stable organisation of leaders maintaining continuity; (2) that the broader the popular mass drawn spontaneously into the struggle, which forms the basis of the movement and participates in it, the more urgent the need for such an organi-sation, and the more solid this organisation must be (for it is much easier for all sorts of demagogues to side-track the more backward sections of the masses); (3) that such an organisation must consist chiefly of people professionally engaged in revolutionary activity; (4) that in an autocratic state, the more we *confine* the membership of such an organisation to people who are profession-ally engaged in revolutionary activity and who have been professionally trained in the art of combating the political police, the more difficult will it be to unearth the organisation; and (5) the *greater* will be the number of people from the working class and from the other social classes who will be able to join the movement and perform active work in it. . . .

PROCLAIMING THE NEW SOVIET
GOVERNMENT (NOVEMBER 1917)

Comrades, the workers' and peasants' revolution, the need of which the Bolsheviks have emphasized many times, has come to pass.

What is the significance of this revolution? Its significance is, in the first place, that we shall have a soviet government, without the participation of bourgeoisie of any kind. The oppressed masses will of themselves form a gov-ernment. The old state machinery will be smashed into bits and in its place will be created a new machinery of government by the soviet organizations. From now on there is a new page in the history of Russia, and the present, third Russian revolution shall in its final result lead to the victory of Socialism.

One of our immediate tasks is to put an end to the war at once. But in order to end the war, which is closely bound up with the present capitalistic system, it is necessary to overthrow capitalism itself. In this work we shall have the aid of the world labor movement, which has already begun to develop in Italy, England, and Germany.

A just and immediate offer of peace by us to the international democracy will find everywhere a warm response among the international proletariat masses. In order to secure the confidence of the proletariat, it is necessary to publish at once all secret treaties.

In the interior of Russia a very large part of the peasantry has said: Enough playing with the capitalists; we will go with the workers. We shall secure the confidence of the peasants by one decree, which will wipe out the private property of the landowners. The peasants will understand that their only salvation is in union with the workers.

We will establish a real labor control on production.

We have now learned to work together in a friendly manner, as is evident from this revolution. We have the force of mass organization which has conquered all and which will lead the proletariat to world revolution.

We should now occupy ourselves in Russia in building up a proletarian socialist state.

Long live the world-wide socialistic revolution.

151

The Plan of Ayala by Emiliano Zapata—1911

Emiliano Zapata (1879–1919) was born in Anenecuilco, Morelos, Mexico. He worked as both sharecropper and horse trainer until he was conscripted into the Mexican army; he eventually held the rank of sergeant. Zapata later became president of his village council and worked for the restoration of peasant land confiscated by the hacendados (large landowners); he adopted the slogan "Land and Liberty." In the Mexican revolution, Zapata sided with Francisco Madero, who took power in 1911. Zapata was the most radical of the peasant leaders and, although he never gained control of the Mexican Revolution, his ideas influenced the course of Mexican history. What does he call for in the Plan of Ayala? Why might his demands have been unpopular with other leaders of the revolution?

I. THE PLAN OF AYALA

The liberating Plan of the sons of the State of Morelos, affiliated with the Insurgent Army which defends the fulfillment of the Plan of San Luis Potosí, with the reforms which they have believed necessary to add for the benefit of the Mexican Fatherland.

From Emiliano Zapata, "The Plan of Ayala," Nov. 29, 1911, trans. Erick D. Langer.

We, the subscribers [to this Plan], constituted in a Revolutionary Council . . .
declare solemnly before the countenance of the civilized world which judges
us and before the Nation to which we belong and love, the principles which
we have formulated to terminate the tyranny which oppresses us and redeem
the Fatherland from the dictatorships which are imposed on us, which are
determined in the following Plan:

1. [Accuses Francisco I. Madero, the leader of the 1910 revolution and President of Mexico, of betraying the Revolution and allying himself with the oppressive old guard in the State of Morelos.]

2. Francisco I. Madero is disavowed as Chief of the Revolution and as President of the Republic, for the above reasons, [and we will] endeavor to overthrow this official.

3. The illustrious General Pascual Orozco, second of the *caudillo* Don Francisco I. Madero, is recognized as Chief of the Liberating Revolution, and in case he does not accept this delicate post, General Emiliano Zapata is recognized as Chief of the Revolution.

4. The Revolutionary Junta of the State of Morelos manifests the following formal points . . . and will make itself the defender of the principles that it will defend until victory or death.

5. The Revolutionary Junta of the State of Morelos will not admit transactions or political compromises until the overthrow of the dictatorial elements of Porfirio Díaz and Francisco I. Madero, since the Nation is tired of false men and traitors who make promises as liberators but once in power, forget them and become tyrants.

6. As an additional part of the Plan which we invoke, we assert that: the fields, woodland, and water which the haciendados [landlords], *científicos* or bosses in the shadow of tyranny and venal justice have usurped, will revert to the possession of the towns or citizens who have their corresponding titles to these properties. [These properties] have been usurped through the bad faith of our oppressors, who maintained all along with arms in hand the above mentioned possession. The usurpers who feel they have the right [to ownership], will demonstrate this before special tribunals which will be established when the Revolution triumphs.

7. In virtue of the fact that the immense majority of the towns and Mexican citizens are not masters of the soil they step upon, suffering horrors of misery without being able to better their social condition at all nor dedicate themselves to industry or agriculture because of the monopoly in a few hands of the land, woodlands, and waters, for this reason [the lands] will be expropriated, with indemnity of the third part of these monopolies to their powerful owners, so that the towns and citizens of Mexico can obtain common lands (*ejidos*), colonies, and legitimate resources for towns or agricultural fields and that above all the lack of prosperity and wellbeing of the Mexican people is improved.

8. The haciendados, *científicos* or bosses who oppose directly or indirectly the present plan, will have their possessions nationalized and two thirds of what they own will be destined for war indemnities, [and] pensions for the widows and orphans of the victims who succumb in the fight for this Plan.

9. To regulate the procedures in regard to the items mentioned above, the laws of disentailment and nationalization will be applied as is appropriate. [The laws] put into effect by the immortal Juarez regarding Church lands can serve as a guide and example, which set a severe example to the despots and conservatives who at all times have tried to impose the ignominious yoke of oppression and backwardness.

10. The insurgent military chiefs of the Republic, who rose up in armed revolt at the behest of Francisco I. Madero to defend the Plan of San Luis Potosí and who now oppose by force the present Plan, are to be judged traitors to the cause they defended and to the Fatherland, given the fact that in actuality many of them to please the tyrants for a handful of coins, or for bribes, are spilling the blood of their brethren who demand the fulfillment of the promises which don Francisco I. Madero made to the Nation.

[11-14. Details the payment of the expenses of war, the administration of the country after the Plan's success, and bids Madero to step down voluntarily.]

15. Mexicans: Consider that the cleverness and the bad faith of one man is spilling blood in a scandalous manner because of his inability to govern; consider that his system of government is putting the Fatherland in chains and by brute force of bayonets trampling under foot our institutions; and as we raised our arms to elevate him to power, today we turn them against him for having gone back on his agreements with the Mexican people and having betrayed the Revolution he initiated; we are not personalists, we are believers in principles not in men.

People of Mexico: Support with your arms in hand this Plan and you will create prosperity and happiness for the Fatherland.

Justicia y ley.
Ayala, 28 of November, 1911.

152

Early Zionist Thought by
Nahum Goldman—1913

The conflict between Arabs and Jews has a long history. Both groups have claimed the same homeland for centuries. In recent times, the conflict has intensified with the growth of the Zionist movement, organized by European Jews in the 1880s as a response to widespread anti-Semitism. The Zionists hoped to re-establish the state of Israel in Palestine. Unfortunately, Palestine in the 1890s was part of the Ottoman Empire and mainly populated by Arabs. When the state of Israel was established in 1948, it seemed to be the realization of the Zionist dream. However, it became a nightmare for both Jews and Palestinian Arabs, who opposed the creation of the new Jewish state. After the first Arab-Israeli War (1948-1949), hundreds of thousands of Palestinians were exiled. These exiles vowed to regain their homeland, thus creating their own version of Zionism. The following document describes the feelings of Nahum Goldman, a leading Zionist, upon first visiting Palestine. Why was he impressed by Palestine? How did his visit increase his Zionist fervor?

NAHUM GOLDMAN

As I have said, I was not a very diligent student and spent a lot of time during the academic year with my parents in Frankfurt and in excursions to the Odenwald or the Neckar Valley. All in all my relationship to the university was not very close, and when the chance of going to Palestine was offered to me in 1913, I jumped at it. A group of students was going there on a visit organized and led by Theodor Zlocisti, one of the oldest German Zionists in Berlin, a physician by profession and a man of literary interests. I was asked if I would like to go along; my expenses would be paid by a wealthy friend of the family. The trip was supposed to last four weeks, but I stayed five months and skipped a whole semester at Heidelberg. . . .

I left the group, which was returning to Germany shortly in any case, and decided really to get to know the country. Although I have been in Palestine probably more than a hundred times since then, I have never again had the opportunity to discover it at such a leisurely yet intensive pace. Free of the

From Nahum Goldman, *The Autobiography of Nahum Goldman: Sixty Years of a Jewish Life* (New York: Holt, Rinehart and Winston, 1969), p. 38–42, 44. Reprinted by permission.

group's daily hikes, receptions, and ceremonies and having decided to stay several months, I could dispose of my time as I pleased.

I spent several weeks in Tel Aviv, which then consisted of only a few streets, several more in Rishon le-Zion and Rehovot, and a week in Rosh Pina in Galilee. But most of my time I spent in Jerusalem, where I rented, in what was then the Russian apartment-house complex, a romantic attic with a balcony. I used to sleep on the balcony when the weather got warm.

A detailed account of colonization in those days is beyond the scope of this book, but it was all in quite a primitive stage, except for a few old-established settlements such as Petah Tiqva, Rishon le-Zion, and one or two others. I was especially impressed by kibbutzim, such as Deganyah and Kinneret, and by the type of young *halutz,* or pioneer, Zionists I encountered for the first time. In Jerusalem I tried to get to know the old *yishuv,* the pre-Zionist Orthodox Jewish community, as well as the new one and had some very impressive encounters with kabbalists and mystics in the Meah Shearim quarter of Jerusalem. . . .

I often used to take long moonlight rides with friends and once, on our way back, we were surrounded by a Bedouin band. They would certainly have robbed us and left us naked on the road if one of my companions, who was familiar with the country, had not advised us to act naturally, to sing and occasionally pat our hip pockets as if we were carrying guns. Apparently this produced the desired effect. After riding along with us for about ten minutes, the Bedouin suddenly scattered. Another time I found myself in a precarious situation when my Arab guide in Jericho arranged for me to be a hidden spectator at an Arab wedding and at the bride's dancing—something forbidden to foreigners under Bedouin law. I had already watched several dances, unforgettable in their wild passion, when my guide rushed up to me, pale with fear, and said that one of the bride's relatives had noticed something and was looking for me. We disappeared as fast as we could and got back to the hotel before it was too late. . . .

But even more than the people and the early achievements of Jewish colonization, the country itself impressed me. Never again was Palestine to have such an impact upon me. For one thing I was younger and more sensitive to such impressions and less distracted by other responsibilities than I was during later visits. The exceptional quality of this curious little territory, which has acquired a unique significance in human history not to be explained by its natural resources or geopolitical situation—what I would like to call its mystical meaning—was brought home to me then as never again. Later it became much more difficult to sense that special aura; one was too distracted by what was happening in and to the country. But at that time Palestine was still untouched. You felt the presence of the mountains without having to think about the settlements that would be established on them. You rode across the plains unmarred by buildings and highways. You traveled very slowly; there were no cars and only a few trains; you usually rode on horseback or in a cart. It took two days to get from Haifa to Jerusalem. One saw the country clearly as if emerging from thousands of years of enchantment. The clearness of the air, the brilliance of the starry sky, the mystery of the austere mountains, made it seem as though its history had grown out of the landscape. In those days it was an extraordinarily peaceful, idealistic country, absorbed in a reverie of its own unique past. In the atmosphere lingered something of the prophets and the great Talmudists, of Jesus and the Apostles, of the Safed kabbalists, and the singers of bygone centuries. . . .

When I left Palestine my Zionism had been enriched by a momentous factor, the country itself. Until then Zionism had been an abstract idea to me, and I had no real conception of what the return of the Jews meant in any concrete sense. My visit gave me that feeling for the soil without which Zinoism is bound to remain quite unsubstantial. From then on I began to understand what it means, not merely negatively in terms of leaving the Diaspora behind, but also positively, as a new beginning in a Jewish homeland.

CHAPTER 19

Science, Medicine, and Technology— 1750–1914 CE

Although there were many advances in technology during the nineteenth century, the documents in this section focus mainly on advances in medicine because of their direct effect on the human condition. Why were Japanese scholars so amazed by the Dutch anatomy book? Can you compare their reaction to that of the seventeenth-century physicians who relied on Galen's teachings?

Is Darwin's work directly related to that of seventeenth-century scientists, who were concerned with infinity and the origin of the world?

Sometimes relatively simple ideas have huge impacts. Such was the case with Long's experimentation with ether and with Semmelweis' insistence that doctors wash their hands. Neither discovery required a sophisticated laboratory or costly experimentation, yet the impact was enormous.

Finally, Freud's research into the workings of the unconscious may have had the greatest impact of all on the human condition. How would you rank these discoveries in order of their impact on alleviating human suffering and increasing human understanding?

153

The Anatomy Lesson
by Genpaku Sugita—1815

During the seventeenth century, the Japanese government had expelled all foreigners, executed all native Christians, and retained only a limited trading connection with the Dutch at Macao. By the end of the eighteenth century, Japanese scholars had begun to realize the cost of this policy of isolation from the West. Japanese scholar Genpaku Sugita obtained a Dutch anatomy text containing the latest Western information and compared it with traditional Chinese medical theories. When they later witnessed the dissection of a corpse, Sugita and his colleagues realized that Japan might benefit from being more open to Western thought and culture. How were they able to understand the Dutch medical book? What did Japanese scholars learn when they compared Chinese and Western medical information after viewing a dissection?

Whenever I met Hiraga Gennai (1729–1779), we talked to each other on this matter: "As we have learned, the Dutch method of scholarly investigation through field work and surveys is truly amazing. If we can directly understand the books written by them, we will benefit greatly. However, it is pitiful that there has been no one who has set his hand on working in this field. Can we somehow blaze this trail? It is impossible to do it in Edo. Perhaps it is best if we ask translators in Nagasaki to make some translations. If one book can be completely translated, there will be an inmeasurable benefit to the country." Every time we spoke in this manner, we deplored the impossibility of implementing our desires. However, we did not vainly lament the matter for long.

Somehow, miraculously I obtained a book on anatomy written in that country. It may well be that the Dutch studies in this country began when I thought of comparing the illustrations in the book with real things. It was a strange and even miraculous happening that I was able to obtain that book in that particular spring of 1771. Then at the night of the third day of the third month, I received a letter from a man by the name of Tokuno Bambei, who was in the service of the then Town Commissioner, Magaribuchi Kai-no-kami. Tokuno stated in his letter that "A post-mortem examination of the body of a condemned criminal by a resident physician will be held tomorrow

"The Anatomy Lesson" by Gempaku Sugita, from *Sources of Japanese History*, ed. by David John Lu (New York: McGraw-Hill, 1974), Vol. I, p. 253–255. Reprinted by permission of M.E. Sharpe, Inc.

at Senjukot-sugahara. You are welcome to "witness it if you so desire." At one time my colleague by the name of Kosugi Genteki had an occasion to witness a post-mortem dissection of a body when he studied under Dr. Yamawaki Toyo of Kyoto. After seeing the dissection first-hand, Kosugi remarked that what was said by the people of old was false and simply could not be trusted. "The people of old spoke of nine internal organs, and nowadays, people divide them into five viscera and six internal organs. That [perpetuates] inaccuracy," Kosugi once said. Around that time (1759) Dr. Toyo published a book entitled *Zoshi (On Internal Organs)*. Having read that book, I had hoped that some day I could witness a dissection. When I also acquired a Dutch book on anatomy, I wanted above all to compare the two to find out which one accurately described the truth. I rejoiced at this unusually fortunate circumstance and my mind could not entertain any other thought. However, a thought occurred to me that I should not monopolize this good fortune, and decided to share it with those of my colleagues who were diligent in the pursuit of their medicine. . . . Among those I invited was one Ryotaku. . . .

The next day, when we arrived at the location . . . Ryotaku reached under his kimono to produce a Dutch book and showed it to us. "This is a Dutch book of anatomy called *Tabulae Anatomicae*. I bought this a few years ago when I went to Nagasaki, and kept it." As I examined it, it was the same book I had and was of the same edition. We held each other's hands and exclaimed: "What a coincidence!" Ryotaku continued by saying: "When I went to Nagasaki, I learned and heard," and opened this book. "These are called *long* in Dutch, they are lungs," he taught us. "This is *hart,* or the heart. When it says *maag* it is the stomach, and when it says *milt* it is the spleen." However, they did not look like the heart given in the Chinese medical books, and none of us were sure until we could actually see the dissection.

Thereafter we went together to the place which was especially set for us to observe the dissection in Kotsugahara. . . . The regular man who performed the chore of dissection was ill, and his grandfather, who was ninety years of age, came in his place. He was a healthy old man. He had experienced many dissections since his youth, and boasted that he dissected a number of bodies. Those dissections were performed in those days by men of the *eta* class. . . . That day, the old butcher pointed to this and that organ. After the heart, liver, gall bladder, and stomach were identified, he pointed to other parts for which there were no names. "I don't know their names. But I have dissected quite a few bodies from my youthful days. Inside of everyone's abdomen there were these parts and those parts." Later, after consulting the anatomy chart, it became clear to me that I saw an arterial tube, a vein, and the suprarenal gland. The old butcher again said, "Every time I had a dissection, I pointed out to those physicians many of these parts, but not a single one of them questioned 'what was this?' or 'what was that?' We compared the body as dissected against the charts both Ryotaku and I had, and could not find a single variance from the charts. The Chinese *Book of Medicine (I Ching)* says that the lungs are like the eight petals of the lotus flower, with three petals hanging in front, three in back, and two petals forming like two ears and that the liver has three petals to the left and four petals to the right. There were no such divisions, and the positions and shapes of intestines and gastric organs were all different from those taught by the old theories. The official physicians, Dr. Okada Yosen and Dr. Fujimoto Rissen, had witnessed dissection seven or eight times. Whenever they witnessed the dissection, they found that the old theories contradicted reality. Each time they were perplexed and could not resolve their doubts. Every time they wrote down what they thought was strange. They wrote in their books, "The more we think of it, there must be fundamental differences in the bodies of Chinese and of the eastern barbarians [i.e., Japanese]." I could see why they wrote this way.

That day, after the dissection was over, we decided that we also should examine the shape of the skeletons left exposed on the execution ground. We collected the bones, and examined a number of them. Again, we were struck by the fact that they all differed from the old theories while conforming to the Dutch charts.

The three of us, Ryotaku, Junan, and I went home together. On the way home we spoke to each other and felt the same way. "How marvelous was our actual experience today. It is a shame that we were ignorant of these things until now. As physicians who serve their masters through medicine, we performed our duties in complete ignorance of the true form of the human body. How disgraceful it is. Somehow, through this experience, let us investigate further the truth about the human body. If we practice medicine with this knowledge behind us, we can make contributions for people under heaven and on this earth." Ryotaku spoke to us. "Indeed, I agree with you wholeheartedly." Then I spoke to my companion. "Somehow if we can translate anew this book called *Tabulae Anatomicae,* we can get a clear notion of the human body inside out. It will have great benefit in the treatment of our patients. Let us do our best to read it and understand it without the help of translators." Ryotaku responded: "I have been wanting to read Dutch books for some time, but there has been no friend who would share my ambitions. I have spent days lamenting it. If both of you wish, I have been in Nagasaki before and have retained some Dutch. Let us use it as a beginning to tackle the book together." After hearing it, I answered, "This is simply wonderful. If we are to join our efforts, I shall also resolve to do my very best". . . .

The next day, we assembled at the house of Ryotaku and recalled the happenings of the previous day. When we faced that *Tabulae Anatomicae,* we felt as if we were setting sail on a great ocean in a ship without oars or a rudder. With the magnitude of the work before us, we were dumbfounded by our own ignorance. However, Ryotaku had been thinking of this for some time, and he had been in Nagasaki. He knew some Dutch through studying and hearing, and knew some sentence patterns and words. He was also ten years older than I, and we decided to make him head of our group and our teacher. At that time I did not know the twenty-five letters of the Dutch alphabet. I decided to study the language with firm determination, but I had to acquaint myself with letters and words gradually.

The First Surgical Operation Under Ether by Crawford Long— 1842

Born in Danielsville, Georgia, Crawford Williamson Long (1815–1879) earned his medical degree from the University of Pennsylvania in 1839. While in college, Long and his friends experimented with inhaling ether. After studying surgery in New York, Long returned to Jefferson, Georgia, to practice medicine. His experience with ether made Long believe that it might be used to alleviate the pain of surgery. Because he had no access to nitrous oxide, he began to experiment with sulfuric ether and found that patients felt no pain when under the effect of the gas. In 1842, he operated on a patient who was unconscious due to ether. The operation was a success and Long performed more surgeries using ether, although he did not publish the results. For this reason, William Morton, a dentist, claimed he was the first to use ether, but Long is credited as the first to use ether to sedate a surgical patient. In the following excerpt, Long discusses his use of ether. How did he realize that ether might ease the pain of surgery?

In the month of December, 1841, or January, 1842, the subject of the inhalation of nitrous oxide gas was introduced in a company of young men assembled at night, in the village of Jefferson, Ga., and the party requested me to prepare them some. I informed them that I had not the requisite apparatus for preparing or using the gas, but that I had an article (sulphuric ether), which would produce equally exhilarating effects and was as safe. The company was anxious to witness its effects: the ether was produced, and all present, in turn, inhaled. They were so much pleased with its effects that they afterwards frequently used it and induced others to use it, and the practice became quite fashionable in the country and some of the contiguous counties. On numerous occasions I inhaled the ether for its exhilarating properties and would frequently at some short time subsequently discover bruises or painful spots on my person which I had no recollection of causing, and which I felt satisfied were received while under the influence of ether. I noticed my friends while etherized, receive falls and blows, which I believed sufficient to cause pain on a person not in a state of anaesthesia, and, on questioning them they uniformly assured me that they did not feel the least pain from these accidents.

From *Source Book of Medical History*, complete with notes by Logan Clendenning
(New York: Dover, 1960), p. 356–358.

Observing these facts I was led to believe that anaesthesia was produced by the inhalation of ether and that its use would be applicable in surgical operations.

The first person to whom I administered ether in a surgical operation was Mr. James M. Venable, who then resided within two miles of Jefferson, and at the present time in Cobb county, Ga. Mr. Venable consulted me on several occasions as to the propriety of removing two small tumors on the back part of his neck, but would postpone from time to time having the operation performed from dread of pain. At length I mentioned to him the fact of my receiving bruises while under the influence of the vapor of ether, without suffering, and, as I knew him to be fond of and accustomed to inhale ether, I suggested to him the probability that the operation might be performed without pain, and suggested to him operating while he was under its influence. He consented to have one tumor removed and the operation was performed the same evening. The ether was given to Mr. Venable on a towel and fully under its influence, I extirpated the tumor. It was encysted and about one-half an inch in diameter. The patient continued to inhale ether during the time of the operation, and seemed incredulous until the tumor was shown to him. He gave no evidence of pain during the operation and assured me after it was over that he did not experience the least degree of pain from its performance. . . .

My third case was a negro boy who had a disease of the toe which rendered amputation necessary, and the operation was performed July 3, 1842, without the boy evincing the slightest degree of pain.

These were all the surgical operations performed by me in the year 1842 upon patients etherized, no other cases occurring in which I believed the inhalation of ether applicable. Since 1842, I have performed one or more operations, annually, on patients in a state of etherization. I procured some certificates in regard to these operations, but not with the same particularity as in regard to the first operations, my sole object being to establish my claim to priority of discovery of the power of ether to produce anaesthesia. However, these certificates can be examined.

Mr. Venable's statement under oath is as follows:

I, James Venable, of the county Cobb and State of Georgia, on oath depose and say, that in the year 1842 I resided at my mother's in Jackson County about two miles from the village of Jefferson, and attended the village academy that year. In the early part of the year the young men of Jefferson and the country adjoining were in the habit of inhaling ether for its exhilarating powers, and I inhaled it frequently for that purpose, and was very fond of its use.

While attending the academy I was frequently in the office of Dr. C. W. Long, and having two tumors on the back of my neck, I several times spoke to him about the propriety of cutting them out, but postponed the operation from time to time. On one occasion we had some conversation about the probability that the tumors might be cut while I was under the influence of ether, without my experiencing pain, and he proposed operating on me while under its influence. I agreed to have one tumor cut out, and had the operation performed that evening after school was dismissed. This was in the early part of the spring of 1842.

I commenced inhaling the ether before the operation was commenced and continued it until the operation was over. I did not feel the slightest pain from the operation and could not believe the tumor was removed until it was shown to me.

A month or two after this time Dr. C. W. Long cut out the other tumor situated on the same side of my neck. In this operation I did not feel the least pain until the last cut was made, when I felt a little pain. In this operation I stopped inhaling the ether before the operation was finished.

I inhaled the ether, in both cases, from a towel, which was the common method of taking it.

JAMES VENABLE

Georgia ⎫ Sworn to before me
Cobb Co., ⎬ Alfred Manes, J.P.
July 23rd, 1849 ⎭

155

From *The Origin of the Species* by Charles Darwin—1859

In its own way as revolutionary as the Communist Manifesto, The Origin of the Species *was written by a very unlikely revolutionary. Charles Darwin (1809–1882) was from a prominent middle-class English family; his grandfather, Josiah Wedgwood, was the founder of the famous ceramics factory. An indifferent student, he failed at both medical and religious studies before finally signing on to a naval expedition to catalog plant and animal life in South America and the Pacific Ocean. During the long voyage, Darwin became an expert naturalist, and the knowledge gained on the expedition led him to formulate his famous theories of natural selection, adaptation, and evolution. Publication of* The Origin of the Species *brought Darwin both fame and controversy, especially when he extended evolution to the human species in* The Descent of Man *(1871). The theory of evolution is still a topic of heated debate today. Why? How does Darwin define natural selection? According to Darwin, what is its purpose? What picture does Darwin create of the struggle for existence?*

From Charles Darwin, *On the Origin of Species by Means of Natural Selection* (New York: D. Appleton and Co., 1883).

STRUGGLE FOR EXISTENCE

Before entering on the subject of this chapter, I must make a few preliminary remarks, to show how the struggle for existence bears on Natural Selection. It has been seen in the last chapter that amongst organic beings in a state of nature there is some individual variability: indeed I am not aware that this has ever been disputed. It is immaterial for us whether a multitude of doubtful forms be called species or sub-species or varieties; what rank, for instance, the two or three hundred doubtful forms of British plants are entitled to hold, if the existence of any well-marked varieties be admitted. But the mere existence of individual variability and of some few well-marked varieties, though necessary as the foundation for the work, helps us but little in understanding how species arise in nature. How have all those exquisite adaptations of one part of the organisation to another part, and to the conditions of life, and of one organic being to another being, been perfected? We see these beautiful co-adaptations most plainly in the woodpecker and the mistletoe; and only a little less plainly in the humblest parasite which clings to the hairs of a quadruped or feathers of a bird; in the structure of the beetle which dives through the water: in the plumed seed which is wafted by the gentlest breeze; in short, we see beautiful adaptations everywhere and in every part of the organic world.

Again, it may be asked, how is it that varieties, which I have called incipient species, become ultimately converted into good and distinct species, which in most cases obviously differ from each other far more than do the varieties of the same species? How do those groups of species, which constitute what are called distinct genera, and which differ from each other more than do the species of the same genus, arise? All these results, as we shall more fully see in the next chapter, follow from the struggle for life. Owing to this struggle, variations, however slight, and from whatever cause proceeding, if they be in any degree profitable to the individuals of a species, in their infinitely complex relations to other organic beings and to their physical conditions of life, will tend to the preservation of such individuals, and will generally be inherited by the offspring. The offspring, also, will thus have a better chance of surviving, for, of the many individuals of any species which are periodically born, but a small number can survive. I have called this principle, by which each slight variation, if useful, is preserved, by the term Natural Selection, in order to mark its relation to man's power of selection. But the expression often used by Mr. Herbert Spencer of the Survival of the Fittest is more accurate, and is sometimes equally convenient. We have seen that man by selection can certainly produce great results, and can adapt organic beings to his own uses, through the accumulation of slight but useful variations, given to him by the hand of Nature. But Natural Selection, as we shall hereafter see, is a power incessantly ready for action, and is as immeasurably superior to man's feeble efforts, as the works of Nature are to those of Art.

Nothing is easier than to admit in words the truth of the universal struggle for life, or more difficult—at least I have found it so—than constantly to bear this conclusion in mind. Yet unless it be thoroughly ingrained in the mind, the whole economy of nature, with every fact on distribution, rarity, abundance, extinction, and variation, will be dimly seen or quite misunderstood. We behold the face of nature bright with gladness, we often see superabundance of food; we do not see or we forget, that the birds which are idly singing round us mostly live on insects or seeds, and are thus constantly destroying life; or we forget how largely these songsters, or their eggs, or their nestlings, are destroyed by birds and beasts of prey; we do not always bear in mind, that, though food may be now superabundant, it is not so at all seasons of each recurring year.

The Term, Struggle for Existence, Used in a Large Sense

I should premise that I use this term in a large and metaphorical sense including dependence of one being on another, and including (which is more important) not only the life of the individual, but success in leaving progeny. Two canine animals, in a time of dearth, may be truly said to struggle with each other which shall get food and live. But a plant on the edge of a desert is said to struggle for life against the drought, though more properly it should be said to be dependent on the moisture. A plant which annually produces a thousand seeds, of which only one on an average comes to maturity, may be more truly said to struggle with the plants of the same and other kinds which already clothe the ground. The mistletoe is dependent on the apple and a few other trees, but can only in a far-fetched sense be said to struggle with these trees, for, if too many of these parasites grow on the same tree, it languishes and dies. But several seedling mistletoes, growing close together on the same branch, may more truly be said to struggle with each other. As the mistletoe is disseminated by birds, its existence depends on them; and it may metaphorically be said to struggle with other fruit-bearing plants, in tempting the birds to devour and thus disseminate its seeds. In these several senses, which pass into each other, I use for convenience' sake the general term of Struggle for Existence.

Geometrical Ratio of Increase

A struggle for existence inevitably follows from the high rate at which all organic beings tend to increase. Every being, which during its natural lifetime produces several eggs or seeds, must suffer destruction during some period of its life, and during some season or occasional year, otherwise, on the principle of geometrical increase, its numbers would quickly become so inordinately great that no country could support the product. Hence, as more individuals are produced than can possibly survive, there must in every case be a struggle for existence, either one individual with another of the same species, or with the individuals of distinct species, or with the physical conditions of life. It is the doctrine of Malthus applied with manifold force to the whole animal and vegetable kingdoms; for in this case there can be no artificial increase of food, and no prudential restraint from marriage. Although some species may be now increasing, more or less rapidly, in numbers, all cannot do so, for the world would not hold them.

There is no exception to the rule that every organic being naturally increases at so high a rate, that, if not destroyed, the earth would soon be covered by the progeny of a single pair. Even slow-breeding man has doubled in twenty-five years, and at this rate, in less than a thousand years, there would literally not be standing-room for his progeny. Linnaeus has calculated that if an annual plant produced only two seeds—and there is no plant so unproductive as this—and their seedlings next year produced two, and so on, then in twenty years there would be a million plants. The elephant is reckoned the slowest breeder of all known animals, and I have taken some pains to estimate its probable minimum rate of natural increase; it will be safest to assume that it begins breeding when thirty years old, and goes on breeding til ninety years old, bringing forth six young in the interval, and surviving till one hundred years old; if this be so, after a period of from 740 to 750 years there would be nearly nineteen million elephants alive, descended from the first pair.

NATURAL SELECTION OR
THE SURVIVAL OF THE FITTEST

How will the struggle for existence, briefly discussed in the last chapter, act in regard to variation? Can the principle of selection, which we have seen is so potent in the hands of man, apply under nature? I think we shall see that it can act most efficiently. Let the endless number of slight variations and individual differences occurring in our domestic productions, and, in a lesser degree, in those under nature, be borne in mind; as well as the strength of the hereditary tendency. Under domestication, it may be truly said that the whole organization becomes in some degree plastic. But the variability, which we almost universally meet with in our domestic productions, is not directly produced, as Hooker and Asa Gray have well remarked, by man; he can neither originate varieties, nor prevent their occurrence; he can only preserve and accumulate such as do occur. Unintentionally he exposes organic beings to new and changing conditions of life, and variability ensues; but similar changes of conditions might and do occur under nature. Let it also be borne in mind how infinitely complex and close-fitting are the mutual relations of all organic beings to each other and to their physical conditions of life; and consequently what infinitely varied diversities of structure might be of use to each being under changing conditions of life. Can it, then, be thought improbable, seeing that variations useful to man have undoubtedly occurred, that other variations useful in some way to each being in the great and complex battle of life, should occur in the course of many successive generations? If such do occur, can we doubt (remembering that many more individuals are born than can possibly survive)that individuals having any advantage, however slight, over others, would have the best chance of surviving and of procreating their kind? On the other hand, we may feel sure that any variation in the least degree injurious would be rigidly destroyed. This preservation of favourable individual differences and variations, and the destruction of those which are injurious, I have called Natural Selection, or the Survival of the Fittest. Variations neither useful nor injurious would not be affected by natural selection, and would be left either a fluctuating element, as perhaps we see in certain polymorphic species, or would ultimately become fixed, owing to the nature of the organism and the nature of the conditions.

We shall best understand the probable course of natural selection by taking the case of a country undergoing some slight physical change, for instance, of climate. The proportional numbers of its inhabitants will almost immediately undergo a change, and some species will probably become extinct. We may conclude, from what we have seen of the intimate and complex manner in which the inhabitants of each country are bound together, that any change in the numerical proportions of the inhabitants, independently of the change of climate itself, would seriously affect the others. If the country were open on its borders, new forms would certainly immigrate, and this would likewise seriously disturb the relations of some of the former inhabitants. Let it be remembered how powerful the influence of a single introduced tree or mammal has been shown to be. But in the case of an island, or of a country partly surrounded by barriers, into which new and better adapted forms could not freely enter, we should then have places in the economy of nature which would assuredly be better filled up, if some of the original inhabitants were in some manner modified; for, had the area been open to immigration, these same places would have been seized on by intruders. In such cases, slight modifications, which in any way favoured the individuals of any species, by better adapting them to their altered conditions, would tend to be preserved; and natural selection would have free scope for the work of improvement.

We have good reason to believe, as shown in the first chapter, that changes in the conditions of life give a tendency to increased variability; and in the foregoing cases the conditions have changed, and this would manifestly be favourable to natural selection, by affording a better chance of the occurrence of profitable variations. Unless such occur, natural selection can do nothing. Under the term of "variations," it must never be forgotten that mere individual differences are included. As man can produce a great result with his domestic animals and plants by adding up in any given direction individual differences, so could natural selection, but far more easily, from having incomparably longer time for action. Nor do I believe that any great physical change, as of climate, or any unusual degree of isolation to check immigration, is necessary in order that new and unoccupied places should be left, for natural selection to fill up by improving some of the varying inhabitants. For as all the inhabitants of each country are struggling together with nicely balanced forces, extremely slight modifications in the structure or habits of one species would often give it an advantage over others; and still further modifications of the same kind would often still further increase the advantage, as long as the species continued under the same conditions of life and profited by similar means of subsistence and defense. No country can be named in which all the native inhabitants are now so perfectly adapted to each other and to the physical conditions under which they live, that none of them could be still better adapted or improved; for in all countries, the natives have been so far conquered by naturalised productions, that they have allowed some foreigners to take firm possession of the land. And as foreigners have thus in every country beaten some of the natives, we may safely conclude that the natives might have been modified with advantage, so as to have better resisted the intruders.

As man can produce, and certainly has produced, a great result by his methodical and unconscious means of selection, what may not natural selection effect? Man can act only on external and visible characters: Nature, if I may be allowed to personify the natural preservation or survival of the fittest, cares nothing for appearances, except in so far as they are useful to any being. She can act on every internal organ, on every shade of constitutional difference, on the whole machinery of life. Man selects only for his own good: Nature only for that of the being which she tends. Every selected character is fully exercised by her, as is implied by the fact of their selection. Man keeps the natives of many climates in the same country; he seldom exercises each selected character in some peculiar and fitting manner; he feeds a long and a short beaked pigeon on the same food; he does not exercise a long-backed or long-legged quadruped in any peculiar manner; he exposes sheep with long and short wool to the same climate. He does not allow the most vigorous males to struggle for the females. He does not rigidly destroy all inferior animals, but protects during each varying season, as far as lies in his power, all his productions. He often begins his selection by some half-monstrous form; or at least by some modification prominent enough to catch the eye or to be plainly useful to him. Under nature, the slightest differences of structure or constitution may well turn the nicely-balanced scale in the struggle for life, and so be preserved. How fleeting are the wishes and efforts of man! how short his time! and consequently how poor will be his results, compared with those accumulated by Nature during whole geological periods! Can we wonder, then, that Nature's productions should be far "truer" in character than man's productions; that they should be infinitely better adapted to the most complex conditions of life, and should plainly bear the stamp of far higher workmanship?

156

Child-Bed Fever by Ignaz Phillip Semmelweis—1861

Childbirth was dangerous for women well into the nineteenth century because of the danger of child-bed fever, an infection of the uterus that was often fatal. Ignaz Semmelweis (1818–1865) was born in Hungary and studied medicine in Vienna. While working at the clinic, he noticed that the death rate from puerperal fever was much greater among women attended by doctors and medical students than among those attended by midwives. In the nineteenth century, doctors did not wash their hands when going from patient to patient or even after autopsying a diseased body and then attending to a living patient. He theorized that doctors were spreading something that caused puerperal fever when they examined patients with unclean hands. As a result, he ordered them to wash their hands in a chlorine solution before examining patients. Unfortunately, the concept of disinfection did not catch on until many years later. In the following excerpt, Semmelweis discusses his findings regarding the cause of puerperal fever. What did he think caused the disease? Did he feel the fever was contagious? How did he think it could be prevented?

Supported by the experiences which I have collected in the course of fifteen years in three different institutions all of which were visited from time to time by puerperal fever to a serious extent, I maintain that puerperal fever, without the exception of a single case, is a resorption fever produced by the resorption of decomposed animal organic material. The first result of this resorption is a blood-dissolution; and exudations result from the blood-dissolution.

The decomposed animal organic material which produces child-bed fever is, in the overwhelming majority of cases, brought to the individual from without, and that is the infection from without; these are the cases which represent child-bed fever epidemics; these are the cases which can be prevented.

In rare cases the decomposed animal matter which when absorbed causes child-bed fever, is produced within the limits of the affected organism. These are the cases of self-infection, and these cases cannot all be prevented.

The source whence the decomposed animal organic material is derived from without is the cadaver of any age, of either sex, without regard to the

From Die Aetiologie, Der Begriff, Une Die Prophylaxis des Kindbettfiebers, Pes, Wein, U. Leipzig, 1861. Trans. from Herbert Thoms' *Selected Readings in Obstetrics and Gynaecology* (Springfield, Ill.: Charles C. Thomas).

antecedent disease, without regard to the fact whether the dead body is that of a puerperal or non-puerperal woman. Only the degree of putrefaction of the cadaver has to be taken into consideration. . . .

At the Obstetric Clinic of the Faculty of Medicine at Pesth, it was physiologic human blood and normal lochia which were the etiological factor of a puerperal fever, inasmuch as they were left for a long time soaking the bed-linen and undergoing decomposition.

The carrier of the decomposed animal organic material is the examining finger, the operating hand, the bed-clothes, the atmospheric air, sponges, the hands of midwives and nurses which come into contact with the excrementa of sick lying-in-women or other patients, and then come again into contact with the genitals of women in labour or just confined; in a word the carrier of the decomposed animal organic material is everything which can be rendered unclean by such material and then come into contact with the genitals of the patient.

The site of infection by the decomposed animal organic material is the internal os uteri and upward from there. The inner surface of the uterus . . . is robbed of its mucosa and presents an area where absorption occurs with extreme readiness. The other parts of the mucosa are well clad with epithelium and do not absorb unless they are wounded. If it is injured any portion of the genitals becomes capable of absorption.

With regard to the time of infection, it seldom occurs during pregnancy because of the inaccessibility of the inner absorbing surface of the uterus by reason of the closure of the os internum. In cases in which the internal os uteri is open during pregnancy infection may occur then, but these cases are rare because there is seldom any need for passing the finger within the cervix uteri.

I neglected to take notes of the cases in which puerperal fever began during pregnancy at the First Obstetric Clinic of Vienna but I believe it to be near the truth if I put down the number of cases as about twenty. By puerperal infection the pregnancy was always interrupted.

The time within which infection most frequently occurs is during the stage of dilatation. This is owing to frequent examinations made with the object of ascertaining the position of the foetus.

A proof of this is that before the introduction of chlorine disinfection nearly all the patients after labour, protracted in the dilatation period, died of puerperal fever.

Infection seldom takes place during the expulsion stage because the surface of the uterus cannot then be reached.

In the third stage, or after-birth period, and during the puerperium, the inner surface of the uterus is accessible, and at this time especially, the atmospheric air loaded with decomposed animal organic materials may gain access to the internal genitals and set up infection. . . .

In the after-birth period and during lying-in, the infection may be produced by the bed-linen coming into contact with the genitals which have been injured in the process of parturition. . . .

Self-infection: The decomposed animal organic material which when absorbed brings on puerperal fever is in rare cases not conveyed to the individual from without but originates within the affected individual owing to the retention of organic material which should have been expelled in child-bed. Before its expulsion decomposition has already begun, and when absorption occurs puerperal fever is produced by Self-infection. These organic materials are the lochia, remnants of decidua, blood coagula which are retained within the cavity of the uterus. Or the decomposed animal organic material is the product of a pathological process, for example, the result of a forcible use of the midwifery forceps causing gangrene of bruised portions of the genital organs and consequent child-bed fever by Self-infection.

When we declare that child-bed fever is a resorption fever in which as the result of absorption a blood-poisoning occurs, and then exudation follows, we do not imply that puerperal fever is peculiar to the lying-in woman and restricted in its incidence to lying-in women. We have met with the disease in pregnant women and in new-born infants without regard to sex. This is the disease which was fatal in the case of Kolletschka; and we find it affecting anatomists, surgeons, and patients who have undergone surgical operations.

Puerperal fever is therefore not a species of disease: puerperal fever is a variety of Pyaemia.

With the expression pyaemia different meanings are bound up: it is therefore necessary to explain what I mean by pyaemia. I understand by pyaemia a blood-poisoning produced by a decomposed animal-organic matter.

A variety of pyaemia I call child-bed fever, because special forms of it occur in the genital sphere of pregnant parturient and puerperal women. . . .

Puerperal fever is not a contagious disease. By contagious disease we understand the sort of disease which itself produces the contagion by which it is propagated, and this contagion again produces in another individual the same disease. Smallpox is a contagious disease because smallpox produces the contagion by which smallpox can be reproduced in another individual. Smallpox produces in another individual smallpox and no other disease. . . . For example, a person suffering from scarlet fever cannot cause smallpox in another individual.

Such is the position with child-bed fever; this disease can be produced in a healthy normal puerperal by a disease which is not puerperal fever. . . .

Puerperal fever is not conveyed to a healthy puerpera unless a decomposed animal-organic material is carried to her. For example, a patient becomes seriously ill with puerperal fever, and when this puerperal fever runs its course without the production of a decomposed animal-organic matter, which appears externally, then is the disease not conveyable to a healthy normal puerpera. But when puerperal fever runs its course in such a way as to produce a decomposed matter appearing externally, then is child-bed fever capable of being conveyed to a normal healthy puerpera. For example, a puerpera is suffering from the malady in the form of septic endometritis . . . from such a patient is puerperal fever capable of being carried.

Puerperal fever is not a contagious disease, but puerperal fever is conveyable from a sick to a sound puerpera by means of a decomposed animal organic materia.

After death the body of every lying-in woman becomes a source of decomposed material which may produce puerperal fever; in the cadaver of the puerpera we consider only the degree of putrefaction. When we have reflected that the overwhelming majority of cases of puerperal fever are produced by infection from outside, and that these cases can be prevented, and that in only a small minority of cases puerperal fever is the result of unavoidable self-infection, the question arises: if all fatal cases, not resulting from puerperal fever, and if all cases of infection from without are prevented by suitable measures, how many lying-in women die as the consequence of self-infection?

It is not possible to answer this question for want of statistics, and we must attain complete control of material and environment so as to banish conveyed infection from our hospitals before we can obtain reliable statistics of self-infection.

157

From *The Interpretation of Dreams* by Sigmund Freud—1899

Modern psychology owes much of its prominence to the work of Sigmund Freud. An Austrian medical doctor, Sigmund Freud (1856–1939 CE) came from a middle-class Jewish family and studied medicine at the University of Vienna. As a specialist in psychiatry, he opened his own practice and began to develop the theories that would later bring him an international reputation. A number of the terms Freud coined have been incorporated into the vernacular, including "ego," "id," and "Oedipus complex." Freud also developed the technique of psychoanalysis. He fled Vienna in 1938 when it was occupied by Hitler's troops, and he died in London in 1939. Perhaps his most important work was on the study of the unconscious. In the following excerpt, Freud discusses the ways dreams can be interpreted. How does he define dreams, and why does he think they occur? Why does Freud believe the interpretation of dreams is important?

I am proposing to show that dreams are capable of interpretation; and any contributions to the solution of the problem which have already been discussed will emerge only as possible byproducts in the accomplishment of my special task. On the hypothesis that dreams are susceptible of interpretation, I at once find myself in disagreement with the prevailing doctrine of dreams— in fact, with all the theories of dreams, excepting only that of Schemer, for "to interpret a dream" is to specify its "meaning," to replace it by something which takes its position in the concatenation of our psychic activities as a link of definite importance and value. But, as we have seen, the scientific theories of the dream leave no room for a problem of dream-interpretation; since, in the first place, according to these theories, dreaming is not a psychic activity at all, but a somatic process which makes itself known to the psychic apparatus by means of symbols. Lay opinion has always been opposed to these theories. It asserts its privilege of proceeding illogically, and although it admits that dreams are incomprehensible and absurd, it cannot summon up the courage to deny that dreams have any significance. Led by a dim intuition, it seems rather to assume that dreams have a meaning, albeit a hidden one; that they are intended as a substitute for some other thought-process, and that we have only to disclose this substitute correctly in order to discover the hidden meaning of the dream.

The unscientific world, therefore, has always endeavored to "interpret" dreams, and by applying one or the other of two essentially different methods. The first of these envisages the dream-content as a whole, and seeks to replace it by another content, which is intelligible and in certain respects analogous. This is symbolic dream-interpretation; and of course it goes to pieces at the very outset in the case of those dreams which are not only unintelligible but confused. The construction which the biblical Joseph placed upon the dream of Pharaoh furnishes an example of this method. The seven fat kine, after which came seven lean ones that devoured the former, were a symbolic substitute for seven years of famine in the land of Egypt, which according to the prediction were to consume all the surplus that seven fruitful years had produced. Most of the artificial dreams contrived by the poets are intended for some such symbolic interpretation, for they reproduce the thought conceived by the poet in a guise not unlike the disguise which we are wont to find in our dreams.

The idea that the dream concerns itself chiefly with the future, whose form it surmises in advance—a relic of the prophetic significance with which dreams were once invested—now becomes the motive for translating into the future the meaning of the dream which has been found by means of symbolic interpretation.

A demonstration of the manner in which one arrives at such a symbolic interpretation cannot, of course, be given. Success remains a matter of ingenious conjecture, of direct intuition, and for this reason dream-interpretation has naturally been elevated into an art which seems to depend upon extraordinary gifts. The second of the two popular methods of dream-interpretation entirely abandons such claims. It might be described as the "cipher method," since it treats the dream as a kind of secret code in which every sign is translated into another sign of known meaning, according to an established key. For example, I have dreamt of a letter, and also of a funeral or the like; I consult a "dream-book," and I find that "letter" is to be translated by "vexation" and "funeral" by "engagement." It now remains to establish a connection, which I am again to assume as pertaining to the future, by means of the rigmarole which I have deciphered.

An ancient and stubbornly retained popular belief seems to have come nearer to the truth of the matter than the opinion of modem science. I must insist that the dream actually does possess a meaning, and that a scientific method of dream-interpretation is possible.

When, after passing through a narrow defile, one suddenly reaches a height beyond which the ways part and a rich prospect lies outspread in different directions, it is well to stop for a moment and consider whither one shall turn next. We are in somewhat the same position after we have mastered this first interpretation of a dream. We find ourselves standing in the light of a sudden discovery. The dream is not comparable to the irregular sounds of a musical instrument, which, instead of being played by the hand of a musician, is struck by some external force; the dream is not meaningless, not absurd, does not pre-suppose that one part of our store of ideas is dormant while another part begins to awake. It is a perfectly valid psychic phenomenon, actually a wish-fulfilment; it may be enrolled in the continuity of the intelligible psychic activities of the waking state; it is built up by a highly complicated intellectual activity. But at the very moment when we are about to rejoice in this discovery a host of problems besets us. If the dream, as this theory defines it, represents a fulfilled wish, what is the cause of the striking and unfamiliar manner in which this fulfilment is expressed?

It is easy to show that the wish-fulfilment in dreams is often undisguised and easy to recognize, so that one may wonder why the language of dreams has not long since been understood. There is, for example, a dream which I can evoke as often as I please, experimentally, as it were. If, in the evening, I eat anchovies, olives, or other strongly salted foods, I am thirsty at night, and there-fore I wake. The waking, however, is preceded by a dream, which has always the same content, namely, that I am drinking. I am drinking long draughts of water; it tastes as delicious as only a cool drink can taste when one's throat is parched; and then I wake, and find that I have an actual desire to drink. The cause of this dream is thirst, which I perceive when I wake. From this sensation arises the wish to drink, and the dream shows me this wish as fulfilled. It thereby serves a function, the nature of which I soon surmise. I sleep well, and am not accustomed to being waked by a bodily need. If I succeed in appeasing my thirst by means of the dream that I am drinking, I need not wake up in order to satisfy that thirst. It is thus a *dream of convenience*. The dream takes the place of action, as elsewhere in life.

If I now declare that wish-fulfilment is the meaning of *every* dream, so that there cannot be any dreams other than wish-dreams, I know beforehand that I shall meet with the most emphatic contradiction. Nevertheless, it is not difficult to parry these objections. It is merely necessary to observe that our doctrine is not based upon the estimates of the obvious dream-content but relates to the thought-content, which, in the course of interpretation, is found to lie behind the dream. Let us compare and contrast the *manifest* and the *latent dream-content.* It is true that here are dreams the manifest content of which is of the most painful nature. But has anyone ever tried to interpret these dreams—to discover their latent thought-content? If not, the two objections to our doctrine are no longer valid; for there is always the possibility that even our painful and terrifying dreams may, upon interpretation, prove to be wish-fulfilments.

She puts a candle into a candlestick; but the candle is broken, so that it does not stand up. The girls at school say she is clumsy; but she replies that it is not her fault.

Here, too, there is an actual occasion for the dream; the day before she had actually put a candle into a candlestick; but this one was not broken. An obvious symbolism has here been employed. The candle is an object which excites the female genitals; its being broken, so that it does not stand upright, signifies impotence on the man's part *(it is not her fault).* But does this young woman, carefully brought up, and a stranger to all obscenity, know of such an application of the candle? By chance she is able to tell how she came by this information. While paddling a canoe on the Rhine, a boat passed her which contained some students, who were singing rapturously, or rather yelling: "When the Queen of Sweden, behind closed shutters, with the candles of Apollo. . . ."

She does not hear or else understand the last word. Her husband was asked to give her the required explanation. These verses are then replaced in the dream-content by the innocent recollection of a task which she once performed *clumsily* at her boarding-school, because of the *closed shutters.* The connection between the theme of masturbation and that of impotence is clear enough. "Apollo" in the latent dream-content connects this dream with an earlier one in which the virgin Pallas figured. All this is obviously not innocent.

THE DREAM-WORK

All other previous attempts to solve the problems of dreams have concerned themselves directly with the manifest dream-content as it is retained in the memory. They have sought to obtain an interpretation of the dream from this content, or, if they dispensed with an interpretation, to base their conclusions concerning the dream on the evidence provided by this content. We, however, are confronted by a different set of data; for us a new psychic material interposes itself between the dream-content and the results of our investigations: the *latent* dream-content, or dream-thoughts, which are obtained only by our method. We develop the solution of the dream from this latent content, and not from the manifest dream-content. We are thus confronted with a new problem, an entirely novel task—that of examining and tracing the relations between the latent dream-thoughts and the manifest dream-content, and the processes by which the latter has grown out of the former.

The dream–thoughts and the dream–content present themselves as two descriptions of the same content in two different languages; or, to put it more clearly, the dream–content appears to us as a translation of the dream–thoughts into another mode of expression, whose symbols and laws of composition we must learn by comparing the origin with the translation. The dream–thoughts we can understand without further trouble the moment we have ascertained them. The dream–content is, as it were, presented in hieroglyphics, whose symbols must be translated, one by one, into the language of the dream–thoughts.

And what of the value of dreams in regard to our knowledge of the future? That, of course, is quite out of the question. One would like to substitute the words: "in regard to our knowledge of the past." For in every sense a dream has its origin in the past. The ancient belief that dreams reveal the future is not indeed entirely devoid of truth. By representing a wish as fulfilled the dream certainly leads us into the future; but this future, which the dreamer accepts as his present, has been shaped in the likeness of the past by the indestructible wish.

CHAPTER 20

Daily Life in the Age of Revolution and Empire—1750–1914 CE

The documents in this section all relate to modernization and change. Several provide descriptions of a country at a given place in time written either by a visitor or by someone writing about his homeland. The others deal directly with modernization of a society, culture or the economy. In the Hai-Lu, an uneducated Chinese visits Europe, an exotic land to him, while Olaudah Equiano and Chinua Achebe write about the recent past and change due to the influence of western culture in Africa. An Indian scholar describes the new city of Calcutta built by the British and a Japanese businessman writes about using European ideas to modernize the Japanese economic system. Finally, a Japanese reformer talks about women's role in 19th century Japan. Which of the documents seem to be most enthusiastic about modernization? Which of the authors would like to continue the process of modernization? Do some regret the changes that modernization has caused?

158

The *Hai Lu*, A Chinese Seaman's Account of Europe by Hsieh Ch'ing Kao—1783–1797

The best primary documents about medieval Asia and Africa are often traveler's accounts. Most of those available in the West were written by Europeans. Accounts of Asian travelers in Europe are relatively rare. The following document is excerpted from the travel notes of a sailor, Hsieh Ch'ing Kao, who traveled throughout Western Europe on a Chinese merchant ship. The author is unknown and was likely a local schoolboy who transcribed this account after Hsieh's return to China. Hsieh was illiterate and went blind in his old age, but his travels were deeply etched in his mind. What kind of information does he recall about each country he visited? Why is it unlikely that Hsieh visited America?

Portugal (called Ta-hsi-yang, or Pu-lu-chi-shih) ". . . has a climate colder than that of Fukien and Kwangtung. Her chief seaport [*Lisbon*] faces the south and is protected by two forts manned by 2000 soldiers and equipped with about four or five hundred cannons. Whenever any ship calls at the port, it is first examined by officials to see whether there is any case of smallpox on board. If there is not, the ship is permitted to enter; otherwise, the ship must wait outside the harbor until all traces of the disease have disappeared. Places of importance are seven in all: Lisbon, Coimbra, Guarda, Vizeu, Villa Real, A-la-chia [?], and Chaves. All these towns are densely settled, garrisoned by heavy forces, and are connected by good land and water routes.

"The people are white in color, and are fond of cleanliness. As to the dress, the men usually wear trousers and short upper clothes, both very much tight-fitting. On special occasions, another piece is worn over the shirt, short in the front and long in the back, just like the wings of a cicada. Women also wear short and tight-fitting upper clothes, but instead of trousers they wear skirts which are sometimes eight or nine folds deep. Among the poor this is made of cotton; among the rich, silk. When rich women go out they often wear a veil made of fine black silk. Both men and women wear leather shoes.

"Monogamy is the prevailing practice. It is only when either the husband or wife has died that the other may remarry. The family of the prospective

From *The Great Chinese Travelers*, ed. by Jeanette Mirsky, 1964, p. 266–271.

bridegroom takes particular pains to find out the size of the bride's dowry before marrying her. Marriages between persons of the same surname are permitted but they are prohibited between children of the same parents. All marriages must receive the sanction of the Church, and it is only after the priest has pronounced his benediction on the couple that a marriage is considered concluded. The marriage ceremonies usually take place in the church.

"Religion plays a dominant part in the lives of these people. Whenever anyone would commit a crime, he would go to the priest in the church and confess his sins and repent, after which he would be absolved by the priest. The priest is strictly forbidden to tell others what he has heard; he would be hanged if he did so. When a king ascends the throne, he does not take a new reign title, but follows the Christian calendar. There are also womenfolk who withdraw from the world and live apart in convents.

"The king of the country is called *li-rei.* His eldest son is called *li-fan-tieh [l'infante]*; his other sons, *pi-lin-hsi-pi [principes]*; his daughters, *pi-lin-so-shih [princezas]*. The Prime Minister is called *kan-tieh [conde]*; the commander-in-chief of the army, *ma-la-chi-tsa [marquesado]*. . . . These officers are usually selected from among the leading citizens of the local community. In order to assist the local officials in their administration of affairs, the home government usually sends out a military official to each region. If the possession is a large one, then three or four officials are sent. If any problem arises, a conference is held of the four local officials and the two central officials from home to decide on the solution and this solution must be in conforrhity with local customs and habits."

Spain ". . . is said to be north-northwest of Portugal and could be reached by sailing in that direction for about eight or nine days from Portugal [*one of Hsieh's mistakes in indicating direction*]. The area of this country is larger than that of Portugal; the people are fierce and wicked. Catholicism is the main religion. Its products are gold, silver, copper, iron, wine, glass, and watches, etc. The silver dollars used in China are manufactured in this country."

England ". . . is located southwest [sic] of France and could be reached by sailing north from St. Helena for about two months. It is a sparsely settled island, separated from the mainland, with a large number of rich families. The dwelling houses have more than one story. Maritime commerce is one of the chief occupations of the English, and wherever there is a region in which profits could be reaped by trading, these people strive for them, with the result that their commercial vessels are to be seen on the seven seas. Commercial traders are to be found all over the country. Male inhabitants from the ages of fifteen to sixty are conscripted into the service of the king as soldiers. Moreover, a large foreign mercenary army is also maintained. Consequently, although the country is small, it has such a large military force that foreign nations are afraid of it.

"Near the sea is Lun-lun [*London*], which is one of the largest cities in the country. In this city is a fine system of waterworks. From the river, which flows through the city, water is raised by means of revolving wheels, installed at three different places, and poured into pipes which carry it to all parts of the city. Anyone desirous of securing water would just have to lay a pipe between his house and the water mains, and water would be available. The water tax for each family is calculated on the number of persons in that family.

"Men and women all wear white ordinarily; for mourning, however, black is used. The army wears a red uniform. Women wear long dresses that sweep the floor, with the upper part tight and the lower part loose. At the waist is a tight belt with a buckle. Whenever there is a celebration of festive occasion, then some young and beautiful girls would be asked to sing and dance to the accompaniment of music. Girls of rich and noble families start to learn these arts when they are very young.

"Whenever English ships meet on the ocean a ship in dire straits, they must rescue all persons on the ill-fated ship, feed and clothe them, and then provide them with sufficient funds to take them back to their native lands. Any captains neglecting to perform such a task would be liable to punishment.

"Among the minerals produced here are gold, silver, copper, tin, and iron. Manufactured articles include tin plate, cotton and woolen goods, clocks, watches, wine, and glass."

Sweden ". . . can be reached by sailing about ten days or more from Holland and about six or seven days from England. The inhabitants of the country are more honest and simple than the English. Her trading vessels carry a blue flag with a white cross. Northwest of Sweden . . . and on the same island and connected with it by land routes is Yung-li-ma-lu-chia [*Denmark, which then included the present Norway*]. The people here have a slightly larger and stronger physique than the Swedes and their customs and habits are similar to those in Sweden. This is the country whose ships fly the yellow flag in Canton.

"*Mieh-li-kan* [*America*] is a small isolated island in the middle of the ocean. It could be reached by sailing west for about ten days from England. Formerly it was part of England but now is an independent country, although the customs and practices of the two countries still remain alike. This land is called Hua-ch'i by the Cantonese. [*Hua-ch'i, "Flowery Flag," refers to the United States flag flown from the ships.*]

"Minerals found in the country include gold, silver, copper, iron, lead, and tin. Manufactured products include tin plate, glass, snuff, wine, woolen and cotton goods. Water transportation in this country is done by means of boats which have wheels on the side and a fire engine in the center. When a strong fire is generated, the wheels are set in motion, thereby propelling the boat forward. The construction of such a boat is clever and ingenious, and other countries are following the example."

159

From *The Interesting Narrative of the Life of Olaudah Equiano*— 1789

An Ibo tribesman from modern-day Nigeria, Olaudah Equiano and his sister were taken from their village by African slave traders when he was 10 years old. Eventually sold to white slave traders, he was shipped to the West Indies, where he was given the name of Gustavus Vasa by his master. Equiano traveled with his master to Canada and Europe, eventually becoming a passionate advocate of abolition. His autobiography provides a fascinating view of both Africa and Europe. In the following excerpt, Equiano talks about his childhood as a member of the Ibo tribe. What status did women have in Ibo society?

MY EARLY LIFE IN EBOE

That part of Africa known by the name of Guinea to which the trade for slaves is carried on extends along the coast above 3,400 miles, from the Senegal to Angola, and includes a variety of kingdoms. Of these the most considerable is the kingdom of Benin, both as to extent and wealth, the richness and cultivation of the soil, the power of its king, and the number and warlike disposition of the inhabitants. . . . This kingdom is divided into many provinces or districts, in one of the most remote and fertile of which, called Eboe, I was born in the year 1745, situated in a charming fruitful vale, named Essaka. The distance of this province from the capital of Benin and the sea coast must be very considerable, for I had never heard of white men or Europeans, nor of the sea, and our subjection to the king of Benin was little more than nominal; for every transaction of the government, as far as my slender observation extended, was conducted by the chiefs or elders of the place. The manners and government of a people who have little commerce with other countries are generally very simple, and the history of what passes in one family or village may serve as a specimen of a nation. My father was one of those elders or chiefs I have spoken of and was styled Embrenché, a term as I remember importing the highest distinction, and signifying in our language a *mark* of grandeur. This mark is conferred on the person entitled to it by cutting the skin across at the top of

From *Equiano's Travels: His Autobiography*, ed. by Paul Edwards (Oxford: Heinemann International, 1967).

the forehead and drawing it down to the eyebrows, and while it is in this situation applying a warm hand and rubbing it until it shrinks up into a thick *weal* across the lower part of the forehead. Most of the judges and senators were thus marked; my father had long borne it. I had seen it conferred on one of my brothers, and I was also *destined* to receive it by my parents. Those Embrenché or chief men decided disputes and punished crimes, for which purpose they always assembled together. The proceedings were generally short, and in most cases the law of retaliation prevailed. I remember a man was brought before my father and the other judges for kidnapping a boy, and although he was the son of a chief or senator, he was condemned to make recompense by a man or woman slave. Adultery, however, was sometimes punished with slavery or death, a punishment which I believe is inflicted on it throughout most of the nations of Africa, so sacred among them is the honour of the marriage bed and so jealous are they of the fidelity of their wives. Of this I recollect an instance— a woman was convicted before the judges of adultery, and delivered over, as the custom was, to her husband, to be punished. Accordingly he determined to put her to death: but it being found just before her execution that she had an infant at her breast, and no woman being prevailed on to perform the part of a nurse, she was spared on account of the child. The men however do not preserve the same constancy to their wives which they expect from them, for they indulge in a plurality, though seldom in more than two. Their mode of marriage is thus: both parties are usually betrothed when young by their parents, (though I have known the males to betroth themselves). On this occasion a feast is prepared, and the bride and bridegroom stand up in the midst of all their friends who are assembled for the purpose, while he declares she is thenceforth to be looked upon as his wife, and that no other person is to pay any addresses to her. This is also immediately proclaimed in the vicinity, on which the bride retires from the assembly. Some time after she is brought home to her husband, and then another feast is made to which the relations of both parties are invited: her parents then deliver her to the bridegroom accompanied with a number of blessings, and at the same time they tie round her waist a cotton string of the thickness of a goose-quill, which none but married women are permitted to wear: she is now considered as completely his wife, and at this time the dowry is given to the new married pair, which generally consists of portions of land, slaves, and cattle, household goods, and implements of husbandry. These are offered by the friends of both parties, besides which the parents of the bridegroom present gifts to those of the bride, whose property she is looked upon before marriage; but after it she is esteemed the sole property of her husband. The ceremony being now ended, the festival begins, which is celebrated with bonfires and loud acclamations of joy accompanied with music and dancing.

We are almost a nation of dancers, musicians, and poets. Thus every great event such as a triumphant return from battle or other cause of public rejoicing is celebrated in public dances, which are accompanied with songs and music suited to the occasion. The assembly is separated into four divisions, which dance either apart or in succession, and each with a character peculiar to itself.

The first division contains the married men, who in their dances frequently exhibit feats of arms and the representation of a battle. To these succeed the married women, who dance in the second division. The young men occupy the third and the maidens the fourth. Each represents some interesting scene of real life, such as a great achievement, domestic employment, a pathetic story, or some rural sport, and as the subject is generally founded on some recent event it is therefore ever new. This gives our dances a spirit and variety which I have scarcely seen elsewhere. We have many musical instruments, particularly drums of different kinds, a piece of music which resembles a guitar, and another much like a stickado. These last are chiefly used by betrothed virgins who play on them on all grand festivals.

As our manners are simple, our luxuries are few. The dress of both sexes is nearly the same. It generally consists of a long piece of calico or muslin, wrapped loosely round the body somewhat in the form of a highland plaid. This is usually dyed blue, which is our favourite colour. It is extracted from a berry and is brighter and richer than any I have seen in Europe. Besides this our women of distinction wear golden ornaments, which they dispose with some profusion on their arms and legs. When our women are not employed with the men in tillage, their usual occupation is spinning and weaving cotton, which they afterwards dye and make into garments. They also manufacture earthen vessels, of which we have many kinds. Among the rest tobacco pipes, made after the same fashion and used in the same manner, as those in Turkey.

Our manner of living is entirely plain, for as yet the natives are unacquainted with those refinements in cookery which debauch the taste: bullocks, goats, and poultry, supply the greatest part of their food. These constitute likewise the principal wealth of the country and the chief articles of its commerce. The flesh is usually stewed in a pan; to make it savoury we sometimes use also pepper and other spices, and we have salt made of wood ashes. Our vegetables are mostly plantains, eadas, yams, beans, and Indian corn. The head of the family usually eats alone; his wives and slaves have also their separate tables. Before we taste food we always wash our hands: indeed our cleanliness on all occasions is extreme, but on this it is an indispensable ceremony. After washing, libation is made by pouring out a small portion of the drink on the floor, and tossing a small quantity of the food in a certain place for the spirits of departed relations, which the natives suppose to preside over their conduct and guard them from evil. They are totally unacquainted with strong or spirituous liquors, and their principal beverage is palm wine. . . .

Our land is uncommonly rich and fruitful, and produces all kinds of vegetables in great abundance. We have plenty of Indian corn, and vast quantities of cotton and tobacco. Our pineapples grow without culture; they are about the size of the largest sugar-loaf and finely flavoured. We have also spices of different kinds, particularly pepper, and a variety of delicious fruits which I have never seen in Europe, together with gums of various kinds and honey in abundance. All our industry is exerted to improve those blessings of nature. Agriculture is our chief employment, and everyone, even the children and women, are engaged in it. Thus we are all habituated to labour from our earliest years. Everyone contributes something to the common stock, and as we are unacquainted with idleness we have no beggars. . . . Deformity is indeed unknown amongst us, I mean that of shape. Numbers of the natives of Eboe now in London might be brought in support of this assertion, for in regard to complexion, ideas of beauty are wholly relative. I remember while in Africa to have seen three negro children who were tawny, and another quite white, who were universally regarded by myself and the natives in general, as far as related to their complexions, as deformed. . . .

Our tillage is exercised in a large plain or common, some hours walk from our dwellings, and all the neighbours resort thither in a body. They use no beasts of husbandry, and their only instruments are hoes, axes, shovels, and beaks, or pointed iron to dig with. Sometimes we are visited by locusts, which come in large clouds so as to darken the air and destroy our harvest. This however happens rarely, but when it does a famine is produced by it. . . . This common is often the theatre of war, and therefore when our people go out to till their land they not only go in a body but generally take their arms with them for fear of a surprise, and when they apprehend an invasion they guard the avenues to their dwellings by driving sticks into the ground, which are so sharp at one end as to pierce the foot and are generally dipped in poison. From what I can recollect of these battles, they appear to have been irruptions of one little state or district on the other to obtain prisoners or booty. Perhaps they were incited to this by those traders who brought the European goods I mentioned amongst us. Such a mode of obtaining slaves in Africa is common, and I believe more are procured this way and by kidnapping than any other. When a trader wants slaves he applies to a chief for them and tempts him with his wares. It is not extraordinary if on this occasion he yields to the temptation with as little firmness, and accepts the price of his fellow creatures liberty with as little reluctance as the enlightened merchant. Accordingly he falls on his neighbours and a desperate battle ensues. If he prevails and takes prisoners, he gratifies his avarice by selling them; but if his party be vanquished and he falls into the hands of the enemy, he is put to death: for as he has been known to foment their quarrels it is thought dangerous to let him survive, and no ransom can save him, though all other prisoners may be redeemed. We have fire-arms, bows and arrows, broad two-edged swords and javelins: we have shields also which cover a man from head to foot. All are taught the use of these weapons; even our women are warriors and march boldly out to fight along with the men. . . . Those prisoners which were not sold or redeemed we kept as slaves: but how different was their condition from that of the slaves in the West Indies! With us they do no more work than other members of the community, even their master; their food, clothing and lodging were nearly the same as theirs, (except that they were not permitted to eat with those who were freeborn), and there was scarce any other difference between them than a superior degree of importance which the head of a family possesses in our state, and that authority which, as such, he exercises over every part of his household. Some of these slaves have even slaves under them as their own property and for their own use.

As to religion, the natives believe that there is one Creator of all things and that he lives in the sun and is girded round with a belt that he may never eat or drink; but according to some he smokes a pipe, which is our own favourite luxury. They believe he governs events, especially our deaths or captivity, but as for the doctrine of eternity, I do not remember to have ever heard of it: some however believe in the transmigration of souls in a certain degree. Those spirits which are not transmigrated, such as their dear friends or relations, they believe always attend them and guard them from the bad spirits or their foes. For this reason they always before eating, as I have observed, put some small portion of the meat and pour some of their drink, on the ground for them, and they often make oblations of the blood of beasts or fowls at their graves. I was very fond of my mother and almost constantly with her. When she went to make these oblations at her mother's tomb, which was a kind of small solitary thatched house, I sometimes attended her. There she made her fibations and spent most of the night in cries and lamentadons. I have been often extremely terrified on these occasions. The loneliness of the place, the darkness of the night, and the ceremony of libation, naturally awful and gloomy, were heightened by my mother's lamentations; and these, concurring with the doleful cries of birds by which these places were frequented, gave an inexpressible terror to the scene.

160

An Indian Scholar Describes Calcutta by Nawab Muhabat Khan—ca. 1800

During the eighteenth century, the greatest of the European trading companies of the era, the British East India Company, governed India for the British Crown while making huge profits from trade with China, India, and Indonesia. Under the rule of the Company, the city of Calcutta, in the steamy mud flats of Bengal, became one of the world's great trading ports. In the following document excerpted from the History of India, *Indian scholar Nawab Muhabat Khan describes his feelings about Calcutta. Unable to do it justice in prose, he turned to poetry to provide a better picture of this*

From *The History of India, as told by its own historians*, by Sir H.M. Elliot, ed. by John Dowson, Vol. VIII (Kitab Mahal: Allahabad).

great port city. Why is the widely traveled Muhabat Khan so impressed by Calcutta? How does he feel about the British who built the city?

Calcutta is a large city, situated on the banks of the Bhágíratí. It is a large port, and the great mart of the trade of the Honourable Company and their dependents. Small vessels called *salap* (sloops?) every year trade with this port from China, Europe, and other countries, and almost at all times some are at anchor there. In these days this city is the residence of the chief English officers, and the city and its dependencies are considered their property. The buildings are built entirely of masonry, plastered with lime or mud. The land, on account of its vicinity to the sea, is very brackish and damp, and hence the houses are raised two or three stories high. The lower apartments are not fit to be inhabited. The buildings are like those of Europe, airy, spacious, and commodious. The city is very large, and all constructed of brick. Besides the English, the Bengalís, Armenians, and other inhabitants, are also opulent merchants. The water of the wells, on account of its brackish quality, is not drinkable. If any person drinks it, he is sure to suffer. In the hot and rainy seasons it becomes peculiarly bitter and saline, and consequently drinking water is procured from tanks. The sea is forty *kos* distant from the city, and the ebb and flow of the tide occur every day and every night. At full moon the bore rushes in for three days with unusual violence. It presents a curious and wonderful scene; it throws some boats on the shore, and breaks others to pieces; those which are not near the shore receive no injury from it, and therefore no boat, large or small, is left there unanchored. In the same manner, towards the end of the lunar month, the water rolls in with great violence for three days and nights. These high floods are called *homán* in the Bengalí language, and that which takes place daily is termed *jowárbháta*.

A mud fort towards the south, outside the city, constructed after the English model, is very marvellous. Its praise is beyond all expression; it is well worth seeing. The wall which encircles it appears in every direction low from the outside, just like the embankment of a tank; but looking at it from the inside it appears high. Very large and lofty buildings are erected within it, and much skill is shown in the entire construction of this fort. There are many other wonderful and excellent works in this city. As regards the beauty of the buildings and various novelties, there is no city like this in the whole of Hindústán, except Sháh-Jahánábád, which is incomparable. Its only defects are that the air is very insalubrious, the water brackish, and the soil damp, to such a degree that the floors of the houses, although made of bricks and lime, are still, from the excess of moisture, always damp, and the walls also are wet to the height of two or three cubits. For four months in the winter the climate is not so unhealthy; but for eight months during the summer and rainy seasons it is very injurious.

Calcutta is a wonderful city, in the country of Bang.
It is a specimen of both China and Farang.

Its buildings are heart–attracting and delightful.
Their heads are exalted to the height of the sky.
The decorations executed in them by skilful persons
Exhibit a variety of good colours and beautiful drawings.
From the beauty of the works of the European artists
The senses of the spectator are overpowered.
The hat-wearing Englishmen who dwell in them
All speak the truth and have good dispositions.
As are the dwellings, so are their occupants.
How can I sufficiently indite their praises?
The roads made of pounded brick are so level,
That the morning breezes sweep away all the dirt from them.
In all the lanes persons whose faces are like the moon take their walks,
So that you would say the earth was bathed in moonlight.
One is like the moon, the other like the planet Jupiter,
The third shows a beauty like that of Venus.
As a multitude of persons like the planets roam in every direction,
The streets take the resemblance of the Milky Way.
You will see, if you go to the bazár, all the excellent things of the world.
All things which are produced in any part of the inhabited world
Are found in its bazár without difficulty.
If I attempt to write in praise of the marvels of the city,
The pen will refuse its office.
But it is well known to all of every degree
That it combines the beauties of China and Farang.
The ground is as level as the face of the sky,
And the roads in it are as straight as the line of the equator.
People go out to walk on them,
And there they meet together like the planets.
Such a city as this in the country of the Bengalís
Nobody has seen or heard of in the world.

161

Modernizing Japan's Economy
by Shibusawa Eiichi—1873

The opening of Japan to the West in the mid-nineteenth century brought many opportunities for young men. Shibusawa Eiichi (1840–1931) was the son of a small businessman who initially was opposed to Western expansion into Japan. However, after visiting the Paris Universal Exposition in 1867–1868, he returned convinced that Japan should modernize its economy. After serving in the Finance Ministry, Shibusawa worked in the private sector, eventually helping to found the Tokyo Stock Exchange and the Tokyo Chamber of Commerce. In the following excerpt from his diary, Shibusawa explains why he decided to go into business on his own. Why did he decide to start his own business? How did he try to blend Western-style business with Japanese culture?

Ito had brought back a mass of materials from America relating to government rules and organization. We had these translated, and with a general picture of our goals in mind, we submitted a memorial recommending a thorough restructuring of government offices. We were told to start with our own ministry. I was given the task of drafting a plan, and in the privacy of my home, I worked for three days and three nights straight without sleeping. My recommendations were forwarded to the Council and eventually adopted. It was also at my suggestion that the American system of bookkeeping—the one still in use today—was adopted. My next assignment was to study banking regulations, but this, I had to admit, was more than I could immediately grasp.

Some time earlier I had gone with Okuma, Ito, and Yoshida Kiyonari to Osaka to inspect the Mint, and spent the trip back thinking about the country's economic future. The government could cudgel its brains and expend all its energies on reforming the currency, revising the tax system, setting up corporate forms of business, and fostering new industries, but as long as the merchants remained in their present state, I doubted that commerce and industry in Japan would ever improve or develop. I wondered whether I should leave government service and devote myself to private business, taking the lead in reviving the spirit of enterprise and developing the country's commerce. When I spoke to Okuma and Ito about this, they said they admired my foresight and ambition but felt my decision premature. My departure, they said, would greatly inconvenience the ministry.

From *Sources of Japanese History*, ed. by David John Lu (New York: McGraw-Hill, 1974), Vol. II, p. 79–80. Reprinted by permission of M.E. Sharpe.

My low opinion of merchants in Japan had been formed to a large extent by my experience at the Tsushoshi, a trading office whose affairs I had been asked to handle since the previous year. I should mention that I was by then assistant deputy vice-minister and charged with general ministerial duties. The Tsushoshi, which had been formed under government directives by influential Tokyo and Osaka merchants in 1868 [1869], was made up of money-exchange houses and firms that dealt in trade and land development. But what had been envisioned as a forerunner of a joint-stock company had turned into an enterprise that consistently lost money, mainly due to inexperience and the inability of the managers to grasp the basic principles and objectives. When I was called in to attend to the Tsushoshi's final dissolution, the merchants I met there were no better than those I remembered from the past. They bowed and scraped the moment they saw a government official, they were uneducated, devoid of initiative, and utterly uninterested in new ideas or innovation.[1] Saddened and exasperated, I had then considered retiring from government and devoting myself to the development of commerce and industry.

Thoroughly discouraged, I went to see Inoue at his home in Kaiunbashi (he was then living in a house owned by Mitsui) and told him I had decided to quit. "To put it bluntly, I see little hope that the government will change its policies. I have no real interest in working at the ministry much longer. I don't like to speak to you like this when I see you working yourself to exhaustion, but if we continue to function in this fashion, I doubt we'll ever be able to put finances in order. I've mentioned this before, but I would rather be in the business world, where I have better hopes for the future. Today, people with any education, ambition, brains, or skills all enter government service and no one goes into private business. That imbalance will prevent us from building a strong country.

The business world around 1873, the year when I resigned my post from the Ministry of Finance, was one filled with inertia. That condition is hard to imagine from the standards we hold for the business world today. There was a tradition of respecting officials and despising common people. All talented men looked to government service as the ultimate goal in their lives, and ordinary students followed their examples. There was practically no one who was interested in business. When people met, they discussed only matters relating to the affairs of the nation and of the world. There was no such thing as practical business education.

It was said that the Meiji Restoration was to bring about equality among the four classes of people. However, in practice, those who engaged in commerce and industry were regarded as plain townspeople as before, and were despised and had to remain subservient to government officials. I knew that conditions such as this would not be allowed to persist. A rigid class structure should not be tolerated. We should be able to treat each other with respect, and make no differentiation between government officials and townspeople. This

---

1 Handwritten manuscript: "Take someone like Minomura Rizaemon at Mutsui, for
  example. That man could barely read."

was essential to our national welfare, as we looked forward to strengthening the country which required wealth to back it up. We needed commerce and industry to attain the goal of becoming a rich nation. Unworthy as I was I thought of engaging in commerce and industry to help promote the prosperity of our nation. I might not have talent to become a good politician, but I was confident that I could make a contribution in the fields of commerce and industry. . . .

As to the question of development of commerce and industry, I felt that to engage in an individually managed shop would be going against the tide of the times, and it was necessary for small business firms to be incorporated into larger ones. In other words, it was necessary to incorporate them, and I decided to devote my energy in this endeavor. As to the laws governing incorporation, I thought about them while studying in France. After my return from France and before my entering into government service, I organized a chamber of commerce in Shizuoka to serve as a model for incorporation in this country. Since that time, I have consistently advocated the advantages of incorporation.

In organizing a company, the most important factor one ought to consider is to obtain the right person to oversee its operation. In the early years of Meiji, the government also encouraged incorporation of companies and organized exchange companies and development companies. The government actively participated in these companies' affairs and saw to it that their various needs were met. However, most of these companies failed because their management was poor. To state it simply, the government failed to have the right men as their managers. I had no experience in commerce and industry, but I also prided myself in the fact that I had greater potential for success in these fields than most of the nongovernmental people at that time.

I also felt that it was necessary to raise the social standing of those who engaged in commerce and industry, and by way of setting an example, I began studying and practicing the teachings of the *Analects of Confucius*. It contains teachings first given more than 2,400 years ago. Yet it supplies the ultimate in practical ethics for all of us to follow in our daily life, and has many golden rules for businessmen to follow. For example there is a saying: "Wealth and respect are what men desire, but unless there be the right way, they are not to be obtained; poverty and lowly position are what men despise, but unless there be the right way, once they are obtained they cannot be abandoned." It shows very clearly how a businessman must act in this world. Thus when I entered the business world, I engaged in commerce and industry in the way consistent with the teachings of the *Analects,* and practiced the doctrine of unity of knowledge and action [as taught by Wang Yang-ming].

From *On Japanese Women*
by Fukuzawa Yukichi—1885

The opening of Japan to the West in the nineteenth century had a powerful effect on Fukuzawa Yukichi (1835–1901). The youngest child of a poor samurai family, Fukuzawa went to school in Osaka, where he became interested in Western culture. Traveling to Europe and the United States in the 1860s, he noted the differences between the culture and education systems of the West compared with those of Japan. As a result, Fukuzawa founded a daily newspaper to educate the Japanese regarding Western culture. He continued to spread his beliefs by founding a university and by writing and speaking about his theories. As a result, he became one of the most controversial Japanese intellectuals of his day. In 1885, Fukuzawa wrote a series of essays on the status of women that were radical even by Western standards and challenged the accepted norms of Japanese gender relations. How did Fukuzawa want to change the way women were educated in Japan? Why? Why did he want Japanese women to be liberated?

Now, mixed marriages, the importing of new stocks of men and women from outside, should certainly be encouraged. This method I shall call the external aid method. Also, one must not neglect the self-aid method, too: that is, to improve the physique of the present Japanese men and women and thereby produce more perfect children. For this purpose, one can consider a number of ways. One of them is to rectify wrong customs concerning food and clothing; another is hygiene, or taking care of diseases and nourishment. Improvement in these important topics in eugenics will undoubtedly be effective.

Besides all these, there is one important topic which, in my opinion, is generally neglected by the whole of society, even by the upper and intellectual classes, which dismiss it lightly. Therefore, in this article, I propose to take this topic up exclusively without referring to the care of diseases and hygiene. The subject I am going to discuss concerns the intellectual and recreational activities of women, which I propose to encourage for the purpose of improving the physical condition of our women. The purpose of my discourse being solely on the improvement of the physical condition, when I discuss the pleasures, I shall at times be touching on the animal nature of human beings. My description may make us appear no different from beasts, and my words may seem dubious to the narrow-minded moralist. However, because the spiritual and the physical phenomena are perfectly distinct affairs, I pray earnestly that my readers will take in my argument without any undue misunderstanding.

My idea for the improvement of our race is to enliven our women's minds and encourage their physical vigor to grow with them, thus to obtain better health and physique for our posterity. In recent years in our country, there have been many discussions on women. But most of them have dwelt on the poor state of their education and their lack of good sense. Some have advocated making them read more or teaching them technical skills to improve their spiritual well-being or encouraged physical exercise for the improvement of their physical growth and the eventual stimulation of their minds, too. These are the common arguments of the advocates of the new civilization.

To me, these arguments are not sufficient to insure the true development of our women. Confucian education, the so-called *Greater Learning for Women* school of thought is simply out of the question, because the more one teaches it the more restricted women become. It is nothing but a philosophy to oppress the mind and, in the process, destroy the physical body too. I am not even satisfied with the so-called new education of civilized men. The reason is that even when women are taught to read and trained in other skills and given plenty of physical training, that education is confined to the school rooms. When they go home, they are treated as the daughters of the family, no different from the old times, and when they marry, they become traditional housewives.

All in all, men and women mold their lives out of the pains and pleasures of life. When their sufferings and pleasures are greater, their lives are that much more fulfilling. This leads to the idea that attempts to increase their sufferings and pleasures will result in heavier responsibilities. For instance, in politics and other worldly affairs, suppose there is a man whose every move influences national affairs, and another whose every utterance and action influences one village; the former person's responsibilities will be heavier than the latter's and his worries and satisfactions will be so much greater than the latter's.

The importance of responsibility being thus, let us examine the actual condition of women in Japan. They are given no responsibility at all. As in the saying "Women have no home of their own anywhere in the world," when she is born, she is brought up in the house which is her father's; when she is grown and married, she lives in a house which is her husband's; when she is old and is being cared for by her son, the house will be her son's. All the family property is her husband's property; women are only allowed to share in the benefits of that property. When the house is poor, the poverty is her husband's poverty; the wife simply follows her husband in the hardship.

It is natural that the work involving the raising and feeding of children falls to the wife, but too often it turns out that she is bringing up her husband's children and not her own. To give proof of this, during her pregnancy, if the husband prays for a male child, the wife too will pray for the same. This is nothing to be wondered at, but often because the husband wants a male child, the wife feels compelled to agree and suffers over it. In an extreme case, if a female baby comes, the husband is dissatisfied and the wife is embarrassed.

When a male child comes, the husband praises his wife and he may even give her a present as an award for her performance. Whether the child is male or female is something determined by nature, and it is, after all, foolish to wish for either sex. But leaving that folly aside, what I wish to stress is that it is a true insult to one's consort to think of awarding her for bearing a male child. Through such an abominable act, the husband regards his wife as a mere instrument for producing children.

Women of our country have no responsibility either inside or outside their homes, and their position is very low. Consequently, their sufferings and pleasures are very small in scale. It has been the custom for hundreds and even thousands of years to make them as feeble as they are, and it is not an easy matter now to lead both their minds and bodies to activity and to vigorous health. There are animated discussions on the education of women. No doubt education will be effective. When taught, women will acquire knowledge and the arts. When the body is exercised, the body will develop. But those attempts will be nothing more than attacking limited areas in a life of confinement and feebleness. . . .

Disrespect for women is a common practice among all the nations of the East, and Japan alone should not be blamed. In neighboring China and Korea, particularly among the middle and upper classes, the women are confined like prisoners within their homes and they are not allowed out. The cruelty the women suffer there is even severer than that suffered by Japanese women. . . .

I by no means intend to advise Japanese women to copy the licentious ways of our neighboring countries. But I do long for the vigor and the freedom of the women of the West. However, looseness and arbitrariness are often unavoidable diseases which go with freedom and activity. I do nor long for these diseases. In the West, women's behavior sometimes goes beyond control: they make light of men; their minds are sharp, but their thoughts may be tarnished and their personal behavior unchaste; they may neglect their own homes and flutter about society like butterflies. Such behavior is no model for Japanese women. To set women's force against men's rampancy is no more than brute force against brute force. If the scheme goes too well and women come out triumphant, the result will be no more than one brute force exchanged for another. I offer no explanation here as my readers must have already appreciated my thoughts. In short, I am not demanding much of men nor any special advantage for women. What I aim at is simply equality between the sexes.

That freedom and pleasure ought to be common possessions of both men and women is a concept that cannot be refuted. When something in limited quantity belongs to two parties, if one party takes a larger share, the other party's share will decrease. This, too, is an irrefutable fact. In Japan today, who enjoys freedom and pleasure in greatest quantities? The answer is that men enjoy them in excessive proportions. As an illustration, let us examine the general customs of our society. There is practically nothing that women are allowed to do but that men cannot do. But there are many, truly countless, things that men are allowed but women not. From the right to possess property, as discussed previously, to all sorts of trivial everyday occurrences: behavior censured as overly forward in a woman is praised as nonchalant and masculine in men; things that are ugly for women are not ugly for men. While a man may play in the gay quarters and enjoy women and wine, his mate will be wasting her youth in the deep confines of a home and even her right to remarry is nullified.

All these are proof of the inequality of sexes. I am not advocating special privileges for women; I only seek to divide the happiness evenly so that both parties can share it evenly. For instance, if men monopolize 99 percent of the right to remarry while women have only 1 percent, I suggest the men give up 49 percent and make the shares even.

The basic purpose of my argument is not to side with women to contest their rights. My purpose is the improvement of the Japanese race. And because it will be impossible to expect women today to bring forth a posterity of better physique, our first necessity is to make our women more active mentally and physically. To make them more active, they must be given more responsibilities and more enjoyments. This is the general gist of my present discourse.

Without our mind, the human body is, after all, no more than an animal's. Suppose there is one male and one female dog, and the male dog is left free to play and roam about while the female dog is chained to a dog-house. Though she is given sufficient food, she is not allowed to play with other dogs or to run on the grass or to romp about on the snow. Furthermore, when the mating season comes, she is still tied to the dog-house with the least freedom. The result is an aggravation of her nerves and weakening of her body.

Suppose this female dog, after all these trials, happens to bear a pup—what kind of pup will it be? Even to me, a person entirely ignorant about the care of dogs, it is clear that the pup will not be a very healthy one. If it is so with a dog, why should it be any different with human beings? The leaders in the forefront of our social progress, if they cannot refute this illustration of the domestic dog, should quickly endeavor to unchain the women of Japan.

163

Things Falls Apart by Chinua Achebe—1900

European imperialism brought modern Western culture to vastly different traditional African societies. Africans were torn between assimilation, rejection, and compromise vis-à-vis Western culture during the colonial period. The following document is an excerpt from a 1958 novel by Chinua Achebe called Things Falls Apart. *Achebe was born in Nigeria to devoutly Christian parents who yet taught him the values of their traditional Igbo society. Although his parents had christened him Albert, he later rejected his British name while attending the University College of Ibadan in Nigeria. Achebe is famous for his novels about the interaction between Western and African culture. Though written much later, the following excerpt provides many insights regarding the choices, changes, and conflicts that Africans faced in 1900. What impact did Christianity appear to have on Africans at this time? Why might Africans have been divided in their response to Western culture and values?*

The missionaries spent their first four or five nights in the marketplace, and went into the village in the morning to preach the gospel. They asked who the king of the village was, but the villagers told them that there was no king. "We have men of high title and the chief priests and the elders," they said.

It was not very easy getting the men of high title and the elders together after the excitement of the first day. But the missionaries persevered, and in the end they were received by the rulers of Mbanta. They asked for a plot of land to build their church.

Every clan and village had its "evil forest." In it were buried all those who died of the really evil diseases, like leprosy and smallpox. It was also the dumping ground for the potent fetishes of great medicine men when they died. An "evil forest" was, therefore, alive with sinister forces and powers of darkness. It was such a forest that the rulers of Mbanta gave to the missionaries. They did not really want them in their clan, and so they made them that offer which nobody in his right senses would accept.

"They want a piece of land to build their shrine," said Uchendu to his peers when they consulted among themselves. "We shall give them a piece of land." He paused, and there was a murmur of surprise and disagreement. "Let

From Chinua Achebe, *Things Fall Apart* (London: William Heinemann Ltd., 1959), p. 138–41, 162–63, 186–88. Copyright © 1959 by Chinua Achebe. Reprinted by permission.

us give them a portion of the Evil Forest. They boast about victory over death. Let us give them a real battlefield in which to show their victory." They laughed and agreed, and sent for the missionaries, whom they had asked to leave them for a while so that they might "whisper together." They offered them as much as the Evil Forest as they cared to take. And to their greatest amazement the missionaries thanked them and burst into song.

"They do not understand," said some of the elders. "But they will understand when they go to their plot of land tomorrow morning." And they dispersed.

The next morning the crazy men actually began to clear a part of the forest and to build their house. The inhabitants of Mbanta expected them all to be dead within four days. The first day passed and the second and third and fourth, and none of them died. Everyone was puzzled. And then it became known that the white man's fetish had unbelievable power. It was said that he wore glasses on his eyes so that he could see and talk to evil spirits. Not long after, he won his first three converts.

Although Nwoye had been attacted to the new faith from the very first day, he kept it secret. He dared not go too near the missionaries for fear of his father. But whenever they came to preach in the open marketplace or the village playground, Nwoye was there. And he was already beginning to know some of the simple stories they told.

"We have now built a church," said Mr. Kiaga, the interpreter, who was now in charge of the infant congregation. The white man had gone back to Umuofia, where he built his headquarters and from where he paid regular visits to Mr. Kiaga's congregation at Mbanta.

"We have now built a church," said Mr. Kiaga, "and we want you all to come in every seventh day to worship the true God."

On the following Sunday, Nwoye passed and repassed the little red-earth and thatch building without summoning enough courage to enter. He heard the voice of singing and although it came from a handful of men it was loud and confident. Their church stood on a circular clearing that looked like the open mouth of the Evil Forest. Was it waiting to snap its teeth together? After passing and re-passing by the church, Nwoye returned home.

It was well known among the people of Mbanta that their gods and ancestors were sometimes long-suffering and would deliberately allow a man to go on defying them. But even in such cases they set their limit at seven market weeks or twenty-eight days. Beyond that limit no man was suffered to go. And so excitement mounted in the village as the seventh week approached since the impudent missionaries built their church in the Evil Forest. The villagers were so certain about the doom that awaited these men that one or two converts thought it wise to suspend their allegiance to the new faith.

At last the day came by which all the missionaries should have died. But they were still alive, building a new red-earth and thatch house for their teacher, Mr. Kiaga. That week they won a handful more converts. And for the first time they had a woman. Her name was Nneka, the wife of Amadi, who was a prosperous farmer. She was very heavy with child.

Nneka had had four previous pregnancies and childbirths. But each time she had borne twins, and they had been immediately thrown away. Her husband and his family were already becoming highly critical of such a woman and were not unduly perturbed when they found she had fled to join the Christians. It was a good riddance. . . .

"Does the white man understand our custom about land?"

"How can he when he does not even speak our tongue? But he says that our customs are bad; and our own brothers who have taken up his religion also say that our customs are bad. How do you think we can fight when our own brothers have turned against us? The white man is very clever. He came quietly and peaceably with his religion. We were amused at his foolishness and allowed him to stay. Now he has won our brothers, and our clan can no longer act like one. He has put a knife on the things that held us together and we have fallen apart." . . .

There were many men and women in Umuofia who did not feel as strongly as Okonkwo about the new dispensation. The white man had indeed brought a lunatic religion, but he had also built a trading store and for the first time palm-oil and kernel became things of great price, and much money flowed into Umuofia. . . .

Mr. Brown [the missionary to the Ibo village] learned a good deal about the religion of the clan and he came to the conclusion that a frontal attack on it would not succeed. And so he built a school and a little hospital in Umuofia. He went from family to family begging people to send their children to his school. But at first they only sent their slaves or sometimes their lazy children. Mr. Brown begged and argued and prophesied. He said that the leaders of the land in the future would be men and women who had learned to read and write. If Umuofia failed to send her children to the school, strangers would come from other places to rule them. They could already see that happening in the Native Court, where the D.C. was surrounded by strangers who spoke his tongue. Most of these strangers came from the distant town of Umuru on the bank of the Great River where the white man first went.

In the end Mr. Brown's arguments began to have an effect. More people came to learn in his school, and he encouraged them with gifts of singlets and towels. They were not all young, these people who came to learn. Some of them were thirty years old or more. They worked on their farms in the morning and went to school in the afternoon. And it was not long before the people began to say that the white man's medicine was quick in working. Mr. Brown's school produced quick results. A few months in it were enough to make one a court messenger or even a court clerk. Those who stayed longer became teachers; and from Umuofia laborers went forth into the Lord's vineyard. New churches were established in the surrounding villages and a few schools with them. From they very beginning religion and education went hand in hand. . . .

"You all know why we are here, when we ought to be building our barns or mending our huts, when we should be putting our compounds in order. My father used to say to me: 'Whenever you see a toad jumping in broad daylight, then know that something is after its life.' When I saw you all pouring into this meeting from all the quarters of our clan so early in the morning, I knew that something was after our life." He paused for a brief moment and then began again:

"All our gods are weeping. Idemili is weeping, Ogwugwu is weeping, Agbala is weeping, and all the others. Our dead fathers are weeping because of the shameful sacrilege they are suffering and the abomination we have all seen with our eyes." He stopped again to steady his trembling voice.

"This is a great gathering. No clan can boast of greater numbers or greater valor. But are we all here? I ask you: Are all the sons of Umuofia with us here?" A deep murmur swept through the crowd.

"They are not," he said. "They have broken the clan and gone their several ways. We who are here this morning have remained true to our fathers, but our brothers have deserted us and joined a stranger to soil their fatherland. If we fight the stranger we shall hit our brothers and perhaps shed the blood of a clansman. But we must do it. Our fathers never dreamed of such a thing, they never killed their brothers. But a white man never came to them. So we must do what our fathers would never have done. Eneke the bird was asked why he was always on the wing and he replied: 'Men have learned to shoot without missing their mark and I have learned to fly without perching on a twig.' We must root out this evil. And if our brothers take the side of evil we must root them out too. And we must do it *now*. We must bale this water now that it is only ankle-deep. . . ."

At this point there was a sudden stir in the crowd and every eye was turned in one direction. There was a sharp bend in the road that led from the market-place to the white man's court, and to the stream beyond it. And so no one had seen the approach of the five court messengers until they had come round the bend, a few paces from the edge of the crowd. Okonkwo was sitting at the edge. . . .

"What do you want here?"

"The white man whose power you know too well has ordered this meeting to stop."

In a flash Okonkwo drew his machete. The messenger crouched to avoid the blow. It was useless. Okonkwo's machete descended twice and the man's head lay beside his uniformed body.

The waiting backcloth jumped into tumultuous life and the meeting was stopped. Okonkwo stood looking at the dead man. He knew that Umuofia would not go to war. He knew because they had let the other messengers escape. They had broken into tumult instead of action. He discerned fright in that tumult. He heard voices asking: "Why did he do it?"

He wiped his machete on the sand and went away.

CHAPTER 21

Arts and Culture— 1750–1914

In this section, most of the documents may be unfamiliar, with the exception of *The White Man's Burden* by Rudyard Kipling. They were chosen because of their insight into non-Western and nontraditional societies of the period, even when they were written by someone from the West. *The Dream of the Red Chamber* provides a glimpse into the lost, insular world of Chinese upper-class life during the eighteenth century. Lafcadio Hearn describes the rules controlling women's hairstyles in nineteenth-century Japan. The last two documents—the tribal song from Uganda and the Navajo chant—describe the cultural traditions of tribal societies during the nineteenth century.

Although Kipling's poem may seem out of place in this section, it provides a view from the other side, that is, the values of European colonialists as opposed to those of the non-Western world. How might Kipling have regarded the Chinese and Japanese cultures depicted in these documents? Would he have appreciated the tribal song and chant?

Most of these documents also contain information about women's roles in society. Do you see similarities between the Chinese, Japanese, and Ugandan documents? Would a modern person be happy in the Navajo world?

164

The Dream of the Red Chamber by Tsao Hsueh-Ch'in—18th century

Published near the end of the eighteenth century, The Dream of the Red Chamber *is an outstanding example of Chinese prose. Its author, Tsao Hsueh-Ch'in (1715–1763), was a member of a once affluent family that had sunk into poverty. A love story that transcends both time and culture, the book features glowing and sensual descriptions of life in an aristocratic Chinese family. The characters act in a realistic manner that reflects the author's personal experience. The following document is a brief excerpt from the novel. How moral are the characters in this story? Do they follow Confucian standards? Is the author subtly critical of Chinese society? If so, how?*

THE DREAM OF THE RED CHAMBER

IN WHICH BLACK JADE IS LOVINGLY WELCOMED BY HER GRANDMOTHER AND PAO-YU IS UNWITTINGLY UPSET BY HIS COUSIN

In the meantime, Black Jade was met by more servants from the Yungkuofu. She had heard a great deal of the wealth and luxury of her grandmother's family and was much impressed by the costumes of the maidservants who had been sent to escort her to the Capital, though they were ordinary servants of the second or third rank. Being a proud and sensitive child, she told herself that she must watch every step and weigh every word so as not to make any mistakes and be laughed at.

From the windows of her sedan chair, she took in the incomparable wealth and splendor of the Imperial City, which, needless to say, far surpassed that of Yangchow. Suddenly she saw on the north side of a street an imposing entrance, consisting of a great gate and a smaller one on either side. Two huge stone lions flanked the approach, and over the main gate there was a panel bearing the characters "ning kuo fu."[1] The center gate was closed, but one of the side doors was open, and under it there were more than a score of manservants lounging

From *Dream of the Red Chamber* by Tsao Hsueh-chin, trans. by Chi-Chen Wang (New York: Anchor Books, 1958), p. 27–47. Reprinted by permission.

1 "Ning kuo fu" means "peace to the country mansion."

about on long benches. A little further to the west, there was another entrance of similar proportions, with the inscription "yung kuo fu"[2] over the main gate. Black Jade's sedan was carried through the side door to the west. After proceeding a distance of an arrow's flight, the bearers stopped and withdrew, as four well-dressed boys of about seventeen came up and took their places. The maidservants alighted from their carriages and followed the sedan on foot until they reached another gate, covered with overhanging flowers. Here the bearers stopped again and withdrew. The maids raised the curtain of the sedan for Black Jade to descend.

Inside the flower-covered gate two verandas led to a passage hall with a large marble screen in the center. Beyond, there was a large court dominated by the main hall with carved beams and painted pillars. From the rafters of the side chambers hung cages of parrots, thrushes, and other pet birds. The maids sitting on the moon terrace of the main hall rose at the approach of Black Jade. "Lao Tai-tai[3] was just asking about Ku-niang,"[4] they said. Then raising the door curtain, they announced, "Lin Ku-niang is here."

As Black Jade entered the door, a silver-haired lady rose to meet her. Concluding that it must be her grandmother, Black Jade was about to kneel before her, but her grandmother took her in her arms and began to weep, calling her many pet names. The attendants all wept at the touching sight. When the Matriarch finally stopped crying, Black Jade kowtowed and was then introduced to her aunts, Madame Hsing and Madame Wang, and to Li Huan, the wife of the late Chia Chu. Turning to the attendants, the Matriarch said, "Ask your young mistresses to come, and tell them they need not go to school today as there is a guest from far away." Presently the three young ladies entered, escorted by their own nurses and maids. Welcome Spring was inclined to plumpness and looked affable. Quest Spring was slender, strong-willed, and independent. Compassion Spring was yet a child.

After the introductions, tea was served. Black Jade answered the endless questions asked by her grandmother and aunts. When did her mother become ill? Who were the doctors called in to attend her? What sort of medicine did they prescribe? When did the funeral take place and who was there? The Matriarch was again in tears as Black Jade told of her mother's illness and death. She said, "Of all my children, I loved your mother best. Now she has preceded me to the grave. And I did not even have a chance to take a last look at her." Again she took Black Jade in her arms and wept.

Though her delicate features were lovely, it was evident that Black Jade was not strong. The Matriarch asked her what medicine she was taking and whether a careful diagnosis had been made.

"I have been like this ever since I can remember," she answered with a wan smile. "Some of the best-known physicians examined me and prescribed all kinds

---

2 "Yung kuo fu" means "may the country mansion long endure."

3 Honorific designation for the mother of the master of the house.

4 Designation for unmarried young ladies.

of medicine and pills, but I did not get any better. I remember that when I was about three years old, a mangy old Buddhist monk came to see my parents and asked them to give me away as a sacrifice to Buddha, saying that I would always be sick unless they let him take me away. The only other remedy, he said, was to keep me from weeping and crying and that I must never be allowed to see any of my maternal relatives. No one paid any attention, of course, to such ridiculous and farfetched talk. For the present, I am taking some ginseng pills."

"We are having some pills made," the Matriarch said, "and I will order some of yours for you."

Suddenly Black Jade heard the sound of laughter in the rear courtyard and the rather loud voice of a young woman saying, "I am late in greeting the guest from the south." Who could this be, Black Jade wondered. Everyone else was quiet and demure. This loud laughter was unsuitable to the general atmosphere of dignity and reserve. As Black Jade was thinking thus to herself, a pretty young woman came in. She was tall and slender and carried herself with grace and self-assurance. She was dressed in brighter colors than the granddaughters of the Matriarch and wore an astonishing amount of jewelry; somehow it seemed to suit her well, but there was a certain hardness about her that did not escape the careful observer.

"You wouldn't know who she is, of course," the Matriarch said to Black Jade, as the latter rose to greet the new arrival, "but she has the sharpest and cleverest tongue in this family. She is what they call a 'hot pepper' in Nanking, so you can just call her that."

One of the cousins came to Black Jade's rescue and introduced "Hot Pepper" as Phoenix, the wife of Chia Lien. Phoenix took Black Jade's hands and looked at her admiringly for a long time before returning her to the Matriarch. "What a beautiful girl!" she said. "Positively the most beautiful thing I've ever seen. No wonder Lao Tai-tai is always talking about her. But how cruel of Heaven to deprive such a lovely thing of her mother." She took out a handkerchief and began to wipe her eyes.

"Are you trying to make me cry all over again?" the Matriarch said. "Moreover, your Mei-mei[5] has just come from a long journey and she is not well. We've just succeeded in quieting her. So don't you upset her again."

"Forgive me," Phoenix said, quickly assuming a smile. "I was so overwhelmed with joy and sorrow at meeting Mei-mei that I quite forgot that Lao Tai-tai mustn't grieve too much." Again she took Black Jade's hands and asked her how old she was, whether she had had a tutor, and what medicine she was taking. She enjoined her not to be homesick, to feel perfectly at home, and not hesitate to ask for anything she wanted, and to report to her if any of the maids should be negligent or disrespectful. "You must remember, Mei-mei, that you are not in a stranger's house," she concluded.

Presently Madame Hsing took Black Jade to pay her respects to Chia Sheh. At the flower-covered gate they entered a carriage, which bore them out

---

5 "Younger sister."

through the western side gate, east past the main entrance, and then entered a black-lacquered gate. It appeared to Black Jade that this compound must formerly have been a part of the garden of the Yungkuofu. It was built on a less pretentious scale than the Yungkuofu proper but it had its verandas, side chambers, flower plots, artificial rocks, and everything else that goes with a well-planned mansion. A number of maids came out to meet Black Jade and Madame Hsing as they entered the inner court. After they were seated in Madame Hsing's room, a maid was sent to inform Chia Sheh of Black Jade's presence. She said when she returned, "Lao-yeh says he is not feeling well and that, since the meeting will only renew their sorrow, he will not see the guest today. He wants Lin Ku-niang to feel at home and to regard her grandmother's house on her own."

Black Jade rose and listened deferentially while the maid delivered the message from her first uncle. Madame Hsing asked her to stay for dinner, but she declined, as etiquette required her to call on her second uncle without delay.

Madame Wang excused Black Jade from her call on Chia Cheng. "He is busy today," she said. "You will see him some other time. But there is something that I must warn you about. You will have no trouble with your sisters. You will all study and embroider together, and I am sure you will be considerate of one another and have no quarrels. But I have my misgivings about that scourge of mine. He is not home now but he will be back later, and you can see for yourself. You must not pay any attention to him. None of his sisters dare to encourage him in the least."

Black Jade had often heard her mother speak of this cousin of hers, how he was born with a piece of jade in his mouth,[6] how his grandmother doted on him and would not suffer his father to discipline him. Madame Wang must be referring to him now. "I have heard Mother speak of this elder brother," the girl said. "But what is there to fear? Naturally I shall be with my sisters, and he will be with the brothers."

"But he has not been brought up like other children," Madame Wang explained. "He lives with Lao Tai-tai and is a good deal with the girls and maids. He behaves tolerably well if left alone but, if any of the girls encourages him in the least, he becomes quite impossible and may say all sorts of wild things. That's why you must not pay any attention to him or take seriously anything he says."

On their way to dinner at the Matriarch's, they passed by Phoenix's compound. Madame Wang pointed it out to Black Jade and said, "You know now where to go if you want anything. "When they arrived in the Matriarch's room, the maids were ready to serve the dinner. There were two chairs on either side of the Matriarch, and Black Jade was ushered by Phoenix to one on the left side nearest to the Matriarch, Black Jade refused the honor, but her grandmother said, "Your aunts and sister-in-law do not dine here. Besides, you are a guest today. So take the seat." Black Jade murmured an apology and

---

6 That is, he was wealthy.

obeyed. Madame Wang sat near the table, while Phoenix and Li Huan stood by and waited upon the Matriarch. The three Springs took their places according to age: Welcome Spring sat on the right, nearest the Matriarch; Quest Spring, second on the left; Compassion Spring, second on the right. Out in the courtyard many maids stood by to carry dishes back and forth from the kitchen. After dinner, the Matriarch dismissed Madame Wang, Li Huan, and Phoenix so that she could talk more freely with her granddaughters.

Suddenly there was a sound of footsteps in the courtyard and a maid announced, "Pao-yu has returned." Instead of the slovenly and awkward boy she expected to see, Black Jade looked upon a youth of great beauty and charm. His face was as bright as the harvest moon, his complexion as fresh as flowers of a spring dawn, his hair as neat as if sculptured with a chisel, his eyebrows as black as if painted with ink. He was gracious even in anger and amiable even when he frowned. He wore a purple hat studded with precious stones and a red coat embroidered with butterflies and flowers. His jade was suspended from his neck by a multicolored silk cord.

Black Jade was startled; so familiar were his features that she felt she must have seen him somewhere before. Pao-yu, on his part, was deeply impressed by her delicate and striking features. Her beautifully curved eyebrows seemed, and yet did not seem, knitted; her eyes seemed, and yet did not seem, pleased. Their sparkle suggested tears, and her soft quick breathing indicated how delicately constituted she was. In repose she was like a fragile flower mirrored in the water; in movement she was like a graceful willow swaying in the wind. Her heart had one more aperture than Pi Kan;[7] she was noticeably more fragile than Hsi Shih.

"It seems that I have seen this Mei-mei before," Pao-yu said, with open admiration.

"Nonsense," the Matriarch said. "How could you have seen her?"

"I may not really have seen her," Pao-yu admitted. "Nevertheless, I feel as if I were meeting a friend whom I have not heard from for years."

"I am glad to hear that," the Matriarch said, "for that ought to mean that you will be good friends."

Pao-yu sat by his cousin and asked her all sorts of questions about the south. "Have you any jade?" he asked finally.

"No, I do not have any," Black Jade answered. "It is rare, and not everybody has it as you do."

Pao-yu suddenly flared up with passion. "Rare indeed!" he cried. "I think it is a most stupid thing. I shall have none of it." He took the jade from his neck and dashed it to the floor. The maids rushed forward to pick it up and as the Matriarch took Pao-yu in her arms and scolded him for venting his anger on the precious object upon which his very life depended. Pao-yu said, weeping, "None of my sisters has anything like it. I am the only one who has it. Now this Mei-mei, who is as beautiful as a fairy, doesn't have any either. What do I want this stupid thing for?"

---

7 This is another way of saying that Black Jade was supersensitive.

"Your Mei-mei did have a piece of jade," the Matriarch fabricated. "But your aunt was so reluctant to part with your Mei-mei that she took the jade from her as a memento. Your Mei-mei said she had none only because she did not want to appear boastful. As a matter of fact, her jade was even better than yours. Now put it back on before your mother hears of this." Pao-yu appeared to be satisfied with the explanation and made no protest when the Matriarch replaced the jade on his neck.

Black Jade was assigned rooms adjoining Pao-yu's in the Matriarch's apartment. As she had brought with her only her nurse and a very young maid named Snow Duck, the Matriarch gave her Purple Cuckoo, one of her own favorite maids. Besides these, Black Jade was given four matrons and four or five maids-of-all-work, the same as the other granddaughters of the Matriarch.

Pao-yu's nurse was called Li Ma; his handmaid was Pervading Fragrance, who had also been a favorite maid of the Matriarch's. She was a good and conscientious girl and faithful to any person to whom she was assigned. Thus when she was in the Matriarch's service, she took thought for no one else. Now that she was Pao-yu's handmaid, she was entirely devoted to him. Originally she was called Pearl, but Pao-yu, because her family name was Hua (flower), gave her a new name, derived from the line, "By the pervading fragrance of the flowers, one knows that the day is warm." She was given to chiding him for his perverse behavior and was often distressed because he would not listen to her advise.

165

Of Women's Hair by Lafcadio Hearn—1894

The American Lafcadio Hearn (1850–1894) went to Japan in the 1890s to study Eastern religions. He learned to speak Japanese and wrote short essays about his experiences in Japan for magazines and books. He became one of the most well-known Western interpreters of Japanese culture and even became a citizen of Japan. In the following excerpt, Hearn describes the symbolism imbedded in the hairstyles of Japanese

From "Of Women's Hair," Lafcadio Hearn, *Glimpses of Unfamiliar Japan*, Vol. II (Cambridge, Mass: The Riverside Press, 1894).

women. Why was the way women wore their hair an important part of Japanese culture? Did women have much choice about wearing the traditional hair style? Would American women have accepted this type of control?

The hair of the younger daughter of the family is very long; and it is a spectacle of no small interest to see it dressed. It is dressed once in every three days; and the operation, which costs four sen, is acknowledged to require one hour. As a matter of fact it requires nearly two. The hairdresser *(kamiyui)* first sends her maiden apprentice, who cleans the hair, washes it, perfumes it, and combs it with extraordinary combs of at least five different kinds. So thoroughly is the hair cleansed that it remains for three days, or even four, immaculate beyond our Occidental conception of things. In the morning, during the dusting time, it is carefully covered with a handkerchief or a little blue towel; and the curious Japanese wooden pillow, which supports the neck, not the head, renders it possible to sleep at ease without disarranging the marvelous structure.

After the apprentice has finished her part of the work, the hairdresser herself appears, and begins to build the coiffure. For this task she uses, besides the extraordinary variety of combs, fine loops of gilt thread or colored paper twine, dainty bits of deliciously tinted crape-silk, delicate steel springs, and curious little basket-shaped things over which the hair is moulded into the required forms before being fixed in place.

The kamiyui also brings razors with her; for the Japanese girl is shaved,—cheeks, ears, brows, chin, even nose! What is there to shave? Only that peachy floss which is the velvet of the finest human skin, but which Japanese taste removes. There is, however, another use for the razor. All maidens bear the signs of their maidenhood in the form of a little round spot, about an inch in diameter, shaven clean upon the very top of the head. This is only partially concealed by a band of hair brought back from the forehead across it, and fastened to the back hair. The girl-baby's head is totally shaved. When a few years old the little creature's hair is allowed to grow except at the top of the head, where a large tonsure is maintained. But the size of the tonsure diminishes year by year, until it shrinks after childhood to the small spot above described; and this, too, vanishes after marriage, when a still more complicated fashion of wearing the hair is adopted.

Such absolutely straight dark hair as that of most Japanese women might seem, to Occidental ideas at least, ill-suited to the highest possibilities of the art of the *coiffeuse*. But the skill of the kamiyui has made it tractable to every aesthetic whim. Ringlets, indeed, are unknown, and curling irons. But what wonderful and beautiful shapes the hair of the girl is made to assume: volutes, jets, whirls, eddying, foliations, each passing into the other blandly as a linking of brush-strokes in the writing of a Chinese master! Far beyond the skill of the Parisian *coiffeuse* is the art of the kamiyui. From the mythical era of the race, Japanese ingenuity has exhausted itself in the invention and the improvement of pretty devices for the dressing of woman's hair; and probably there have never been so many beautiful fashions of wearing it in any other country as there have been in Japan. These have changed through the centuries; sometimes becoming wondrously intricate of design, sometimes exquisitely simple,—as in that gracious custom, recorded for us in so many quaint drawings, of allowing the long black tresses to flow unconfined below the waist. But every mode of which we have any pictorial record had its own striking charm. Indian, Chinese, Malayan, Korean ideas of beauty found their way to the Land of the Gods, and were appropriated and transfigured by the finer native conceptions of comeliness. Buddhism, too, which so profoundly influenced all Japanese art and thought, may possibly have influenced fashions of wearing the hair; for its female divinities appear with the most beautiful coiffures. Notice the hair of a Kwannon or a Benten, and the tresses of the Tennin,—those angel-maidens who float in azure upon the ceilings of the great temples.

Not less than fourteen different ways of dressing the hair are practiced by the *coiffeuses* of Izumo; but doubtless in the capital, and in some of the larger cities of eastern Japan, the art is much more elaborately developed. The hairdressers (*kamiyui)* go from house to house to exercise their calling, visiting their clients upon fixed days at certain regular hours. The hair of little girls from seven to eight years old is in Matsue dressed usually after the style called O-tabako-bon, unless it be simply "banged." In the O-tabako-bon ("honorable smoking-box" style) the hair is cut to the length of about four inches all round except above the forehead, where it is clipped a little shorter; and on the summit of the head it is allowed to grow longer and is gathered up into a peculiarly shaped knot, which justifies the curious name of the coiffure. As soon as the girl becomes old enough to go to a female public day-school, her hair is dressed in the pretty, simple style called katsurashita, or perhaps in the new, ugly, semi-foreign "bundle-style" called sokuhatsu, which has become the regulation fashion in boarding-schools. For the daughters of the poor, and even for most of those of the middle classes, the public-school period is rather brief; their studies usually cease a few years before they are marriageable, and girls marry very early in Japan. The maiden's first elaborate coiffure is arranged for her when she reaches the age of fourteen or fifteen, at earliest. From twelve to fourteen her hair is dressed in the fashion called Omoyedzuki; then the style is changed to the beautiful coiffure called jorowage. There are various forms of this style, more or less complex. A couple of years later, the jorowage yields place in the turn to the shinjocho ("new-butterfly" style), or the shimada, also called takawage. The shinjocho style is common, is worn by women of various ages, and is not considered very genteel. The shimada, exquisitely elaborate, is; but the more respectable the family, the smaller the form of this coiffure; geisha and joro wear a larger and loftier variety of it, which properly answers to the name takawage, or "high coiffure." Between eighteen and twenty years of age the maiden again exchanges this style for another termed Tenjingaeshi; between twenty and twenty-four years of age she adopts the fashion called mitsuwage, or the "triple coiffure" of three loops; and a somewhat similar but still more complicated coiffure, called mitsuwakudzushi is worn by young women of from twenty-five to twenty-eight. Up to that age every change in the fashion of wearing the hair has been in the direction of elaborateness and complexity. But after twenty-eight a Japanese woman is no longer considered young, and there is only one more coiffure for her,—the mochiriwage or bobai, the simple and rather ugly style adopted by old women.

But the girl who marries wears her hair in a fashion quite different from any of the preceding. The most beautiful, the most elaborate, and the most costly of all modes is the bride's coiffure, called hanayome, a word literally signifying "flower-wife." The structure is dainty as its name, and must be seen to be artistically appreciated. Afterwards the wife wears her hair in the styles called kumesa or maruwage, another name for which is katsuyama. The kumesa style is not genteel, and is the coiffure of the poor; the maruwage or katsuyama is refined. In former times the samurai women wore their hair in two particular styles: the maiden's coiffure was ichogaeshi, and that of the married folk katahajishi. It is still possible to see in Matsue a few katahajishi coiffures.

The hair of dead women is arranged in the manner called tabanegaini, somewhat resembling the shimada extremely simplified, and without ornaments of any kind. The name tabanegami signifies hair tied into a bunch, like a sheaf of rice. This style must also be worn by women during the period of mourning.

Ghosts, nevertheless, are represented with hair loose and long, falling weirdly over the face. And no doubt because of the melancholy suggestiveness of its drooping branches, the willow is believed to be the favorite tree of ghosts. Thereunder, 'tis said, they mourn in the night, mingling their shadowy hair with the long disheveled tresses of the tree.

As the hair of the Japanese woman is her richest ornament, it is of all her possessions that which she would most suffer to lose; and in other days the man too manly to kill an erring wife deemed it vengeance enough to turn her away with all her hair shorn off. Only the greatest faith or the deepest love can prompt a woman to the voluntary sacrifice of her entire *chevelure,* though partial sacrifices, offerings of one or two long thick cuttings, may be seen suspended before many an Izunio shrine.

What faith can do in the way of such sacrifice, he best knows who has seen the great cables, woven of women's hair, that hang in the vast Hongwanji temple at Kyoto. And love is stronger than faith, though much less demonstrative. According to ancient custom a wife bereaved sacrifices a portion of her hair to be placed in the coffin of her husband, and buried with him. The quantity is not fixed: in the majority of cases it is very small, so that the appearance of the coiffure is thereby nowise affected. But she who resolves to remain forever loyal to the memory of the lost yields up all. With her own hand she cuts off her hair, and lays the whole glossy sacrifice—emblem of her youth and beauty—upon the knees of the dead.

It is never suffered to grow again.

166

"The White Man's Burden" by Rudyard Kipling—1899

Born in India to a civil servant, Rudyard Kipling (1865–1936) was one of the most renowned British authors of the late nineteenth and early twentieth centuries. Sent to boarding school in England, Kipling was lonely and unhappy there and returned to India as soon as possible. Much of his work both supported and stressed imperial themes. Kipling won the Nobel Prize for Literature in 1907 and supported Britain with a patriot's fervor during World War I, despite the loss of his only son in battle. The following poem was actually addressed to Americans after their venture into colonialism with the Spanish-American War. What did Kipling mean by the "white man's burden?" How did he feel about the native populations of the white man's colonies?

Take up the White Man's burden—
Send forth the best ye breed—
Go bind your sons to exile
To serve your captives' need;
To wait in heavy harness,
On fluttered folk and wild—
Your new-caught, sullen peoples,
Half-devil and half-child.

Take up the White Man's burden—
In patience to abide,
To veil the threat of terror
And check the show of pride;
By open speech and simple,
An hundred times made plain,
To seek another's profit,
And work another's gain.

Take up the White Man's burden—
The savage wars of peace—
Fill full the mouth of Famine
And bid the sickness cease;
And when your goal is nearest

From Rudyard Kipling, "The White Man's Burden," in *Rudyard Kipling's Verse: 1885–1918* (Garden City, NY: Doubleday, 1920).

The end for others sought,
Watch Sloth and heathen Folly
Bring all your hope to nought.

Take up the White Man's burden—
No tawdry rule of kings,
But toil of serf and sweeper—
The tale of common things.
The ports ye shall not enter,
The roads ye shall not tread,
Go make them with your living,
And mark them with your dead.

Take up the White Man's burden—
And reap his old reward:
The blame of those ye better,
The hate of those ye guard—
The cry of hosts ye humour
(Ah, slowly!) toward the light:—
"Why brought ye us from bondage,
"Our loved Egyptian night?"

Take up the White Man's burden—
Ye dare not stoop to less—
Nor call too loud on Freedom
To cloak your weariness;
By all ye cry or whisper,
By all ye leave or do,
The silent, sullen peoples
Shall weigh your Gods and you.

Take up the White Man's burden—
Have done with childish days—
The lightly proffered laurel,
The easy, ungrudged praise.
Comes now, to search your manhood
Through all the thankless years,
Cold, edged with dear-bought wisdom,
The judgment of your peers!

167

"Prayer to Thunder," a Navajo Night Chant—20th century

At the beginning of the twentieth century, there was an interest in preserving the rich literature of the Navajo. The following excerpt comes from a Navajo ceremonial chant translated and transcribed in 1902. An important part of Navajo culture is the belief that people must always live in harmony with nature. What does the chant tell you about Navajo life and religion?

FROM THE NIGHT CHANT[1]

Prayer to Thunder[2]

In Tsegíhi,[3]
In the house made of the dawn,
In the house made of the evening twilight,
In the house made of the dark cloud,
In the house made of the he-rain,   5
In the house made of the dark mist,
In the house made of the she-rain,[4]
In the house made of pollen,[5]
In the house made of grasshoppers,
Where the dark mist curtains the doorway,   10
The path to which is on the rainbow,
Where the zigzag lightning stands high on top,
Where the he-rain stands high on top,
Oh, male divinity![6]

From *The Night Chant: A Navaho Ceremony*, trans. by Washington Matthews, 1902.

1 Both selections' translated by Washington Matthews.

2 In performance each line of the prayer is first recited by the chanter, then repeated by the patient.

3 Pronounced *tsay-gee'-hee*, a distant canyon and site of the *house made of dawn* (line 2), a prehistoric ruin, regarded as the home of deities.

4 Rain without thunder. He-rain: rain with thunder.

5 Emblem of peace, of happiness, of prosperity [Translator's note].

6 Thunder, regarded as a bird.

With your moccasins of dark cloud, come to us.   15
With your leggings of dark cloud, come to us.
With your shirt of dark cloud, come to us.
With your headdress of dark cloud, come to us.
With your mind enveloped in dark cloud, come to us.
With the dark thunder above you, come to us soaring.   20
With the shapen cloud at your feet, come to us soaring.
With the far darkness made of the dark cloud
     over your head, come to us soaring.
With the far darkness made of the he-rain
     over your head, come to us soaring.
With the far darkness made of the dark mist
     over your head, come to us soaring.
With the far darkness made of the she-rain
     over your head, come to us soaring.   25
With the zigzag lightning flung out on high
     over your head, come to us soaring.
With the rainbow hanging high over your head,
     come to us soaring.
With the far darkness made of the dark cloud on
     the ends of your wings, come to us soaring.
With the far darkness made of the he-rain on
     the ends of your wings, come to us soaring.
With the far darkness made of the dark mist on
     the ends of your wings, come to us soaring.   30
With the far darkness made of the she-rain on
     the ends of your wings, come to us soaring.
With the zigzag lightning flung out on high on
     the ends of your wings, come to us soaring.
With the rainbow hanging high on the ends of
     your wings, come to us soaring.
With the near darkness made of the dark cloud, of
     the he-rain, of the dark mist, and of the
     she-rain, come to us.
With the darkness on the earth, come to us.   35
With these I wish the foam floating on the flowing
     water over the roots of the great corn.
I have made your sacrifice.
I have prepared a smoke[7] for you.
My feet restore for me.
My limbs restore for me.   40
My body restore for me.
My mind restore for me.

---

7 Printed reed filled with native tobacco, offered as a sacrifice.

My voice restore for me.
Today, take out your spell for me.
Today, take away your spell for me. 45
Away from me you have taken it.
Far off from me it is taken.
Far off you have done it.
Happily I recover.
Happily my interior becomes cool. 50
Happily my eyes regain their power.
Happily my head becomes cool.
Happily my limbs regain their power.
Happily I hear again.
Happily for me *the spell*[8] is taken off. 55
Happily may I walk.
Impervious to pain, may I walk.
Feeling light within, may I walk.
With lively feelings, may I walk.
Happily abundant dark clouds I desire. 60
Happily abundant dark mists I desire.
Happily abundant passing showers I desire.
Happily an abundance of vegetation I desire.
Happily an abundance of pollen I desire.
Happily abundant dew I desire. 65
Happily may fair white corn, to the ends of the
    earth, come with you.
Happily may fair yellow corn, to the ends of the
    earth, come with you.
Happily may fair blue corn, to the ends of the
    earth, come with you.
Happily may fair corn of all kinds, to the ends
    of the earth, come with you.
Happily may fair plants of all kinds, to the ends
    of the earth, come with you. 70
Happily may fair goods of all kinds, to the ends
    of the earth, come with you.
Happily may fair jewels of all kinds, to the ends
    of the earth, come with you.
With these before you, happily may they come
    with you.
With these behind you, happily may they come
    with you.
With these below you, happily may they come
    with you. 75

---

8 Words added by the translator.

With these above you, happily may they come
  with you.
With these all around you, happily may they
  come with you.
Thus happily you accomplish your tasks.
Happily the old men will regard you.
Happily the old women will regard you.   80
Happily the young men will regard you.
Happily the young women will regard you.
Happily the boys will regard you.
Happily the girls will regard you.
Happily the children will regard you.   85
Happily the chiefs will regard you.
Happily, as they scatter in different directions,
  they will regard you.
Happily, as they approach their homes, they will
  regard you.
Happily may their roads home be on the trail of pollen.
Happily may they all get back.   90
In beauty I walk.
With beauty before me, I walk.
With beauty behind me, I walk.
With beauty below me, I walk.
With beauty above me, I walk.   95
With beauty all around me, I walk.
It is finished in beauty,
It is finished in beauty,
It is finished in beauty,
It is finished in beauty.   100

Finishing Song

From the pond in the white valley—
The young man doubts it—
He takes up his sacrifice,
With that he now heals.
With that your kindred thank you now   5

From the pools in the green meadow[9]—
The young woman doubts it—

---

9 A contrast of landscapes, of the beginning and end of a stream. It rises in a green valley
  in the mountains and flows down to the lower plains, where it spreads into a single sheet
  of water. As the dry season approaches, it shrinks, leaving a white saline efflorescence
  called alkali. The male is associated with the sterile, unattractive alkali flat in the first
  stanza, while the female is named with the pleasant mountain meadow in the second
  stanza [adapted from Translator's note].

He takes up his sacrifice,[10]
With that he now heals.
With that your kindred thank you now.   10

---

10 The deity accepts the sacrificial offering (see n. 7, p. 498) and effects the healing that
     benefits the patient and his kindered—though young men and young women, with the
     irreverence of youth, may doubt the truth of the ceremony.

168

A Mother to Her First Born (Lango, Uganda)—Not Determined

Poetry has always been an important part of African tribal society. Freedom from colonial rule has resulted in a new wave of contemporary African poetry that celebrates its land and culture. Often the theme of these poems concerns love between either man and woman or mother and child or love for the homeland. In the following poem from Ugandan oral tradition, the love the mother has for her child is universally accessible and yet is distinctly African. Why is this mother so proud to have a male child? Why is bearing a child important to her status in tribal society?

Speak to me, child of my heart.
Speak to me with your eyes, your round, laughing eyes,
Wet and shining as Lupeyo's bull-calf.

Speak to me, little one,
5 Clutching my breast with your hand,
So strong and firm for all its littleness.
It will be the hand of a warrior, my son,
A hand that will gladden your father.

From *Heritage of African Poetry: An Anthology of Oral and Written Poetry*, ed. by Isidore Okpewho (Longman Group, UK, 1985).

See how eagerly it fastens on me:
10   It thinks already of a spear:
It quivers as at the throwing of a spear.
Oh son, you will have a warrior's name and be a leader
     of men.
And your sons, and your son's sons, will remember you long
     after you have slipped into the darkness.
But I, I shall always remember your hand clutching me so.
15   I shall recall how you lay in my arms,
And looked at me so, and so,
And how your tiny hands played with my bosom.
And when they name you great warrior, then will my eyes be
     wet with remembering.
And how shall we name you, little warrior?
20   See, let us play at naming.
It will not be a name of despisal, for you are my first-born.
Not as Nawal's son is named will you be named.
Our gods will be kinder to you than theirs.
Must we call you 'Insolence' or 'Worthless One'?
25   Shall you be named, like a child of ill fortune, after the dung of cattle?
Our gods need no cheating, my child:
They wish you no ill.
They have washed your body and clothed it with beauty.
They have set a fire in your eyes.
30   And the little, puckering ridges of your brow—
Are they not the seal of their finger-prints when they fashioned you?
They have given you beauty and strength, child of my heart,
And wisdom is already shining in your eyes,
And laughter.
35   So how shall we name you, little one?
Are you your father's father, or his brother, or yet another?
Whose spirit is it that is in you, little warrior?
Whose spear-hand tightens round my breast?
Who lives in you and quickens to life, like last year's melon seed?
40   Are you silent, then?
But your eyes are thinking, thinking, and glowing like the eyes
     of a leopard in a thicket.
Well, let be.
At the day of naming you will tell us.
O my child, now indeed I am happy.
45   Now indeed I am a wife!—
No more a bride, but a Mother-of-one.
Be splendid and magnificent, child of desire.
Be proud, as I am proud.
Be happy, as I am happy.
50   Be loved, as now I am loved.

Child, child, child, love I have had from my man.
But now, only now, have I the fullness of love.
Now, only now, am I his wife and the mother of his first-born.
His soul is safe in your keeping, my child, and it was I, I, I,
    who have made you.
55   Therefore am I loved.
Therefore am I happy.
Therefore am I a wife.
Therefore have I great honour.
You will tend his shrine when he is gone.
60   With sacrifice and oblation you will recall his name year by year.
He will live in your prayers, my child,
And there will be no more death for him, but everlasting life
    springing from your loins.
You are his shield and spear, his hope and redemption from
    the dead.
Through you he will be reborn, as the saplings in the Spring.
65   And I, I am the mother of his first-born.
Sleep, child of beauty and courage and fulfilment, sleep.
I am content.

CHAPTER 22

Religion and Philosophy — 1914–Present

The first three documents in this section were written by philosophers. They deal with the rationale for existence, gender roles, and national identity. The last three documents look at the role of the Catholic Church in modern times, offering both radical and traditional solutions to world problems. In the first document, Sartre explains his view of existentialism. Would Pascal have agreed with his argument? Does Sartre provide an adequate reason for "existence" to citizens of the twenty-first century?

Many of the documents in this reader have dealt with progress and change over time. Did Simone de Beauvoir feel that modern women have more freedom and opportunities or that they were still controlled by cultural values of the past? Octavio Paz wrote about Latin American identity. According to Paz, what is at the heart of Mexican culture and identity? How does it differ from the West? Has it been influenced by Western culture in a positive way?

In the last three documents, Gustavo Gutierrez and Oscar Romero, both Catholic priests, talk about helping the poor through social reform in Latin America, and Mother Teresa discusses her work with the helpless and poor in India. Although all of them had the same goals, each had a very different idea about what role the Church should play in modern society. Which plan do you think would be ultimately most successful? Is there a place for each in the world? Has the impact of liberation theology been positive or negative? What, if anything, do they have in common with Catholic leaders of the past?

169

From "Existentialism and Humanism" by Jean-Paul Sartre—1948

A native Parisian, Jean-Paul Sartre (1905–1980) was educated in Paris and at German universities. He taught philosophy during the 1930s at La Havre and Paris but was captured by the Nazis while serving as an Army meteorologist. Sartre was a prisoner of war in Germany before returning to his teaching position and participating in the French resistance to German occupation. Sartre considered himself an athiestic existentialist. He wrote extensively on the subject and incorporated his ideas into several novels, plays, and critical essays; Simone de Beauvoir was his long-time collaborator and companion. Sartre was considered one of the most respected postwar French intellectuals. In the following excerpt, Sartre defends his views of existentialism. How does he define existentialism? Why does he say there are two kinds of existentialists? What does he mean by "athiestic existentialism"?

What, then, is this that we call existentialism? Most of those who are making use of this word would be highly confused if required to explain its meaning. For since it has become fashionable, people cheerfully declare that this musician or that painter is "existentialist." A columnist in *Clartés* signs himself "The Existentialist," and, indeed, the word is now so loosely applied to so many things that it no longer means anything at all. . . . All the same, it can easily be defined.

The question is only complicated because there are two kinds of existentialists. There are, on the one hand, the Christians, amongst whom I shall name Jaspers and Gabriel Marcel, both professed Catholics; and on the other the existential atheists, amongst whom we must place Heidegger as well as the French existentialists and myself. What they have in common is simply the fact that they believe that *existence* comes before *essence*—or, if you will, that we must begin from the subjective. What exactly do we mean by that?

If one considers an article of manufacture—as, for example, a book or a paper-knife—one sees that it has been made by an artisan who had a conception of it; and he has paid attention, equally, to the conception of a paper-knife and to

From *Existentialism and Humanism* by Jean-Paul Sartre, trans. by Philip Mairet (London: Metheun & Co. Ltd, p. 25–42. Reprinted by permission.

the pre-existent technique of production which is a part of that conception and is, at bottom, a formula. Thus the paper-knife is at the same time an article producible in a certain manner and one which, on the other hand, serves a definite purpose, for one cannot suppose that a man would produce a paper-knife without knowing what it was for. Let us say, then, of the paper-knife that its essence—that is to say the sum of the formulae and the qualities which made its production and its definition possible—precedes its existence. The presence of such-and-such a paper-knife or book is thus determined before my eyes. Here, then, we are viewing the world from a technical standpoint, and we can say that production precedes existence.

When we think of God as the creator, we are thinking of him, most of the time, as a supernal artisan. Whatever doctrine we may be considering, whether it be a doctrine like that of Descartes, or of Leibniz himself, we always imply that the will follows, more or less, from the understanding or at least accompanies it, so that when God creates he knows precisely what he is creating. Thus, the conception of man in the mind of God is comparable to that of the paper-knife in the mind of the artisan: God makes man according to a procedure and a conception, exactly as the artisan manufactures a paper-knife, following a definition and a formula. Thus each individual man is the realisation of a certain conception which dwells in the divine understanding. In the philosophic atheism of the eighteenth century, the notion of God is suppressed, but not, for all that, the idea that essence is prior to existence; something of that idea we still find everywhere, in Diderot, in Voltaire and even in Kant. Man possesses a human nature; that "human nature," which is the conception of human being, is found in every man; which means that each man is a particular example of a universal conception, the conception of Man. In Kant, this universality goes so far that the wild man of the woods, man in the state of nature and the bourgeois are all contained in the same definition and have the same fundamental qualities. Here again, the essence of man precedes that historic existence which we confront in experience.

Atheistic existentialism, of which I am a representative, declares with greater consistency that if God does not exist there is at least one being whose existence comes before its essence, a being which exists before it can be defined by any conception of it. That being is man or, as Heidegger has it, the human reality. What do we mean by saying that existence precedes essence? We mean that man first of all exists, encounters himself, surges up in the world—and defines himself afterwards. If man as the existentialist sees him is not definable, it is because to begin with he is nothing. He will not be anything until later, and then he will be what he makes of himself. Thus, there is no human nature, because there is no God to have a conception of it. Man simply is. Not that he is simply what he conceives himself to be, but he is what he wills, and as he conceives himself after already existing—as he wills to be after that leap toward existence. Man is nothing else but that which he makes of himself. That is the first principle of existentialism. And this is what people call its "subjectivity," using the word as a reproach against us. But what do we mean to say by this, but that man is of a greater dignity than a stone or a table? For we mean to say that man primarily exists—that man is, before all else, something which propels itself towards a future and is aware that it is doing so. Man is, indeed, a project which possesses a subjective life, instead of being a kind of moss, or a fungus or a cauliflower. Before that projection of the self nothing exists; not even in the heaven of intelligence: man will only attain existence when he is what he purposes to be. Not, however, what he may wish to be. For what we usually understand by wishing or willing is a conscious decision taken—much more often than not—after we have made ourselves what we are. I may wish to join a party, to write a book or to marry—but in such a case what is usually called my will is probably a manifestation of a prior and more spontaneous decision. If, however, it is true that existence is prior to essence, man is responsible for what he is. Thus, the first effect of existentialism is that it puts every man in possession of himself as he is, and places the entire responsibility for his existence squarely upon his own shoulders. And, when we say that man is responsible for himself, we do not mean that he is responsible only for his own individuality, but that he is responsible for all men. The word "subjectivism" is to be understood in two senses, and our adversaries play upon only one of them. Subjectivism means, on the one hand, the freedom of the individual subject and, on the other, that man cannot pass beyond human subjectivity. It is the latter which is the deeper meaning of existentialism. When we say that man chooses himself, we do mean that every one of us must choose himself; but by that we also mean that in choosing for himself he chooses for all men. For in effect, of all the actions a man may take in order to create himself as he wills to be, there is not one which is not creative, at the same time, of an image of man such as he believes he ought to be. To choose between this or that is at the same time to affirm the value of that which is chosen; for we are unable ever to choose the worse. What we choose is always the better; and nothing can be better for us unless it is better for all. If, moreover, existence precedes essence and we will to exist at the same time as we fashion our image, that image is valid for all and for the entire epoch in which we find ourselves. Our responsibility is thus much greater than we had supposed, for it concerns mankind as a whole. If I am a worker, for instance, I may choose to join a Christian rather than a Communist trade union. And if, by that membership, I choose to signify that resignation is, after all, the attitude that best becomes a man, that man's kingdom is not upon this earth, I do not commit myself alone to that view. Resignation is my will for everyone, and my action is, in consequence, a commitment on behalf of all mankind. Or if, to take a more personal case, I decide to marry and to have children, even though this decision proceeds simply from my situation, from my passion or my desire, I am thereby committing not only myself, but humanity as a whole, to the practice of monogamy. I am thus responsible for myself and for all men, and I am creating a certain image of man as I would have him to be. In fashioning myself I fashion man.

   This may enable us to understand what is meant by such terms—perhaps a little grandiloquent—as anguish, abandonment and despair. As you will soon see, it is very simple. First, what do we mean by anguish? The existentialist frankly states that man is in anguish. His meaning is as follows: When a man commits himself to anything, fully realising that he is not only choosing what he will be, but is thereby at the same time a legislator deciding for the whole of mankind—in such a moment a man cannot escape from the sense of complete and profound responsibility. There are many, indeed, who show no such anxiety. But we affirm that they are merely disguising their anguish or are in flight from it. Certainly, many people think that in what they are doing they commit no one but themselves to anything: and if you ask them, "What would happen if everyone did so?" they shrug their shoulders and reply, "Everyone does not do so." But in truth, one ought always to ask oneself what would happen if everyone did as one is doing; nor can one escape from that disturbing thought except by a kind of self-deception. The man who lies in self-excuse, by saying "Everyone will not do it," must be ill at ease in his conscience, for the act of lying implies the universal value which it denies. By its very disguise his anguish reveals itself. This is the anguish that Kierkegaard called "the anguish of Abraham." You know the story: An angel commanded Abraham to sacrifice his son: and obedience was obligatory, if it really was an angel who had appeared and said, "Thou, Abraham, shalt sacrifice thy son." But anyone in such a case would wonder, first, whether it was indeed an angel and secondly, whether I am really Abraham. Where are the proofs? A certain mad woman who suffered from hallucinations said that people were telephoning to her, and giving her orders. The doctor asked, "But who is it that speaks to you?" She replied: "He says it is God." And what, indeed, could prove to her that it was God? If an angel appears to me, what is the proof that it is an angel; or, if I hear voices, who can prove that they proceed from heaven and not from hell, or from my own subconsciousness or some pathological condition? Who can prove that they are really addressed to me?

Who, then, can prove that I am the proper person to impose, by my own choice, my conception of man upon mankind? I shall never find any proof whatever; there will be no sign to convince me of it. If a voice speaks to me, it is still I myself who must decide whether the voice is or is not that of an angel. If I regard a certain course of action as good, it is only I who choose to say that it is good and not bad. There is nothing to show that I am Abraham: nevertheless I also am obliged at every instant to perform actions which are examples. Everything happens to every man as though the whole human race had its eyes fixed upon what he is doing and regulated its conduct accordingly. So every man ought to say, "Am I really a man who has the right to act in such a manner that humanity regulates itself by what I do." If a man does not say that, he is dissembling his anguish. Clearly, the anguish with which we are concerned here is not one that could lead to quietism or inaction. It is anguish pure and simple, of the kind well known to all those who have borne responsibilities. When, for instance, a military leader takes upon himself the responsibility for an attack and sends a number of men to their death, he chooses to do it and at bottom he alone chooses. No doubt he acts under a higher command, but its orders, which are more general, require interpretation by him and upon that interpretation depends the life of ten, fourteen, or twenty men. In making the decision, he cannot but feel a certain anguish. . . .

And when we speak of "abandonment"—a favourite word of Heidegger—
we only mean to say that God does not exist, and that it is necessary to draw
the consequences of his absence right to the end. The existentialist is strongly
opposed to a certain type of secular moralism which seeks to suppress God at
the least possible expense. Towards 1880, when the French professors endeav-
oured to formulate a secular morality, they said something like this:—God is a
useless and costly hypothesis, so we will do without it. However, if we are to
have morality, a society and a law-abiding world, it is essential that certain values should be taken seriously; they must have an *a priori* existence ascribed to
them. It must be considered obligatory *a priori* to be honest, not to lie, not to
beat one's wife, to bring up children and so forth; so we are going to do a little
work on this subject, which will enable us to show that these values exist all
the same, inscribed in an intelligible heaven although, of course, there is no
God. In other words—and this is, I believe, the purport of all that we in France
call radicalism—nothing will be changed if God does not exist; we shall redis-
cover the same norms of honesty, progress and humanity, and we shall have disposed of God as an out-of-date hypothesis which will die away quietly of
itself. The existentialist, on the contrary, finds it extremely embarrassing that
God does not exist, for there disappears with Him all possibility of finding values in an intelligible heaven. There can no longer be any good *a priori,* since
there is no infinite and perfect consciousness to think it. It is nowhere written
that "the good" exists, that one must be honest or must not lie, since we are
now upon the plane where there are only men. Dostoevski once wrote "If
God did not exist, everything would be permitted"; and that, for existentialism, is the starting point. Everything is indeed permitted if God does not exist,
and man is in consequence forlorn, for he cannot find anything to depend
upon either within or outside himself. He discovers forthwith that he is without excuse. For if indeed existence precedes essence, one will never be able to
explain one's action by reference to a given and specific human nature; in other
words, there is no determinism—man is free, man *is* freedom. Nor, on the
other hand, if God does not exist, are we provided with any values or com-
mands that could legitimise our behaviour. Thus we have neither behind us,
nor before us in a luminous realm of values, any means of justification or
excuse. We are left alone, without excuse. That is what I mean when I say that
man is condemned to be free. Condemned, because he did not create himself,
yet is nevertheless at liberty, and from the moment that he is thrown into this
world he is responsible for everything he does. The existentialist does not
believe in the power of passion. He will never regard a grand passion as a
destructive torrent upon which a man is swept into certain actions as by fate,
and which, therefore, is an excuse for them. He thinks that man is responsible
for his passion. Neither will an existentialist think that a man can find help
through some sign being vouchsafed upon earth for his orientation: for he
thinks that the man himself interprets the sign as he chooses. He thinks that
every man, without any support or help whatever, is condemned at every
instant to invent man. As Ponge has written in a very fine article, "Man is the
future of man." That is exactly true. Only, if one took this to mean that the

future is laid up in Heaven, that God knows what it is, it would be false, for then it would no longer even be a future. If, however, it means that, whatever man may now appear to be, there is a future to be fashioned, a virgin future that awaits him—then it is a true saying. But in the present one is forsaken.

170

From *The Second Sex* by Simone de Beauvoir—1949

The Parisian Simone de Beauvoir (1908–1949) received a Catholic education and earned a degree in philosophy from the Sorbonne. She taught philosophy in evening college until she met Jean-Paul Sartre; they became lifelong partners but rejected marriage as a bourgeois institution. de Beauvoir gave up teaching for writing in the 1930s. She produced both existential novels and academic articles and also edited the influential journal Modern Times. *In* The Second Sex, *de Beauvoir discusses the subjugation of women throughout history. The book became an important work in the new women's movement. According to de Beauvoir, how have women struggled against male domination? Do you agree with her that men and women think differently? Why or why not? Have the problems she wrote about been resolved today? Why or why not?*

I n a sense her whole existence is waiting, since she is confined in the limbo of immanence and contingence, and since her justification is always in the hands of others. She awaits the homage, the approval of men, she awaits love, she awaits the gratitude and praise of her husband or her lover. She awaits her support, which comes from man; whether she keeps the checkbook or merely gets a weekly or monthly allowance from her husband, it is necessary for him to have drawn his pay or obtained that raise if she is to be able to pay the grocer or buy a new dress. She waits for man to put in an appearance, since her economic dependence places her at his disposal; she is only one element in masculine life while man is her whole existence. The husband has his occupations outside the home, and the wife has to put up with his absence all day long; the lover—passionate as he may be—is the one who decides on their meetings and separations in accordance with his obligations. In bed, she awaits the male's desire, she awaits—sometimes anxiously—her own pleasure.

All she can do is arrive later at the rendezvous her lover has set, not be ready at the time designated by her husband; in that way she asserts the importance of her own occupations, she insists on her independence; and for the moment she becomes the essential subject to whose will the other passively submits. But these are timid attempts at revenge; however persistent she may be in keeping men waiting, she will never compensate for the interminable hours she has spent in watching and hoping, in awaiting the good pleasure of the male.

Woman is bound in a general way to contest foot by foot the rule of man, though recognizing his over-all supremacy and worshipping his idols. Hence that famous "contrariness" for which she has often been reproached. Having no independent domain, she cannot oppose positive truths and values of her own to those asserted and upheld by males; she can only deny them. Her negation is more or less thoroughgoing, according to the way respect and resentment are proportioned in her nature. But in fact she knows all the faults in the masculine system, and she has no hesitation in exposing them. . . .

It is understandable, in this perspective, that woman takes exception to masculine logic. Not only is it inapplicable to her experience, but in his hands, as she knows, masculine reasoning becomes an underhand form of force; men's undebatable pronouncements are intended to confuse her. The intention is to put her in a dilemma: either you agree or you do not. Out of respect for the whole system of accepted principles she should agree; if she refuses, she rejects the entire system. But she cannot venture to go so far; she lacks the means to reconstruct society in different form. Still, she does not accept it as it is. Halfway between revolt and slavery, she resigns herself reluctantly to masculine authority. On each occasion he has to force her to accept the consequences of her halfhearted yielding. Man pursues that chimera, a companion half slave, half free: in yielding to him, he would have her yield to the convincingness of an argument, but she knows that he has himself chosen the premises on which his rigorous deductions depend. As long as she avoids questioning them, he will easily reduce her to silence; nevertheless he will not convince her, for she senses his arbitrariness. And so, annoyed, he will accuse her of being obstinate and illogical; but she refuses to play the game because she knows the dice are loaded.

Woman does not entertain the positive belief that the truth is something *other* than men claim; she recognizes, rather, that there *is not* any fixed truth. It is not only the changing nature of life that makes her suspicious of the principle of constant identity, nor is it the magic phenomena with which she is surrounded that destroy the notion of causality. It is at the heart of the masculine world itself, it is in herself as belonging to this world that she comes upon the ambiguity of all principle, of all value, of everything that exists. She knows that masculine morality, as it concerns her, is a vast hoax. Man pompously thunders forth his code of virtue and honor; but in secret he invites her to disobey it, and he even counts on this disobedience; without it, all that splendid façade behind which he takes cover would collapse. . . .

Woman has the same faults because she is a victim of the same paternalistic oppression; she has the same cynicism because she sees man from top to toe, as a valet sees his master. But it is clear that none of woman's traits manifest an originally perverted essence or will: they reflect a situation. "There is dissimulation everywhere under a coercive regime," says Fourier. "Prohibition and contraband are inseparable in love as in trade." And men know that woman's faults indicate her situation so well that, anxious to maintain the hierarchy of sexes, they encourage in their companions the very traits that merit their contempt. No doubt the husband or lover is irritated by the faults of the particular woman he lives with, and yet when they extoll the charms of femininity in general, they believe it to be inseparable from its defects. If woman is not faithless, futile, cowardly, indolent, she loses her seductiveness. . . .

Not accepting logical principles and moral imperatives, skeptical about the laws of nature, woman lacks the sense of the universal; to her the world seems a confused conglomeration of special cases. This explains why she believes more readily in the tittle-tattle of a neighbor than in a scientific explanation. No doubt she respects the printed book, but she respectfully skims the pages of type without getting at the meaning; on the contrary, the anecdote told by some unknown in a waiting line or drawing-room at once takes on an overwhelming authority. Within her sphere all is magic; outside, all is mystery. She is unfamiliar with the criterion of plausibility; only immediate experience carries convication—her own experience, or that of others if stated emphaticaaly enough. As for her own self, she feels she is a special case because she is isolated in her home and hence does not come into active contact with other women; she is always expecting that destiny and men will make an exception in her favor. She believes in her intuitions much more firmly than in universally valid reasoning; she readily admits that they come from God or from some vague world-spirit; regarding some misfortune or accident she calmly thinks: "That will not happen to me." Regarding benefits, on the other hand, she imagines that "an exception will be made in my case": she rather expects special favors. The storekeeper will give her a discount, the policeman will let her through without a pass; she has been taught to overestimate the value of her smile, and no one has told her that all women smile. It is not that she thinks herself more extraordinary than her neighbor: she does not make the comparison. And for the same reason experience rarely shows her how wrong she is: she meets with one failure after another, but she does not sum them up in a valid conclusion.

This shows why women do not succeed in building up a solid counter-universe whence they can challenge the males; now and then they rail at men in general, they tell what happens in the bedroom or at childbirth, they exchange horoscopes and beauty secrets. But they lack the conviction necessary to build this grievance-world their resentment calls for; their attitude toward man is too ambivalent. Doubtless he is a child, a necessitous and vulnerable body, he is a simpleton, a bothersome drone, a mean tyrant, a vain egotist; but he is also the liberating hero, the divinity who bestows values. His desire is gross appetite, his embrace a degrading duty; yet his fire and virile force seem like demiurgic power. When a woman says ecstatically: "He is a man!" she evokes at once the sexual vigor and the social effectiveness of the man she admires. In both he displays the same creative superiority; she does not conceive of his being a great artist, a great man of business, a general, a leader, without being a potent lover, and thus his social successes always have a sexual attractiveness; inversely, she is quick to see genius in the man who satisfies her desires. . . .

The ambiguity of woman's feelings toward man is found again in her general attitude toward herself and the world. The domain in which she is confined is surrounded by the masculine universe, but it is haunted by obscure forces of which men are themselves the playthings; if she allies herself with these magical forces, she will come to power in her turn. Society enslaves Nature; but Nature dominates it. The Spirit flames out beyond Life: but it ceases to burn when life no longer supports it. Woman is justified by this equivocation in finding more verity in a garden than in a city, in a malady than in an idea, in a birth than in a revolution; she endeavors to reestablish that reign of the earth, of the Mother, in order to become again the essential in face of the inessential. But as she, also, is an existent having transcendence, she can give value to that domain where she is confined only by transfiguring it: she lends it a transcendent dimension. Man lives in a consistent universe that is a reality conceivable in thought. Woman is at grips with a magical reality that defies thought, and she escapes from it through thoughts without real content. Instead of taking up her existence, she contemplates in the clouds the pure Idea of her destiny; instead of acting, she sets up her own image in the realm of imagination: that is, instead of reasoning, she dreams. Hence the fact that while being "physical," she is also artificial, and while being earthy, she makes herself ethereal. Her life is passed in washing pots and pans, and it is a glittering novel; man's vassal, she thinks she is his idol; carnally humiliated, she is all for Love. Because she is condemned to know only the factual contingence of life, she makes herself priestess of the Ideal.

This ambivalence is evident in the way woman regards her body. It is a burden: worn away in service to the species, bleeding each month, proliferating passively, it is not for her a pure instrument for getting a grip on the world but an opaque physical presence; it is no certain source of pleasure and it creates lacerating pains; it contains menaces: woman feels endangered by her "insides." It is a "hysteric" body, on account of the close connection of the endocrine secretions with the nervous and sympathetic systems that control the muscles and the viscera. Her body displays reactions for which the woman denies responsibility; in sobs, vomiting, convulsions, it escapes her control, it betrays her; it is her most intimate verity, but it is a shameful verity that she keeps hidden. And yet it is also her glorious double; she is dazzled in beholding it in the mirror; it is promised happiness, work of art, living statue; she shapes it, adorns it, puts it on show. When she smiles at herself in the glass, she forgets her carnal contingence; in the embrace of love, in maternity, her image is destroyed.

But often, as she muses on herself, she is astonished to be at one and the same time that heroine and that flesh.

Nature similarly presents a double face to her, supplying the soup kettle and stimulating mystical effusions. When she became a housekeeper and a mother, woman renounced her free roaming of field and wood, she preferred the quiet cultivation of her kitchen garden, she tamed the flowers and put them in vases; yet she is still entranced with moonlight and sunset. In the terrestrial fauna and flora she sees food and ornament before all; but in them a sap circulates which is nobility and magic. Life is not merely immanence and repetition: it has also a dazzling face of light; in flowery meadows it is revealed as Beauty. Attuned to nature by the fertility of her womb, woman is also swept by its animating breeze, which is spirit. And to the extent that she remains unsatisfied and, like the young girl, feels unfulfilled and unlimited, her soul, too, will be lost to sight down roads stretching endlessly on, toward unbounded horizons. Enslaved as she is to her husband, her children, her home, it is ecstasy to find herself alone, sovereign on the hillsides; she is no longer mother, wife, housekeeper, but a human being; she contemplates the passive world, and she remembers that she is wholly a conscious being, an irreducible free individual. Before the mystery of water and the leap of summits, the male's supremacy fades away. Walking through the heather, dipping her hand in the stream, she is living not for others, but for herself. Any woman who has preserved her independence through all her servitudes will ardently love her own freedom in Nature. Others will find there only pretexts for refined raptures; and they will hesitate at twilight between the danger of catching cold and an ecstasy of the soul.

171

The Labyrinth of Solitude by Octavio Paz—1961

Octavio Paz (1914–1998) was a Latin American poet whose work was known inter-nationally as well as in Latin America. He was born in Mexico City, Mexico. Although his grandfather was a novelist, his father worked for Emiliano Zapata, the Mexican rev-olutionary. When Zapata was assassinated, the family briefly moved to the United States. Although Paz attended the National University in Mexico, he left school; his ambition was to be a poet. He fought on the Republican side during the Spanish Civil War, but he became disillusioned with Communism by the beginning of the Cold War. Paz also worked as a journalist and later became a Mexican diplomat. Late in life, he taught Spanish studies at many American universities. In the following document, he tries to determine the essence of the Mexican character and show how it differs from that of North America and Europe. Why, according to Paz, do Mexicans have a sense of iso-lation? What seems to define their society?

I. LABYRINTH OF SOLITUDE

The minority of Mexicans who are aware of their own selves do not make up a closed or unchanging class. They are the only active group, in comparison with the Indian-Spanish inertia of the rest, and every day they are shaping the country more and more into their own image. And they are also increasing. They are conquering Mexico. We can all reach the point of knowing ourselves to be Mexicans. It is enough, for example, simply to cross the border: almost at once we begin to ask ourselves, at least vaguely, the same questions that Samuel Ramos asked in his *Profile of Man and Culture in Mexico.* I should confess that many of the reflections in this essay occurred to me outside of Mexico, during a two-year stay in the United States. I remember that whenever I attempted to examine North American life, anxious to discover its meaning, I encountered my own question-ing image. That image, seen against the glittering background of the United States, was the first and perhaps the profoundest answer which that country gave to my questions. Therefore, in attempting to explain to myself some of the traits of the present-day Mexican, I will begin with a group for whom the fact that they are Mexicans is a truly vital problem, a problem of life or death.

When I arrived in the United States I lived for a while in Los Angeles, a city inhabited by over a million persons of Mexican origin. At first sight, the visitor is surprised not only by the purity of the sky and the ugliness of the dispersed and ostentatious buildings, but also by the city's vaguely Mexican atmosphere, which cannot be captured in words or concepts. This Mexicanism—delight in decorations, carelessness and pomp, negligence, passion and reserve—floats in the air. I say "floats" because it never mixes or unites with the other world, the North American world based on precision and efficiency. It floats, without offering any opposition; it hovers, blown here and there by the wind, sometimes breaking up like a cloud, sometimes standing erect like a rising skyrocket. It creeps, it wrinkles, it expands and contracts; it sleeps or dreams; it is ragged but beautiful. It floats, never quite existing, never quite vanishing.

Something of the same sort characterizes the Mexicans you see in the streets. They have lived in the city for many years, wearing the same clothes and speaking the same language as the other inhabitants, and they feel ashamed of their origin; yet no one would mistake them for authentic North Americans. I refuse to believe that physical features are as important as is commonly thought. What distinguishes them, I think, is their furtive, restless air: they act like persons who are wearing disguises, who are afraid of a stranger's look because it could strip them and leave them stark naked. When you talk with them, you observe that their sensibilities are like a pendulum, but a pendulum that has lost its reason and swings violently and erratically back and forth. This spiritual condition, or lack of a spirit, has given birth to a type known as the *pachuco*. The *pachucos* are youths, for the most part of Mexican origin, who form gangs in Southern cities; they can be identified by their language and behavior as well as by the clothing they affect. They are instinctive rebels, and North American racism has vented its wrath on them more than once. But the *pachucos* do not attempt to vindicate their race or the nationality of their forebears. Their attitude reveals an obstinate, almost fanatical will-to-be, but this will affirms nothing specific except their determination—it is an ambiguous one, as we will see—not to be like those around them. The *pachuco* does not want to become a Mexican again; at the same time he does not want to blend into the life of North America. His whole being is sheer negative impulse, a tangle of contradictions, an enigma. Even his very name is enigmatic: *pachuco*, a word of uncertain derivation, saying nothing and saying everything. It is a strange word with no definite meaning; or, to be more exact, it is charged like all popular creations with a diversity of meanings. Whether we like it or not, these persons are Mexicans, are one of the extremes at which the Mexican can arrive.

Since the *pachuco* cannot adapt himself to a civilization which, for its part, rejects him, he finds no answer to the hostility surrounding him except this angry affirmation of his personality. Other groups react differently. The Negroes, for example, oppressed by racial intolerance, try to "pass" as whites and thus enter society. They want to be like other people. The Mexicans have suffered a less violent rejection, but instead of attempting a problematical adjustment to society, the *pachuco* actually flaunts his differences. The purpose of his grotesque dandyism and anarchic behavior is not so much to point out the injustice and incapacity of a society that has failed to assimilate him as it is to demonstrate his personal will to remain different.

It is not important to examine the causes of this conflict, and even less so to ask whether or not it has a solution. There are minorities in many parts of the world who do not enjoy the same opportunities as the rest of the population. The important thing is this stubborn desire to be different, this anguished tension with which the lone Mexican—an orphan lacking both protectors and positive values—displays his differences. The *pachuco* has lost his whole inheritance: language, religion, customs, beliefs. He is left with only a body and a soul with which to confront the elements, defenseless against the stares of everyone. His disguise is a protection, but it also differentiates and isolates him: it both hides him and points him out.

II. THE OTHER MEXICO

These pages are both a postscript to a book I wrote some twenty years ago and, equally, a preface to another, unwritten book. I have alluded in two of my works, *The Labyrinth of Solitude and Corriente alterna [Alternating Current],* to that unwritten book: the theme of Mexico leads to a reflection upon the fate of Latin America. Mexico is a fragment, a part, of a vaster history. I know that that reflection should be a recovery of our true history, from the time of Spanish domination and the failure of our revolution of independence—a failure that corresponds to those of Spain in the nineteenth and twentieth centuries—to our own day. I also know that the book should deal with the problem of development, taking it as its central theme. . . .

. . . the models of development that the West and East offer us today are compendiums of horrors. Can we devise more humane models that correspond to what we are? As people on the fringes, inhabitants of the suburbs of history, we Latin Americans are uninvited guests who have sneaked in through the West's back door, intruders who have arrived at the feast of modernity as the lights are about to be put out. We arrive late everywhere, we were born when it was already late in history, we have no past or, if we have one, we spit on its remains, our peoples lay down and slept for a century, and while asleep they were robbed and now they go about in rags, we have not been able to save even what the Spaniards left us when they departed, we have stabbed one another . . . Despite all this, and despite the fact that our countries are inimical to thought, poets and prose writers and painters who equal the best in the other parts of the world have sprung up here and there, separately but without interruption. Will we now, at last, be capable of thinking for ourselves? Can we plan a society that is not based on the domination of others and that will not end up like the chilling police paradises of the East or with the explosions of disgust and hatred that disrupt the banquet of the West?

172

A Theology of Liberation by Gustavo Gutierrez—1973

In Latin America, the majority of people are peasants with little power and often little hope. In recent years, the Catholic clergy has begun to side with poor workers in increasing numbers. A Peruvian Jesuit, Gustavo Gutierrez (1928–) is considered to be the father of liberation theology. Much of his writing is based on Marxist thought and has contributed to the anticapitalist and anti-American sentiments of many Central and South Americans. In the following excerpt, Gutierrez discusses the problems facing the Church in Latin America today. What does he say are the options of the Latin American Church? What does he mean by the "theory of dependence"? What is his vision for Latin America?

THE OPTION BEFORE THE LATIN AMERICAN CHURCH

We have seen that one of the most fruitful functions of theology—and one in which we are particularly interested in this work—is critical reflection, the fruit of a confrontation between the Word accepted in faith and historical praxis.

Historical developments can help us to discover unsuspected facets of revelation as well as to understand the nature of the Church in greater depth, express it better, and adjust it more successfully to our times. For this reason the commitment of Christians in history constitutes a true *locus theologicus*.

In this connection it is useful to recall, at least in broad outline, the new awareness of the reality of the continent which Latin Americans have acquired as well as the way in which they understand their own liberation. We will also look at the options which important sectors of the Church are making here in the only predominantly Christian continent among those inhabited by oppressed peoples. The Latin American Church indeed faces peculiar and acute problems related to the process of liberation.

From *A Theology of Liberation* by Gustavo Gutierrez, trans. and ed. by Sister Caridad Inda and John Eagleson, 1988. Reprinted by permission of Orbis Books, Maryknoll, NY.

THE PROCESS OF LIBERATION
IN LATIN AMERICA

Dependence and *liberation* are correlative terms. An analysis of the situation of dependence leads one to attempt to escape from it. But at the same time participation in the process of liberation allows one to acquire a more concrete living awareness of this situation of domination, to perceive its intensity, and to want to understand better its mechanisms. This participation likewise highlights the profound aspirations which play a part in the struggle for a more just society.

An Awareness of the Latin American Reality

After a long period of real ignorance of its own reality (except for a brief period of optimism induced by vested interests) Latin America is now progressing from a partial and anecdotal understanding of its situation to a more complete and structural one.

The most important change in the understanding of the Latin American reality lies, first, in going beyond a simple, tearful description with an attendant accumulation of data and statistics, and, second, in having no false hopes regarding the possibility of advancing smoothly and by preestablished steps towards a more developed society. The new approach consists in paying special attention to the root causes of the situation and considering them from a historical perspective. This is the point of view which Latin Americans are beginning to adopt in the face of the challenge of an ever more difficult and contradictory situation.

The Decade of Developmentalism

Latin America in the '50s was characterized by great optimism regarding the possibility of achieving self-sustained economic development. To do this it was necessary to end the stage of *foreign-oriented growth* (exportation of primary products and importation of manufactured products), which made the Latin American countries dependent exclusively upon foreign trade. The more developed countries in the area had already begun to do this. There would then begin an *inward development*. By means of the substitution of imports, expansion of the internal market, and full industrialization, this would lead to an independent society. Fernando Henrique Cardoso and Enzo Faletto wrote that "it could not be denied that at the beginning of the decade of the '50s some of the necessary preconditions were present for this new stage in the Latin American economy, at least in countries such as Argentina, Mexico, Chile, Colombia and Brazil. This approach was based on a favorable set of historical circumstances and was theoretically formulated in serious economic studies. In the political sphere, it was adopted by the populist movements which at different times and with varying influence arose in Latin America.

The developmentalist policies current at that time were supported by international organizations. From their point of view underdeveloped countries thus were considered backward, having reached a lower level than the developed countries. They were obligated, therefore, to repeat more or less faithfully the historical experience of the developed countries in their journey towards modern society. For those located in the heart of the Empire, this modern society was characterized by high mass consumption.

Developmentalist policies did not yield the expected results. One of their proponents acknowledged that "after more than half of the decade of the '60s has passed, the *gap* between the two worlds is growing bigger, rather than slowly decreasing as was expected.... While from 1960 to 1970 the developed nations will have increased their wealth by 50 percent, the developing countries, two-thirds of the world's population, will continue to struggle in poverty and frustration." The developmentalist approach has proven to be unsound and incapable of interpreting the economic, social, and political evolution of the Latin American continent.

The Theory of Dependence

For some time now, another point of view has been gaining ground in Latin America. It has become ever clearer that underdevelopment is the end result of a process. Therefore, it must be studied from a historical perspective, that is, in relationship to the development and expansion of the great capitalist countries. The underdevelopment of the poor countries, as an overall social fact, appears in its true light: as the historical byproduct of the development of other countries. The dynamics of the capitalist economy lead to the establishment of a center and a periphery, simultaneously generating progress and growing wealth for the few and social imbalances, political tensions, and poverty for the many.

The imbalance between developed and underdeveloped countries—caused by the relationships of dependence—becomes more acute if the cultural point of view is taken into consideration. The poor, dominated nations keep falling behind; the gap continues to grow. The underdeveloped countries, in relative terms, are always farther away from the cultural level of the center countries; for some it is difficult ever to recover the lost ground. Should things continue as they are, we will soon be able to speak of two human groups, two kinds of people: "Not only sociologists, economists, and political theorists, but also psychologists and biologists have pointed with alarm to the fact that the incessant widening of the distance between the developed and the underdeveloped countries is producing a marked separation of two human groups; this implies the appearance, in a short time, of a true anthropological differentiation.... At each level of progress and each stage of development, the industrialized countries advance and accumulate strength which allows them to reach new collective goals of a number and degree much higher than those attainable by the underdeveloped countries."

The Liberation Movement

To characterize Latin America as a dominated and oppressed continent naturally leads one to speak of liberation and above all to participate in the process. Indeed, *liberation* is a term which expresses a new posture of Latin Americans.

The failure of reformist efforts has strengthened this attitude. Among more alert groups today, what we have called a new awareness of Latin American reality is making headway. They believe that there can be authentic development for Latin America only if there is liberation from the domination exercised by the great capitalist countries, and especially by the most powerful, the United States of America. This liberation also implies a confrontation with these groups' natural allies, their compatriots who control the national power structure. It is becoming more evident that the Latin American peoples will not emerge from their present status except by means of a profound transformation, a *social revolution,* which will radically and qualitatively change the conditions in which they now live. The oppressed sectors within each country are becoming aware—slowly, it is true—of their class interests and of the painful road which must be followed to accomplish the breakup of the status quo. Even more slowly they are becoming aware of all that the building of a new society implies.

There is also present in this process of liberation, explicitly or implicitly, a further ramification which it is well to keep in mind. The liberation of our continent means more than overcoming economic, social, and political dependence. It means, in a deeper sense, to see the becoming of mankind as a process of the emancipation of man in history. It is to see man in search of a qualitatively different society in which he will be free from all servitude, in which he will be the artisan of his own destiny. It is to seek the building up of *a new man.* Ernesto Che Guevara wrote, "We revolutionaries often lack the knowledge and the intellectual audacity to face the task of the development of a new human being by methods different from the conventional ones, and the conventional methods suffer from the influence of the society that created them."

This vision is what in the last instance sustains the liberation efforts of Latin Americans. But in order for this liberation to be authentic and complete, it has to be undertaken by the oppressed people themselves and so must stem from the values proper to these people. Only in this context can a true cultural revolution come about.

173

Liberation Theology by Archbishop Oscar Romero—1979

Born in Ciudad Barrios, a town in the mountainous east of El Salvador, Oscar Romero (1917–1980) was the second of seven children. At age 13, he declared that he had a vocation to the priesthood. Romero had a relatively conservative career as a priest, but that changed when he became archbishop of San Salvador in February 1977. He began to speak out for the poor and oppressed of San Salvador, and he worked with them for social justice. He spoke and wrote passionately against injustice and about the need for reform. In March 1980, he preached a sermon against repression of the people by Salvadoran soldiers; the next day, he was murdered while saying mass. Conservatives in the government were determined to repress the revolution against their policies that was supported by Romero. The following document is an excerpt from a speech he made in the United States in 1979. What kind of reforms did Romero hope to achieve for El Salvador? Did he feel that violence in the cause of social justice was appropriate? Do you see any elements of Marxism in this speech?

VIOLENCE

Violence is the outstanding characteristic of my poor country at the present time. Full of anguish, I must agree with the final document of Puebla:† the "muted cry" of persons pleading for liberation that never came is now "loud and clear, and increasing in volume and intensity." It comes from blood-stained and tragic experiences.

At the base of all violence is social injustice, accurately called "structural violence," which is our greatest social evil now. As Puebla says, this is "the most devastating and humiliating kind of scourge," a "situation of inhuman poverty" finding expression in "infant mortality, lack of adequate housing, health problems, starvation salaries, unemployment and underemployment, malnutrition, job certainty, compulsory mass migrations, etc."

Together with this structural violence, we have suffered "repressive violence" from the state, which, justifying itself with the ideology of "national security," considers "subversive" any attempt at liberation of the people. It pretends to justify

---

From Archbishop Oscar Romero, *Voice of the Voiceless: The Four Pastoral Letters and Other Statements*, trans. by Michael J. Walsh, 1985, p. 169–170, 172–173. Reprinted by permission of Orbis Books, Maryknoll, NY.

† Romero refers throughout these passages to conferences of the Latin American bishops, including one held at Medellín, Colombia, in 1968, and another held at Puebla, Mexico, in 1979.

murder, disappearances, arbitrary imprisonment, acts of terrorism, kidnappings, and acts of torture," all of which show "a complete lack of respect for the dignity of the human person." From January to June of this year alone there have been 406 assassinations and 307 political arrests, all due to this violence.

From these two kinds of violence, oppression and repression, pour forth what Medellín calls "the explosive revolutions of despair," which have claimed at least 95 victims among us in this same period. Side by side with this tragic play of violence, and as the cause of it, there is a scandalous moral deterioration. As Puebla puts it: "Latin American countries are experiencing the heavy burden of economic and institutional crises, and clear symptoms of corruption and violence." Pastoral concern must point out here, painfully, a horrible inventory of infidelities to and betrayals of Christian and moral values, as much in public administration as in personal affairs. Everywhere we see what the Lord called "the mystery of iniquity."

Something new came to light in El Salvador on October 15. A coup d'état planned and carried out by young officers of the armed forces, overthrew, without bloodshed, the regime of General Carlos Humberto Romero. But it has not checked the "spiral of violence." The unexpected change brought about by the military was declared a "rupture with the past." A pledge was given to clean up corruption and to change in depth the structures that nourish violence. With this purpose in mind, honest and competent citizens have joined the new government as a guarantee of good and innovating intentions. Never before in the history of our country have we had a government making such promises as the present one.

Unfortunately, despite the hopes of liberation that our church has supported with prudent criticism, repressive actions of security forces have continued to erupt, and leftist groups multiply their violent activities. For the latter the military insurrection is not a real change, but simply a new face for the same repression. Change, they say, will come only through a process of popular insurrection. They are engaged in a so-called prolonged popular rebellion whose final objective is the seizure of power.

On the other hand, the "extreme right," the privileged minority, constitutes the main obstacle to the necessary socio-economic reforms. This minority is highly reactionary when its selfish interests are at stake. Therefore it maintains the oppression, the structural violence; instead of helping a government that proposes the necessary changes, the right continues to press for a government of repressive violence.

This coup d'état and the platform of the new government bring a breath of hope to the people. In the midst of the crisis there are many positive aspects that allow us to perceive, with a solid basis in reality, that Salvadorans are capable of finding peace, a peace based on justice and attained through the price of our people's liberation. Our people have those great human and Christian values that the church esteems and feels duty-bound to strengthen and to pursue in offering guidance in the spirit of the gospel and the light of faith. Outstanding among these values are the spirit of service, the experience of love, the spirit of solidarity, of responsibility, industry, courage. One of the most basic is the sense of community with which Salvadorans are capable of overcoming selfishness and sterile divisiveness.

PROPHETIC DENUNCIATION

We have done nothing but comply with the fiery words of Pope John Paul II:

> It is necessary that injustice be given its correct designation: the exploitation of some human beings by others, the exploitation of a people by the state, by institutions, by the structures of economic systems, or of regimes that sometimes operate callously. It is necessary to give the correct name to every social injustice, to every act of discrimination or violence inflicted on human beings, whether on persons themselves, or their spirit, or their consciences, or their convictions.

The evangelical stress of this denunciation is not inspired by hate or by revenge but by the love of the Lord who "does not want the death of sinners but their conversion and life."

THE UNMASKING OF IDOLATRY

It is part of our prophetic function to invoke the greatness of the only Lord to overthrow absolutisms that offend God and destroy human dignity. I have pointed out three principal idolatries:

1. The idolatry of wealth and private property, which inclines persons toward the ideal of "having more" and lessens their interest in "being more." It is this absolutism that supports the structural violence and oppression of our people.

2. The idolatry of power, which under the new label of "national security" has often contributed to strengthening "the totalitarian or authoritarian character of governments based on the use of force, leading to the abuse of power and the violation of human rights."

3. The idolatry of political organizations, which certain popular political groups fall into when they no longer seek the interest of the people who originally inspired them, but rather subordinate the people to the interest of ideologies and organizations. During the last few weeks, this absolutism of radical leftist groups has caused great violence in El Salvador. They want to hinder the stabilization of the new government at any cost, so that their own strategy of popular insurrection may prevail. They refuse any type of dialogue and their only language is violence, which in turn provokes new repressive violence. Many are the dead and wounded, and great is the damage caused by this new game of provocation and repression.

The church feels that it is a part of its evangelical mission to unmask these destructive absolutisms and guide humankind to the one and only Absolute and to human fellowship.

The Nobel Peace Prize Address
by Mother Teresa—1979

Although born in Yugoslavia, Mother Teresa (1910–1997) spent most of her long life in the slums of Calcutta, India. Young Agnes Gonxha Bojxhiu knew at an early age that she would become a nun. When she joined the Irish Loretto order, she chose the name Teresa after the sixteenth-century mystic Teresa of Avila. Sent to India in 1931, she taught at St. Mary's High School in Calcutta until 1948, but she was so moved by the condition of the poor that she gained permission to work amongst the poorest of the poor in the Calcutta slums. Without funds, she started an open-air school for poor children. She soon gained both volunteer helpers and funding for her mission. In 1950, she received permission from the Church to start her own order, The Missionaries of Charity. Their primary task was to love and care for the unwanted. The Society of Missionaries is now an international order with both active and contemplative branches of nuns, brothers, and priests who care for the homeless poor. In addition, there are more than a million workers worldwide who support the work of the Missionaries of Charity. Mother Teresa's work has been honored throughout the world with awards such as the Nobel Peace Prize. What does Mother Teresa feel are some of the problems with family life today? Why is she opposed to abortion? What seems to bring her the greatest joy?

As we have gathered here together to thank God for the Nobel Peace Prize I think it will be beautiful that we pray the prayer of St. Francis of Assisi which always surprises me very much—we pray this prayer every day after Holy Communion, because it is very fitting for each one of us, and I always wonder that so many hundreds of years ago as St. Francis of Assisi composed this prayer that they had the same difficulties that we have today, as we recite this prayer that fits very nicely for us also. I think some of you already have got it—so we will pray together. . . .

Let us thank God for the opportunity that we all have together today, for this gift of peace that reminds us that we have been created to live that peace, and Jesus became man to bring that good news to the poor. He being God became man in all things like us except sin, and he proclaimed very clearly that he had come to give the good news. The news was peace to all of good will and this is something that we all want—the peace of heart—and God loved

---

the world so much that he gave his son—it was a giving—it is as much as if to say it hurt God to give, because he loved the world so much that he gave his son, and he gave him to Virgin Mary, and what did she do with him?

As soon as he came in her life—immediately she went in haste to give that good news, and as she came into the house of her cousin, the child—the unborn child—the child in the womb of Elizabeth, lit with joy. He, that little unborn child, was the first messenger of peace. He recognized the Prince of Peace, he recognized that Christ has come to bring the good news for you and for me. And as if that was not enough—it was not enough to become a man—he died on the cross to show that greater love, and he died for you and for me and for that leper and for that man dying of hunger and that naked person lying in the street not only of Calcutta, but of Africa, and New York, and London, and Oslo—and insisted that we love one another as he loves each one of us. And we read that in the Gospel very clearly—love as I have loved you—as I love you—as the Father has loved me, I love you—and the harder the Father loved him, he gave him to us, and how much we love one another, we, too, must give to each other until it hurts. It is not enough for us to say: I love God, but I do not love my neighbor. St. John says you are a liar if you say you love God and you don't love your neighbor. How can you love God whom you do not see, if you do not love your neighbor whom you see, whom you touch, with whom you live. And so this is very important for us to realize that love, to be true, has to hurt. It hurt Jesus to love us, it hurt him. And to make sure we remember his great love he made himself bread of life to satisfy our hunger for his love. Our hunger for God, because we have been created for that love. We have been created in his image. We have been created to love and be loved, and then he has become man to make it possible for us to love as he loved us. He makes himself the hungry one—the naked one—the homeless one—the sick one—the one in prison—the lonely one—the unwanted one—and he says: You did it to me. Hungry for our love, and this is the hunger of our poor people. This is the hunger that you and I must find, it may be in our own home.

I never forget an opportunity I had in visiting a home where they had all these old parents of sons and daughters who had just put them in an institution and forgotten maybe. And I went there, and I saw in that home they had everything, beautiful things, but everybody was looking towards the door. And I did not see a single one with their smile on their face. And I turned to the sister and I asked: How is that? How is it that the people they have everything here, why are they all looking towards the door, why are they not smiling? I am so used to see the smile on our people, even the dying ones smile, and she said: This is nearly every day, they are expecting, they are hoping that a son or daughter will come to visit them. They are hurt because they are forgotten, and see—this is where love comes. That poverty comes right there in our own home, even neglect to love. Maybe in our own family we have somebody who is feeling lonely, who is feeling sick, who is feeling worried, and these are difficult days for everybody. Are we there, are we there to receive them, is the mother there to receive the child?

I was surprised in the waste to see so many young boys and girls given into drugs, and I tried to find out why—why is it like that, and the answer was: Because there is no one in the family to receive them. Father and mother are so busy they have no time. Young parents are in some institution and the child takes back to the street and gets involved in something.

We are talking of peace. These are things that break peace, but I feel the greatest destroyer of peace today is abortion, because it is a direct war, a direct killing—direct murder by the mother herself. And we read in the Scripture, for God says very clearly: Even if a mother could forget her child—I will not forget you—I have curved you in the palm of my hand. We are curved in the palm of His hand, so close to Him that unborn child has been curved in the hand of God. And that is what strikes me most, the beginning of that sentence, that even if a mother *could* forget, something impossible—but even if she could forget—I will not forget you. And today the greatest means—the greatest destroyer of Peace is abortion. And we who are standing here—our parents wanted us. We would not be here if our parents would do that to us. Our children, we want them, we love them, but what of the millions? Many people are very, very concerned with the children in India, with the children of Africa where quite a number die, maybe of malnutrition, of hunger and so on, but millions are dying deliberately by the will of the mother. And this is what is the greatest destroyer of peace today. Because if a mother can kill her own child—what is left for me to kill you and you to kill me—there is nothing between. And this I appeal in India, I appeal everywhere: Let us bring the child back, and this year being the child's year: What have we done for the child?

At the beginning of the year I told, I spoke everywhere and I said: Let us make this year that we make every single child born, and unborn, wanted. And today is the end of the year, have we really made the children wanted? I will give you something terrifying. We are fighting abortion by adoption, we have saved thousands of lives, we have sent words to all the clinics, to the hospitals, police stations—please don't destroy the child, we will take the child. So every hour of the day and night it is always somebody, we have quite a number of unwedded mothers—tell them come, we will take care of you, we will take the child from you, and we will get a home for the child. And we have a tremendous demand for families who have no children, that is the blessing of God for us.

And also, we are doing another thing which is very beautiful—we are teaching our beggars, our leprosy patients, our slum dwellers, our people of the street, natural family planning. And in Calcutta alone in six years—it is all in Calcutta—we have had 61,273 babies less from the families who would have had, but because they practise this natural way of abstaining, of self-control, out of love for each other. We teach them the temperature meter[1] which is very beautiful, very simple, and our poor people understand. And you know what they have told me? Our family is healthy, our family is united, and we can have a baby whenever we want. So clear—those people in the street, those beggars—and I think that if our people can do like that how much more you and

---

1 For determining when conception is most likely to occur.

all the others who can know the ways and means without destroying the life that God has created in us. The poor people are very great people. They can teach us so many beautiful things. The other day one of them came to thank us and said: You people who have evolved chastity you are the best people to teach us family planning. Because it is nothing more than self-control out of love for each other. And I think they said a beautiful sentence. And these are people who maybe have nothing to eat, maybe they have not a home where to live, but they are great people. The poor are very wonderful people. One evening we went out and we picked up four people from the street. And one of them was in a most terrible condition—and I told the sisters: You take care of the other three, I take this one that looked worse.

So I did for her all that my love can do, I put her in bed, and there was such a beautiful smile on her face. She took hold of my hand, said one word: Thank you—and died.

I could not help but examine my conscience before her, and I asked what would I say if I was in her place. And my answer was very simple. I would have tried to draw a little attention to myself, I would have said I am hungry, that I am dying, I am cold, I am in pain, or something, but she gave me much more— she gave me her grateful love. And she died with a smile on her face. As that man said whom we picked up from the drain, half eaten with worms, and we brought him to the home: I have lived like an animal in the street, but I am going to die like an angel, loved and cared for. And it was so wonderful to see the greatness of that man who could speak like that, who could die like that without blaming anybody, without cursing anybody, without comparing any- thing. Like an angel—this is the greatness of our people. And that is why we believe what Jesus has said: I was hungry—I was naked—I was homeless—I was unwanted, unloved, uncared for—and you did it to me. I believe that we are not real social workers. We may be doing social work in the eyes of the people, but we are really contemplatives in the heart of the world. For we are touching the body of Christ 24 hours. We have 24 hours in this presence, and so you and I. You too try to bring that presence of God in your family, for the family that prays together stays together. And I think that we in our family, we don't need bombs and guns, to destroy to bring peace—just get together, love one another, bring that peace, that joy, that strength of presence of each other in the home. And we will be able to overcome all the evil that is in the world. There is so much suffering, so much hatred, so much misery, and we with our prayer, with our sacrifice are beginning at home.

Love begins at home, and it is not how much we do, but how much love we put in the action that we do. It is to God Almighty—how much we do it does not matter, because He is infinite, but how much love we put in that action. How much we do to Him in the person that we are serving. Some time ago in Calcutta we had great difficulty in getting sugar, and I don't know how the word got around to the children, and a little boy of four years old, Hindu boy, went home and told his parents: I will not eat sugar for three days, I will give my sugar to Mother Teresa for her children. After three days his father and mother brought him to our house. I had never met them before, and this little one could scarcely pronounce my name, but he knew exactly what he had come to do. He knew that he wanted to share his love. And this is why I have received such a lot of love from you all. From the time that I have come here I have simply been surrounded with love, and with real, real understanding love. It could feel as if everyone in India, everyone in Africa is somebody very special to you. And I felt quite at home I was telling Sister today. I feel in the Convent with the Sisters as if I am in Calcutta with my own Sisters. So completely at home here, right here. And so here I am talking with you—I want you to find the poor here, right in your own home first. And begin love there. Be that good news to your own people. And find out about your nextdoor neighbors—do you know who they are?

I had the most extraordinary experience with a Hindu family who had eight children. A gentleman came to our house and said: Mother Teresa, there is a family with eight children, they had not eaten for so long—do something. So I took some rice and I went there immediately. And I saw the children— their eyes shining with hunger—I don't know if you have ever seen hunger. But I have seen it very often. And she took the rice, she divided the rice, and she went out. When she came back I asked her—where did you go, what did you do? And she gave me a very simple answer: They are hungry also. What struck me most was that she knew—and who are they, a Muslim family—and she knew. I didn't bring more rice that evening because I wanted them to enjoy the joy of sharing. But there were those children, radiating joy, sharing the joy with their mother because she had the love to give. And you see this is where love begins—at home, and I want you—and I am very grateful for what I have received. It has been a tremendous experience and I go back to India—I will be back by next week, the 15th I hope—and I will be able to bring your love.

And I know well that you have not given from your abundance, but you have given until it has hurt you. Today the little children they gave—I was so surprised—there is so much joy for the children that are hungry. That the children like themselves will need love and care and tenderness, like they get so much from their parents. So let us thank God that we have had this opportunity to come to know each other, and this knowledge of each other has brought us very close. And we will be able to help not only the children of India and Africa, but will be able to help the children of the whole world, because as you know our Sisters are all over the world.

And with this Prize that I have received as a Prize of Peace, I am going to try to make the home for many people that have no home. Because I believe that love begins at home, and if we can create a home for the poor—I think that more and more love will spread. And we will be able through this understanding love to bring peace, be the good news to the poor. The poor in our own family first, in our country and in the world. To be able to do this, our Sisters, our lives have to be woven with prayer. They have to be woven with Christ to be able to understand, to be able to share. Because today there is so much suffering—and I feel that the passion of Christ is being relived all over again—are we there to share that passion, to share that suffering of people. Around the world, not only in the poor countries, but I found the poverty of the West so much more difficult to remove. When I pick up a person from the street, hungry, I give him a plate of rice, a piece of bread, I have satisfied. I have removed that hunger. But a person that is shut out, that feels unwanted, unloved, terrified, the person that has been thrown out from society—that poverty is so hurtable and so much, and I find that very difficult. Our Sisters are working amongst that kind of people in the West. So you must pray for us that we may be able to be that good news, but we cannot do that without you, you have to do that here in your country. You must come to know the poor, maybe our people here have material things, everything, but I think that if we all look into our own homes, how difficult we find it sometimes to smile at each other, and that the smile is the beginning of love. And so let us always meet each other with a smile, for the smile is the beginning of love, and once we begin to love each other naturally we want to do something.

So you pray for our Sisters and for me and for our Brothers, and for our co-workers that are around the world. That we may remain faithful to the gift of God, to love Him and serve Him in the poor together with you. What we have done we would not have been able to do if you did not share with your prayers, with your gifts, this continual giving. But I don't want you to give me from your abundance, I want that you give me until it hurts. The other day I received 15 dollars from a man who has been on his back for twenty years, and the only part that he can move is his right hand. And the only companion that he enjoys is smoking. And he said to me: I do not smoke for one week, and I send you this money. It must have been a terrible sacrifice for him, but see how beautiful, how he shared, and with that money I bought bread and I gave to those who are hungry with a joy on both sides, he was giving and the poor were receiving. This is something that you and I—it is a gift of God to us to be able to share our love with others. And let it be as it was for Jesus. Let us love one another as he loved us. Let us love Him with undivided love. And the joy of loving Him and each other—let us give now—that Christmas is coming so close. Let us keep that joy of loving Jesus in our hearts. And share that joy with all that we come to touch with. And that radiating joy is real, for we have no reason not to be happy because we have Christ with us. Christ in our hearts, Christ in the poor that we meet, Christ in the smile that we give and the smile that we receive. Let us make that one point: That no child will be unwanted, and also that we meet each other always with a smile, especially when it is difficult to smile.

I never forget some time ago about 14 professors came from the United States from different universities. And they came to Calcutta to our house. Then we were talking about that they had been to the home for the dying. We have a home for the dying in Calcutta, where we have picked up more than 36,000 people only from the streets of Calcutta, and out of that big number more than 18,000 have died a beautiful death. They have just gone home to God; and they came to our house and we talked of love, of compassion, and then one of them asked me: Say, Mother, please tell us something that we will remember, and I said to them: Smile at each other, make time for each other in your family. Smile at each other.

And then another one asked me: Are you married, and I said: Yes, and I find it sometimes very difficult to smile at Jesus because he can be very demanding sometimes. This is really something true, and there is where love comes—when it is demanding, and yet we can give it to Him with joy. Just as I have said today, I have said that if I don't go to Heaven for anything else I will be going to Heaven for all the publicity because it has purified me and sacrified me and made me really something ready to go to Heaven. I think that this is something, that we must live life beautifully, we have Jesus with us and He loves us. If we could only remember that God loves me, and I have an opportunity to love others as he loves me, not in big things, but in small things with great love, then Norway becomes a nest of love. And how beautiful it will be that from here a centre for peace has been given. That from here the joy of life of the unborn child comes out. If you become a burning light in the world of peace, then really the Nobel Prize is a gift of the Norwegian people. God bless you!

CHAPTER 23

Law, Government, Revolution, and War—1914–Present

The postmodern world has seen revolution and change in many lands. It started with the new nations created from the Ottoman and Austro-Hungarian Empires after World War I, the Russian Revolution of 1917, and the spread of Communism into Europe and Asia.

Strong currents of nationalism were present throughout the twentieth century and into the twenty-first. Nationalist movements spread through the Middle East, Western and Eastern Europe, Latin America, Asia, and Africa; some have been successful and others have failed. Many governments adopted socialist governments during the twentieth century, either through revolution or the ballot box.

Do you see any similarities between the selections from Marcus Garvey, Jomo Kenyatta, and Desmond Tutu regarding nationalist goals? What were their hopes for Africa?

Gandhi is best known for the practice of nonviolence; when did he say violence was necessary? Does Mao's discussion of the problems with revolution build on Marx and Engels' document in the preceding section? How is it different? Hitler and Castro both wanted to establish a socialist state; do you see any similarities in what they hoped to accomplish? How did the British welfare state differ from the German and Cuban models? Does reading the documents on Arab nationalism help you understand current issues in the Middle East? What role does the Islamic religion play in the struggle?

The Doctrine of the Sword by Mohandas K. Gandhi—1920

Mohandas K. Gandhi (1869–1948) was born into a middle-class Hindu family. He was sent to England to study law and then worked for 20 years to defend the rights of immigrants to South Africa. He returned to India in 1914, eventually becoming the leader of the Indian National Congress. He developed the policy of stayagraha, that is, nonviolent civil disobedience in public acts of defiance against British rule to gain Indian independence. As a result, he was jailed several times. He participated in the post–World War II negotiations with Britain that resulted in Indian independence but was shot to death by a Hindu fanatic in 1948. Although Gandhi is best known for his policy of nonviolent resistance, in the following document he explains the true meaning of nonviolence and explains the difference between nonviolence and cowardice. When, according to Gandhi, should Indians choose violence? How does he explain the difference between nonviolence and weakness?

I WOULD risk violence a thousand times rather than risk the emasculation of a whole race.

VIOLENCE THE CHOICE

I do believe that, where there is only a choice between cowardice and violence, I would advise violence. . . . I would rather have India resort to arms in order to defend her honour than that she should, in a cowardly manner, become or remain a helpless witness to her own dishonor.

But I believe that nonviolence is infinitely superior to violence, forgiveness is more manly than punishment. Forgiveness adorns a soldier . . . But abstinence is forgiveness only when there is the power to punish; it is meaningless when it pretends to proceed from a helpless creature. . . .

But I do not believe India to be helpless. . . . I do not believe myself to be a helpless creature. . . . Strength does not come from physical capacity. It comes from an indomitable will.

We do want to drive out the best in the man, but we do not want on that account to emasculate him. And in the process of finding his own status, the beast in him is bound now and again to put up his ugly appearance.

"The Doctrine of the Sword" by Mohandas K. Ghandi, 1920.

The world is not entirely governed by logic. Life itself involves some kind of violence and we have to choose the path of least violence.

NO COWARDICE

I want both the Hindus and Mussalmans to cultivate the cool courage to die without killing. But if one has not that courage, I want him to cultivate the art of killing and being killed rather than, in a cowardly manner, flee from danger. For the latter, in spite of his flight, does commit mental himsa. He flees because he has not the courage to be killed in the act of killing.

My method of nonviolence can never lead to loss of strength, but it alone will make it possible, if the nation wills it, to offer disciplined and concerted violence in time of danger.

My creed of nonviolence is an extremely active force. It has no room for cowardice or even weakness. There is hope for a violent man to be some day non-violent, but there is none for a coward. I have, therefore, said more than once . . . that, if we do not know how to defend ourselves, our women and our places of worship by the force of suffering, i.e., nonviolence, we must, if we are men, be at least able to defend all these by fighting.

No matter how weak a person is in body, if it is a shame to flee, he will stand his ground and die at his post. This would be nonviolence and bravery. No matter how weak he is, he will use what strength he has in inflicting injury on his opponent, and die in the attempt. This is bravery, but not nonviolence. If, when his duty is to face danger, he flees, it is cowardice. In the first case, the man will have love or charity in him. In the second and third cases, there would be a dislike or distrust and fear.

My nonviolence does admit of people, who cannot or will not be nonviolent, holding and making effective use of arms. Let me repeat for the thousandth time that nonviolence is of the strongest, not of the weak.

To run away from danger, instead of facing it, is to deny one's faith in man and God, even one's own self. It were better for one to drown oneself than live to declare such bankruptcy of faith.

SELF-DEFENCE BY VIOLENCE

I have been repeating over and over again that he who cannot protect himself or his nearest and dearest or their honour by non-violently facing death may and ought to do so by violently dealing with the oppressor. He who can do neither of the two is a burden. He has no business to be the head of a family. He must either hide himself, or must rest content to live for ever in helplessness and be prepared to crawl like a worm at the bidding of a bully.

The strength to kill is not essential for self-defence; one ought to have the strength to die. When a man is fully ready to die, he will not even desire to offer violence. Indeed, I may put it down as a self-evident proposition that the desire to kill is in inverse proportion to the desire to die. And history is replete with instances of men who, by dying with courage and compassion on their lips, converted the hearts of their violent opponents.

Nonviolence cannot be taught to a person who fears to die and has no power of resistance. A helpless mouse is not nonviolent because he is always eaten by pussy. He would gladly eat the murderess if he could, but he ever tries to flee from her. We do not call him a coward, because he is made by nature to behave no better than he does.

But a man who, when faced by danger, behaves like a mouse, is rightly called a coward. He harbors violence and hatred in his heart and would kill his enemy if he could without hurting himself. He is a stranger to nonviolence. All sermonizing on it will be lost on him. Bravery is foreign to his nature. Before he can understand nonviolence, he has to be taught to stand his ground and even suffer death, in the attempt to defend himself against the aggressor who bids fair to overwhelm him. To do otherwise would be to confirm his cowardice and take him further away from nonviolence.

Whilst I may not actually help anyone to retaliate, I must not let a coward seek shelter behind nonviolence so-called. Not knowing the stuff of which nonviolence is made, many have honestly believed that running away from danger every time was a virtue compared to offering resistance, especially when it was fraught with danger to one's life. As a teacher of nonviolence I must, so far as it is possible for me, guard against such an unmanly belief.

Self-defence. . . . is the only honourable course where there is unreadiness for self-immolation.

Though violence is not lawful, when it is offered in self-defence or for the defence of the defenceless, it is an act of bravery far better than cowardly submission. The latter befits neither man nor woman. Under violence, there are many stages and varieties of bravery. Every man must judge this for himself. No other person can or has the right.

176

On African Nationalism
by Marcus Garvey—1923

After World War I, nationalist movements began to blossom in Africa. Marcus Garvey (1887–1940) was born in Jamaica and held many jobs until he found his calling as a crusader for black nationalism. Garvey is best known as the founder of the Back to Africa movement in the 1920s. Garvey believed that people of African ancestry should "redeem" Africa and that the European Colonial powers should give up their colonies. Who was the audience for this speech? What did Garvey want them to accomplish?

MARCUS GARVEY PREACHES
AFRICAN REVOLUTION

George Washington was not God Almighty. He was a man like any Negro in this building, and if he and his associates were able to make a free America, we too can make a free Africa. Hampden, Gladstone, Pitt and Disraeli were not the representatives of God in the person of Jesus Christ. They were but men, but in their time they worked for the expansion of the British Empire, and today they boast of a British Empire upon which "the sun never sets." As Pitt and Gladstone were able to work for the expansion of the British Empire, so you and I can work for the expansion of a great African Empire. Voltaire and Mirabeau were not Jesus Christs, they were but men like ourselves. They worked and overturned the French Monarchy. They worked for the Democracy which France now enjoys, and if they were able to do that, we are able to work for a democracy in Africa. Lenin and Trotsky were not Jesus Christs, but they were able to overthrow the despotism of Russia, and today they have given to the world a Social Republic, the first of its kind. If Lenin and Trotsky were able to do that for Russia, you and I can do that for Africa. Therefore, let no man, let no power on earth, turn you from this sacred cause of liberty. I prefer to die at this moment rather than not to work for the freedom of Africa. If liberty is good for certain sets of humanity it is good for all. Black men, Colored men, Negroes have as much right to be free as any other race that God Almighty ever created, and we desire freedom that is unfettered, freedom that is unlimited, freedom that will give us a chance and opportunity

From Marcus Garvey, "Redeeming the African Motherland," in *Philosophy and Opinions of Marcus Garvey*, Vol. I, ed. by Amy Jacques Garvey (New York: University Publishing House, 1923).

to rise to the fullest of our ambition and that we cannot get in countries where other men rule and dominate.

We have reached the time when every minute, every second must count for something done, something achieved in the cause of Africa. We need the freedom of Africa now, therefore, we desire the kind of leadership that will give it to us as quickly as possible. You will realize that not only individuals, but governments are using their influence against us. But what do we care about the unrighteous influence of any government? Our cause is based upon righteousness. And anything that is not righteous we have no respect for, because God Almighty is our leader and Jesus Christ our standard bearer. We rely on them for that kind of leadership that will make us free, for it is the same God who inspired the Psalmist to write "Princes shall come out of Egypt and Ethiopia shall stretch out her hands unto God." At this moment methinks I see Ethiopia stretching forth her hands unto God and methinks I see the Angel of God taking up the standard of the Red, the Black and the Green, and saying "Men of the Negro Race, Men of Ethiopia, follow me." Tonight we are following. We are following 400,000,000 strong. We are following with a determination that we must be free before the wreck of matter, before the crash of worlds.

It falls to our lot to tear off the shackles that bind Mother Africa. Can you do it? You did it in the Revolutionary War. You did it in the Civil War; You did it at the Battles of the Marne and Verdun; You did it in Mesopotamia. You can do it marching up the battle heights of Africa. Let the world know that 400,000,000 Negroes are prepared to die or live as free men. Despise us as much as you care. Ignore us as much as you care. We are coming 400,000,000 strong. We are coming with our woes behind us, with the memory of suffering behind us—woes and suffering of three hundred years—they shall be our inspiration. My bulwark of strength in the conflict of freedom in Africa, will be the three hundred years of persecution and hardship left behind in this Western Hemisphere. The more I remember the suffering of my fore-fathers, the more I remember the lynchings and burnings in the Southern States of America, the more I will fight on even though the battle seems doubtful. Tell me that I must turn back, and I laugh you to scorn. Go on! Go on! Climb ye the heights of liberty and cease not in well doing until you have planted the banner of the Red, the Black and the Green on the hilltops of Africa.

"Strength means to excel in the profession of death . . ." by Sami Shawkat—1933

In the following document, Sami Shawkat, the Iraqi director of education in 1933, addresses students in Baghdad. What does he feel is most needed for a strong Iraq/Arab society? Why does he refer to Germany, India, and Egypt in this speech?

Tomorrow, your headmaster Mr. Darwish al-Miqdadi will visit the Ministry of Defense to discuss with its senior officials the curriculum of your military studies. Do you know what these studies are and why they are introduced this year into the curricula of our schools? I have called you together today to explain this point.

We often hear and read that there is no political independence without economic independence, or that there can be no independence without knowledge. But Egypt, whose income has for many years now exceeded her expenditure by millions of pounds, and who has the best universities and schools and the greatest scholars in the Near East, has had her independence delayed up to now. The treasuries of the Indian rajas contain hundreds of millions of gold pieces and vast numbers of precious stones; India herself has more than twenty-five large universities from which graduate annually thousands of young men with diplomas in higher studies. Yet India is a colony. The proportion of the educated in Syria amounts to 76 per cent, and the majority of her population is not different in progress, civilization or culture from the peoples of southern Europe, but in spite of this, unfortunately, we still find her deprived of independence. On the other hand, the Afghans, who lead the life of the fourteenth century and whose treasuries have never been filled with gold, are independent. And here is our neighbor, the Kingdom of Saudi Arabia, whose inhabitants live on dates and camels' milk, in whose schools no modern arts are taught, and whose culture has not crossed the boundaries of religion; she too is independent. And Arab Yemen is also independent, in spite of her lack of money.

Money and learning, therefore, are not all that is needed for the independence of nations, nor are they the only axe with which to strike down the walls of imperialism and sever the chains of humiliation.

From Sami Shawkat in *Arab Nationalism: An Anthology* ed. by Sylvia G. Haim (Berkeley, CA: University of California Press, 1962).

But . . .

There is something else more important than money and learning for preserving the honor of a nation and for keeping humiliation and enslavement at bay.

That is strength.

Strength is the soil on which the seed of justice burgeons; the nation which has no strength is destined to humiliation and enslavement. Riches without strength are a cause of humiliation and enslavement; as for knowledge without strength, it only produces crying and weeping on the part of the weak, and mockery on the part of the strong. This weeping and mocking will sometimes go on for tens, even hundreds, of years, as has happened in India and other countries.

Strength, as I use the word here, means to excel in the Profession of Death.

The nation which does not excel in the Profession of Death with iron and fire will be forced to die under the hooves of the horses and under the boots of a foreign soldiery. If to live is just, then killing in self-defense is also just. Had Mustafa Kemal not had, for his revolution in Anatolia, forty thousand officers trained in the Profession of Death, we would not have seen Turkey restoring in the twentieth century the glories of Yavouz Sultan Selim. Had not Pahlavi had thousands of officers well versed in the sacred profession we would not have seen him restoring the glory of Darius. And had Mussolini not had tens of thousands of Black Shirts well versed in the Profession of Death he would not have been able to put on the temples of Victor Emmanuel the crown of the first Caesars of Rome.

In the Balkans, the Albanian nation is independent, and in the Near East Arab Iraq is independent; in Albania the reed has prospered and in Iraq the cedar. The reed bush casts its shade over no more than a few centimeters of ground, no matter how tall it grows; but the cedar tree, after only a few years of growth, casts its shade over tens and hundreds of meters. Iraq's horizon of hope extends to all the Arab countries, whereas it is not in the power of Albania to look beyond its boundaries. Sixty years ago, Prussia used to dream of uniting the German people. What is there to prevent Iraq, which fulfilled her desire for independence ten years ago, from dreaming to unite all the Arab countries?

On the banks of this great river which we see morning and evening Harun al-Rashid established his throne, and from this sandy shore he ruled more than 200 million souls. We will not deserve to take pride in him and to claim that we are his descendants if we do not restore what he built and what the enemies of the Arabs destroyed. The spirit of Harun al-Rashid and the spirit of al-Ma'mun want Iraq to have in a short while half a million soldiers and hundreds of airplanes. Is there in Iraq a coward who will not answer their call? Your military studies this year, oh youths, are those lessons of strength which the country needs and which our glorious history demands. If we do not want death under the hooves of the horses and the boots of the foreign armies, it is our duty to perfect the Profession of Death, the profession of the army, the sacred military profession. This year, the lessons will be confined to the Central Secondary School in the capital, but in the future they will extend to all the secondary schools in the country, as well as to all the teachers' training colleges.

On then, oh young men, to Strength. On to the perfection of the sacred Profession of Death. Lift up high the banner of Faisal, the successor of Harun al-Rashid.

178

The First Arab Students' Congress Manifesto—1938

World War I brought many changes to the Middle East. The first was the disintegration of the Ottoman Empire, which resulted from its alliance with Germany and Austria. By the mid-1920s, the Republic of Turkey had become the Middle East's first modern (secular) state under Kemal Ataturk. Although Egypt and Iraq seemingly gained independence in the 1930s, Europeans still dominated the area and went back on their promise to recognize Arab independence in exchange for their support of the Allies during World War I. As a result, modern Arab nationalism gradually became a force in the Middle East. The following pact defines Arab nationalist beliefs. What did the students feel should be the main goal of Arab nationalists? What were their concerns about the Jewish Zionist movement?

I. Our National Pact

I am an Arab, and I believe that the Arabs constitute one nation. The sacred right of this nation is to be sovereign in her own affairs. Her ardent nationalism drives her to liberate the Arab homeland, to unite all its parts, and to found political, economic, and social institutions more sound and more compatible than the existing ones. The aim of this nationalism is to raise up the standard of living and to increase the material and the spiritual good of the people; it also aspires to share in working for the good of the human collectivity; it strives to realize this by continuous work based on national organization.

From Sami Shawkat in *Arab Nationalism: An Anthology* ed. by Sylvia G. Haim (Berkeley, CA: University of California Press, 1962).

I pledge myself to God, that I will strive in this path to my utmost, putting the national interest above any other consideration.

II. First Principles

The Arabs: All who are Arab in their language, culture, and loyalty, . . . those are the Arabs. The Arab is the individual who belongs to the nation made up of those people.

The Arab Homeland: It is the land which has been, or is, inhabited by an Arab majority, in the above sense, in Asia and Africa. As such it is a whole which cannot be divided or partitioned. It is a sacred heritage no inch of which may be trifled with. Any compromise in this respect is invalid and is national treason.

Arab Nationalism: It is the feeling for the necessity of independence and unity which the inhabitants of the Arab lands share. . . . It is based on the unity of the homeland, of language, culture, history, and a sense of the common good.

The Arab Movement: It is the new Arab renaissance which pervades the Arab nation. Its motive force is her glorious past, her remarkable vitality and the awareness of her present and future interests. This movement strives continuously and in an organized manner toward well-defined aims. These aims are to liberate and unite the Arab homeland, to found political, economic, and social organizations more sound than the existing ones, and to attempt afterward to work for the good of the human collectivity and its progress. These aims are to be realized by definite means drawn from the preparedness of the Arabs and their particular situation, as well as from the experience of the West. They will be realized without subscribing to any particular creed of the modern Western ones such as Fascism, Communism, or Democracy.

The Arab National Idea: It is a national idea which proscribes the existence of racial, regional, and communal fanaticisms. It respects the freedom of religious observance, and individual freedoms such as the freedom of opinion, work, and assembly, unless they conflict with the public good. The Arab national idea cannot be contradictory to the good of real racial and religious minorities; it aims rather at treating all sincere patriots on the principle of equality of rights and duties.

III. Foreign Elements in the Arab Countries

We have said that the Arab countries belong to the Arabs and that benefits therefrom must accrue to them. By Arabs we mean those whom the political report has included under this appellation. As for those elements who are not Arabized and who do not intend to be Arabized but are, rather, intent on putting obstacles in the way of the Arab nation, they are foreign to the Arab nation. The most prominent problem of this kind is that of the Jews in Palestine.

If we looked at the Jews in Palestine from an economic angle we would find that their economy is totally incompatible with the Arab economy. The Jews are attempting to build up a Jewish state in Palestine and to bring into this state great numbers of their kind from all over the world. Palestine is a small country, and they will therefore have to industrialize it so that this large number of inhabitants can find subsistence. And in order to make their industry a success they will have to find markets for their products. For this they depend on the Arab market; their products will therefore flood the Arab countries and compete with Arab industries. This is very harmful to the Arabs.

Moreover, Palestine, placed as it is between the Arab countries in Asia and Africa, occupies an important position in land, sea, and air communications. A foreign state in Palestine will impede these communications and have a harmful effect on commerce. And even if the Jews in Palestine presented no danger other than the economic, this would be enough for us to oppose them and to put an end to their intrigues, so that we may ensure for our country a happy and glorious future.

Among the dangerous alien elements in the Arab countries are the foreign colonies such as the Italians in Tripolitania, the French, and the Frenchified Jews in Tunisia, Algeria, and Morocco. The danger of these elements is akin to that of the Jews in Palestine, even though less prominent and less critical.

179

Problems of China's Revolutionary War by Mao Zedong—1936

Born into a well-off peasant family in the Hunan province, Mao Zedong (1893–1976) participated in a revolution against the Manchu as a university student in 1911. Shortly afterwards, he became a Marxist and one of the first members of the Chinese Communist party. Mao decided that the usually discounted peasants and not the workers were the revolutionary force needed to defeat the Kuomintang. In 1934, surrounded by Chiang Kai-shek's troops, Mao and 100,000 Communist troops and officials broke out and

From Mao Zedong, *Selected Works* (New York: International Publishers, 1954), Vol. I.

made the Long March of over 6,000 miles to safety in mountainous Kansu province. There, Mao built up his forces in readiness for the long struggle against the Japanese and the Kuomintang. The following excerpts contain the gist of his plan. What role did Mao feel the Communist party should play in the revolution? How do his ideas compare with Lenin's? What did he think were the four unique characteristics of China's revolutionary war?

THE CHINESE COMMUNIST PARTY AND CHINA'S REVOLUTIONARY WAR

The chief enemies in China's revolutionary war are imperialism and the feudal forces. Although the Chinese bourgeoisie may take part in the revolutionary war on certain historical occasions, yet owing to its selfish character and its lack of political and economic independence, it is neither willing nor able to lead China's revolutionary war to complete victory. The masses of the Chinese peasantry and of the urban petty bourgeoisie are willing to take part actively in the revolutionary war and to bring about its complete victory. They are the main forces in the revolutionary war, yet small-scale production, which is their characteristic and limits their political outlook, renders them unable to give correct leadership in the war. Thus, in an era when the proletariat has already appeared on the political stage, the responsibility of leadership in China's revolutionary war inevitably falls on the shoulders of the Chinese Communist Party. At such a time any revolutionary war will certainly end in defeat if the leadership of the proletariat and the Communist Party is lacking or is forsaken. For of all the social strata and political groups in semicolonial China only the proletariat and the Communist Party are the most open-minded and unselfish, possess the most farsighted political outlook and the highest organizational quality, and are also the readiest to learn with an open mind from the experiences of the advanced proletariat of the world and its parties as well as to apply what they have learned in their own undertakings....

CHARACTERISTICS OF CHINA'S REVOLUTIONARY WAR

1. The Importance of the Subject

People who will not admit, who do not know, or who do not care to know that China's revolutionary war has its own characteristics have treated the war waged by the Red Army against the Kuomintang forces as similar in nature to wars in general or the civil war in the Soviet Union.[1] The experience of the civil war in the Soviet Union directed by Lenin and Stalin has indeed a world-wide

---

1 The reference is to the postrevolutionary struggle between the Bolsheviks and their opponents from 1917 to 1921.

significance. All Communist Parties, including the Chinese Communist Party, regard this experience and its theoretical summing-up by Lenin and Stalin as their guiding compass. Yet this does not mean that we are to make use of this experience mechanically under our own conditions. China's revolutionary war is distinguished by many characteristics from the civil war in the Soviet Union. Failure to reckon with these characteristics or denial of them is of course erroneous. This point has been fully proved in the ten years of our war. . . .

2. What Are the Characteristics of China's Revolutionary War?

What then are the characteristics of China's revolutionary war?

I think there are four.

The first is that China is a vast semicolonial country which is unevenly developed both politically and economically. . . .

The unevenness of political and economic development in China—the coexistence of a frail capitalist economy and a preponderant semi-feudal economy; the coexistence of a few modern industrial and commercial cities and the boundless expanses of stagnant rural districts; the coexistence of several millions of industrial workers on the one hand and, on the other, hundreds of millions of peasants and handicraftsmen under the old régime; the coexistence of big warlords controlling the Central government and small warlords controlling the provinces; the coexistence of two kinds of reactionary armies, i.e., the so-called Central army under Chiang Kai-shek and the troops of miscellaneous brands under the warlords in the provinces; and the coexistence of a few railway and steamship lines and motor roads on the one hand and, on the other, the vast number of wheel-barrow paths and trails for pedestrians only, many of which are even difficult for them to negotiate. . . .

The second characteristic is the great strength of the enemy.

What is the situation of the Kuomintang, the enemy of the Red Army? It is a party that has seized political power and has relatively stabilized it. It has gained the support of the principal counter-revolutionary countries in the world. It has remodeled its army, which has thus become different from any other army in Chinese history and on the whole similar to the armies of the modern states in the world; its army is supplied much more abundantly with arms and other equipment than the Red Army, and is greater in numerical strength than any army in Chinese history, even than the standing army of any country in the world. . . .

The Chinese Red Army is confronted with such a powerful enemy. This is the second characteristic of China's revolutionary war. This characteristic inevitably makes the war waged by the Red Army different in many ways from wars in general, from the civil war in the Soviet Union and from the Northern Expedition.[2]

The third characteristic is that the Red Army is weak and small. . . .

---

2 The military campaign the Kuomintang pursued between 1926 and 1928 to break the
 hold of the warlords on central north China.

Our political power is dispersed and isolated in mountainous or remote regions, and is deprived of any outside help. In economic and cultural conditions the revolutionary base areas are more backward than the Kuomintang areas. The revolutionary bases embrace only rural districts and small towns. They were extremely small in the beginning and have not grown much larger since. Moreover, they are often shifted and the Red Army possesses no really consolidated bases. . . .

The fourth characteristic is the Communist Party's leadership and the agrarian revolution.

This characteristic is the inevitable result of the first one. It gives rise to the following two features. On the one hand, China's revolutionary war, though taking place in a period of reaction in China and throughout the capitalist world, can yet be victorious because it is led by the Communist Party and supported by the peasantry. Because we have secured the support of the peasantry, our base areas, though small, possess great political power and stand firmly opposed to the political power of the Kuomintang which encompasses a vast area; in a military sense this creates colossal difficulties for the attacking Kuomintang troops. The Red Army, though small, has great fighting capacity, because its men under the leadership of the Communist Party have sprung from the agrarian revolution and are fighting for their own interests, and because officers and men are politically united.

On the other hand, our situation contrasts sharply with that of the Kuomintang. Opposed to the agrarian revolution, the Kuomintang is deprived of the support of the peasantry. Despite the great size of its army it cannot arouse the bulk of the soldiers or many of the lower-rank officers, who used to be small producers, to risk their lives voluntarily for its sake. Officers and men are politically disunited and this reduces its fighting capacity. . . .

STRATEGIC DEFENSIVE

Military experts of new and rapidly developing imperialist countries like Germany and Japan positively boast of the advantages of strategic offensive and condemn strategic defensive. Such an idea is fundamentally unsuitable for China's revolutionary war. Such military experts point out that the great shortcoming of defense lies in the fact that, instead of gingering up the people, it demoralizes them. But that applies only to countries where class contradictions are sharp and the war benefits only the reactionary ruling strata or the reactionary groups in power. Our case is different. Under the slogan of safeguarding the revolutionary base areas and safeguarding China, we can rally the greatest majority of the people to fight single-mindedly, because we are the victims of oppression and aggression. The Red Army of the Soviet Union defeated its enemies also by defensive warfare during the civil war. It not only carried on the war under the slogan of defending the Soviets when the imperialist powers organized the Whites[3] for an onslaught, but also carried out military mobilization under the slogan of defending the capital when the October Uprising was being prepared. Defensive battles in a just war can not only exercise a lulling influence on the politically alien elements but mobilize the backward sections of the masses to join in the war.

When Marx said that once an armed uprising is started there must not be a moment's pause in the attack, he meant that the masses, having taken the enemy by surprise in an uprising, must not allow the reactionary ruling classes any chance to retain or recover their political power, but must seize this moment to spring a surprise attack on the nation's reactionary ruling forces, and that they must never feel satisfied with the victories they have won, underrate the enemy, relent in their attacks on the enemy, or hesitate to go forward so as to miss the chance of annihilating the enemy and court failure for the revolution. This is correct. This does not mean, however, that we revolutionaries should not adopt defensive measures even when we are already locked in a battle with an enemy stronger than ourselves and are hard pressed by him. Anyone who thinks so would be a prize idiot.

Our past war was on the whole an offensive against the Kuomintang, though militarily it assumed the form of smashing the enemy's campaigns of "encirclement and annihilation."

In military terms, our warfare consists in the alternate adoption of the defensive and the offensive. It makes no difference to us whether our offensive is regarded as following the defensive or preceding it, because the turning-point comes when we smash the campaigns of "encirclement and annihilation." It remains a defensive until a campaign of "encirclement and annihilation" is smashed, and then it immediately begins as an offensive; they are but two phases of the same thing, as one campaign of "encirclement and annihilation" of the enemy is closely followed by another. Of the two phases, the defensive phase is more complicated and more important than the offensive phase. It involves numerous problems of how to smash the campaign of "encirclement and annihilation." The basic principle is for active defense and against passive defense.

In the civil war, when the Red Army surpasses the enemy in strength, there will no longer be any use for strategic defensive in general. Then our only directive will be strategic offensive. Such a change depends on an overall change in the relative strength of the enemy and ourselves. The only defensive measures that remain will be of a partial character.

---

3 In the Russian civil war, the opponents of the "Reds," or Bolsheviks.

180

From *Mein Kampf* by
Adolf Hitler—1924

The totalitarian state in the West was defined by Adolf Hitler in his political tract,
Mein Kampf. *Hitler (1889–1945) was born in Austria-Hungary and served bravely*
in World War I. A disillusioned veteran, he turned to race-based politics and soon
became the leader of the Nationalist Socialist German Worker's Party (Nazis). While
imprisoned for a failed political coup, he wrote Mein Kampf *("My Struggle"), which*
outlined his political theories for the creation of a totalitarian state. Hitler rose to power
during the political turmoil of the 1930s and founded the Third Reich in 1933. His
attempts to create a Greater Germany while implementing a destructive racial policy
resulted in the Holocaust and plunged Germany into total war with the Allied powers.
In the end, Germany was defeated and Hitler committed suicide in a Berlin bunker in
1945. What are the main goals of a "folkish" state according to Hitler? How does this
compare with the goals of Stalin or the British welfare state?

HITLER DEFINES THE STATE

Anyone who believes today that a folkish National Socialist state must distinguish itself from other states only in a purely mechanical sense, by a superior
construction of its economic life—that is, by a better balance between rich and
poor, or giving broad sections of the population more right to influence the
economic process, or by fairer wages by elimination of excessive wage differ-
entials—has not gone beyond the most superficial aspect of the matter and has
not the faintest idea of what we call a philosophy. All the things we have just
mentioned offer not the slightest guaranty of continued existence, far less of
any claim to greatness. A people which did not go beyond these really superficial reforms would not obtain the least guaranty of victory in the general struggle of nations. A movement which finds the content of its mission only in such
a general leveling, assuredly just as it may be, will truly bring about no great
and profound, hence real, reform of existing conditions, since its entire activity
does not, in the last analysis, go beyond externals, and does not give the people
that inner armament which enables it, with almost inevitable certainty I might
say, to overcome in the end those weaknesses from which we suffer today. . . .

The folkish state must care for the welfare of its citizens by recognizing in all and everything the importance of the value of personality, thus in all fields preparing the way for that highest measure of productive performance which grants to the individual the highest measure of participation.

And accordingly, the folkish state must free all leadership and especially the highest—that is, the political leadership—entirely from the parliamentary principle of majority rule—in other words, mass rule—and instead absolutely guarantee the right of the personality.

From this the following realization results:

The best state constitution and state form is that which, with the most unquestioned certainty, raises the best minds in the national community to leading position and leading influence.

But as, in economic life, the able men cannot be appointed from above, but must struggle through for themselves, and just as here the endless schooling, ranging from the smallest business to the largest enterprise, occurs spontaneously, with life alone giving the examinations, obviously political minds cannot be "discovered." Extraordinary geniuses permit of no consideration for normal mankind.

From the smallest community cell to the highest leadership of the entire Reich, the state must have the personality principle anchored in its organization.

There must be no majority decisions, but only responsible persons, and the word "council" must be restored to its original meaning. Surely every man will have advisers by his side, but *the decision will be made by one man.*

The principle which made the Prussian army in its time into the most wonderful instrument of the German people must some day, in a transferred sense, become the principle of the construction of our whole state conception: *authority of every leader downward and responsibility upward.*

Even then it will not be possible to dispense with those corporations which today we designate as parliaments. But their councillors will then actually give counsel; responsibility, however, can and may be borne only by *one* man, and therefore only he alone may possess the authority and right to command.

Parliaments as such are necessary, because in them, above all, personalities to which special responsible tasks can later be entrusted have an opportunity gradually to rise up.

This gives the following picture:

The folkish state, from the township up to the Reich leadership, has no representative body which decides anything by the majority, but only *advisory bodies* which stand at the side of the elected leader, receiving their share of work from him, and in turn if necessary assuming unlimited responsibility in certain fields, just as on a larger scale the leader or chairman of the various corporations himself possesses.

As a matter of principle, the folkish state does not tolerate asking advice or opinions in special matters—say, of an economic nature—of men who, on the basis of their education and activity, can understand nothing of the subject. It, therefore, divides its representative bodies from the start into *political and professional chambers.*

In order to guarantee a profitable cooperation between the two, a special *senate* of the élite always stands over them.

In no chamber and in no senate does a vote ever take place. They are working institutions and not voting machines. The individual member has an advisory, but never a determining, voice. The latter is the exclusive privilege of the responsible chairman.

This principle—absolute responsibility unconditionally combined with absolute authority—will gradually breed an élite of leaders such as today, in this era of irresponsible parliamentarianism, is utterly inconceivable.

Thus, the political form of the nation will be brought into agreement with that law to which it owes its greatness in the cultural and economic field.

★ ★ ★

As regards the possibility of putting these ideas into practice, I beg you not to forget that the parliamentary principle of democratic majority rule has by no means always dominated mankind, but on the contrary is to be found only in brief periods of history, which are always epochs of the decay of peoples and states.

But it should not be believed that such a transformation can be accomplished by purely theoretical measures from above, since logically it may not even stop at the state constitution, but must permeate all other legislation, and indeed all civil life. Such a fundamental change can and will only take place through a movement which is itself constructed in the spirit of these ideas and hence bears the future state within itself.

Hence the National Socialist movement should today adapt itself entirely to these ideas and carry them to practical fruition within its own organization, so that some day it may not only show the state these same guiding principles, but can also place the completed body of its own state at its disposal.

181

Britain Converts to a Welfare State—1942–1948

The years during which World War II raged in Europe brought a distinct shift towards governmental responsibility for social welfare in Great Britain. These concepts were first detailed in the Beveridge Report, created in 1942 and first put into effect in 1948. How do the goals of this report differ from those of the Nazi state? What role did the British people play in the changes that were implemented?

BRITAIN PLANS THE WELFARE STATE (1942)

In proceeding from this first comprehensive survey of social insurance to the next task—of making recommendations—three guiding principles may be laid down at the outset.

The first principle is that any proposals for the future, while they should use to the full the experience gathered in the past, should not be restricted by consideration of sectional interests established in the obtaining of that experience. Now, when the war is abolishing landmarks of every kind, is the opportunity for using experience in a clear field. A revolutionary moment in the world's history is a time for revolutions, not for patching.

The second principle is that organisation of social insurance should be treated as one part only of a comprehensive policy of social progress. Social insurance fully developed may provide income security; it is an attack upon Want. But Want is one only of five giants on the road of reconstruction and in some ways the easiest to attack. The others are Disease, Ignorance, Squalor and Idleness.

The third principle is that social security must be achieved by co-operation between the State and the individual. The State should offer security for service and contribution. The State in organising security should not stifle incentive, opportunity, responsibility; in establishing a national minimum, it should leave room and encouragement for voluntary action by each individual to provide more than that minimum for himself and his family. . . .

Abolition of want requires, first, improvement of State insurance, that is to say provision against interruption and loss of earning power. All the principal causes of interruption or loss of earnings are now the subject of

From "Report by Sir William Beveridge," *Social Insurance and Allied Services* (Cmd. 6404), London, Her Majesty's Stationery Office, 1942, p. 6–8, 13, 158–159.

schemes of social insurance. If, in spite of these schemes, so many persons unemployed or sick or old or widowed are found to be without adequate income for subsistence according to the standards adopted in the social surveys, this means that the benefits amount to less than subsistence by those standards or do not last as long as the need, and that the assistance which supplements insurance is either insufficient in amount or available only on terms which make men unwilling to have recourse to it. None of the insurance benefits provided before the war were in fact designed with reference to the standards of the social surveys. Though unemployment benefit was not altogether out of relation to those standards, sickness and disablement benefit, old age pensions and widows' pensions were far below them, while workmen's compensation was below subsistence level for anyone who had family responsibilities or whose earnings in work were less than twice the amount needed for subsistence. To prevent interruption or destruction of earning power from leading to want, it is necessary to improve the present schemes of social insurance in three directions: by extension of scope to cover persons now excluded, by extension of purposes to cover risks now excluded, and by raising the rates of benefit.

Abolition of want requires, second, adjustment of incomes, in periods of earning as well as interruption of earning, to family needs, that is to say in one form or another it requires allowances for children. Without such allowances as part of benefit or added to it, to make provision for large families, no social insurance against interruption of earnings can be adequate. But, if children's allowances are given only when earnings are interrupted and are not given during earning also, two evils are unavoidable. First, a substantial measure of acute want will remain among the lower paid workers as the accompaniment of large families. Second, in all such cases, income will be greater during unemployment or other interruptions of work than during work.

★ ★ ★

There is here an issue of principle and practice on which strong arguments can be advanced on each side by reasonable men. But the general tendency of public opinion seems clear. After trial of a different principle, it has been found to accord best with the sentiments of the British people that in insurance organised by the community by use of compulsory powers each individual should stand in on the same terms; none should claim to pay less because he is healthier or has more regular employment. In accord with that view, the proposals of the Report mark another step forward to the development of State insurance as a new type of human institution, differing both from the former methods of preventing or alleviating distress and from voluntary insurance. The term "social insurance" to describe this institution implies both that it is compulsory and that men stand together with their fellows. The term implies a pooling of risks except so far as separation of risks serves a social purpose. There may be reasons of social policy for adjusting premiums to risks, in order to give a stimulus for avoidance of danger, as in the case of industrial accident and disease. There is no longer an admitted claim of the individual citizen to share in national insurance and yet to stand outside it, keeping the advantage of his individual lower risk whether of unemployment or of disease or accident. . . .

A comprehensive national health service will ensure that for every citizen there is available whatever medical treatment he requires, in whatever form he requires it, domiciliary or institutional, general, specialist or consultant, and will ensure also the provision of dental, ophthalmic and surgical appliances, nursing and midwifery and rehabilitation after accidents. Whether or not payment towards the cost of the health service is included in the social insurance contribution, the service itself should

   (i) be organised, not by the Ministry concerned with social insurance, but by Departments responsible for the health of the people and for positive and preventive as well as curative measures;

 (ii) be provided where needed without contribution conditions in any individual case.

Restoration of a sick person to health is a duty of the State and the sick person, prior to any other consideration. The assumption made here is in accord with the definition of the objects of medical service as proposed in the Draft Interim Report of the Medical Planning Commission of the British Medical Association:

"(a) to provide a system of medical service directed towards the achievement of positive health, of the prevention of disease, and the relief of sickness;

 (b) to render available to every individual all necessary medical services, both general and specialist, and both domiciliary and institutional."

The Resurgence of Islam by
Hasan Al-Bana—ca. 1940s

Islam is currently one of the most vital of the world's great religions. Traditional Islamic societies have turned away from the influences of the West to embrace traditional Muslim religion and culture. Mosque attendance has increased and many Islamic women have returned to wearing traditional dress. At the same time, Islam has become an increasingly potent political force, dating from the overthrow of the Shah of Iran in 1979 and extending to the current Iraq conflict. The commentary by Hasan Al-Bana (1906–1949) details the ideas that still form the core of much contemporary Muslim thought. Al-Bana was an Egyptian who formed the Muslim Brotherhood, a secret and politically powerful organization in the Middle East. Al-Bana was not an admirer of Western influence in the Arab world. Although he died before the current problems in the Middle East came to a head, his words preview what was to come. What does he say is wrong with the West? What does he claim is the strength of the Islamic faith? How does he compare the influence of socialism and democracy on the Arab world?

When we observe the evolution in the political, social, and moral spheres of the lives of nations and peoples, we note that the Islamic world—and, naturally, in the forefront, the Arab world—gives to its rebirth an Islamic flavor. This trend is ever-increasing. Until recently, writers, intellectuals, scholars, and governments glorified the principles of European civilization, gave themselves a Western tint, and adopted a European style and manner; today, on the contrary, the wind has changed, and reserve and distrust have taken their place. Voices are raised proclaiming the necessity for a return to the principles, teachings, and ways of Islam, and, taking into account the situation, for initiating the reconciliation of modem life with these principles, as a prelude to a final "Islamization."

This development worries a good number of governments and Arab powers, which, having lived during the past generations in a state of mind that had retained from Islam only lessons of fanaticism and inertia, regarded the Muslims only as weak drudges or as nations easily exploitable by colonialism. In trying to understand the new movement ... these governments have produced all sorts of possible interpretations: "It is the result," said some, "of the growth of extremist organizations and fanatical groups." Others explained that it was a

From Kemal Karpat, ed., *Political and Social Thought in the Contemporary Middle East* (New York: Praeger, 1968), p. 118–121. Reprinted by permission of Greenwood Publishing Group, Inc., Westport, CT.

reaction to present-day political and economic pressures, of which the Islamic nations had become aware. Finally, others said, "It is only a means whereby those seeking government or other honors may achieve renown and position."

Now all these reasons are, in our opinion, as far as possible from the truth; for this new movement can only be the result of the following three factors, which we will now examine.

The first of the three is the failure of the social principles on which the civilization of the Western nations has been built. The Western way of life—bounded in effect on practical and technical knowledge, discovery, invention, and the flooding of world markets with mechanical products—has remained incapable of offering to men's minds a flicker of light, a ray of hope, a grain of faith, or of providing anxious persons the smallest path toward rest and tranquillity. Man is not simply an instrument among others. Naturally, he has become tired of purely materialistic conditions and desires some spiritual comfort. But the materialistic life of the West could only offer him as reassurance a new materialism of sin, passion, drink, women, noisy gatherings, and showy attractions which he had come to enjoy. Man's hunger grows from day to day: he wants to free his spirit, to destroy this materialistic prison and find space to breathe the air of faith and consolation.

The second factor—the decisive factor in the circumstances—is the discovery by Islamic thinkers of the noble, honorable, moral, and perfect content of the principles and rules of this religion, which is infinitely more accomplished, more pure, more glorious, more complete, and more beautiful than all that has been discovered up till now by social theorists and reformers. For a long time, Muslims neglected all this, but once God had enlightened their thinkers and they had compared the social rules of their religion with what they had been told by the greatest sociologists and the cleverest leading theorists, they noted the wide gap and the great distance between a heritage of immense value on one side and the conditions experienced on the other. Then, Muslims could not but do justice to the spirit and the history of their people, proclaiming the value of this heritage and inviting all peoples—nonpracticing Muslims or non-Muslims—to follow the sacred path that God had traced for them and to hold to a straight course.

The third factor is the development of social conditions between the two murderous world wars (which involved all the world powers and monopolized the minds of regimes, nations, and individuals) which resulted in a set of principles of reform and social organization that certain powers, in deciding to put them into practice, have taken as an instructional basis. . . .

Thus, German Nazism and Italian Fascism rose to the fore; Mussolini and Hitler led their two peoples to unity, order, recovery, power, and glory. In record time, they ensured internal order at home and, through force, made themselves feared abroad. Their regimes gave real hope, and also gave rise to thoughts of steadfastness and perseverance and the reuniting of different, divided men around the words "chief" and "order." In their resolutions and speeches, the Führer and the Duce began to frighten the world and to upset their epoch. . . .

The star of socialism and Communism, symbol of success and victory, shone with an increasing brilliance; Soviet Russia was at the head of the collectivist camp. She launched her message and, in the eyes of the world, demonstrated a system which had been modified several times in thirty years. The democratic powers—or, to use a more precise expression, the colonialist powers, the old ones worn out, the new ones full of greed—took up a position to stem the current. The struggle intensified, in some places openly, in others under cover, and nations and peoples, perplexed, hesitated at the crossroads, not knowing which way was best; among them were the nations of Islam and the peoples of the Qur'ān the future, whatever the circumstances, is in the hands of God, the decision with history, and immortality with the most worthy.

This social evolution and violent, hard struggle stirred the minds of Muslim thinkers; the parallels and the prescribed comparisons led to a healthy conclusion: to free themselves from the existing state of affairs, to allow the necessary return of the nations and peoples to Islam.

183

The Kenya Africa Union Is Not the Mau Mau by Jomo Kenyatta—1952

Jomo Kenyatta (1893–1978) was the first president of Kenya. He campaigned for land reform and political rights for many years in England and Africa. After returning to Kenya in 1946, Kenyatta was accused of being one of the leaders of the Mau Mau uprising and was imprisoned and later exiled. (The Mau Mau was a secret Kenyan organization of mainly Kikuyu tribesmen who used terror to force the English from Kenya.) After his release, Kenyatta worked with the British to write a constitution for Kenya, which gained its independence in 1963. Kenyatta served first as prime minister and then as president when Kenya became a republic in 1964. He restored stability to the state and later died in office. What does Kenyatta say are the most pressing problems facing Kenyans? Why does he say that the Kenya Africa Union is not the Mau Mau?

From F.D. Cornfield, *The Origins and Growth of Mau Mau*, Sessional Paper No. 5 of 1959–1960 (Nairobi: 1960).

SPEECH AT THE KENYA AFRICAN UNION
MEETING AT NYERI, JULY 26, 1952

. . . I want you to know the purpose of K.A.U. It is the biggest purpose the African has. It involves every African in Kenya and it is their mouthpiece which asks for freedom. K.A.U. is you and you are the K.A.U. If we unite now, each and every one of us, and each tribe to another, we will cause the implementation in this country of that which the European calls democracy. True democracy has no colour distinction. It does not choose between black and white. We are here in this tremendous gathering under the K.A.U. flag to find which road leads us from darkness into democracy. In order to find it we Africans must first achieve the right to elect our own representatives. That is surely the first principle of democracy. We are the only race in Kenya which does not elect its own representatives in the Legislature and we are going to set about to rectify this situation. We feel we are dominated by a handful of others who refuse to be just. God said this is our land. Land in which we are to flourish as a people. We are not worried that other races are here with us in our country, but we insist that we are the leaders here, and what we want we insist we get. We want our cattle to get fat on our land so that our children grow up in prosperity; we do not want that fat removed to feed others. He who has ears should now hear that K.A.U. claims this land as its own gift from God and I wish those who are black, white or brown at this meeting to know this. K.A.U. speaks in daylight. He who calls us the *Mau Mau* is not truthful. We do not know this thing *Mau Mau*. We want to prosper as a nation, and as a nation we demand equality, that is equal pay for equal work. Whether it is a chief, headman or labourer be needs in these days increased salary. He needs a salary that compares with a salary of a European who does equal work. We will never get our freedom unless we succeed in this issue. We do not want equal pay for equal work tomorrow—we want it right now. Those who profess to be just must realize that this is the foundation of justice. It has never been known in history that a country prospers without equality. We despise bribery and corruption, those two words that the European repeatedly refers to. Bribery and corruption is prevalent in this country, but I am not surprised. As long as a people are held down, corruption is sure to rise and the only answer to this is a policy of equality. If we work together as one, we must succeed.

Our country today is in a bad state for its land is full of fools—and fools in a country delay the independence of its people. K.A.U. seeks to remedy this situation and I tell you now it despises thieving, robbery and murder for these practices ruin our country. I say this because if one man steals, or two men steal, there are people sitting close by lapping up information, who say the whole tribe is bad because a theft has been committed. Those people are wrecking our chances of advancement. They will prevent us getting freedom. If I have my own way, let me tell you I would butcher the criminal, and there are more criminals than one in more senses than one. The policeman must arrest an offender, a man who is purely an offender, but lie must not go about picking up people with a small horn of liquor in their hands and march them in procession with his fellow policemen to Government and say he has got a *Mau Mau* amongst the Kikuyu people. The plain clothes man who hides in the hedges must, I demand, get the truth of our words before be flies to Government to present them with false information. I ask this of them who are in the meeting to take heed of my words and do their work properly and justly. . . .

. . . Do not be scared of the few policemen under those trees who are holding their rifles high in the air for you to see. Their job is to seize criminals, and we shall save them a duty today. I will never ask you to be subversive but I ask you to be united, for the day of Independence is the day of complete unity and if we unite completely tomorrow, our independence will come tomorrow. This is the day for you to work bard for your country, it is not words but deeds that count and the deeds I ask for come from your pockets. The biggest subscribers to K.A.U. are in this order. First, Thomson's Falls branch, second, Elburgon branch and third Gatundu branch. Do you, in Nyeri branch, want to beat them? Then let us see your deeds come forth.

I want to touch on a number of points, and I ask you for the hundredth time to keep quiet whilst I do this. We want self-government, but this we will never get if we drink beer. It is harming our country and making people fools and encouraging crime. It is also taking all our money. Prosperity is a prerequisite of independence and, more important, the beer we are drinking is harmful to our birthrate. You sleep with a woman for nothing if you drink beer. It causes your bones to weaken and if you want to increase the population of the Kikuyu you must stop drinking.

. . . K.A.U. is not a fighting union that uses fists and weapons. If any of you here think that force is good, I do not agree with you: remember the old saying that he who is hit with a rungu returns, but he who is hit with justice never comes back. I do not want people to accuse us falsely—that we steal and that we are *Mau Mau*. I pray to you that we join hands for freedom and freedom means abolishing criminality. Beer harms us and those who drink it do us harm and they may be the so-called *Mau Mau*. Whatever grievances we have, let us air them here in the open. The criminal does not, want freedom and land—he wants to line his own pocket. Let us therefore demand our rights justly. The British Government has discussed the land problem in Kenya and we hope to have a Royal Commission to this country to look into the land problem very shortly. When this Royal Commission comes, let us show it that we are a good peaceful people and not thieves and robbers.

Program for Cuba by
Fidel Castro—1956

Fidel Alejandro Castro Ruz (1926–) was born into a wealthy Cuban farming family and educated at Jesuit schools. He became radicalized and in 1959 helped to overthrow Fulgencio Batista's dictatorship as the leader of the 26th of July movement. He then turned Cuba into the first Communist state in the Americas, despite the opposition of the United States. Holding the title of premier until 1976, he then became the president of the Council of State and the Council of Ministers. Castro has held the office of First Secretary of the Cuban Communist Party since it was formed in 1965. Castro believes that socialism is the only hope for Latin America. What does he feel needs to be done?

CASTRO'S PROGRAM

When we speak of the people we do not mean the comfortable ones, the conservative elements of the nation, who welcome any regime of oppression, any dictatorship, any despotism, prostrating themselves before the master of the moment until they grind their foreheads into the ground. When we speak of struggle, the people means the vast unredeemed masses to whom all make promises and whom all deceive; we mean the people who yearn for a better, more dignified and more just nation; who are moved by ancestral aspirations of justice, for they have suffered injustice and mockery generation after generation; who long for great and wise changes in all aspects of their life; people who, to attain the changes, are ready to give even the very last breath of their lives, when they believe in something or in someone, especially when they believe in themselves. . . . The people we counted on in our struggle were these:

Seven hundred thousand Cubans without work, who desire to earn their daily bread honestly without having to emigrate in search of a livelihood.

Five hundred thousand farm labourers inhabiting miserable shacks (*bohíos*), who work four months of the year and starve during the rest, sharing their misery with their children; who have not an inch of land to till, and whose existence would move any heart not made of stone.

Four hundred thousand industrial labourers and stevedores whose retirement funds have been embezzled, whose benefits are being taken away, whose

From Fidel Castro, "History Will Absolve Me," Moncada Trial Defense Speech, Santiago, Cuba, October 16, 1956 (London: Jonathan Capte, 1958). First published in Cuba, 1957.

homes are wretched quarters, whose salaries pass from the hands of the boss to those of the money-lender (*garrotero*), whose future is a pay reduction and dismissal, whose life is eternal work and whose only rest is in the tomb.

One hundred thousand small farmers who live and die working on land that is not theirs, looking at it with sadness as Moses looked at the promised land, to die without ever owning it; who, like feudal serfs, have to pay for the use of their parcel of land by giving up a portion of its products; who cannot love it, improve it, beautify it, nor plant a lemon or an orange tree on it, because they never know when a sheriff will come with the rural guard to evict them from it.

Thirty thousand teachers and professors who are so devoted, dedicated and necessary to the better destiny of future generations and who are so badly treated and paid.

Twenty thousand small business men, weighted down by debts, ruined by the crisis and harangued by a plague of grafting and venal officials.

Ten thousand young professionals: doctors, engineers, lawyers, veterinarians, school teachers, dentists, pharmacists, newspapermen, painters, sculptors, etc., who come forth from school with their degrees, anxious to work and full of hope, only to find themselves at a dead end with all doors closed, and where no ear hears their clamour or supplication.

These are the people, the ones who know misfortune and, therefore, are capable of fighting with limitless courage!

To the people whose desperate roads through life have been paved with the bricks of betrayals and false promises, we were not going to say: "We will eventually give you what you need," but rather—"Here you have it, fight for it with all your might, so that liberty and happiness may be yours!"

In the brief of this case, the five revolutionary laws that would have been proclaimed immediately after the capture of the Moncada Barracks and would have been broadcasted to the nation by radio should be recorded. It is possible that Colonel Chaviano may deliberately have destroyed these documents, but even if he has done so I remember them.

The First Revolutionary Law would have returned power to the people and proclaimed the Constitution of 1940 the supreme Law of the State, until such time as the people should decide to modify or change it. And, in order to effect its implementation and punish those who had violated it, there being no organization for holding elections to accomplish this, the revolutionary movement, as the momentous incarnation of this sovereignty, the only source of legitimate power, would have assumed all the faculties inherent in it, except that of modifying the Constitution itself: in other words, it would have assumed the legislative, executive and judicial powers. . . .

The Second Revolutionary Law would have granted property, non-mortgageable and non-transferable, to all planters, non-quota planters, lessees, share-croppers, and squatters who hold parcels of five *caballerías* of land or less, and the State would indemnify the former owners on the basis of the rental which they would have received for these parcels over a period of ten years.

The Third Revolutionary Law would have granted workers and employees the right to share thirty per cent of the profits of all the large industrial,

mercantile and mining enterprises, including the sugar mills. The strictly agricultural enterprises would be exempt in consideration of other agrarian laws
which would be implemented.

The Fourth Revolutionary Law would have granted all planters the right
to share fifty-five per cent of the sugar production and a minimum quota of
forty thousand *arrobas* for all small planters who have been established for three
or more years.

The Fifth Revolutionary Law would have ordered the confiscation of all
holdings and ill-gotten gains of those who had committed frauds during previous regimes, as well as the holdings and ill-gotten gains of all their legatees and
heirs. To implement this, special courts with full powers would gain access to
all records of all corporations registered or operating in this country, in order
to investigate concealed funds of illegal origin, and to request that foreign governments extradite persons and attach holdings rightfully belonging to the
Cuban people. Half of the property recovered would be used to subsidize
retirement funds for workers and the other half would be used for hospitals,
asylums and charitable organizations.

185

My vision for South Africa by Desmond Tutu—1979

*The son of a teacher and a domestic servant, Desmond Tutu (1931–) grew up in
the gold-mining area of South Africa. His family moved to Johannesburg when he was
12 years old and he attended high school there. After graduating from college and teaching high school, Tutu studied to become an Anglican priest. He later became an anti-
apartheid activist, winner of the 1984 Nobel Peace Prize, and the first black Anglican
Archbishop of Cape Town, South Africa. In the following excerpt, Tutu describes his
dream for the future of South Africa. What does freedom mean to Tutu? Why doesn't
he favor capitalism? How does his utopia appear to an American?*

From "My Vision for South Africa" from *Crying in the Wilderness* by Desmond Tutu, ed. by
John Webster. Introduction and notes copyright © 1982 by John Webster. Text copyright
© Desmond Tutu. Reprinted by permission.

We should all have the freedom to become fully human. That is basic to my understanding of society—that God created us without any coercion, freely for freedom. Responsibility is a nonsense except in the context of freedom—freedom to accept or reject alternative options, freedom to obey or disobey. God, who alone has the perfect right to be a totalitarian, has such a tremendous respect for our freedom to be human, that he would much rather see us go freely to hell than compel us to go to heaven.

According to the Bible, a human being can be a human being only because he belongs to a community. A person is a person through other persons, as we say in our African idiom. And so separation of persons because of biological accidents is reprehensible and blasphemous. A person is entitled to a stable community life, and the first of these communities is the family. A stable family life would be of paramount importance in my South Africa.

There would be freedom of association, of thought and of expression. This would involve freedom of movement as well. One would be free to go wherever one wanted, to associate with whomsoever one wished. As adult humans we would not be subject to draconian censorship laws. We can surely decide for ourselves what we want to read, what films to view and what views to have. We must not be frog-marched into puritanism.

Because we are created in the image of God one of our attributes is creativity. South Africa is starved of the great things many of her children can create and do, because of artificial barriers, and the refusal to let people develop to their fullest potential. When one has been overseas and seen for example the Black Alvin Alley dance group, which performed modern ballet to standing room only crowds at Covent Garden, then one weeps for how South Africa has allowed herself to be cheated of such performances by her own inhabitants. How many potentially outstanding people are being denied the opportunity to get on?

When I think of the splendid young people I have met, who despite some horrendous experiences at the hands of the system, have emerged quite unscathed with bitterness, and who have a tremendous humanity and compassion, then I weep because we are so wantonly wasteful of human resources. We need a course on human ecology.

I lay great stress on humaneness and being truly human. In our African understanding, part of Ubantu—being human—is the rare gift of sharing. This concept of sharing is exemplified at African feasts even to this day, when people eat together from a common dish, rather than from individual dishes. That means a meal is indeed to have communion with one's fellows. Blacks are beginning to lose this wonderful attribute, because we are being inveigled by the excessive individualism of the West. I loathe Capitalism because it gives far too great play to our inherent selfishness. We are told to be highly competitive, and our children start learning the attitudes of the ratrace quite early. They mustn't just do well at school—they must sweep the floor with their rivals. That's how you get on. We give prizes to such persons, not so far as I know to those who know how best to get on with others, or those who can coax the best out of others. We must delight in our ulcers, the symbols of our success.

So I would look for a socio-economic system that placed the emphasis on sharing and giving, rather than on self-aggrandisement and getting. Capitalism is exploitative and I can't stand that. We need to engage the resources that each person has. My vision includes a society that is more compassionate and caring, in which 'superfluous appendages' [*the government's way of describing families of black workers*] are unthinkable, where young and old are made to feel wanted, and that they belong and are not resented. It is a distorted community that trundles its aged off into soulless institutions. We need their accumulated wisdom and experience. They are splendid for helping the younger to feel cared for; certainly that has been the experience in the extended family.

I believe too that in a future South Africa we must be supportive of the family. The nuclear family is not geared to stand all the strains placed on it by modern day pressures. Then-are things we can survive better in a group than singly. I know there are pressures in the extended family, but I need to be persuaded that these are greater than those presently haunting the nuclear family.

Basically I long and work for a South Africa that is more open and more just; where people count and where they will have equal access to the good things of life, with equal opportunity to live, work, and learn. I long for a South Africa where there will be equal and untram melled access to the courts of the land, where detention without trial will be a thing of the hoary past, where bannings and other such arbitrary acts will no longer be even so much as mentioned, and where the rule of law will hold sway in the fullest sense. In addition, all adults will participate fully in political decision making, and in other decisions which affect their lives. Consequently they will have the vote and be eligible for election to all public offices. This South Africa will have integrity of territory with a common citizenship, and all the rights and privileges that go with such a citizenship, belonging to all its inhabitants.

Clearly, for many people, what I have described is almost a Utopia, and we cannot reach that desired goal overnight. Black leaders would, I feel, be willing to go back to the black community, and say: 'Hold on—things are moving in the right direction' if certain minimum conditions were pledged and met, even in stages, by the white powers that be. These are:

(A) Abolition of the Pass Laws.

(B) The immediate halting of population removals.

(C) The scrapping of Bantu Education, and a move towards a unitary educational system.

(D) A commitment to call a National Convention.

These would be significant steps towards realising the vision.

186

The Resurgence of Islam by Ayatollah Murtada Mutahhari—ca. 1980s

Ayatollah Murtada Mutahhari, one of the leaders of the successful revolution in Iran in 1979, talks about the motivation of the Shiite revolutionaries. What were the Shiite complaints about the Shah? What were the goals of the revolution? Do Al-Bana and Ayatollah Mutahhari seem to have the same goals? Do these documents provide any insight into the current problems in the Middle East?

AYATULLAH MURTADA MUTAHHARI

Scholars and knowledgeable persons in contemporary history concede that in the second half of our century in almost all or at least in a large number of Islamic countries Islamic movements have been in ascent openly or secretly. These are practically directed against despotism, capitalist colonialism or materialistic ideologies subscribing to colonialism in its new shape. Experts on political affairs acknowledge that after having passed through a period of mental crisis the Muslims are once again struggling to reestablish their "Islamic identity" against the challenges of capitalist West and the communist East. But in no Islamic country has this type of movement gained as much of depth and extent as in Iran since the year 1960. Nor is there a parallel to the proportions which the Iranian movement has obtained. It, therefore, becomes necessary to analyze this remarkably significant event of history.

Like all natural occurrences, social and political events, also tend to differ from one another in their behaviours. All historical movements cannot be considered identical in their nature. The nature of the Islamic movement is in no case similar to the French revolution or to the great October revolution of Russia.

The current Iranian movement is not restricted to any particular class or trade union. It is not only a labour, an agrarian, a student, an intellectual or a bourgeois movement. Within its scope fall one and all in Iran, the rich and the poor, the man and the woman, the school boy and the scholar, the warehouse man and the factory labourer, the artisan and the peasant, the clergy and the teacher, the literate and the illiterate, one and all. An announcement made by

From John J. Donohue and John L. Esposito, eds., *Islam in Transition: Muslim Perspectives* (New York: Oxford University Press, 1982), p. 308–313. Reprinted by permission.

the preceptor of the highest station guiding the movement is received in the length and breadth of the country with equal enthusiasm by all classes of the people. . . .

This movement is one of the glaring historical proofs which falsifies the concept of materialistic interpretation of history and that of the dialectics of materialism according to which economy is recognised as the cornerstone of social structure and a social movement is considered a reflection of class struggle. . . .

The awakened Islamic conscience of our society has induced it to search for Islamic values. This is the conscience of the cumulative enthusiasms of all classes of people, including perhaps some of the hereby dissident groups, which has galvanized them into one concerted upsurge.

The roots of this movement shall have to be traced in the events that occurred during the last half century in our country [during the reign of the Pahlavi shahs, 1925–1979] and the way these events came into conflict with the Islamic spirit of our society.

It is evident that during the last half century, there have been events which adopted a diametrically opposite direction as far as the nobler objectives of Islam were concerned and which aimed at nullifying the aspirations of the well-meaning reformers for the last century. This state of affairs could not continue for long without reaction.

What happened in Iran during the last half century may be summed up as under:

1. Absolute and barbaric despotism.

2. Denial of freedom of every kind.

3. A new type of colonialism meaning an invisible and dangerous colonialism embracing political, economic and cultural aspects of life.

4. Maintaining distance between religion and politics. Rather, divorcing politics from religion.

5. An attempt at leading Iran back to the age of ignorance of pre-Islamic days. . . .

6. Effecting a change and corrupting the rich Islamic culture and replacing it with the ambiguous Iranian culture.

7. Gruesome killing of Iranian Muslims, imprisonment and torture of the alleged political prisoners.

8. Ever increasing discrimination and cleavage among the classes of society despite so-called reforms.

9. Domination of non-Muslim elements over the Muslim elements in the government and other institutions.

10. Flagrant violation of Islamic laws either directly or by perpetrating corruption in the cultural and social life of the people.

11. Propaganda against Persian literature (which has always been the protector and upholder of Islamic spirit) under the pretext of purifying the Persian language of foreign terminology.

12. Severing relations with Islamic countries and flirting with non-Islamic and obviously with anti-Islamic countries like Israel.

What is the objective pursued by the movement and what does it want? Does it aim at democracy? Does it want to liquidate colonialism from our country? Does it rise to defend what is called in modem terminology as human rights? Does it want to do away with discrimination, inequality? Does it want to uproot oppression? Does it want to undo materialism and so forth and so on?

In view of the nature of the movement and its roots as already brought under consideration and also in view of the statements and announcements given out by the leaders of the movement, what one may gather as an answer to these questions is "Yes" as well as "No."

"Yes" because all the objectives mentioned above form the very crux of it. And "No" because the movement is not limited to only these or any one of these objectives. An Islamic movement cannot, from the point of its objective, remain a restricted affair, because Islam, in its very nature, is "an indivisible whole" and with the realization of any of the objectives set before it, its role does not cease to be.

★ ★ ★

No movement can be led successfully without leadership. But who should be the leader or the group of leaders when the movement is an Islamic one in its nature and when its objective is exclusively Islam?

Evidently the leadership should, in the first place, fulfill the general conditions of the task before it. Then the leaders must be deeply Islamic, fully conversant with the ethical, social, political and spiritual philosophy of Islam. They must have the knowledge of Islam's universal vision, its insight about empirical matters like the creation, the origin, the creator of the universe, the need for creation of the universe, etc. They must have the deep knowledge of Islam's views and stipulations on man and his society. It is of great importance that the leaders must have a clear picture of the Islamic ideology of man's relations with his society; his manner and method of framing the social order; his abilities of defending and pursuing certain things and resisting others; his ultimate objectives and the means of attaining those objectives, etc.

It is obvious that only such persons can lead as have been brought up under the pure Islamic culture having perfectly mastered the branches of religious learning and Islamic sciences, the Qur`ān, tradition, jurisprudence, etc. It is, therefore, only ecclesiastics who qualify for the leadership of such a movement.

CHAPTER 24

Science, Medicine, and Technology— 1914–Present

Tremendous benefits to society have resulted from the scientific and technological advances of postmodern scientists who have built on the work of scientific pioneers from preceding centuries. In many cases, these advances have changed the way we live as well as the world we live in. Nevertheless, many seemingly beneficial scientific discoveries have had some extremely harmful consequences. The documents in this section all take a negative position regarding the consequences of advances in science and technology during the postmodern era. They deal only indirectly with advances in medicine.

Because of the wars that ravaged the world during the last century, many nations encouraged their scientists to develop new weapons that were deadlier than any others yet known. This resulted in the creation of chemical weapons such as poison gas in World War I and the atomic bomb in World War II. The medical profession was helpless and unprepared to treat the victims of these weapons and each still has the potential to destroy the entire world. What is the destructive potential of chemical weapons and atomic bombs in the postmodern era? Is there any way they can be controlled?

Space travel was the dream of Renaissance scientists such as Leonardo da Vinci and Giordano Bruno, but it wasn't until after World War II that both the United States and the Soviet Union developed rocket systems capable of launching humans into space. In the United States, NASA developed a series of space shuttles that could carry astronauts into space for extended stays; until the Challenger explosion, the shuttle had an enviable safety record. According to the Challenger document, what was the main problem faced by the government in maintaining a regular schedule of space shuttle flights? How does the author feel about allowing civilians to travel on shuttles?

Providing enough food to feed the world's growing population is still a major concern, especially in third-world countries with booming populations. The growth in world population after Word War II led to an exponential increase in the use of chemicals to aid agricultural production with little concern to possible side effects. Rachel Carson was one of the first scientists to voice her concern regarding the dangers involved with the wholesale use of pesticides by farmers and individuals. Do you agree with Carson that our attempts to "control" nature are arrogant and outdated? What kind of world does Carson envision if scientific attempts to control nature increase food production? How do you think she would feel about genetic engineering and cloning?

Finally, predictions of the future are always interesting. Which model in the last document do you think is most accurate? Have some of the predictions already come true?

187

The First Poison Gas Attack—
1915

The First World War saw the unleashing of a variety of new weapons developed in modern laboratories. One of the most deadly and insidious was poison gas. Both the French and Germans experimented with the use of gaseous irritants in grenades and shells in 1914 in an attempt to break the stalemate of trench warfare. However, the first use of poison gas was on April 22, 1915, at the beginning of the Second Battle of Ypres. The Germans unleashed a cloud of greenish-yellow chlorine gas on British, Canadian, French, and Algerian troops. Its effect was deadly; within seconds of inhaling the gas, victims' respiratory organs were destroyed, causing them to choke and gasp for breath. The following excerpt comes from the diary of Anthony R. Hossack, who served in the Queen Victoria Rifles during World War I and witnessed the first use of poison gas. What was the soldiers' reaction to the use of poison gas? Were they prepared to counteract it? Why do you think everyone was surprised at the Germans' use of poison gas?

It was Thursday evening, April 22nd, 1915. In a meadow off the Poperinghe-Ypres road, the men of the Queen Victoria Rifles were taking their ease. We had just fought our first big action in the fight for Hill 60.

We had had a gruelling time, and had left many of our comrades on its slopes. We survivors were utterly spent and weary; but we felt in good heart, for only an hour ago we had been personally congratulated by Sir John French, also the Army Commander, General Smith-Dorrien.

Now some of us were stretched out asleep on the grass, others making preparations for a much-needed toilet. Our cooks were preparing a meal, and on our right a squad of Sappers were busily erecting huts in which we were to sleep. Alas! We never used them! As the sun was beginning to sink, this peaceful atmosphere was shattered by the noise of heavy shell-fire coming from the north-west, which increased every minute in volume, while a mile away on our right a 42-cm shell burst in the heart of the stricken city of Ypres.

As we gazed in the direction of the bombardment, where our line joined the French, six miles away, we could see in the failing light the flash of shrapnel with here and there the light of a rocket. But more curious than anything was a low cloud of yellow-grey smoke or vapour, and, underlying everything, a dull confused murmuring.

From "Memoirs & Diaries: The First Gas Attack" by Anthony R. Hossack. First published in *Everyman at War*, ed. by D.B. Purdom, 1930.

Suddenly down the road from the Yser Canal came a galloping team of horses, the riders goading on their mounts in a frenzied way; then another and another, till the road became a seething mass with a pall of dust over all.

Plainly something terrible was happening. What was it? Officers, and Staff officers too, stood gazing at the scene, awestruck and dumbfounded; for in the northerly breeze there came a pungent nauseating smell that tickled the throat and made our eyes smart. The horses and men were still pouring down the road, two or three men on a horse, I saw, while over the fields streamed mobs of infantry, the dusky warriors of French Africa; away went their rifles, equipment, even their tunics that they might run the faster.

One man came stumbling through our lines. An officer of ours held him up with levelled revolver, "What's the matter, you bloody lot of cowards?" says he. The Zouave was frothing at the mouth, his eyes started from their sockets, and he fell writhing at the officer's feet. "Fall in!" Ah! we expected that cry; and soon we moved across the fields in the direction of the line for about a mile. The battalion is formed into line, and we dig ourselves in.

It is quite dark now, and water is being brought round, and we hear how the Germans have, by the use of poison gas, driven a French army corps out of the line, creating a huge gap which the Canadians have closed *pro tem*. A cheer goes up at this bald statement, though little we knew at what a cost those gallant souls were holding on.

About midnight we withdrew from our temporary trenches and marched about for the rest of the night, till at dawn, we were permitted to snatch what sleep we could under a hedge.

About the middle of the morning we were on the move again, to the north, and were soon swinging along through Vlamertinghe. About two miles out of that town we halted in a field. By this time we had joined up with the remainder of our Brigade, the 13th, and, after a meal had been served, we were ordered to dump our packs and fall in by companies. Here our company commander, Captain Flemming, addressed us.

"We are," he said, "tired and weary men who would like to rest; however, there are men more weary than we who need our help. We may not have to do much; we may have to do a great deal. Whatever happens, fight like hell. I shall at any rate." A few moments more—then off we go again towards that incessant bombardment, which seemed to come closer every minute.

The Scottish Borderers led the Brigade, followed by the Royal West Rents, then ourselves—all with bayonets fixed, for we were told to be prepared to meet the Germans anywhere on the road.

We were now in the area of the ill-fated French Colonial Corps. Ambulances were everywhere, and the village of Brielen, through which we passed, was choked with wounded and gassed men. We were very mystified about this gas, and had no protection whatever against it.

Shortly after passing through Brielen we turned to the left down a road which led to the Canal, along the south side of which ran a steep spoil bank, and, as the head of our battalion reached this, we halted. We could see nothing of what went on on the other side, but knew by the rattle of musketry that there was something doing.

So there was, for when we finally crossed the pontoon we found that the Jocks had met the Germans on the north bank and had bundled them helter-skelter up the slope to Pilckem. This saved us any dirty work for that day, so we spent the rest of it till midnight in carrying supplies and ammunition to the Jocks and Kents, and afterwards lay in reserve on the Canal bank. It froze hard that night, and after the sweating fatigue of carrying boxes of S.A.A. all night we were literally aching with cold.

All night there seemed to be a spasmodic bombardment all round the Salient. Next morning about 12 o'clock the Adjutant, Captain Culme-Seymour, was chatting to Captain Flemming a few paces away from where I was lying, when up rushed a breathless despatch rider and handed him a message, which he read aloud to Flemming.

I caught three words, "Things are critical." In about five minutes the Colonel had the battalion on the move. We moved off in double file by companies, our company leading; as we did so a big shell burst in the midst of "D" Company, making a fearful mess.

We moved on quickly, like a gigantic serpent, with short halts now and then. As we skirted Ypres there was a roar of swift-moving thunder and a 17-inch shell, which seemed to be falling on top of us, burst a quarter of a mile away, covering us with dirt.

Over meadows and fields green with young crops which would never be harvested, past cows peacefully grazing that had had their last milking, we went, passing curiously unperturbed peasants, who watched us from the farms and cottages.

As we crossed the Roulers road a lone cavalryman came galloping down it, hatless and rolling in his saddle as though drunk. Some wag throws a ribald jest at him. He turns his ashy face towards us, and his saddle it seems is a mass of blood. Above us a Taube appears and, hovering over us, lets fall a cascade of glittering silver like petals. A few moments more and shells begin to fall about us in quantities, and gaps begin to appear in our snakelike line.

We pass a field battery; it is not firing, as it has nothing to fire, and its commander sits weeping on the trail of one of his useless guns. We quicken our pace, but the shelling gets heavier. It seems to be raining shrapnel. Captain Flemming falls, but struggles to his feet and waves us on with encouraging words.

We double across a field, and in a few moments come on to the road again. Here was action indeed, for barely had we reached the road and started to work our way towards St. Julien, than we found ourselves amongst a crowd of Canadians of all regiments jumbled up anyhow, and apparently fighting a desperate rearguard action.

They nearly all appeared to be wounded and were firing as hard as they could. A machine gun played down the road. Then comes an order: "Dig in on the roadside." We all scrambled into the ditch, which, like all Flanders ditches, was full of black, liquid mud, and started to work with entrenching tools—a hopeless job.

A woman was bringing jugs of water from a cottage a few yards away; evidently she had just completed her week's washing, for a line of garments fluttered in the garden.

"Dig! Dig, for your lives!" shouts an officer. But, dig! How can we? 'Tis balers we need.

A detonation like thunder, and I inhale the filthy fumes of a 5.9 as I cringe against the muddy bank. The German heavies have got the road taped to an inch. Their last shell has pitched on our two M.G. teams, sheltering in the ditch on the other side of the road. They disappear, and all we can hear are groans so terrible they will haunt me for ever.

Kennison, their officer, stares dazed, looking at a mass of blood and earth. Another crash and the woman and her cottage and water jars vanish and her pitiful washing hangs in a mocking way from her sagging clothes line. A bunch of telephone wires falls about us. To my bemused brain this is a catastrophe in itself, and I curse a Canadian Sapper beside me for not attempting to mend them.

He eyes me vacantly, for he is dead. More and more of these huge shells, two of them right in our midst. Shrieks of agony and groans all round me. I am splashed with blood. Surely I am hit, for my head feels as though a battering-ram has struck it. But no, I appear not to be, though all about me are bits of men and ghastly mixtures of khaki and blood.

The road becomes a perfect shambles. For perhaps half a minute a panic ensues, and we start to retire down the road. But not for long. Colonel Shipley stands in the centre of the road, blood streaming down his face. The gallant Flemming lies at his feet, and the Adjutant, Culme-Seymour, stands in a gateway calmly lighting a cigarette.

"Steady, my lads!" says the Colonel. "Steady, the Vics! Remember the regiment." The panic is ended.

"This way," says Seymour. "Follow me through this gate here." As we dash through the gate, I catch a glimpse of our M.O. working in an empty gun-pit like a butcher in his shop. Many were the lives he saved that day.

Once through the gate we charge madly across a field of young corn. Shrapnel and machine-gun bullets are cracking and hissing everywhere. Ahead of us is a large farm, and advancing upon it at almost right angles to ourselves is a dense mass of German infantry.

We are carrying four extra bandoliers of ammunition as well as the rest of our equipment. Shall I ever get there? My limbs ache with fatigue and my legs are like lead. But the inspiring figure of Seymour urges us on, yet even he cannot prevent the thinning of our line or the gaps being torn in it by the German field gunners, whom we can now plainly see.

At last we reach the farm, and we follow Culme-Seymour round to its further side. The roar of enemy machine guns rises to a crazy shrieking, but we are past caring about them, and with a sob of relief we fall into the farm's encircling trench.

Not too soon either, for that grey mass is only a few hundred yards off, and "Rapid fire! Let 'em have it, boys!" and don't we just. At last a target, and one that we cannot miss. The Germans fall in scores, and their batteries limber up and away. At last we have our revenge for the discomfort of the afternoon. But the enemy re-form and come on again, and we allow them to come a bit nearer, which they do. We fire till our rifles are almost too hot to hold, and the few survivors of our mad quarter of an hour stagger back.

The attack has failed, and we have held them, and thank God that we have, for, as our next order tells us, "This line must be held at all costs. Our next is the English Channel."

And hold it we did, through several more big attacks, though the enemy set fire to the farm and nearly roasted us, though our numbers dwindled and we were foodless and sleepless, till, thirty-six hours later, we were relieved in a misty dawn, and crept back through burning Ypres for a few hours' respite.

Anthony R. Hossack joined the Queen Victoria Rifles at the beginning of the War and served with them on the Western Front from early 1915 till after the Battle of Arras, where, in July 1917, he was wounded, returning to France at the end of February 1918, when he was attached to the M.G. Battalion of the 9th (Scottish) Division, and, after coming through the retreat from St. Quentin, was taken prisoner in the battle for Mt. Kemmel.

188

The Bombing of Hiroshima—1945

The culmination of the top-secret Manhattan project, under which the best scientists of the world worked to develop an atomic bomb, was the dropping of the bomb on the Japanese city of Hiroshima on August 6, 1945. Approximately 80,000 people died immediately, and tens of thousands of others suffered terrible burns and radiation poisoning. Unfortunately, no one seemed to realize at the time the horrible potential of atomic and hydrogen bombs. Almost all Americans supported the use of the bomb when they heard of it, because they wanted to end the costly war with Japan. Today, 60 years later, there is much controversy over the decisions made in 1945. The following excerpt relates the experience of a Hiroshima schoolgirl the day the bomb hit. How did Michicho survive

From Yamaoka Michiko, "Eight Hundred Meters from the Hypocenter," in Haruko Taya Cook and Theodore F. Cook, *Japan at War: An Oral History* (New York: The New Press, 1992), p. 384–387. Reprinted by permission.

the blast of the bomb? How did she feel about Americans after the bomb was dropped? What were her thoughts on the morality of using the bomb?

That year, on August 6, I was in the third year of girls' high school, fifteen years old. I was an operator at the telephone exchange. We had been mobilized from school for various work assignments for more than a year. My assigned place of duty was civilian, but we, too, were expected to protect the nation. We were tied by strong bonds to the country. We'd heard the news about the Tokyo and Osaka bombings, but nothing had dropped on Hiroshima. Japan was winning. So we still believed. We only had to endure. I wasn't particularly afraid when B-29s flew overhead.

That morning I left the house at about seven forty-five. I heard that the B-29s had already gone home. Mom told me, "Watch out, the B-29s might come again." My house was one point three kilometers from the hypocenter. My place of work was five hundred meters from the hypocenter. I walked toward the hypocenter in an area where all the houses and buildings had been deliberately demolished for fire breaks. There was no shade. I had on a white shirt and *monpe*. As I walked there, I noticed middle-school students pulling down houses at a point about eight hundred meters away from the hypocenter. I heard the faint sound of planes as I approached the river. The planes were tricky. Sometimes they only pretended to leave. I could still hear the very faint sound of planes. Today, I have no hearing in my left ear because of the damage from the blast. I thought, how strange, so I put my right hand above my eyes and looked up to see if I could spot them. The sun was dazzling. That was the moment.

There was no sound. I felt something strong. It was terribly intense. I felt colors. It wasn't heat. You can't really say it was yellow, and it wasn't blue. At that moment I thought I would be the only one who would die. I said to myself, "Goodbye, Mom."

They say temperatures of seven thousand degrees centigrade hit me. You can't really say it washed over me. It's hard to describe. I simply fainted. I remember my body floating in the air. That was probably the blast, but I don't know how far I was blown. When I came to my senses, my surroundings were silent. There was no wind. I saw a slight threadlike light, so I felt I must be alive. I was under stones. I couldn't move my body. I heard voices crying, "Help! Water!" It was then I realized I wasn't the only one. I couldn't really see around me. I tried to say something, but my voice wouldn't come out.

"Fire! Run away! Help! Hurry up!" They weren't voices but moans of agony and despair. "I have to get help and shout," I thought. The person who rescued me was Mom, although she herself had been buried under our collapsed house. Mom knew the route I'd been taking. She came, calling out to me. I heard her voice and cried for help. Our surroundings were already starting to burn. Fires burst out from just the light itself. It didn't really drop. It just flashed.

It was beyond my mother's ability. She pleaded, "My daughter's buried here, she's been helping you, working for the military." She convinced soldiers nearby to help her and they started to dig me out. The fire was now blazing.

"Woman, hurry up, run away from here," soldiers called. From underneath the stones I heard the crackling of flames. I call to her. "It's all right. Don't worry about me. Run away." I really didn't mind dying for the sake of the nation. Then they pulled me out by my legs.

Nobody there looked like human beings. Until that moment I thought incendiary bombs had fallen. Everyone was stupefied. Humans had lost the ability to speak. People couldn't scream, "It hurts!" even when they were on fire. People didn't say, "It's hot!" They just sat catching fire.

My clothes were burnt and so was my skin. I was in rags. I had braided my hair, but now it was like a lion's mane. There were people, barely breathing, trying to push their intestines back in. People with their legs wrenched off. Without heads. Or with faces burned and swollen out of shape. The scene I saw was a living hell.

Mom didn't say anything when she saw my face and I didn't feel any pain. She just squeezed my hand and told me to run. She was going to go rescue my aunt. Large numbers of people were moving away from the flames. My eyes were still able to see, so I made my way towards the mountain, where there was not fire, toward Hijiyama. On this flight I saw a friend of mine from the phone exchange. She'd been inside her house and wasn't burned. I called her name, but she didn't respond. My face was so swollen she couldn't tell who I was. Finally, she recognized my voice. She said, "Miss Yamaoka, you look like a monster!" That's the first time I heard that word. I looked at my hands and saw my own skin was hanging down and the red flesh exposed. I didn't realize my face was swollen up because I was unable to see it.

The only medicine was tempura oil. I put it on my body myself. I lay on the concrete for hours. My skin was now flat, not puffed up anymore. One or two layers had peeled off. Only now did it become painful. A scorching sky was overhead. The flies swarmed over me and covered my wounds, which were already festering. People were simply left lying around. When their faint breathing became silent, they'd say, "This one's dead," and put the body in a pile of corpses. Some called for water, and if they got it, they died immediately.

Mom came looking for me again. That's why I'm alive today. I couldn't walk anymore. I couldn't see anymore. I was carried on a stretcher as far as Ujina, and then from there to an island where evacuees were taken. On the boat there I hear voices saying, "Let them drink water if they want. They'll die either way." I drank a lot of water.

I spent the next year bedridden. All my hair fell out. When we went to relatives' houses later they wouldn't even let me in because they feared they'd catch the disease. There was neither treatment nor assistance for me. Those people who had money, people who had both parents, people who had houses, they could go to the Red Cross Hospital or the Hiroshima City Hospital. They could get operations. But we didn't have any money. It was just my Mom and I. Keloids° covered my face, my neck. I couldn't even move my neck. One

---

° Dense scar tissue.

eye was hanging down. I was unable to control my drooling because my lip had been burned off. I couldn't get any treatments at a hospital, so my mother gave me massages. Because she did that for me, my keloids aren't as bad as they would have been. My fingers were all stuck together. I couldn't move them. The only thing I could do was sew shorts, since I only needed to sew a straight line. I had to do something to earn money.

The Japanese government just told us we weren't the only victims of the war. There was no support or treatment. It was probably harder for my Mom. Once she told me she tried to choke me to death. If a girl had terrible scars, a face you couldn't be born with, I understand that even a mother could want to kill her child. People threw stones at me and called me Monster. That was before I had my many operations. I only showed this side of my face, the right hand side, when I had to face someone. Like I'm sitting now.

A decade after the bomb, we went to America. I was one of the twenty-five selected by Norman Cousins to be brought to America for treatment and plastic surgery. We were called the Hiroshima Maidens. The American government opposed us, arguing that it would be acknowledging a mistake if they admitted us to America, but we were supported by many civilian groups. We went to Mount Sinai Hospital in New York and spent about a year and a half undergoing treatment. I improved tremendously. I've now had thirty-seven operations, including efforts at skin grafts.

When I went to America I had a deep hatred toward America. I asked myself why they ended the war by a means which destroyed human beings. When I talked about how I suffered, I was often told, "Well, you attacked Pearl Harbor!" I didn't understand much English then, and it's probably just as well. From the American point of view, they dropped that bomb in order to end the war faster, in order to create more damage faster. But it's inexcusable to harm human beings in this way. I wonder what kind of education there is now in America about atomic bombs. They're still making them, aren't they?

189

Report on the Space Shuttle Challenger Accident by Richard P. Feynman—1988

Manned flight into space—first by rocket and then by the space shuttle—as developed by the United States was made possible by advances in rocketry technology during the late 1960s and early '70s. The first space shuttle rolled off the assembly line in September 1976 and began testing in January 1977. By popular demand, its name came from the science fiction television show Star Trek. Five shuttles were eventually built, and until the loss of the Challenger on January 28, 1986, the space shuttle program had an impressive safety record. Before exploding 73 seconds into its mission, The Challenger had flown the most voyages of the shuttle fleet. All seven crew members died, including Christa McAuliffe, who had been selected to be the first teacher in space. In the following excerpt, Dr. Richard P. Feynman (1918-1988), a professor of theoretical physics and winner of the Nobel Prize in Physics, discusses the problems associated with the space shuttle program. What does Feynman say was the problem with maintaining a regular schedule of shuttle flights? Why does he feel that civilians should not fly on shuttle missions? What recommendations does he make for future flights?

I t appears that there are enormous differences of opinion as to the probability of a failure with loss of vehicle and of human life. The estimates range from roughly 1 in 100 to 1 in 100,000. The higher come from the working engineers, and the very low figures from management. What are the causes and consequences of this lack of agreement? Since 1 part in 100,000 would imply that one could put a Shuttle up each day for 300 years expecting to lose only one, we could properly ask "What is the cause of management's fantastic faith in the machinery?"

If a reasonable launch schedule is to be maintained, engineering often cannot be done fast enough to keep up with the expectations of originally conservative certification criteria designed to guarantee a very safe vehicle. In these situations, subtly, and often with apparently logical arguments, the criteria are altered so that flights may still be certified in time. They therefore fly in a relatively unsafe condition, with a chance of failure of the order of a percent (it is difficult to be more accurate).

Official management, on the other hand, claims to believe the probability of failure is a thousand times less. One reason for this may be an attempt to

From "Personal observations on the reliability of the Shuttle" by Richard P. Feynman in Appendix to the Presidential Commission Report on the Space Shuttle Challenger Accident.

assure the government of NASA perfection and success in order to ensure the supply of funds. The other may be that they sincerely believed it to be true, demonstrating an almost incredible lack of communication between themselves and their working engineers.

In any event this has had very unfortunate consequences, the most serious of which is to encourage ordinary citizens to fly in such a dangerous machine, as if it had attained the safety of an ordinary airliner. The astronauts, like test pilots, should know their risks, and we honor them for their courage. Who can doubt that McAuliffe was equally a person of great courage, who was closer to an awareness of the true risk than NASA management would have us believe?

Let us make recommendations to ensure that NASA officials deal in a world of reality in understanding technological weaknesses and imperfections well enough to be actively trying to eliminate them. They must live in reality in comparing the costs and utility of the Shuttle to other methods of entering space. And they must be realistic in making contracts, in estimating costs, and the difficulty of the projects. Only realistic flight schedules should be proposed, schedules that have a reasonable chance of being met. If in this way the government would not support them, then so be it. NASA owes it to the citizens from whom it asks support to be frank, honest, and informative, so that these citizens can make the wisest decisions for the use of their limited resources.

For a successful technology, reality must take precedence over public relations, for nature cannot be fooled.

190

Silent Spring—1962—
Rachel Carson

Born on a farm in western Pennsylvania, Rachel Carson (1907–1964) earned a Master's Degree in Zoology and was hired as a junior biologist for the Bureau of Fisheries. Eventually Carson became chief of publications for the US Fish and Wildlife Service. Carson's love and respect for nature led her to write a series of books about the natural world that were immensely popular. Her concern about the growing use of chemical fertilizers and pesticides in the late fifties caused her to write Silent Spring. Although she was vilified by many for her courageous stand, before her death President Kennedy called for testing of the chemicals Carson discussed in her book. What is Carson's view of the relationship between nature and humankind? Do you think her views about the use of chemicals are needlessly alarmist? What is the role of the environmental movement in today's world?

The history of life on earth has been a history of interaction between living things and their surroundings. To a large extent, the physical form and the habits of the earth's vegetation and its animal life have been molded by the environment. Considering the whole span of earthly time, the opposite effect, in which life actually modifies its surroundings, has been relatively slight. Only within the moment of time represented by the present century has one species—man—acquired significant power to alter the nature of his world.

During the past quarter century this power has not only increased to one of disturbing magnitude but it has changed in character. The most alarming of all man's assaults upon the environment is the contamination of air, earth, rivers, and sea with dangerous and even lethal materials. This pollution is for the most part irrecoverable; the chain of evil it initiates not only in the world that must support life but in living tissues is for the most part irreversible. In this now universal contamination of the environment, chemicals are the sinister and little-recognized partners of radiation in changing the very nature of the world—the very nature of its life. Strontium 90, released through nuclear explosions into the air, comes to the earth in rain or drifts down as fallout, lodges in soil, enters into the grass or corn or wheat grown there, and in time takes up its abode in the bones of a human being, there to remain until his death. Similarly, chemicals sprayed on croplands or forests or gardens lie long in the soil, entering into living organisms, passing from one to another in a chain of poisoning and death. Or they pass mysteriously by underground streams until they emerge and, through the alchemy of air and sunlight, combine into new forms that kill vegetation, sicken cattle, and work unknown harm on those who drink from once pure wells. As Albert Schweitzer has said, "Man can hardly even recognize the devils of his own creation."

It look hundreds of millions of years to produce the life that now inhabits the earth—eons of time in which that developing and evolving and diversifying life reached a state of adjustment and balance with its surroundings. The environment, rigorously shaping and directing the life it supported, contained elements that were hostile as well as supporting. Certain rocks gave out dangerous radiation; even within the light of the sun, from which all life draws its energy, there were short-wave radiations with power to injure. Given time—time not in years but in millennia—life adjusts, and a balance has been reached. For time is the essential ingredient; but in the modern world there is no time.

The rapidity of change and the speed with which new situations are created follow the impetuous and heedless pace of man rather than the deliberate pace of nature. Radiation is no longer merely the background radiation of rocks, the bombardment of cosmic rays, the ultraviolet rays of the sun that have existed before there was any life on earth; radiation is now the unnatural creation of man's tampering with the atom. The chemicals to which life is asked to make its adjustment are no longer merely the calcium and silica and copper and all the rest of the minerals washed out of the rocks and carried in rivers to the sea; they are the synthetic creations of man's inventive mind, brewed in his laboratories, and having no counterparts in nature.

To adjust to these chemicals would require time on the scale that is nature's; it would require not merely the years of a man's life but the life of generations. And even this, were it by some miracle possible, would be futile, for the new chemicals come from our laboratories in an endless stream; almost five hundred annually find their way into actual use in the United States alone. The figure is staggering and its implications are not easily grasped—500 new chemicals to which the bodies of men and animals are required somehow to adapt each year, chemicals totally outside the limits of biologic experience.

Among them are many that are used in man's war against nature. Since the mid-1940's over 200 basic chemicals have been created for use in killing insects, weeds, rodents, and other organisms described in the modern vernacular as "pests" and they are sold under several thousand different brand names.

These sprays, dusts, and aerosols are now applied almost universally to farms, gardens, forests, and homes—nonselective chemicals that have the power to kill every insect, the "good" and the "bad," to still the song of birds and the leaping of fish in the streams, to coat the leaves with a deadly film, and to linger on in the soil—all this though the intended target may be only a few weeds or insects. Can anyone believe it is possible to lay down such a barrage of poisons on the surface of the earth without making it unfit for all life? They should not be called "insecticides," but "biocides."

The whole process of spraying seems caught up in an endless spiral. Since DDT was released for civilian use, a process of escalation has been going on in which ever more toxic materials must be found. This has happened because insects, in a triumphant vindication of Darwin's principle of the survival of the fittest, have evolved super races immune to the particular insecticide used, hence a deadlier one has always to be developed—and then a deadlier one than that. . . .

The "control of nature" is a phrase conceived in arrogance, born of the Neanderthal age of biology and philosophy, when it was supposed that nature exists for the convenience of man. The concepts and practices of applied entomology for the most part date from that Stone Age of science. It is our alarming misfortune that so primitive a science has armed itself with the most modern and terrible weapons, and that in turning them against the insects it has also turned them against the earth.

191

From *A Scenario for America and the World* by Herman Kahn, William Brown, and Leon Martel—1976

The beginning of the new millennium in 2000 brought a host of predictions for the future. The document that follows is a forecast that was published by Herman Kahn, William Brown, and Leon Martel in 1976. Kahn, a mathematician and physicist, was a defense analyst from 1946 to 1961 for the RAND Corporation, a nonprofit think tank often used by the Department of Defense. The table that follows was printed at the front of the book and provides four scenarios ranging from pessimistic (Neo-Malthusian) to very optimistic. Thirty years later, the table still provides food for thought. How might your basic attitude towards life affect which scenario you think is correct? Have any of the strategies proposed in 1976 already been adopted somewhere in the world? Which policies do you think governments should adopt to create the best possible future for their people?

Four Views of the Earth-Centered Perspective

A. Convinced Neo-Malthusian	B. Guarded Pessimist	C. Guarded Optimist	D. Technology-and-Growth Enthusiast
1. BASIC WORLD MODEL			
Finite pie. Most global nonrenewable resources can be estimated accurately enough (within a factor of 5) to demonstrate the reality of the running-out phenomenon. Whatever amounts of these resources are consumed will forever be denied to others. Current	*Uncertain-pie.* The future supply and value of both old and new materials are necessarily uncertain. Past projections of the future availability of materials usually have been gross underestimates. One can concede this could happen again, but current estimates	*Growing pie.* Past technological and economic progress suggests that increasing current production is likely to increase further the potential for greater production and that progress in one region encourages similar developments everywhere. Thus as the rich get	*Unlimited pie.* The important resources are capital, technology and educated people. The greater these resources, the greater the potential for even more. There is no persuasive evidence that any meaningful limits to growth are in sight—or

(Continued)

Tables from *The Next 200 Years* by Herman Kahn, p. 10–16. Reprinted by permission of HarperCollins, Inc.

Four Views of the Earth-Centered Perspective (*continued*)

A. Convinced Neo-Malthusian	B. Guarded Pessimist	C. Guarded Optimist	D. Technology-and-Growth Enthusiast
estimates show we will be running out of many critical resources in the next 50 years. The existing remainder of the pie must be shared more fairly among the nations of the world and between this generation and those to follow. Because the pie shrinks over time, any economic growth that makes the rich richer can only make the poor poorer.	seem relatively reliable. Current exponential growth clearly risks an early exhaustion of some critical materials. Prudence requires immediate conservation of remaining resources. Excessive conservation poses small risks while excessive consumption would be tragic.	richer, the poor also benefit. Higher consumption in the developed world tends to benefit all countries. Excessive caution tends to maintain excessive poverty. Some caution is necessary in selected areas, but both the "least risk" and the "best bet" paths require continued and rapid technological and economic development.	are desirable—except for population growth in some LDCs.[1] If any very long-term limits set by a "finite earth" really exist, they can be offset by the vast extraterrestrial resources and areas that will become available soon. Man has always risen to the occasion and will do so in the future despite dire predictions from the perennial doomsayers who have always been scandalously wrong.

2. TECHNOLOGY AND CAPITAL

Largely illusory or counterproductive. Proposed technological solutions to problems of pollution or scarce resources are shortsighted illusions that only compound the difficulties. Even on a moderate scale this approach would only further deplete crucial resources while avoiding the real problems and prolonging the poverty of the LDCs. Any future economic development should be restricted to the Third World and should include some transfer of existing capital	*Mostly diminishing returns.* Generally, despite many exceptions, the future will bring diminishing marginal returns from new investments, and the effort required for economic gains will increase dramatically. The technology, capital equipment and other efforts required to obtain minerals and food in increasingly marginal situations will accelerate the approaching exhaustion of many resources and substantially increase pollution and shortages—possibly to lethal	*Required for progress.* Despite some dangers, only new technology and capital investment can increase production; protect and improve the environment; hold down the cost of energy, minerals and food; provide economic surpluses with which to improve living standards in the LDCs; and prepare prudently for any potential unexpected catastrophes. We must be alert for problems resulting from inadequately understood innovations, inappropriate growth and/or natural	*Solves almost all problems.* Some current problems have resulted from careless application of technology and investment, but none is without a remedy. It is not paradoxical that technology which caused problems can also solve them—it only requires mankind's attention and desire. There is little doubt that sufficient land and resources exist for continual progress on earth. Most current problems are the result of too little technology and capital, not too much. In any case man's

1 Less–developed countries.

Four Views of the Earth-Centered Perspective *(continued)*

A. Convinced Neo-Malthusian	B. Guarded Pessimist	C. Guarded Optimist	D. Technology-and-Growth Enthusiast
assets from the over developed nations. A completely new approach is needed for the long term.	levels. Until practical solutions to these problems have appeared, we must turn away from technology and investment.	causes. However, we should proceed with energy and confidence even while exercising great caution and constantly reassessing future risks and benefits.	desire for expansion into new frontiers will lead eventually to the colonization of the solar system and effectively unlimited *lebensraum*.[2]

3. MANAGEMENT AND DECISION-MAKING

A. Convinced Neo-Malthusian	B. Guarded Pessimist	C. Guarded Optimist	D. Technology-and-Growth Enthusiast
Failure is almost certain. The complexities, rigidities and ideological differences among nations and their institutions make it inconceivable that present human organizations, even with computer assistance, could sufficiently comprehend and effectively act to solve our most important problems. A drastic redesign is needed to circumvent the thrust toward bigness, to permit much more local and decentralized decision-making, and to live and work on a manageable human scale. More emphasis is needed on the community and regional level—much less on big business, big government and big organizations generally.	*Likely failure.* The rapidity of change, growing complexity and increasing conflicting interests make effective management of resources, control of pollution and resolution of social conflicts too difficult. Some slowdown and simplification of issues are imperative—even if they require drastic actions. If we don't reform voluntarily, more painful political and economic changes may be imposed on us by the catastrophic events made inevitable by failure to act soon. (Note that there is a wide range of altitudes here toward central planning and local decision-making, but almost all of them mistrust the current "unfree market.")	*Moderately successful.* Systematic internalization of current external costs and normal economic mechanisms can make most private organizations adequately responsive to most problems. A practical degree of public regulation and a low degree of international cooperation can handle the rest, if somewhat awkwardly. Outstanding management is rare but usually not essential as most institutions learn from experience—if often slowly and painfully. (But good management can reduce the number and intensity of painful experiences.) Except for wars, shocks as great as the oil shock and other 1973–74 experiences are rare, and yet existing systems reacted adequately—and survived.	*Not a serious problem.* We flatter ourselves that current issues are more important and difficult than ever. Actually there is usually nothing very special happening. Mankind always has faced difficult and dangerous problems and poor solutions resulted in high costs. Sometimes there is even a Darwinian selection—the successes surviving and the failures disappearing. Progress has made the stakes today less dramatic. Modern communication and information systems and sophisticated organizations provide a capability for rapid adjustments to reality whenever changes are required and government interference is not counterproductive.

(Continued)

---

2 German for "living space."

Four Views of the Earth-Centered Perspective (continued)

A. Convinced Neo-Malthusian	B. Guarded Pessimist	C. Guarded Optimist	D. Technology-and-Growth Enthusiast
4. RESOURCES			
Steady depletion. Mankind is steadily, and often rapidly, depleting the earth's potential resources for foods, fuels and minerals, and overwhelming its capability to absorb or recycle pollutants. Catastrophic results for some of these resources may be postponed until the 21st century, but food, energy and some minerals already appear to be critically short for the near term. All signs point to catastrophe for the medium-and long-term future.	*Continual difficulties.* The basic problem of limited resources may be insoluble. Even when sufficient resources exist, politics, incompetent management, poor planning and slow responses make effective solutions difficult under conditions of exponentially increasing demand. Where resources are becoming scarce and unrelenting demands for growth are coupled with incompetence, intolerable pressures are generated and disaster becomes probable. A more cautious approach to growth seems clearly desirable.	*Generally sufficient.* Given slow but steady technological and economic progress and an ultimate world population below 30 billion, it should be feasible to attain economic living standards markedly better than current ones. With rapid progress and good management generally, even higher economic levels and an outstanding quality of life become possible. Economic success enhances national capabilities to resolve specialized resource issues as they arise. However, the tendency toward cartels coupled with political conflicts could create short-term problems in maintaining adequate supplies at reasonable prices.	*Economics and technology can provide superb solutions.* The earth is essentially bountiful in all of the important resources. Sudden large price fluctuations tend to be "self-correcting" within a few years although they can be misinterpreted as basic shortages (as in 1973–74).[3] Near-term prices are certainly important, but we have often lived with short-term problems. Trust in the economics of the market system, confidence in emerging technological solutions and a little patience will remedy the current resource issues just as they have in the past.
5. CURRENT GROWTH			
Carcinogenic. Current population and economic production are akin to a spreading cancer. They are already more than the earth can sustain in a steady state. Future economic or population growth will	*Large potential for disaster.* Even if roughly current levels of production could be indefinitely sustained, continued exponential growth in population and production eventually must lead to	*Probable transition to stability.* Although current projections are uncertain, social and cultural forces inherent in both developing and affluent societies appear likely to limit the world population to	*Desirable and healthy.* No obvious limits are apparent. Even with current technological potential, growth (except perhaps in a few of the poorest nations) is and will be purely a matter of human choice, not of

---

3 In the wake of the so-called Yom Kippur War between Israel and the Arab states in
   1973, Muslim nations that were members of OPEC curtailed oil production and
   declared an embargo on oil exports to the United States. Before the embargo ended in
   1974, oil prices had quadrupled in the United States.

Four Views of the Earth-Centered Perspective *(continued)*

A. Convinced Neo-Malthusian	B. Guarded Pessimist	C. Guarded Optimist	D. Technology-and-Growth Enthusiast
hasten and increase the magnitude of the future tragedy. The current demand for continued economic growth and the likelihood of a greatly increased world population only imply a steady worsening of the present extremely dangerous conditions.	exhausted resources and hazardous pollution. Few positive human values would be served by continued mindless growth. We must learn that demand is not need. Unless drastic voluntary reforms limit future growth, catastrophes stemming from limited resources and high pollution levels are likely to make these reforms mandatory before long.	about three times the current level and average per capita production to about two or three times the current U.S. level. There seems to be more than enough energy, resources and space for most populations, assuming that a relatively small number of people put forth the necessary efforts and others do not interfere.	natural limitations, Problems always exist, but solutions always emerge—often as a result of the dynamism of growth. We do not know man's ultimate fate, but truly fantastic economic and technological capabilities are likely to be included as both a means and an end (e.g., they probably include self-reproducing automation and space colonization in the next century).

6. INNOVATION AND DISCOVERY

A trap. New discoveries of resources, new technologies and new projects may postpone the immediate need for drastic actions, but not for long. Such postponement will make eventual collapse earlier and more severe. Prudence demands immediate restraint, cutbacks and a basic change in values and objectives. The time for short-run palliatives is past.	*Increasingly ineffective.* The basic solution is to increasingly limit demands, not to encourage a desperate search for new inventions that might suffice temporarily but would exacerbate long-run problems, by increasing environmental damage and depletion of resources, while encouraging current growth and deferring hard decisions. Although technological solutions may buy some time, it has become increasingly important to use this time constructively and avoid the undue economic expansion that new discoveries encourage.	*Usually effective.* New resources, new technology and economic growth often produce new problems, but they still do solve current problems, improve efficiency and upgrade the quality of life. Also, they increase the toughness and flexibility of the economy and society (i.e., provide insurance against bad luck or incompetence). With good management, they also can help to reduce population growth, conserve expensive minerals, improve nutrition within the poorer countries and generally improve future prospects.	*Mankind's greatest hope.* New and improving technologies (agronomy, electronics, genetics, power generation and distribution, information processing, etc.) aided by fortuitous discoveries (e.g., ocean nodules) further man's potential for solving current perceived problems and for creating an affluent and exciting world. Man is now entering the most creative and expansive period of his history. These trends will soon allow mankind to become the "master" of the solar system.

(Continued)

Four Views of the Earth-Centered Perspective (*continued*)

A. Convinced Neo-Malthusian	B. Guarded Pessimist	C. Guarded Optimist	D. Technology-and-Growth Enthusiast

7. INCOME GAPS AND POVERTY

A. Convinced Neo-Malthusian	B. Guarded Pessimist	C. Guarded Optimist	D. Technology-and-Growth Enthusiast
Destined to tragic conclusions. The major consequeces of industrialization and economic growth have been to enrich the few while exploiting and improverishing the many. The gap between rich and poor as well as the total misery in the world are at all-time highs—and growing. Meanwhile natural resources, the heritage of the poor countries, are being consumed by the rich, thereby denying the poor any real hope for better living conditions—even temporarily.	*Increasing and threatening.* Income gaps have been increasing and may lead to dangerous responses. A drastic decrease in income among the poor may even be likely soon. Worldwide class warfare may emerge following a series of desperate political crises. These are not only possible but may be imminent as a consequence of the gaps and the exploitation of the mineral resources of the LDCs. A more equitable income distribution has become a most urgent matter.	*Declining absolute poverty.* World-wide, the threat of absolute poverty. (i.e., possible large-scale famine) is likely soon to be forever abolished. Some income gaps may increase during the next century, but some will decrease. Generally, incomes of both rich and poor will increase. Both the gaps and improving technology will tend to accelerate development in poor countries. Attempts to force a rapid equalization of income would guarantee only failure and tragic consequences.	*A misformulated problem.* Western civilization required about 200 years to change from general poverty to general affluence. Because of their success and continuing advances in technology, many of the current LDCs will be able to make a similar transition within 50 years. All countries can be expected to become wealthy within the next 200 years. Any lesser scenario would be unreasonable or an expression of very bad luck and/or bad management.

9. QUALITY OF LIFE

A. Convinced Neo-Malthusian	B. Guarded Pessimist	C. Guarded Optimist	D. Technology-and-Growth Enthusiast
Ruined. Through excessive growth, mankind has become the most destructive species in history and may yet increase the extend of this damage manyfold. Indeed, a point of no return may have been passed already, mostly because of the persistent and growing potential for nuclear warfare. In any event, the values that lead toward a satisfying and wholesome life have already been largely destroyed in the developed nations.	*In conflict with much growth.* Continued economic development or population growth might well mean further deterioration of the environment, overcrowding, suburban sprawl and a society suitable more for machines than human beings. Priorities must change; market demand is not the same as need; GNP is not wealth, high technology not the same as a good life; automation and appliances do not necessarily increase human happiness.	*More gains than losses.* If environmental protection, health, safety and other considerations are neglected, growth would be accompanied by an unnecessary destruction of important values. However, much of what some elites claim to be destructive others consider constructive (e.g., a pipeline). With adequate internalization of the appropriate costs (by society's criteria), complaints from unhappy factions might still be loud or visible but would be generally inappropriate.	*A meaningless phrase and issue.* Disgruntled or un-happy people often oppose real progress for romantic, class, selfish or other reasons. They are not representative of the nation and need not be taken at face value. In a changing world, some elites may not benefit much or may even lose somewhat. But most people would benefit and gain expectations for an even better future.

CHAPTER 25

Daily Life in the Postmodern World— 1914–Present

Modernization during the twentieth century caused upheaval and change in countries such as the Soviet Union and China, where the economy was restructured and expanded by government intervention and control. Millions of people were displaced due to the ravages of war and the creation of new states, whereas others were imprisoned because they criticized their governments. In China, the relaxation of rules against capitalism allowed peasants to become entrepreneurs with some success. Modernization provided opportunities for women in some areas, yet all women did not share in the rights and opportunities accorded them in some societies in the years after World War II.

How did Stalin and Nkrumah hope to change the economic structure of their countries? What role did the people have in these decisions? How did the establishment of the new state of Israel change life for the Palestinians? Did the revolution in Iran help the cause of women who supported it? Why or why not? Compare the status of women in Japan, Uganda, and India. In which of these societies did women benefit most from modernization? In which did modernization negatively undermine traditional culture? In which country did modernization change women's lives in a positive manner?

192

Memories of Childhood by
Yevgeny Yevtushenko—1938

The following document is an excerpt from the autobiography of the Soviet Union's most famous poet, Yevgeny Yevtushenko. He wrote about his childhood in Russia during the era of Stalinist collectivization and political repression. How does this excerpt help you to understand Soviet attitudes towards Stalin in the late 1930s? What seems to have been the reason for their loyalty to him?

YEVGENY YEVTUSHENKO
REMEMBERS HIS CHILDHOOD

I was born on July 18, 1933, in Siberia, at Zima Junction, a small place near Lake Baikal. My surname, Yevtushenko, is Ukrainian.

Long ago, at the end of the last century, my great-grandfather, a peasant from the Zhitomir Province, was deported to Siberia for having "let out the red rooster" in his landlord's house. This is the Russian peasant way of saying that he had set fire to his house. That's probably the origin of my inclination to reach for that red rooster whenever I meet anyone with a landlord's mentality.

No one in our family uttered the word "Revolution" as if he were making a speech. It was uttered quietly, gently, a shade austerely. Revolution was the religion of our family.

My grandfather, Yermolay Yevtushenko, a soldier who could barely read, was one of the organizers of the peasant movement in the Urals and in eastern Siberia. Later, under the Soviet regime he studied at a military academy, became a brigade commander, and held the important post of deputy commander of artillery in the Russian Republican Army. But even in his commander's uniform he remained the peasant he had always been and kept his religious faith in Revolution.

I last saw him in 1938. I was five then. I remember our conversation very well.

My grandfather came into my room. I had already undressed and was lying in bed. He sat down on the edge of my bed. He had in his hands a box of liqueur-filled chocolates. His eyes, usually mischievous and smiling, that night

From Yevgeny Yevtushenko, *A Precocious Autobiography*, trans. Andrew R. MacAndrew (New York: E.P. Dutton, 1936), p. 14–17. Copyright © 1963 by E.P. Dutton. Reprinted by permission of Penguin Group (USA), Inc.

looked at me from under his gray prickly crew-cut with a tired and sad expression. He offered me the box of chocolates and then pulled a bottle of vodka out of the pocket of his cavalry breeches.

"I want us to have a drink together," he said. "You have the candy and I'll have the vodka."

He slapped the bottom of the bottle with the flat of his hand and the cork shot out. I fished a chocolate out of the box.

"What shall we drink to?" I asked, trying hard to sound grown-up.

"To the Revolution," my grandfather said with grim simplicity.

We touched glasses—that is, my candy touched his bottle—and we drank.

"Now go to sleep," Grandfather said.

He switched off the light but remained sitting on my bed.

It was too dark for me to see his face but I felt that he was looking at me.

Then he began to sing softly. He sang the melancholy songs of the chain gangs, the songs of the strikers and the demonstrators, the songs of the Civil War.

And listening to them I went to sleep. . . .

I never saw my grandfather again. My mother told me he had gone away for a long trip. I didn't know that on that very night he had been arrested on a charge of high treason. I didn't know that my mother stood night after night in that street with the beautiful name, Marine Silence Street, among thousands of other women who were also trying to find out whether their fathers, husbands, brothers, sons were still alive. I was to learn all this later.

Later I also found out what had happened to my other grandfather, who similarly had vanished. He was Rudolph Gangnus, a round-shouldered gray-bearded mathematician of Latvian origin, whose textbooks were used to teach geometry in Soviet schools. He was arrested on a charge of spying for Latvia.

But at this time I knew nothing.

I went with my father and mother to watch the holiday parades, organized workers' demonstrations, and I would beg my father to lift me up a little higher.

I wanted to catch sight of Stalin.

And as I waved my small red flag, riding high in my father's arms above that sea of heads, I had the feeling that Stalin was looking right at me.

I was filled with a terrible envy of those children my age lucky enough to be chosen to hand bouquets of flowers to Stalin and whom he gently patted on the head, smiling his famous smile into his famous mustache.

To explain away the cult of Stalin's personality by saying simply that it was imposed by force is, to say the least, rather naive. There is no doubt that Stalin exercised a sort of hypnotic charm.

Many genuine Bolsheviks who were arrested at that time utterly refused to believe that this had happened with his knowledge, still less on his personal instructions. Some of them, after being tortured, traced the words "Long live Stalin" in their own blood on the walls of their prison.

Did the Russian people understand what was really happening?

I think the broad masses did not. They sensed intuitively that something was wrong, but no one wanted to believe what he guessed at in his heart. It would have been too terrible.

The Russian people preferred to work rather than to think and to analyze. With a heroic, stubborn self-sacrifice unprecedented in history they built power station after power station, factory after factory. They worked in a furious desperation, drowning with the thunder of machines, tractors, and bulldozers the cries that might have reached them across the barbed wire of Siberian concentration camps.

193

A Palestinian Exile Remembers by Fawzi Turki—1948

In contrast to the joy of the Israelis upon the creation of the state of Israel in 1948 is the recollection of Fawzi Turki. This young Palestinian, along with his parents, sisters, and brother was forced into exile at the end of the first Arab–Israeli War. They ended up in a refugee camp in Beirut, Lebanon, along with many other Palestinians, yet they never gave up the hope of returning to Palestine. How do Turki's attitudes and desires compare with those of Nahum Goldman? What might drive Palestinians to acts of violence to regain their homeland? Why might the Jews retaliate so fiercely?

Abreeze began to blow as we moved slowly along the coast road, heading to the Lebanese border—my mother and father, my two sisters, my brother and I. Behind us lay the city of Haifa, long the scene of bombing, sniper fire, ambushes, raids, and bitter fighting between Palestinians and Zionists. Before us lay the city of Sidon and indefinite exile. Around us the waters of the Mediterranean sparkled in the sun. Above us eternity moved on unconcerned, as if God in his heavens watched the agonies of men, as they walked on crutches, and smiled. And our world had burst, like a bubble, a bubble that had engulfed us within its warmth. From then on I would know only crazy sorrow and watch the glazed eyes of my fellow Palestinians burdened by loss and devastated by pain.

April 1948. And so it was the cruelest month of the year; but there were crueler months, then years. . . .

From Fawaz Turki, *The Disinherited: Journal of a Palestinian Exile* (New York: Monthly Review Press, 1972), p. 43–45, 47–48, 54. Copyright © 1972 by Monthly Review Press. Reprinted by permission of the Monthly Review Foundation.

After a few months in Sidon, we moved again, a Palestinian family of six heading to a refugee camp in Beirut, impotent with hunger, frustration, and incomprehension. But there we encountered other families equally helpless, equally baffled, who like us never had enough to eat, never enough to offer books and education to their children, never enough to face an imminent winter. In later years, when we left the camp and found better housing and a better life outside and grew up into our early teens, we would complain about not having this or that and would be told by our mothers: "You are well off, boy! Think of those still living there in the camps. Just think of them and stop making demands." We would look out the window and see the rain falling and hear the thunder. And we would remember. We would understand. We would relent as we thought "of those still living there."

Man adapts. We adapted, the first few months, to life in a refugee camp. In the adaptation we were also reduced as men, as women, as children, as human beings. At times we dreamed. Reduced dreams. Distorted ambitions. One day, we hoped, our parents would succeed in buying two beds for me and my sister to save us the agonies of asthma, intensified from sleeping on blankets on the cold floor. One day, we hoped, there would be enough to buy a few pounds of pears or apples as we had done on those special occasions when we fought and sulked and complained because one of us was given a smaller piece of fruit than the others. One day soon, we hoped, it would be the end of the month when the UNRWA rations arrived and there was enough to eat for a week. One day soon, we argued, we would be back in our homeland.

The days stretched into months and those into a year and yet another. Kids would play in the mud of the winters and the dust of the summers, while "our problem" was debated at the UN and moths died around the kerosene lamps. A job had been found for me in a factory not far from the camp, where I worked for six months. I felt pride in the fact that I was a bread earner and was thus eligible to throw my weight around the house, legitimately demand an extra spoonful of sugar in my tea, and have my own money to spend on comic books and an occasional orange on the side. I had even started saving to buy my own bed, but I was fired soon after that.

A kid at work had called me a two-bit Palestinian and a fist fight ensued. The supervisor, an obese man with three chins and a green stubble that covered most of his face and reached under his eyes, came over to stop the fight. He decided I had started it all, slapped me hard twice, deducted three lira from my wages for causing trouble (I earned seven lira a week), paid me the rest, called me a two-bit Palestinian, and, pointing to my blond hair, suggested I had a whore mother and shoved me out the door.

I went to the river and sat on the grass to eat my lunch. I was shaken more by the two-bit-Palestinian epithet than by the plight of being unemployed. At home and around the camp, we had unconsciously learned to be proud of where we came from and to continue remembering that we were Palestinians. If this was stigmatic outside, there it was an identity to be known, perpetuated, embraced. My father, reproaching us for an ignoble offense of some kind, would say: "You are a Palestinian." He would mean: as a Palestinian one is not expected to stoop that low and betray his tradition. If we came home affecting a Lebanese accent, our mother would say: "Hey, what's wrong with your own accent? You're too good for your own people or something? You want to sound like a foreigner when we return to Haifa? What's wrong with you, hey?"

* * *

Our Palestinian consciousness, instead of dissipating, was enhanced and acquired a subtle nuance and a new dimension. It was buoyed by two concepts: the preservation of our memory of Palestine and our acquisition of education. We persisted in refusing the houses and monetary compensation offered by the UN to settle us in our host countries. We wanted nothing short of returning to our homeland. And from Syria, Lebanon, and Jordan, we would see, a few miles, a few yards, across the border, a land where we had been born, where we had lived, and where we felt the earth. "This is my land," we would shout, or cry, or sing, or plead, or reason. And to that land a people had come, a foreign community of colonizers, aided by a Western world in a hurry to rid itself of guilt and shame, demanding independence from history, from heaven, and from us.

194

The Age of Women in Japan by Keiko Higuchi—1980

By 1979, Japan was well on its way to recovery after the devastating losses of World War II. Postwar economic growth had been tremendous, and the standard of living in Japan was now close to that of the United States. Modernization also had a great impact on women's roles in Japan. Patriarchal attitudes were still powerful; women who sought careers in the business world or academia often faced many obstacles, while a declining birth rate and increased life expectancy forced many to reconsider traditional female roles. In the following document, Keiko Higuchi, a Japanese feminist, discusses the changes she saw in the attitudes of Japanese women by 1980. What does she think would have the most impact on the lives of Japanese women? Do you see any similarities between the lives of Japanese and American women in 1980?

From Higuchi Keiko, "Japanese Women in Transition," *Japan Quarterly* 29 (July–Sept. 1982): 311, 313–18.

"The Age of Women"—so ran the catch-phrase adorning a Japanese newspaper advertisement on New Year's Day 1979, the eye of the 80s. The ad went on in part to say: "Dazzling—simply dazzling, the women of today. Mothers and daughters taking off suddenly on trips abroad, or giving up their diets and going in for yoga instead. Expressing themselves freely, without fear or hesitation, these are women who know the art of enjoying life to the full . . . Today's women are off the sidelines to stay."

The slogan notwithstanding, this message is probably best understood as a gift of flattery from male salesmen to female buyers. Beginning with this advertisement, the decade of the 80s has come with increasing frequency to be called "the age of women." And yet one has the distinct sense that before yielding any substantial results, the term was quickly taken over by the advertising industry as a piece of "fashion." In any case, the emergence of language such as this in newspaper advertising is surely a sign of change in the situation of Japanese women. . . .

The consciousness of Japanese women is now in a state of transition. Their attitude toward the idea that "men should work outside the home, women inside" has changed greatly in the last 10 years. In a 1972 survey of attitudes on women's issues undertaken by the Prime Minister's Office, over 80 percent of women respondents agreed with the idea as stated above. But in a similar survey conducted in 1976, the year after International Women's Year, those concurring that "men work, and women stay home" were 49 percent, while 40 percent disagreed and 11 percent were undecided. The wording of the question as well as the range of possible answers vary, making simple comparisons difficult, but it would seem clear at any rate that doubts regarding the traditional idea of sex-differentiated work roles are rapidly growing. In 1979 the Prime Minister's Office conducted another survey posing the same questions as in 1976, but this time, in response to the assertion that "men work and women stay home," pollees were evenly divided among "agree," "disagree" and "don't know," with each answer drawing a response in the 30th percentile. When the question pertains to "men" and "women," people are somewhat likely to go against the traditional view, but when the words "husbands" and "wives" are substituted, resistance declines. Acceptance of sex-differentiated work roles is still deep-rooted in Japan.

Among the younger generation, however, there is possibility for more rapid change. In the 1979 survey by the Prime Minister's Office, the assertion by 25 percent of unmarried women that they had "no wish to marry" attracted wide notice. Japanese have a high marriage rate, so much so that they have been called a people "fond of marrying": by age 50, 97 percent of both men and women have been married at least once. The Prime Minister's Office asked the same question in 1972, but at that time only 14 percent of women declared themselves uninterested in marrying. In the 1979 survey, a mere 12 percent of men selected the same response, thus revealing a gap in attitudes toward marriage between the sexes. Moreover, women responding that "a woman's happiness lies in marriage" went down from 40 percent to 32 percent.

Yearly surveys by Nippon Recruit Center, an employment agency, on "attitudes of female university students toward employment" show that until the late 70s, even among graduates of four-year colleges, those desiring to work "until retirement age" amounted to scarcely 20 percent. In the 1981 survey, however, 41 percent of respondents (19 percent for junior college graduates) gave that answer. The most frequently given answer was to work "until a child is born, then again after the child is older" (58.7 percent). Significantly, those who said simply, "until marrying" or "until a child is born"—thus relegating work to a brief period early in their lifetimes—were in the minority for the first time at 25.3 percent or one quarter of the sample. For Japan, where women are held to be at a particular disadvantage in combining marriage and a career, and where long-term female employment is much rarer than in Europe and America, such a shift in attitudes is truly remarkable. . . .

In the Tokyo residential area where I live, around 10 every morning housewives clad in short, above-the-knee outfits get on their bikes, tennis rackets in baskets, and pedal off in a row for the local tennis court. A conspicuous change in the last 10 years has been the phenomenal growth in large cities nationwide of housewives' hobby and culture centers, sponsored by newspapers, broadcasting companies, department stores and even big businesses. Women in their 30s and 40s, freed from the burden of caring for small children, flock to tennis courts and culture centers out of a desire to be with others like themselves—a hunger, perhaps, for companionship—as they seek the pattern for the latter half of their lives. In the past, Japanese women were referred to by their husbands as *kanai*, meaning literally "inside the house"—and that is exactly where they stayed. Today, as women step out more and more in search of entertainment, education and a wide variety of activities, one sometimes hears a man say of his wife, "She's no *kanai*; she's my *kagai* ('outside the house')."

But housewives commuting to tennis courts and cultural enrichment centers are, after all, outnumbered by those commuting to work. The number of female employees is steadily increasing, and at present nearly 70 percent are married. In addition, more than half of all unemployed housewives aged 40 and above "would like to work." By far their biggest motivation is to bring the family budget out of the red. Although real earnings of household heads have declined in the last few years, the standard of living has held its own, thanks largely to increases in wives' earnings.

Not long ago, when I was in a department store, two clerks called out to me one after the other. They told me they had heard me speak at a lecture meeting sponsored by a grade-school PTA. Both of them are active as PTA members while holding down part-time jobs in a department store. The day of the lecture meeting, they said, they had taken off work to attend. I could not help feeling struck by this clear example of change. It wasn't many years ago that at PTA meetings one frequently heard the complaint that "so many women have jobs nowadays, there's nobody to work for the PTA." Some ladies even went so far as to take part-time jobs only when officers' elections came around, and then plead work as an excuse to decline. Now many women manage successfully to juggle work outside the home with active participation in community affairs. Working housewives have become so commonplace that it can no longer be said that "PTA is for mothers who don't work."

Toward the end of April 1982, the Ministry of Labor published results of a "Basic survey on Wage Structure in 1981." According to these results, although until recently male workers attained their top earning power in their 50s, now male wages have begun to peak earlier, in the 45–50 age bracket. "My husband's earnings will peak when he's in his 40s—so I'd better go to work to help out the budget." This sort of determination appears to be spreading rapidly among Japanese women.

Women in Japan are stepping out of the house in ever-swelling numbers. Yet men persist in clinging to the notion that "women's work is in the home." Those most critical of sex-differentiated labor roles are not men, but women. It appears inevitable, therefore, that discord will arise between the sexes.

Conflict between husband and wife is apt to arise from the work overload of working wives. The belief that household affairs are the wife's exclusive responsibility is deeply ingrained in Japanese society, and many women would in fact regard their husband's entrance into the kitchen as an unwelcome intrusion. According to a 1976 research survey by the Prime Minister's Office on "Lifestyles in Society," unemployed housewives spend an average of five hours and 54 minutes each day on housework and childcare, compared to three hours and 29 minutes for those with outside jobs. Husbands of unemployed wives, for their part, contribute an average of seven minutes daily to the same tasks, while for husbands of working women the figure is an astounding six minutes. Thus, utterly betraying the expectation that "it is only natural for the husband to help out around the house if the wife works too," Japenese married men reign as *shujin* ("husband"; literally, "master") in their homes, and whether or not the wife has an outside job they do virtually no housework.

The husband expects his wife to look after the home, and in the home he seeks a place of recreation and relaxation in which to garner strength for the coming day's work. This is the view of the wife's role, and of the function of the home, given often in Japanese textbooks for the lower, compulsory levels of school. The husband, behaving exactly as the textbooks predict he will, hands over his pay envelope to his wife without even looking inside. Most big corporations nowadays transfer paychecks directly to employees' bank accounts, but the wife remains firmly in charge of home finances. The husband sees the act of turning over his entire salary to his wife simultaneously as an expression of love and a fulfillment of obligation. The wife, however, has begun to entertain misgivings about an existence spent for the most part waiting passively at home for her husband's return.

The profound changes in the lifestyles of Japanese women surely have few precedents anywhere in the world. It is well known that Japanese women expend more love and energy on their children than on their husbands. But the children who are objects of so much maternal devotion have decreased drastically in number per family while average life expectancies have continued to rise. In 1940, a woman whose youngest child had just entered school had only 7.6 years of life remaining; in 1978, the number of years she could count on had jumped to 44. After the youngest child marries, moreover, she and her husband can still look forward to nearly a score of years of married life. . . .

The new women's liberation movement which spread to Japan in the early 70s brought pressure for change in the lives of both men and women. And the U.N.'s Decade for Women forced the Japanese government to face up to many of the issues involved. At the same time, the extremely rapid aging of Japanese society—a phenomenon without precedent or equal in the world—is forcing upon us, willy-nilly, a reevaluation of relationships between the sexes, married and unmarried alike.

Aged people (those 65 years old and above) now comprise a mere 9 percent of the population of Japan, but in the coming 30 to 40 years it is anticipated that their numbers will swell to more than 23 percent. No advanced nation has yet experienced a society in which one out of every four people is elderly.

The life span of Japanese women is approaching 80 years. The question of how middle-aged Japanese women are to spend the latter half of this extended lifetime is one that must be asked. With marriage as the single-minded goal of their youth, followed by harried years of caring for husband and children, they have had little time for self-reflection; now, realizing after their children are grown or their husband retires that without a personal goal they will be unable to face the loneliness of widowhood, these women are full of consternation. Among Japanese aged 65 and over, those whose spouse is living account for 80 percent of the men, but only one in three of women. Soon there will be one million old people living alone in Japan, 80 percent of them female. Their income, moreover, is less than half that of men. And of those looking after elderly invalids in their own homes, as many as 90 percent are women. Lately the idea that "the problems of old age are women's problems" is voiced more and more often at women's gatherings. . . .

The traditional life-patterns for Japanese men and women—until very recently thought natural and common-sensical—are now, under the pressures of a highly developed, rapidly aging industrial society, in a period of transition, as people seek to put them in a new frame of reference.

195

The Revolution that Failed Women by Zand Dokht—1981

Despite the fact that the Pahlavi regimes of the Shahs (1925–1979) gave women politi-cal rights and encouraged them to abandon the veil and seek an education, millions of women supported the 1979 revolution. They were disgusted with the corruption of the Shah's government and participated in the massive public demonstrations that occurred before the revolution. Unfortunately, many of these same women were bitterly disap-pointed when the Islamic Republic of Ayatollah Khomeini reinstated traditional Islamic roles for women. In response, they formed the Women's Solidarity Committee to protect women's rights in Iran, but the organization was later banned within the country. The organization still exists outside Iran, however. The following excerpt comes from one of their publications. Why did so many Iranian women support the revolution that curtailed their freedom? In what ways did the successful revolution affect their role in society?

When Khomeini created his Islamic Republic in 1979, he relied on the institution of the family, on support from the women, the mer-chants, and the private system of landownership. The new Islamic constitution declared women's primary position as mothers. The black veil, symbol of the position of women under Islam, was made compulsory. Guards were posted outside government offices to enforce it, and women were sacked from their jobs without compensation for refusing to wear the veil. The chair-man of the Employment Office, in an interview with the government's women's magazine said, "We can account for 100,000 women government employees being sacked as they resisted the order of the revolutionary govern-ment when it was demanded of them to put the veil on."

Schools were segregated, which meant that women were barred from some technical schools, even from some religious schools, and young girls' education in the villages was halted. Lowering the marriage age for girls to 13, reinstating polygamy and *Sighen* (temporary wives), the two major pillars of Islam, meant that women did not need education and jobs, they only needed to find husbands.

The Ayatollahs in their numerous public prayers, which grew to be the only possible national activity, continuously gave sermons on the advantages of marriage, family, and children being brought up on their mother's lap. They preached that society would be pure, trouble free, criminal-less (look at the

From *Third World/Second Sex* by Miranda Davies (London: Zed Books, 1983), p. 152–149. Reprinted by permission of Zed Books, Ltd.

youth problem in the West) if everybody married young, and if men married as many times as possible (to save the unprotected women who might otherwise become prostitutes). The government created a marriage bank at a time when half the working population was unemployed, whereby men were given huge sums—around £3,500—to get married. Another *masterpiece* of the revolutionary Islamic government was to create a system of arranged marriages in prisons, between men and women prisoners, to "protect" women after they leave prison.

Because abortion and contraception are now unobtainable, marriage means frequent pregnancy. If you are 13 when you get married, it is likely that you will have six children by the time you are 20. This, in a country where half the total population are already under 16, is a tragedy for future generations.

Religious morality demands that all pleasures and entertainments be banned. Wine, music, dancing, chess, women's parts in theater, cinema and television—you name it, Khomeini banned it. He even segregated the mountains and the seas, for male and female climbers and swimmers.

But compulsory morality, compulsory marriage, and the compulsory wearing of the veil did not create the Holy Society that Khomeini was after; but public lashings, stonings, chopping of hands and daily group executions sank Iran into the age of Barbarism.

Perhaps nowhere else in the world have women been murdered for walking in the street open-faced. The question of the veil is the most important issue of women's liberation in Muslim countries. The veil, a long engulfing black robe, is the extension of the four walls of the home, where women belong. The veil is the historical symbol of woman's oppression, seclusion, denial of her social participation and equal rights with men. It is a cover which defaces and objectifies women. To wear or not to wear the veil, for Muslim women is "the right to choose." . . .

Why do women, workers and unemployed, support this regime which has done everything in its power to attack their rights and interests? The power of Islam in our culture and tradition has been seriously underestimated . . . and it was through this ideology that Khomeini directed his revolutionary government. The clergy dealt with everyday problems and spoke out on human relationships, sexuality, security and protection of the family and the spiritual needs of human beings. It was easy for people to identify with these issues and support the clergy, although nobody knew what they were later to do. When Khomeini asked for sacrifices—"we haven't made the Revolution in order to eat chicken or dress better"—women (so great in the art of sacrifice) and workers accepted these anti-materialist ideas. . . .

Women's attraction to Khomeini's ideas was not based simply on his Islamic politics, but also on the way he criticized the treatment of women—as secretaries and media sex objects—under the Shah's regime. Women were genuinely unsatisfied and looking for change. Some educated Iranian women went back to Iran from America and Europe to aid the clergy with the same messages, and became the government's spokeswomen. They put on the veil willingly, defended Islamic virtues and spiritual values while drawing from their own experiences in the West. They said it was cold and lonely, Western women were only in pursuit of careers and self-sufficiency, and that their polygamous sexual relationships had not brought them liberation, but confusion and exploitation. These women joined ranks with an already growing force of Muslim women, to retrieve the tradition of true/happy Muslim women—in defense of patriarchy.

The mosque is not just a place of prayer, it is also a social club for women. It provides a warm, safe room for women to meet, chat or listen to a sermon, and there are traditional women-only parties and picnics in gardens or holy places. Take away these traditional and religious customs from women is the Shah—with his capitalist and imperialist reforms, irrelevant to women's needs—tried to do and a huge vacuum is left. Khomeini stepped in to fill that vacuum. The reason why Khomeini won was that the Shah's social-economic program for women was dictatorial, bureaucratic, inadequate (especially in terms of health education) and therefore irrelevant to women's needs. What little the Shah's reform brought to women was just a token gesture. Women dissatisfied with the Shah's reform felt that they had benefited little from him and would not miss it if it was taken away.

196

A Chinese Peasant Maps His Road to Wealth by Wang Xin—1984

The following document was part of an article printed in the Beijing Review *in 1984. The author, a peasant who lived through the turmoil of the Communist revolution as well as the reforms of Deng Xiaoping, relates his family's quest for wealth. Obviously, Wang Xin benefited from the new economic policies, because by 1984 his family was one of the 22 wealthiest in China. Can you see any elements of Confucian tradition in Wang's narrative? Would you consider him a capitalist?*

From Wang Xin with Yang Xiaobing, "A Peasant Maps His Road to Wealth," *Beijing Review*, 27 (12 Nov. 1984), p. 28–30. Reprinted by permission.

There is a long story behind my family's prosperity. My family's history is closely linked with the history of the Chinese society. So let me start my story with the rise and fall of the country.

In 1941, I was born to a poor peasant family in Pinggu County. At the time, my family had 10 members from three generations, but we had no farmland at all. My grandpa and his brother had to work for the landlord. My father and his brother wove at home and traded their coarse cloth at the market for some food. While peddling their handmade cloth, they had to be alert and evasive to avoid being forced to bribe the police.

One winter day, my grandpa's brother had two fingers bit off while feeding cattle for the landlord. The landlord simply dismissed him when he saw he was no longer useful. This made our lives even worse. My grandma had no other way to earn money but to pick wild jujubes in the mountains, which were ground up and mixed with wild herbs to make something like a bun.

At the time, my grandparents and parents wanted to work hard and get rich. Their desire, however, was merely a dream.

BRIGHT DAWN

In 1949 New China was founded and we peasants became masters of the country. Land reform was carried out, with feudalist land ownership abolished and farmland returned to the tillers. All the 300 peasant families in my village got shares of farmland, averaging 0.2 hectare per person. For us peasants, this really meant something to live on.

During the land reform, the landlords' surplus rooms were confiscated and the extra rooms were distributed among the poor. My family moved from a three-room thatched house into a tile-roofed house with seven rooms. Though only a small child at the time, I clearly remember how happy the peasants were.

In 1951 the agricultural collectivization movement got underway in my village. We first got organized into mutual-aid production teams and then into elementary agricultural co-operatives, pooling our land and sharing the dividends. In 1956 we switched to the advanced agricultural co-operatives and put our farmland into public ownership. The principle of "to each according to his work" was followed. The removal of land boundary stakes made it possible to develop a unified farming plan on a larger scale and created favourable conditions for water conservation projects and agricultural mechanization.

With the land under public ownership, all the villagers met to discuss how to use their farmland and how to distribute the income. This was completely different from preliberation days when we had no land at all.

During those years, since everyone worked hard and the government provided the co-operative with preferential loans and farm tools, production grew rapidly. The grain output, for instance, grew from 2,250 kg per hectare before 1949 to 4,225 kg in 1956. I remember my family got more than enough wheat that year. We lived quite well during those years.

In July of 1957, our village was hit by a hailstorm. With crops ruined, old people worried that they would have to go begging as they had in the past when natural disasters struck. But when the government heard about our problems, it exempted us from agricultural taxes for that whole year, shipped in grain seeds and potato seedlings and urged us to tide over the difficulty while developing production. By relying on the collective strength of the village and everybody's hard work, no one ran short of food.

In 1957 something important happened to me. I was enrolled in the county's middle school after I graduated from the primary school in my village. Before me, for generations all my family had been illiterate.

TWISTS AND TURNS

In 1958 we got organized into the people's commune, which brought about some desirable changes, but also resulted in some baffling developments.

A people's commune usually consisted of several villages (a village was usually an advanced co-operative). To see many people working on a vast expanse of land was really a spectacular view. Soon after the founding of the people's commune, a tractor station was set up to oversee ploughing and sowing.

The year of 1959, however, was chaotic. Some people said we had arrived at real communism. All the people in my village ate at the same canteen, free of charge. We produced hundreds of thousands of kilogrammes of sweet potatoes. But nobody wanted them. The result was that all the potatoes rotted in the fields. Some people were prone to boasting and exaggeration. There was a 0.13 hectare plot of farmland by my middle school. About 2,500 kg of wheat seeds were sown and people said it would yield 100,000 kg. But, in reality, it produced only 250 kg (because far too many seeds were sown). Though the Central Committee of the Chinese Communist Party later criticized this mistake of being boastful and exaggerating, much of wealth had already been wasted. The negative impacts of such actions were felt for years.

The people's commune authorities also gave some arbitrary and impractical orders. Our village had a piece of land which should have been planted with soybeans. Some cadres of the people's commune, however, ordered us to grow carrots. Another piece of land which had already been planted with sweet potatoes was designated for soybeans. All these illogical orders resulted in sizeable losses.

It now becomes clear that the inclination to boast and give arbitrary orders came from "Leftist" thinking.

Of course, the people's commune did some good. The most visible improvements were the water conservation projects. I myself took part in building several big projects.

In 1960 I came back home after graduation from junior middle school. My family of 10 members was then broken up into several small ones. I moved in with my uncle and his wife. Peasants from surrounding villages were then building the Haizi Reservoir, which would irrigate almost 10,000 hectares, one-third of the county's total farmland. The builders, in addition to getting subsidies from the state, were paid in cash by the people's commune and received food rations. This made it attractive work and made it possible for the people's commune to mobilize enough people to build the big projects. The water conservaton projects on which I worked are still benefiting the people.

I got married in 1962 and later had two sons and one daughter. More mouths need more money. I managed to increase the income for my family. The next year, I spent my spare time collecting firewood in the winter and growing melons on my family's private plot in the summer. The extra work brought in more than 400 yuan. Our life was pretty good.

In 1966, the chaotic "cultural revolution" began. I could no longer collect firewood or grow melons because these were seen as capitalist undertakings. We peasants, unlike workers who have regular wages, had to work in the fields or we would have had nothing to eat. So our agricultural production continued as usual.

In retrospect, my life improved steadily after I began working. But I always thought I could have done much better. I was held back. In 1969, I was elected deputy leader of the brigade in charge of sideline production. One day I bought some eggs from a state chicken farm in order to hatch chickens for the brigade. I sold some of the surplus eggs and made 100 yuan for the brigade. I was shocked when I was criticized for selling the eggs. I was labelled a capitalist speculator.

AFFLUENCE BEGINS

It is only in recent years that I have been able to work hard and grow prosperous without restrictions.

In 1979 I learnt from newspapers and broadcasts that the Party had adopted flexible policies in the countryside. The contract responsibility system, which guaranteed more pay for more work, became popular in my village. The new policies allowed us peasants to become the real masters of agriculture and set us free to work hard and make more money. I wondered what I could do to get wealthy.

In 1981, I chose to raise chickens. I spent 380 yuan to buy 500 chicks. I was then a Communist Party member and the brigade's deputy leader. What I did raised some eyebrows in the village, but it didn't affect my job. The policy supported me. I got rich by working hard. Nothing wrong. I earned 850 yuan that year.

I then expanded the scope of my chicken business. The state credit co-operative offered me loans and encouraged me to forge ahead. I read books and studied to learn how to raise chickens scientifically. I also learnt how to treat chicken diseases such as diarrhoea and typhoid fever. In 1982, I sold the state 6,000 chickens for 9,000 yuan. With my income from the brigade and other household sidelines. I earned a total of more than 10,000 yuan, a figure larger than my combined income for the previous 10 years. The county recognized my achievements and rewarded me.

The Party policy is to bring into full play everyone's enthusiasm for production. It creates more wealth for the country and provides a good life for the peasants. Being among the first in my county to get rich, I'd like to lead others to prosperity.

Wang Shuchen has eight family members, but only two are able men. They have had a hard time. I explained the Party's policy to him and asked if he would like to raise chickens, too. I lent him 580 yuan, saying, "Please use this money to raise chickens. If the chickens die, I won't ask for the money back." Because he was less experienced in raising chickens, I went to his home several times every day to help him write observation notes, make plans for buying chicken feed, keep balance sheets and cure chicken diseases. Last year Wang earned more than 5,000 yuan from his chicken business alone.

197

Traditional Versus Nuclear Families in Modern India—1985

Since ancient times, the traditional extended family has been the most important unit of Indian society among Hindus. It was the center of economic as well as religious and social life and was perhaps even more important than social caste. Historically, it was a patriarchal family in which women were subject to male control. However, it also contained the husband's close paternal relatives—uncles, aunts, cousins, nephews, and nieces—who provided some security during times of economic and social distress. In recent times, modern secular Indians have moved away from Hindu tradition. Their families are nuclear rather than extended, and women seem to have more opportunity and freedom. However, according to the author of the following document, the rise of the modern nuclear family is not without problems for Indian women. What does Viji Srinivasan, a writer for the Times of India, *say are the problems Indian women face in*

From Viji Srinivasa, "My Son, My Son," *The Times of India* (Bombay), *Sunday Review*, 11 May 1985, p. 1.

a traditional Hindu family? Why might they have problems in becoming modern, assertive woman within a nuclear family?

Durga Devi cries as if her heart would break. "We lived happily for 15 years, my husband and I. Then he began to live with his younger brother's widow in front of my eyes . . . now, the work in Sewa-Mithila helps me to get over the grief."

Sarayu Devi is petrified. "I am a child-widow. From the age of 12. I have been living with my husband's elder brother's family as an unpaid drudge, wearing only white saris, no jewellery, not even a glass bangle. Yesterday I returned home from my first day's work at Sewa-Mithila. My brother-in-law's eyes were bloodshot. He had spread a mattress in the open courtyard. He held a pot of sindhur in his hand and lunged at me. You will go to work and lie with someone there? No, I'll lie with you first, right here. Then at least my younger brother's soul will rest in peace."

Both of them are poor women painters in Madhubani district of Bihar, and are members of the Self-Employed Women's Association, Mithila.

I interview 65 of Sewa-Mithila's women painters . . . slowly a pattern emerges . . . every problem in the world seems to be represented here—their husbands are alcoholic, or mentally ill, or, had tuberculosis or leprosy and had hidden it: or are deceitful, or manipulative, or irresponsible, or promiscuous. Only two painters say they are happy.

This profile comes up again and again, wherever poor women's organisations and organisations working against violence on women in India, document women's lives—the Annapurnas of Bombay; the lace-makers of Narsapur; the fisherwomen of Madras; the painters of Madhubani; the victims of dowry harassment in Delhi; the clerical women's union in Trivandrum.

And gradually a pattern emerges, as I think through the lives of the thousands of women I have interviewed. . . .

What do all these men and women have in common? [E]specially the lowest income, low-income and lower middle class Hindu families? *They are caste-centred families.* They are characterised by being joint families which participate in the ritualistic basis of the Hindu religion; having respect for the kin-group and a fear of kin-group censure; having socio-religious obligations towards the caste-community, and deference towards male authority; seeing support of parents as a moral duty for sons; and, last, but not least, having a domestic status for women, lacking a basic dignity.

These basic characteristics are certainly found to a greater or lesser degree in the lower and the lowest income groups, from the uppermost castes to the lowermost castes.

It may be argued that the lowest castes do not have these characteristics—their women are more free to divorce and remarry, their women cannot afford to be "secluded" etc. But it is also true that as these castes move upwards economically, their value-system changes into the value-system of typical caste-centred families.

As the group moves slightly upwards in economic terms (lower middle class), the basic characteristics of caste-centred families hold good, but additional characteristics emerge—the role of the woman is seen as being subordinate to the man's: there are invisible fears of going against this subordination; the joint family is viewed as being symbolic of the ethical framework of a Hindu household; there is the Hindu ideal that a husband is next only to God; there is family solidarity which in [times] of distress supports individuals on a long-term basis; women's self-effacement, self-sacrifice, complete subordination to male authority [and] submissiveness are seen as virtues. The older generation demands respect and concern based on their traditional position and they exercise power on the same basis, in important decisions such as education, taking up jobs, arranging marriages, etc.; the husband–wife relationship is not seen as pivotal, the wife is not dependent on the husband for companionship; she keeps a low profile with respect to her in-laws; and, in addition, concepts such as pollution with regard to women, avoidance, child marriage, widow's situation viewed as being unlucky, etc., flourish.

As opposed to this, as one moves upwards classwise, there is a multicaste secular society with "secular" families (e.g., the urban middle class, the urban elite). Its characteristics are: a nuclear family; children are brought up without the ritualistic basis of the Hindu religion; girls and women receive a somewhat western-oriented higher education; women use their education to establish their individual sphere of influence in the outside world. The secular families give her greater freedom of choice and scope for expression. Parental authority over her is present but diminishing. She is too confident to regard male authority as final, and she is not disciplined enough to subordinate herself entirely to male authority. But she has a distant admiration for self-sacrifice, subordination, timidity and modesty and values and cherishes the traditional wife ideal. She is modest, quiet, yet self-reliant, is job-worthy and has new skills.

These traits prepare her for two different roles, not compatible with each other, and she is extremely vulnerable to the competing demands of these two roles.

She is less tolerant of domination by in-laws, her independence is enhanced, she retains or tries to retain control over her income, she sees her husband and children in an exclusive relationship; the child–parent relationship is more equal. She wants to develop her interests and personality. She is not willing to accept a marriage on the basis of subjugation of her own interests. She has a sense of her own identity as separate from that of the man and has a personal desire to live fully and express herself fully. She is prepared to take second place in the husband–wife relationship, only if given with respect and consideration. She is not prepared to accept one standard of behaviour for the man and another for the woman. She has a greater sense of her rights.

But, often, she has very little competitiveness with respect to her husband, she is not ambitious for herself, and is not interested in competing with his ambition: she is willing to consider him as the head of the family. . . .

The modern Indian woman has a work-ethic, has efficiency and self-reliance; has discipline; but she is also non-individualistic, non-competitive, does not want complete freedom of action. She has a commitment to marriage, a commitment to the family. She is willing to serve men without fear or loss of self-respect, but wants respect and understanding.

But, a man in a secular family wants his wife to be non-aggressive and non-assertive in relation to him and his family. He still prefers not to recognise the change in women's psychology once they are equal partners in supporting a family. He does not want a challenge to his supremacy, he does not want a relationship of mutual respect, he wants a mere vehicle of his wishes, he wants a passive partner with no demands of her own. He is not psychologically prepared to set aside his comforts. He is unable to profit from the liberal attitudes of secular society.

The older generation still views the daughter-in-law as wholly subordinate to their wishes. They demand respect and concern based on their traditional position and they exercise power on the same basis. . . .

The logic of modern ideas is selectively accepted by Hindu men to the detriment of Hindu women. The man expects her to be completely traditional and pliable, to fit in with his own standards of feminine behaviour; to accept an unfair distribution of work, unreasonable dowry demands. He feels that he has to be obeyed; that it is his privilege to decide what his wife can do. He has been exposed to "modern" conflicts longer than women. He has been able to "manage" different demands by dominating his wife in a non-rational manner. He counts on the absolute stability of his marriage, which can be shaken only by him. In spite of being highly educated and responsible, he has not yet accurately judged the mental makeup of the modern Indian woman.

We bring up our daughters with an understanding of the discipline required in day-to-day life and for a self-reliant way of life; we give them confidence, we give them strength. We give our daughters modesty, humility, self-sacrifice, a commitment to marriage, a commitment to family—as we have always done in the old way of life. But now we also give our daughters skills, and a work-ethic; we give her a modern education—we give her the capabilities to be independent—this is the new way of life. . . .

But we "spoil" our sons. We bring them up saying: "You are so important. You will live with us and take care of us in our old age. Your sisters will go away to another home. You will bring a daughter-in-law to our home. She will bring a dowry. Your sisters have to be given a dowry—so they are a burden.

"But you are our wealth. Your wife will take care of you. You have no need to step into the kitchen. There is no need for you to learn to cook, to sew, to bring water, to bring fuel and fodder, to sweep and clean, to wash dirty vessels and clothes, to wash cows, to make cow-dung cakes, she will do it all. Your role is different. You are the one to do our funeral rites, you are the one to offer *pinda* to us and to our ancestors. Without you there is no salvation for us. You are crucial and you are wonderful . . . Of course, we love your sisters, but differently." . . .

Indian society is still in a painful transition from the old world to the new. Indian women are achieving the transition with strength and dignity. Let us bring up at least the new generations of our sons and daughters to face the transition with courage. Then only will Indian women and men realize their full potential.

198

The Women of Uganda by Jane Perlez—1991

This relatively recent article from the New York Times *discusses the problems facing African women. What causes the pain and drudgery these women endure? How has the modern world impacted these women? Are their problems insurmountable? How could they improve their lives?*

Namutumba, Uganda—When 28-year-old Safuyati Kawuda married the man she remembers as "handsome and elegant," her husband scraped together the bride price: five goats and three chickens. The animals represented a centuries-old custom intended to compensate Mrs. Kawuda's father for losing the labor of his daughter.

In the decade since, Mrs. Kawuda has rarely seen her husband, who long ago left this hot and dusty village for a town 70 miles away. She has accepted her husband's acquisition of two other wives and has given birth to five of his 13 children.

Instead of laboring for her father she has toiled for her husband instead—hauling firewood, fetching water, digging in the fields, producing the food the family eats, and bearing and caring for the children.

Like Mrs. Kawuda, women in rural Africa are the subsistence farmers. They produce, without tractors, oxen, or even plows, more than 70 percent of the continent's food, according to the World Bank. Back-breaking hand cultivation is a job that African men consider to be demeaning "women's work." The male responsibility is generally to sell the food the women produce. But as urbanization has stepped up, men have gone to the cities in search of other jobs, leaving women like Mrs. Kawuda alone.

MANY INEQUALITIES

The discrepancy between the physical labor of women and men is accompanied by other pervasive inequalities. In the vast majority of African countries, women do not own or inherit land. Within families, boys are encouraged to go to school, girls are not. In many places, women treat wife-beating as an accepted practice. The Uganda Women's Lawyers Association recently embarked on a campaign to convince women that wife-battering is not a sign of a man's love.

Recent surveys in Africa show other significant disparities between men and women. In 10 African countries, according to the United Nations Children's Fund, women and children together make up 77 percent of the population. Yet in only 16 percent of the households in those countries do the women have the legal right to own property.

Despite calls by the United Nations for the improvement of the lives of African women and efforts by the World Bank to finance projects focused on women, little has been done to improve the dismal status of rural women, African and Western experts say. With the continent's worsening economies in the 1980's, women suffered even more.

"The poor, the majority of whom are women, have had to take on additional work burdens in order to cope with cutbacks in social services and the increased cost of living," the Weekly Review, a magazine in Kenya, reported last year.

NO EXPECTATIONS

Mrs. Kawuda has never attended school. She cannot read or write, although her husband can. She has no radio. The farthest she has been from home is Jinja, 70 miles away. She has no expectations of a better life because she has known nothing else. But her ignorance of the outside world does not stop her from knowing her life is unrelentingly tough. She knows that in her bones.

"Everything is difficult," Mrs. Kawuda said, as she bent over to hoe cassava, her bare, rough feet splattered with dark dirt. "It's more of a problem than it used to be to find firewood. If you can't find wood on the ground, you have to cut it and there is no one to help you. Digging in the fields is the most difficult. I don't like it."

Mrs. Kawuda shares her world of perpetual fatigue with her five children; her husband's second wife, Zainabu Kasoga, 27, and her four children. Her husband's third wife—"the town wife"—lives in Jinja, where the husband, 31-year-old Kadiri Mpyanku, a tea packer, spends most of his time.

When the husband visited Mrs. Kawuda on a recent weekend, he brought enough sugar for three days and a packet of beans. Mrs. Kawuda said she was dependent on him for clothes and other essentials, and money that she said he did not always have. In most households in the area, the men also live most of the time in either Jinja or Kampala, the capital.

Here in the village, 120 miles northeast of Kampala, Mrs. Kawuda and Mrs. Kasoga run a household with another woman, the wife of their husband's brother, Sayeda Naigaga, 20, and her three children.

The women live without running water or electricity in three small, mud-wall structures. In the outdoor courtyard, life grinds on: the peeling and chopping of food, eating by adults and feeding of infants, washing, bathing, weaving and the receiving of guests all take place on the orange clay ground, packed smooth by the passage of bare feet.

In the old days, Ugandan men built separate houses for each wife, but such luxuries disappeared with the collapse of the economy. Mrs. Kawuda and her five children sleep in one room of the main shelter and Mrs. Kasoga and her four children in another. When their husband is around, he shuttles between the two bedrooms.

Mrs. Kawuda is of the Bisoga tribe, the second largest in Uganda and one where polygamy is common. Sexual and marriage mores differ in various parts of Africa. The Uganda Women's Lawyers Association estimates that 50 percent of marriages in Uganda are polygamous and, according to United Nations figures, a similar percentage exists in West Africa.

In Kenya, the Government's Women's Bureau estimates that about 30 percent of the marriages are polygamous. However, because of the economic burden of keeping several wives and families, the practice is declining, the bureau says.

Often the wives in a polygamous marriage are hostile toward each other. But perhaps as a survival instinct, Mrs. Kawuda and Mrs. Kasoga are friendly, taking turns with Mrs. Naigaga to cook for the 15-member household.

Days start with the morning ritual of collecting water. For these Ugandan women, the journey to the nearest pond takes half an hour. The six-gallon cans, when full of water, are heavy on the trip home.

Digging in the fields is the most loathed of the chores, but also the one the women feel most obliged to do since the family's food supply comes from what they grow. As they work under the sun, the women drape old pieces of clothing on their heads for protection. The youngest child, 2-year-old Suniya clings to her mother's back while Mrs. Kawuda hunches over, swinging a hoe, a sight as pervasive in rural Africa as an American mother gliding a cart along the aisles of a supermarket. "Having a baby on your back is easy," Mrs. Kawuda said. "When you are eight months pregnant and digging, it is more difficult."

VISITING HUSBAND "SUPERVISES"

There was no possibility the husband would help in the fields. It was his job to "supervise," said Mrs. Kawuda, ridiculing a suggestion that he might pitch in.

When he arrived late on a recent Saturday night, Mr. Mpyanku was treated as the imperious ruler by the children, some of whom tentatively came to greet him. He was barely acknowledged by the women, who seemed a little fearful and immediately served tea.

By early Sunday morning, he had disappeared to the nearby trading post to be with his male friends. "He has gone to discuss business with his friends," Mrs. Kawuda said. "What business can I discuss with him? Will we talk to him about digging cassava?"

Mrs. Kawuda said her husband had promised not to take any more wives. "But you never know what he thinks," she said. "I can't interfere in his affairs. If I did, he would say: 'Why is she poking her nose into my affairs?' "

Fertility and children remain at the center of rural marriage in Africa. Large numbers of children improve a household's labor pool and provide built-in security for parents in old age.

Mrs. Kawuda said she wanted one more child, in the hopes of its being another boy. After that, she said, she would use an injectible form of contraceptive. It is a method popular among African rural women because it can be used without their husband's knowledge. But in reality, contraception was an abstraction to Mrs. Kawuda since she had no idea where to get it. She had never heard of condoms.

AIDS BECOMES A CONCERN

A recent concern for African women is AIDS, which like much else in their lives they seem powerless to control. Unconvinced by her husband's assurance that he is faithful to his town wife, Mrs. Kawuda said: "He can say it's all right, we need not worry. But you never know what he does in town. He fears AIDS, too. But he messes around too much."

A worldly person compared to his wives, Mr. Mpyanku speaks reasonable English and has traveled to Kenya.

He described himself as the provider of cash for the rural family. But Mr. Mpyanku's emphasis is on his own livelihood and his urban life.

He rode the most comfortable form of transportation home, a nonstop minibus from Jinja that cost about $1.50, instead of the cheaper taxi at $1. He would do the same on his return.

Yet his oldest child, a daughter, Maliyamu, 10, missed much of her schooling last year. Her report card said her $7 in school fees had not been paid. It was a cheerless sign that Mrs. Kawuda's daughter would, like her mother, remain uneducated and repeat for another generation the cycle of female poverty and punishing physical labor.

CHAPTER 26

Arts and Culture in the Post Modern World— 1914—Present

The last century produced a vast amount of literature, much of it dealing with the carnage of war. The first four documents all describe life experiences during World War I. "Munition Wages," a satirical English music hall song, deals with women who worked in munitions factories during the war. Do you think the author of this ballad felt that factory workers faced considerable danger? Did she think the women who worked in the factories received the respect they deserved for their efforts?

The next three documents deal with combat experiences during World War I. All were written by veterans of the war. Remarque and Junger served in the German army and Sassoon was a British soldier. Are there some commonalities in their experiences? Which accounts are the most critical of authority? Who do they blame for the slaughter?

Wild Grass by Lu Xun and the poems of Senghor are more evocative of a particular culture and time. What image do you get of 1920's China and 1950's Africa after reading these poems? How do they compare with earlier Chinese and African literature?

Finally, the last two documents relate some of the horrors of World War II and the postwar period in the Soviet Union, and yet they also provide some insights into the durability and strength of the human spirit. How and why were some people able to survive the Holocaust and German labor camps?

199

"Munition Wages," a Musical Parody by Madeline Ida Bedford —1917

While their husbands and boyfriends were at the front, English women got factory jobs to support the war effort. It was popularly believed that they earned high wages, allowing them to live the good life. In reality, the factories were both dangerous and dirty, and the women worked long hours for relatively little pay. How does the author of this document really feel about her factory job? Does it appear that some men were upset by the relatively good wages women were paid for war work?

A MUSICAL PARODY
MADELINE IDA BEDFORD

Munition Wages
Earning high wages? Yus,
Five quid a week.
A woman, too, mind you,
I calls it dim sweet.

Ye'are asking some questions—
But bless yer, here goes:
I spends the whole racket
On good times and clothes.

* * *

We're all here today, mate,
Tomorrow—perhaps dead,
If Fate tumbles on us
And blows up our shed.

Madeline Ida Bedford, "Munition Wages" as printed in Agenal Woollacott, *On Her Their Lives Depend: Munitions Workers in the Great War* (Berkeley, CA: University of California Press, 1994), p. 125.

Afraid! Are yer kidding?
With money to spend!
Years back I wore tatters,
Now—silk stockings, mi friend!

I've bracelets and jewellery,
Rings envied by friends;
A sergeant to swank with,
And something to lend.

I drive out in taxis,
Do theatres in style.
And this is mi verdict—
It is jolly worth while.

Worth while, for tomorrow
If I'm blown to the sky,
I'll have repaid mi wages
In death—and pass by.

200

"Counter-Attack" by Siegfried Sassoon—1918

The hell of trench warfare during World War I was the source of poetry as well as novels. Born into the gentry of Kent, England, Siegfried Sassoon (1886-1967) was educated at Marlborough and Cambridge universities, where he was mainly interested in writing poetry and fox hunting. He enlisted in the army and served in the Royal Welsh Fusiliers. After his brother's death, Sassoon fought recklessly at the front, but as the war dragged on, he became increasingly disgusted with the conflict. Unlike many others, Sassoon survived the war and had a successful literary career. The following poem was written late in the war. What is the theme of this poem? How does it compare with All Quiet on the Western Front *and* Storm of Steel?

SIEGFRIED SASSOON,
"COUNTER-ATTACK"

We'd gained our first objective hours before
While dawn broke like a face with blinking eyes,
Pallid, unshaved and thirsty, blind with smoke.
Things seemed all right at first. We held their line,
With bombers posted, Lewis guns well placed,
And clink of shovels deepening the shallow trench.

The place was rotten with dead; green clumsy legs
High-booted, sprawled and grovelled along the saps;
And trunks, face downward, in the sucking mud,
Wallowed like trodden sand-bags loosely filled;
And naked sodden buttocks, mats of hair,
Bulged, clotted heads slept in the plastering slime.
And then the rain began,—the jolly old rain!

A yawning soldier knelt against the bank,
Staring across the morning blear with fog;
He wondered when the Allemands* would get busy;
And then, of course, they started with five-nines
Traversing, sure as fate, and never a dud.
Mute in the clamour of shells he watched them burst

Spouting dark earth and wire with gusts of hell,
While posturing giants dissolved in drifts of smoke.
He crouched and flinched, dizzy with galloping fear,
Sick for escape,—loathing the strangled horror
And butchered, frantic gestures of the dead.

An officer came blundering down the trench:
"Stand-to and man the fire-step!" On he went . . .
Gasping and bawling, "Fire-step . . . counter-attack!"
Then the haze lifted. Bombing on the right
Down the old sap: machine guns on the left;
And stumbling figures looming out in front.
"O Christ, they're coming at us!" Bullets spat,

And he remembered his rifle . . . rapid fire . . .
And started blazing wildly . . . then a bang
Crumpled and spun him sideways, knocked him out
To grunt and wiggle: none heeded him; he choked

---

* Germans.

And fought the flapping veils of smothering gloom,
Lost in a blurred confusion of yells and groans . . .
Down, and down, and down, he sank and drowned,
Bleeding to death. The counter-attack had failed.

201

From *The Storm of Steel* by Ernst Junger—1920

A middle-class German youth with an adventurous spirit, Ernst Junger (1895–1998) enlisted in the French Foreign legion in 1912. At the outbreak of World War I, the 19-year-old Junger returned to Germany and enlisted in the army, soon becoming a lieutenant on the Western Front. He served in the trenches and was decorated for bravery. After the war, Junger studied natural science and philosophy and began a career as a writer. Junger's first novel, the semi-autobiographical Storm of Steel, *was admired by the Nazis, but Junger did not join the Nazi party. He did, however, enlist in the German army at the start of World War II, although he supported few of the Nazis' causes. Though increasingly critical of Hitler, he survived the war and became active in the cause of peace and European unity. The following excerpt describes the lives of German soldiers in the trenches. Does Junger's experience during the war seem to have been positive? How does Junger's* Storm of Steel *compare with Remarque's* All Quiet on the Western Front? *Why might the Nazis' have admired this book?*

THE AUTHOR'S PREFACE

I was, a nineteen-year-old lieutenant in command of a platoon, and my part of the line was easily recognizable from the English side by a row of tall shell-stripped trees that rose from the ruins of Monchy. My left flank was bounded by the sunken road leading to Berlesau–Bois, which was in the hands of the English; my right was marked by a sap running out from our lines, one that

From *Storm of Steel* by Ernst Junger, trans. by Basil Crieghton (New York: Doubleday, 1919).

helped us many a time to make our presence felt by means of bombs and rifle grenades.

Today there is no secret about what those trenches concealed, and a book such as this may, like a trench map years after the event, be read with sympathy and interest by the other side. But here not only the blue and red lines of the trenches are shown, but the blood that beat and the life that lay hid in them.

Time only strengthens my conviction that it was a good and strenuous life, and that the war, for all its destructiveness, was an incomparable schooling of the heart. The front-line soldier whose foot came down on the earth so grimly and harshly may claim this at least, that it came down cleanly. Warlike achievements are enhanced by the inherent worth of the enemy.

On the 23d of August we were transported in lorries to Le Mesnil. Our spirits were excellent, though we knew we were going to be put in where the battle of Somme was at its worst. Chaff and laughter went from lorry to lorry. We marched from Le Mesnil at dusk to Sailly-Saillisel, and here the battalion dumped packs in a large meadow and paraded in battle order.

Artillery fire of a hitherto unimagined intensity rolled and thundered on our front. Thousands of twitching flashes turned the western horizon into a sea of flowers. All the while the wounded came trailing back with white, dejected faces, huddled into the ditches by the gun and ammunition columns that rattled past.

A man in a steel helmet reported to me as guide to conduct my platoon to the renowned Combles, where for the time we were to be in reserve. Sitting with him at the side of the road, I asked him, naturally enough, what it was like in the line. In reply I heard a monotonous tale of crouching all day in shell holes with no one on either flank and no trenches communicating with the rear, of unceasing attacks, of dead bodies littering the ground, of maddening thirst, of wounded and dying, and of a lot besides. The face half-framed by the steel rim of the helmet was unmoved; the voice accompanied by the sound of battle droned on, and the impression they made on me was one of unearthly solemnity. One could see that the man had been through horror to the limit of despair and there had learned to despise it. Nothing was left but supreme and superhuman indifference.

"Where you fall, there you lie. No one can help you. No one knows whether he will come back alive. They attack every day, but they can't get through. Everybody knows it is life and death."

As far as we could see in the darkness, Combles was utterly shot to bits. The damage seemed to be recent, judging from the amount of timber among the ruins and the contents of the houses slung over the road. We climbed over numerous heaps of debris—rather hurriedly, owing to a few shrapnel shells—and reached our quarters. They were in a large, shot-riddled house. Here I established myself with three sections. The other two occupied the cellar of a ruin opposite.

At 4 a.m. we were aroused from our rest on the fragments of bed we had collected, in order to receive steel helmets. It was also the occasion of discovering a sack of coffee beans in a corner of the cellar; whereupon there followed a great brewing of coffee.

After breakfast I went out to have a look round. Heavy artillery had turned a peaceful little billeting town into a scene of desolation in the course of a day or two. Whole houses had been flattened by single direct hits or blown up so that the interiors of the rooms hung over the chaos like the scenes on a stage. A sickly scent of dead bodies rose from many of the ruins, for many civilians had been caught in the bombardment and buried beneath the wreckage of their homes. A little girl lay dead in a pool of blood on the threshold of one of the doorways.

The square in front of the ruins of the church had been particularly hard hit. Here was the entrance to the catacombs, a very ancient underground passage with recesses here and there in which were crowded the staffs of all the units engaged. It was said that the civilians had opened up the entrance with pickaxes when the bombardment began. It had been walled up and kept secret from the Germans during the whole of their occupation. The streets were reduced to narrow paths winding circuitously round and over heaps of timber and masonry. Quantities of fruit and vegetables were going to waste in the churned-up gardens.

A plentiful supply of "iron rations" provided us with a dinner that we cooked in the kitchen, and concluded, needless to say, with strong coffee. I then settled myself in an armchair upstairs. From letters scattered about I saw that the house belonged to a brewer, Lesage. Cupboards and chests of drawers were thrown open; there was an overturned washstand, a sewing machine, and a perambulator. The pictures and the looking glasses on the walls were all broken. Drawers had been pulled out and emptied, and a yard deep all over the floor were underclothes, corsets, books, papers, bedroom tables, broken glass, bottles, notebooks, chair legs, coats, cloaks, lamps, curtains, window frames, doors torn from their hinges, lace, photographs, oil paintings, albums, broken boxes, hats, flower pots, and torn wall paper, all tangled up together in wild confusion.

In the course of the afternoon the firing increased to such a degree that single explosions were no longer audible. There was nothing but one terrific tornado of noise. From seven onward the square and the houses round were shelled at intervals of half a minute with fifteen-centimeter shells. There were many duds among them, which all the same made the houses rock. We sat all this while in our cellar, round a table, on armchairs covered in silk, with our heads propped on our hands, and counted the seconds between the explosions. Our jests became less frequent, till at last the foolhardiest of us fell silent, and at eight o'clock two direct hits brought down the next house.

From nine to ten the shelling was frantic. The earth rocked and the sky boiled like a gigantic cauldron.

Hundreds of heavy batteries were concentrated on and round Combles. Innumerable shells came howling and hurtling over us. Thick smoke, ominously lit up by Very lights, veiled everything. Head and ears ached violently, and we could only make ourselves understood by shouting a word at a time. The power of logical thought and the force of gravity seemed alike to be suspended. One had the sense of something as unescapable and as unconditionally fated as a catastrophe of nature. An N.C.O. of No. 3 platoon went mad.

At ten this carnival of hell gradually calmed down and passed into a steady drum fire. It was still certainly impossible to distinguish one shell from another.

At last we reached the front line. It was held by men cowering close in the shell holes, and their dead voices trembled with joy when they heard that we were the relief. A Bavarian sergeant major briefly handed over the sector and the Very-light pistol.

My platoon formed the right wing of the position held by the regiment. It consisted of a shallow sunken road which had been pounded by shells. It was a few hundred meters left of Guillemont and a rather shorter distance right of Bois-de-Trônes. We were parted from the troops on our right, the Seventy-sixth Regiment of Infantry, by a space about five hundred meters wide. This space was shelled so violently that no troops could maintain themselves there.

As I had no idea how far off the enemy were, I warned my men to be ready for the worst. We all remained on guard. I spent the night with my batman and two orderlies in a hole perhaps one yard square and one yard deep.

When day dawned we were astonished to see, by degrees, what a sight surrounded us.

The sunken road now appeared as nothing but a series of enormous shell holes filled with pieces of uniform, weapons, and dead bodies. The ground all round, as far as the eye could see, was plowed by shells. You could search in vain for one wretched blade of grass. This churned-up battlefield was ghastly. Among the living lay the dead. As we dug ourselves in we found them in layers stacked one upon the top of another. One company after another had been shoved into the drum fire and steadily annihilated. The corpses were covered with the masses of soil turned up by the shells, and the next company advanced in the place of the fallen.

The sunken road and the ground behind were full of German dead; the ground in front, of English. Arms, legs, and heads stuck out stark above the lips of the craters. In front of our miserable defenses there were torn-off limbs and corpses over many of which cloaks and ground sheets had been thrown to hide the fixed stare of their distorted features. In spite of the heat no one thought for a moment of covering them with soil.

The village of Guillemont was distinguished from the landscape around it only because the shell holes there were of a whiter color by reason of the houses which had been ground to powder. Guillemont railway station lay in front of us. It was smashed to bits like a child's plaything. Delville Wood, reduced to matchwood, was farther behind.

Day had scarcely dawned when an English flying man descended on us in a steep spin and circled round incessantly like a bird of prey, while we made for our holes and cowered there. Nevertheless, the observer's sharp eyes must have spied us out, for a siren sounded its deep, long-drawn notes above us at short intervals. After a little while it appeared that a battery had received the signal. One heavy shell after another came at us on a flat trajectory with incredible fury. We crouched in our refuges and could do nothing. Now and then we lit a cigar and threw it away again. Every moment we expected a rush of earth to bury us. The sleeve of Schmidt's coat was torn by a big splinter.

At three in the afternoon the men came in from the left flank and said they could stick it no longer, as their shelters were shot to bits. It cost me all my callousness to get them back to their posts.

Just before ten at night the left flank of the regimental front was heavily shelled, and after twenty minutes we came in for it too. In a brief space we were completely covered in dust and smoke, and yet most of the hits were just in front or just behind. While this hurricane was raging I went along my platoon front. The men were standing, rifle in hand, as though carved in stone, their eyes fixed on the ground in front of them. Now and then by the light of a rocket I saw the gleam of helmet after helmet, bayonet after bayonet, and I was filled with pride at commanding this handful of men that might very likely be pounded into the earth but could not be conquered. It is in such moments that the human spirit triumphs over the mightiest demonstrations of material force. The fragile body, steeled by the will, stands up to the most terrific punishment.

202

From *All Quiet on the Western Front* by Erich Maria Remarque—1929

Much has been written about the inhumanity and brutality of trench warfare during World War I. One of the most powerful was the book All Quiet on the Western Front. *Erich Maria Remarque (1898–1970) was drafted into the German army at the age of 18 and served on the Western Front. After the war, Remarque pursued a career as a sports car driver and sports writer while establishing himself as a writer. His powerful antiwar novel was banned by the Nazis. Remarque, who was opposed to Nazi policy, left Germany when they came to power. How does* All Quiet on the Western Front *differ from* Storm of Steel? *Why would the first be banned and the second admired by the Nazis? Who does Paul blame for the plight of the German soldiers?*

From *All Quiet on the Western Front* by Erich Maria Remarque. Reprinted by permission.

At last it grows quiet. The fire has lifted over us and is now dropping on the reserves. We risk a look. Red rockets shoot up to the sky. Apparently there's an attack coming.

Where we are it is still quiet. I sit up and shake the recruit by the shoulder. "All over, kid! It's all right this time."

He looks round him dazedly. "You'll get used to it soon," I tell him. . . .

He goes off. Things become quieter, but the cries do not cease. "What's up, Albert?" I ask.

"A couple of columns over there got it in the neck."

The cries continued. It is not men, they could not cry so terribly.

"Wounded horses," says Kat.

It's unendurable. It is the moaning of the world, it is the martyred creation, wild with anguish, filled with terror, and groaning.

We are pale. Detering stands up. "God! For God's sake! Shoot them."

He is a farmer and very fond of horses. It gets under his skin. Then as if deliberately the fire dies down again. The screaming of the beasts becomes louder. One can no longer distinguish whence in this now quiet silvery land-scape it comes; ghostly, invisible, it is everywhere, between heaven and earth it rolls on immeasurably. Detering raves and yells out: "Shoot them! Shoot them, can't you? damn you again!"

"They must look after the men first," says Kat quietly.

We stand up and try to see where it is. If we could only see the animals we should be able to endure it better. Müller has a pair of glasses. We see a dark group, bearers with stretchers, and larger black clumps moving about. Those are the wounded horses. But not all of them. Some gallop away in the distance, fall down, and then run on farther. The belly of one is ripped open, the guts trail out. He becomes tangled in them and falls, then he stands up again.

Detering raises up his gun and aims. Kat hits it in the air. "Are you mad—?"

Detering trembles and throws his rifle on the ground.

We sit down and hold our ears. But this appalling noise, these groans and screams penetrate, they penetrate everywhere.

We can bear almost anything. But now the sweat breaks out on us. We must get up and run no matter where, but where these cries can no longer be heard. And it is not men, only horses.

From the dark group stretchers move off again. Then single shots crack out. The black heap convulses and then sinks down. At last! But still it is not the end. The men cannot overtake the wounded beasts which fly in their pain, their wide open mouths full of anguish. One of the men goes down on one knee, a shot—one horse drops—another. The last one props itself on its forelegs and drags itself round in a circle like a merry-go-round; squatting, it drags round in circles on its stiffened forelegs, apparently its back is broken. The soldier runs up and shoots it. Slowly, humbly, it sinks to the ground.

We take our hands from our ears. The cries are silenced. Only a long-drawn, dying sigh still hangs on the air.

Then only again the rockets, the singing of the shells and the stars there—most strange.

Detering walks up and down cursing: "Like to know what harm they've done." He returns to it once again. His voice is agitated, it sounds almost digni-fied as he says: "I tell you it is the vilest baseness to use horses in the war."

. . .

The days go by and the incredible hours follow one another as a matter of course. Attacks alternate with counter-attacks and slowly the dead pile up in the field of craters between the trenches. We are able to bring in most of the wounded that do not lie too far off. But many have long to wait and we listen to them dying.

For one of them we search two days in vain. He must be lying on his belly and unable to turn over. Otherwise it is hard to understand why we cannot find him; for it is only when a man has his mouth close to the ground that it is impossible to gauge the direction of his cry.

He must have been badly hit—one of those nasty wounds neither so severe that they exhaust the body at once and a man dreams on in a half-swoon, nor so light that a man endures the pain in the hope of becoming well again. Kat thinks he has either a broken pelvis or a shot through the spine. His chest cannot have been injured otherwise he would not have such strength to cry out. And if it were any other kind of wound it would be possible to see him moving.

He grows gradually hoarser. The voice is so strangely pitched that it seems to be everywhere. The first night some of our fellows go out three times to look for him. But when they think they have located him and crawl across, next time they hear the voice it seems to come from somewhere else altogether.

We search in vain until dawn. We scrutinized the field all day with glasses, but discover nothing. On the second day the calls are fainter; that will be because his lips and mouth have become dry.

Our Company Commander has promised next turn of leave with three days extra to anyone who finds him. That is a powerful inducement, but we would do all that is possible without that for his cry is terrible. Kat and Kropp even go out in the afternoon, and Albert gets the lobe of his ear shot off in consequence. It is to no purpose, they come back without him.

It is easy to understand what he cries. At first he called only for help—the second night he must have had some delirium, he talked with his wife and his children, we often detected the name Elise. To-day he merely weeps. By evening the voice dwindles to a croaking. But it persists still through the whole night. We hear it so distinctly because the wind blows toward our line. In the morning when we suppose he must already have long gone to his rest, there comes across to us one last gurgling rattle.

The days are hot and the dead lie unburied. We cannot fetch them all in, if we did we should not know what to do with them. The shells will bury them. Many have their bellies swollen up like balloons. They hiss, belch, and make movements. The gases in them make noises.

The sky is blue and without clouds. In the evening it grows sultry and the heat rises from the earth. When the wind blows toward us it brings the smell of blood, which is very heavy and sweet. This deathly exhalation from the shell-holes seems to be a mixture of chloroform and putrefaction, and fills us with nausea and retching.

. . .

Although we need reinforcement, the recruits give us almost more trouble than they are worth. They are helpless in this grim fighting area, they fall like flies. Modern trench-warfare demands knowledge and experience; a man must have a feeling for the contours of the ground, an ear for the sound and character of the shells, must be able to decide beforehand where they will drop, how they will burst, and how to shelter from them.

The young recruits of course know none of these things. They get killed simply because they hardly can tell shrapnel from high-explosive, they are mown down because they are listening anxiously to the roar of the big coal-boxes falling in the rear, and miss the light, piping whistle of the low spreading daisy-cutters. They flock together like sheep instead of scattering, and even the wounded are shot down like hares by the airmen.

Their pale turnip faces, their pitiful clenched hands, the fine courage of these poor devils, the desperate charges and attacks made by the poor brave wretches, who are so terrified that they dare not cry out loudly, but with battered chests, with torn bellies, arms and legs only whimper softly for their mothers and cease as soon as one looks at them.

Their sharp, downy, dead faces have the awful expressionlessness of dead children.

It brings a lump into the throat to see how they go over, and run and fall. A man would like to spank them, they are so stupid, and to take them by the arm and lead them away from here where they have no business to be. They wear grey coats and trousers and boots, but for most of them the uniform is far too big, it hangs on their limbs, their shoulders are too narrow, their bodies too slight; no uniform was ever made to these childish measurements.

Between five and ten recruits fall to every old hand.

. . .

Bombardment, barrage, curtain-fire, mines, gas, tanks, machine-guns, hand-grenades—words, words, but they hold the horror of the world.

Our faces are encrusted, our thoughts are devastated, we are weary to death; when the attack comes we shall have to strike many of the men with our fists to waken them and make them come with us—our eyes are burnt, our hands are torn, our knees bleed, our elbows are raw.

How long has it been? Weeks—months—years? Only days. We see time pass in the colorless faces of the dying, we cram food into us, we run, we throw, we shoot, we kill, we lie about, we are feeble and spent, and nothing supports us but the knowledge that there are still feebler, still more spent, still more helpless ones there who, with staring eyes, look upon us as gods that escape death many times.

We show them how to take cover from aircraft, how to simulate a dead man when one is overrun in an attack, how to time hand-grenades so that they explode half a second before hitting the ground; we teach them to fling themselves into holes as quick as lightning before the shells with instantaneous fuses; we show them how to clean up a trench with a handful of bombs; we explain the difference between the fuse-length of the enemy bombs and our own; we put them wise to the sound of gas shells;—show them all the tricks that can save them from death.

They listen, they are docile—but when it begins again, in their excitement they do everything wrong.

Haie Westhus drags off with a great wound in his back through which the lung pulses at every breath. I can only press his hand; "It's all up, Paul," he groans and he bites his arm because of the pain.

We see men living with their skulls blown open; we see soldiers run with their two feet cut off, they stagger on their splintered stumps into the next shell-hole; a lance-corporal crawls a mile and a half on his hands dragging his smashed knee after him; another goes to the dressing station and over his clasped hands bulge his intestines; we see men without mouths, without jaws, without faces; we find one man who has held the artery of his arm in his teeth for two hours in order not to bleed to death. The sun goes down, night comes, the shells whine, life is at an end.

Still the little piece of convulsed earth in which we lie is held. We have yielded no more than a few hundred yards of it as a prize to the enemy. But on every yard there lies a dead man.

203

From *Wild Grass* by Lu Xun— 1927

China's literary tradition is the oldest in the world. For thousands of years, Chinese poets and writers have provided vivid pictures of society and life in the Confucian tradition. Despite his small body of work, Lu Xun (1881–1936) (Zhou Shuren was his real name; Lu Xun was his pen name) is considered the father of modern Chinese literature. A disenchanted intellectual born into a family of scholar-officials and educated in the traditional Confucian classics, he wrote the following poem during a period of struggle and confusion in China, when the past was giving way to revolution and change. What view did Lu Xun seem to have of his world? How does the world of Lu Xun compare to the Navajo vision set forth in the night chant?

From "Wild Grass" by Lu Xun from *Renditions*, No. 26 (Autumn 1986), Hong Kong Research Centre for Translation of The Chinese University of Hong Kong, p. 151–153.

WILD GRASS[1]

Special thanks to D. E. Pollard

Epigraph

When I am silent, I am fulfilled; when I am about to speak, I then feel empty.

My past life is dead. At this death I greatly rejoice, because I know from this death that my life once existed. The dead life has decayed. I greatly rejoice, because I know from this decay that my life was not empty.

The soil of life has been cast upon the surface of the land. Tall trees do not grow from it, only wild grass. For this I am to blame.

Wild grass has no deep roots, it bears no pretty flowers, no pretty leaves. But it drinks in dew and water, sucks in the flesh and blood of long dead corpses, and wrests its existence from each and every thing. When it is alive, it is always trampled on, cut down, until it dies and decays.

But I am at ease, joyful. I will laugh; I will sing.

Naturally I love my wild grass, but I hate the ground which uses it for decoration.

Under the crust the subterranean fire is blazing. When it erupts, its lava will consume all the wild grass, all the tall trees. Whereupon nothing will be left to decay.

But I am at ease, joyful. I will laugh; I will sing.

Heaven and earth are so still and silent, I cannot laugh or sing. Even if heaven and earth were not so still and silent, perhaps I still would not be able to do so. At this juncture of light and darkness, life and death, past and future, I offer this clump of wild grass before friends and foes, men and beasts, the loving and the unloving as my witness.

For my sake, and for the sake of friends and foes, men and beasts, those loving and unloving, I hope that death and decay will come speedily to this grass. If not, then I will not have lived, and this would be an even greater misfortune than death and decay.

Perish, wild grass, and with it, my epigraph.

April 26, 1927

Autumn Night

Through the window I can see two trees in my backyard. The one is a date tree, the other is also a date tree.

---

1 Translated by Ng Mau-sang.

The night sky above is strange and distant. Never in my life have I seen such a strange and distant sky. He seems intent on forsaking the world and staying out of people's sight. But now he is winking—with eyes of a few dozen stars, utterly blue, and cold. A smile hovers around his mouth, seeming to him to be very profound, and thereupon he begins to spread frost on the wild flowers and wild grass in my courtyard.

I do not know the names of these flowers and grasses, or what people call them. I remember a plant which put forth a tiny flower—the flower is still in bloom, but she is even tinier, trembling in the cold, dreaming. She dreams of the coming of spring, of autumn, of a skinny poet wiping his tears on her last petal, telling her that autumn may come, winter may come, but eventually spring will come, when butterflies will fly gaily about, and the bees will sing their spring song. Thereupon she smiles, although she has turned red in the piercing cold and remains curled up.

The date trees have shed all their leaves. Some time ago, a boy or two still came to beat them for the dates that others had left behind. Now, not a single one is left, even the leaves have all fallen. The date tree understands the dream of the tiny pink flower, that after autumn spring will come; he also knows the dream of the fallen leaves, that after spring there is still autumn.

He has shed all his foliage, leaving only the trunk; he is relieved from bending under his load of leaves and fruit, and now enjoys stretching himself. But a few boughs are still hanging down, nursing the wounds caused by the poles that struck him for his dates, while the longest and straightest of his boughs are like iron, silently piercing the strange and distant sky, making him wink his wicked eyes; piercing the full moon in the sky, making her go pale with embarrassment.

The wickedly winking sky turns an even deeper, perturbed blue. He seems intent on escaping from men, on avoiding the date tree, leaving only the moon behind. But the moon has secretly hid herself in the east. Only the naked trunk is still like iron, silently piercing the strange and distant sky, determined to pierce it to death, regardless of how and how often he winks his seductive eyes.

With a sharp shriek, a vicious bird of the night flies past.

I suddenly hear a slight tittering in the middle of the night, so soft that it seems not to want to awaken those who are asleep, though the titter echoes across the surrounding air. In the dead of night, there is no one about. I instantly recognize that this laughter is coming from my own mouth. Put to flight by the sound, I go back into my room, and immediately raise the wick of my lamp.

The glass pane of the back window rattles; many insects are still blindly battering against it. Shortly afterwards, a few squeeze in, probably through the holes in the paper covering. Once inside, they knock against the glass lampshade, making yet more rattling sounds. One plunges in from above, and runs into the flame. It is a real flame, I think. But two or three rest panting on the paper lampshade. The lampshade was replaced only last night, its snow-white paper folded in a wave-like pattern, with a sprig of scarlet jasmine painted in one corner.

When the scarlet jasmine blossoms, the date tree will again dream the dream of the tiny pink flower; it will grow lushly and bend in an arc. I hear again the midnight laughter, and immediately cut the train of my thought.

I look at these little insects still resting on the snow-white paper—their heads big and tails small, like sunflower seeds, only half the size of a grain of wheat. How lovely and pitiable they are in their emerald hue.

I yawn, and light a cigarette, puffing out the smoke. I stare at the lamp and pay silent tribute to these dainty heroes in emerald green.

204

Poems by Leopold Sedar Senghor—1950s

Although he is better known as the president of Senegal (1960–1981), Leopold Sedar Senghor (1906–2001) was also one of the most talented and acclaimed African poets. The Francophone Senghor was educated in France and served in the French army during World War II; he was the first African member of the Academie Francaise. Senghor was famous for using the term "negritude" to mean identification with blackness in a way that transcended cultural and ethnic division and was a precursor of Afrocentrism. His poetry covers a variety of topics including traditional African themes and the problems of postcolonial Africa. How does Senghor use the poem "Black Woman" to express negritude? Does it have anything in common with the traditional tribal chant in this section? What are the main themes of these poems?

BLACK WOMAN

Naked woman, black woman
Dressed in your color[1] that is life, in your form that is beauty!
I grew up in your shadow. The softness of your hands
Shielded my eyes, and now at the height of Summer and Noon,
From the crest of a charred hilltop I discover you, Promised Land[2]   5
And your beauty strikes my heart like an eagle's lightning flash.

From *The Collected Poetry by Leopold Sedar Senghor*, trans. by Melvin Dixon. Reprinted by permission of University of Virginia Press.

1 A reference to the green vegetation of the African landscape, to which the black woman is assimilated.

2 The analogy with the Israelites in the Old Testament of the Bible confers a religious note on this poem

Naked woman, dark woman
Ripe fruit with firm flesh, dark raptures of black wine,
Mouth that gives music to my mouth
Savanna of clear horizons, savanna quivering to the fervent caress   10
Of the East Wind,[3] sculptured tom-tom, stretched drumskin
Moaning under the hands of the conqueror
Your deep contralto voice[4] is the spiritual song of the Beloved.

Naked woman, dark woman
Oil no breeze can ripple, oil soothing the thighs   15
Of athletes and the thighs of the princes of Mali[5]
Gazelle with celestial limbs, pearls are stars
Upon the night of your skin. Delight of the mind's riddles,
The reflections of red gold from your shimmering skin
In the shade of your hair, my despair   20
Lightens in the close suns of your eyes.

Naked woman, black woman
I sing your passing beauty and fix it for all Eternity
before jealous Fate reduces you to ashes to nourish the roots of life.

PRAYER TO THE MASKS

Masks![1] O Masks!
Black mask, red mask, you white-and-black masks
Masks of the four cardinal points where the Spirit blows
I greet you in silence!
And you, not the least of all, Ancestor with the lion head.[2]   5
You keep this place safe from women's laughter
And any wry, profane smiles[3]

---

3 The Harmattan, a dry, sharp wind that blows from the Sahara, northeast of Senegal, between November and April.

4 An allusion to the vocal register of Marian Anderson (1897–1993), an African American singer famous for her rendering of Negro spirituals.

5 The ancient empire of the West African savanna.

1 Representatives of the spirits of the ancestors. In African belief, the ancestors inhabit the immaterial world beyond the visible, from there offering protection to their living descendants.

2 The animal totem of Senghor's family. His father bore the Serer name Diogoye ("Lion"). A totem is an animal or plant that is closely associated with a family, sometimes considered to be a member of the family.

3 Ancestral masks are usually kept in an enclosure, a sacred place forbidden to women and uninitiated males. There is also a suggestion here that Senghor will protect them from the patronizing gaze of white people.

You exude the immortal air where I inhale
The breath of my Fathers.
Masks with faces without masks, stripped of every dimple   10
And every wrinkle
You created this portrait, my face leaning
On an altar of blank paper[4]
And in your image, listen to me!
The Africa of empires is dying—it is the agony   15
Of a sorrowful princess
And Europe, too, tied to us at the navel.
Fix your steady eyes on your oppressed children
Who give their lives like the poor man his last garment.
Let us answer "present" at the rebirth of the World   20
As white flour cannot rise without the leaven.[5]
Who else will teach rhythm to the world
Deadened by machines and cannons?
Who will sound the shout of joy at daybreak to wake orphans and the
   dead?
Tell me, who will bring back the memory of life   25
To the man of gutted hopes?
They call us men of cotton, coffee, and oil
They call us men of death.
But we are men of dance, whose feet get stronger
As we pound upon firm ground.[6]   30

LETTER TO A PRISONER

Ngom! Champion of Tyâné![1]
It is I who greet you, I your village neighbor, your heart's neighbor.
I send you my white[2] greeting like the dawn's white cry,
Over the barbed wires of hate and stupidity,
And I call you by your name and your honor.   5

---

4 An ironic reference to Senghor's Western education.

5 An ingredient (for example, yeast) in baked goods that make them rise; also a biblical
   image.

6 A reference to Antaeus, who in Greek mythology drew strength by touching the earth
   with his feet.

1 A Serer female name. The direct address with which the poem opens is a convention of
   oral poetry. Ngom, a comrade in the German prisoner-of-war camp, is addressed by his
   praise name as a champion wrestler, whose exploits in the arena bring honor to his
   beloved, Tyâné. In the poem, Senghor shares his experience of wartime Paris; to which
   he has returned after his release from the camp, with the Africans whom he left behind.

2 Wan, melancholic.

My greetings to Tamsia Dargui Ndyâye, who lives off parchments[3]
That give him a subtle tongue and long thin fingers,[4]
To Samba Dyouma, the poet, whose voice is the color of flame[5]
And whose forehead bears the signs of his destiny,
To Nyaoutt Mbodye and to Koli Ngom, your namesake   10
And to all those who, at the hour when the great arms
Are sad like branches beaten by the sun, huddle at night
Shivering around the dish of friendship.

I write you from the solitude of my precious—and closely guarded—
Residence of my black skin. Fortunate are my friends   15
Who know nothing of the icy walls and the brightly lit
Apartments that sterilize every seed on the ancestors' masks
And even the memories of love.
You know nothing of the good white bread, milk, and salt,
Or those substantial dishes that do not nourish,   20
That separate the refined from the boulevard crowds,
Sleepwalkers who have renounced their human identity
Chameleons[6] deaf to change, and their shame locks you
In your cage of solitude.
You know nothing of restaurants and swimming pools   25
Forbidden to noble black blood
And Science and Humanity erecting their police lines
At the borders of negritude.[7]
Must I shout louder? Tell me, can you hear me?
I no longer recognize white men, my brothers,   30

---

3 Implies intellectual and spiritual nourishment. *Tamsir:* a title for a learned man,
  equivalent to "doctor."

4 Of the ascetic man of letters.

5 A reference to Dyouma's golden voice and the passionate content of his lyrics. Oral
  poets sang or declaimed their compositions.

6 A reference to those French people who collaborated with the German forces of the
  Occupation.

7 Here, a collective term for the black race, in its historical circumstance the world over.

205

I Lived to Tell the Horrors
of Treblinka—1944

*Beginning in 1935, increasingly repressive legislation was passed against the Jews by
the German Reichstag. In* Mein Kampf, *Hitler laid the foundation for the Holocaust
of Jews in Europe during World War II. Jews were identified and transported to concentration camps, where they were exterminated. Communists, gypsies, Jehovah's
Witnesses, Protestants, and Catholics who opposed Hitler, as well as those considered to
be mentally or physically weak, also died in the camps. More than 10 million people
died; more than half were Eastern and Western European Jews. The following excerpt
is an anonymous account of a Treblinka survivor. How did people try to escape from the
camp? What is most horrifying about this account?*

I left Warsaw on July 27, 1942, and wandered through many towns to escape
deportation. We did not know then what "deportation" implied, but we had
a foreboding that it was synonymous with death. Thousands had already
been deported and nothing had been heard from them.

In the town of—, I was detained by Polish police and kept in a cell for four
weeks.

I failed to convince my fellow-prisoners that we should attempt to escape.
They thought it was impossible. Our guards forewarned us that ten hostages
would be shot for each Jew who escaped. We were 110 Jews, guarded by
48 gendarmes. One day we were led to the railroad station where the tracks
were blocked by cars packed with Jews. A sixtieth car was awaiting our arrival.
I was one of 84 people, men and women, crowded into this car, which had a
single window near the roof. When comrade Z and I attempted to use the
window for escape, we were prevented forcibly by others, who feared they
would be shot if we succeeded.

Arrival at Treblinka

At 7 in the morning, the train arrived at Malkina, where it was divided into six
sections, each containing ten cars. My car was shunted with nine others to a
branch line. Some 15 minutes later, we arrived at the Treblinka station; the
train continued for another five minutes, entered a forest and passed through a

From "I lived to Tell the Horrors of Treblinka," Anonymous, Feb. 1944 in *Fifty Years Ago:
Darkness before Dawn. Planning Guide for Commemoration Programs* (Washington D.C.: U.S.
Holocaust Memorial Museum, 1994), p. 158–159.

big gate. The doors opened suddenly. At each side stood guards armed with sticks and whips, shouting in Polish, Ukrainian and German, "Quick, get out!" To evade the beatings, we desperately scrambled to get ahead of one another. Twelve Ukrainians, with rifles aimed at us, reinforced the guards who, in turn, were reinforced by other men, guns in hand, holding ferocious dogs by their leashes.

We were ordered to stand in formation. An S.S. official, watch in hand, shouted an order: "I give you one minute to take your shoes and stockings off, tie them together and hold them in your hands. One minute—or you'll be shot."

We were ordered to run . . . and to return through the "corridor." The guards lashed us furiously. Some of us crumbled and died. We were barefooted and as the ground was rubble-spattered, our soles bled. We were ordered to throw our shoes into a pile of clothes, some three stories high, and to return through the "corridor."

Whippers and Whipped

Finally we were ordered to halt and the women were marched off to a square covered by a thatch roof. Later we saw them marched past, nude, toward a fenced-off area. They vanished behind a gate.

We were ordered to undress and run back and forth between the clothing pile and the spot where we had undressed—all the time through the "corridor" of madly yelling guards.

From the direction of the high fence there came a horrible moaning which lasted for a minute or two. I observed that the men with whips and sticks forming the outer wall of the "corridor," were Jews themselves—derelict, half-mad individuals, prodded by Ukrainians who pressed guns into their backs.

When we again reached the clothes-pile, I jumped onto it, grabbed a pair of pants and a jacket, picked up a cane and forced my way among the guards forming the "corridor."

With all the others, I shouted hysterically and waved my cane. S.S. men, standing to the side, watching the sadistic orgy with satisfaction, pulled out all well-built Jews.

"Hospital"—Nazi Style

At the sound of a sharp whistle, we were rushed to the train, where we formed two rows at the doors of each car. Ten more cars had arrived from one of which an old Jew tumbled. An S.S. man ordered one of the guards to take him to "the hospital." Then I, too, was ordered to take an old man to "the hospital."

I did not know what was meant by "the hospital," but I followed the first guard. We walked toward an area from which thick smoke rose, and stopped at a pit ten meters in width and ten meters in depth. I could see smouldering human bodies at the bottom. I followed the motions of the "veterans." We undressed the old Jews and seated them at the edge of the pit, their feet dangling. Some more were brought here. Ukrainian guards whipped them once and immediately they dropped into the smouldering pit.

I learned that the veterans had been here for some three weeks, others for no more than three or four days. Every morning, one or two of the beaters' group were led away, never to be seen again.

The fenced-off enclosure from which came the frequently horrifying moans, followed by a dreadful silence, was known as "the court of death." Two Jewish youths, employed as gravediggers, escaped from there and sought to lose themselves among us. They told us that there were eight barracks with room for 7,000.

All who arrived on the trains, excepting those who were assigned as "beaters," were led into the barracks and told they would receive baths and showers. The barracks were sealed and gas let in. Those outside waiting their turn soon grasped what was happening and sought to stampede. But then S.S. men and Ukrainians with ferocious dogs appeared and kept them back. The doors were sealed for 15 minutes at a time, and when they opened, all who had been locked in were dead.

Five hundred men were assigned to the one task of removing the corpses and throwing them into the burning pit. Five hundred Jews—mental derelicts, servants of death, half-dead themselves. There were at least ten suicides daily among them. All bore the stench of carrion, because of their work.

In the far corner of our yard there was a hut in which lived the essential laborers—carpenters, locksmiths, electricians, tailors—and 12 musicians. Brought here from Warsaw some months before the official deportations began they had constructed a camp and were still employed at such labors. They wore yellow patches on their clothing and were kept separate from us. The musicians were assigned to play for the Nazis at their orgies.

I was at Treblinka for four days, during which Jews arrived from Holland, France, Vienna and all parts of Poland, only to disappear behind the fence of "the court [of] death."

Blueprint for Escape

Escape during the day was impossible, for we were under constant guard from the moment we were marched out at 6 A.M. until 7 P.M., when we were locked in again.

We decided that we must find some way to remain outside the barracks at night. One evening, at 6 P.M., I tied my comrades into a bundle of clothing and placed them on the pile. One who had refused to escape himself tied me into a bundle, as I had done with my comrades, and placed me on the hill. After 6 P.M., silence settled on the camp. We disentangled ourselves and with the pressure of our bodies, we dug a big pit in the clothes-pile in order to be able to see without being seen. Every half hour the guard passed the clothing hill, and frequently the spotlight was turned on it. We were able to tell the time by the change of the watch.

Evading the spotlight, we crept slowly toward the pit, using its vapors, rising thicker at night than during the day, as a smoke-screen. We faced the first barbed-wire fence. The soil was soft under it and we dug with our hands and knives and finally passed through. We found ourselves in a forest, walked straight ahead and soon faced another barbed-wire fence. As the soil here was hard, we could not dig, and were compelled to climb the barbed wire.

Bruised and cut, we got across. Soon we faced a third barbed-wire barrier. We climbed this one, too.

We reached Warsaw on the morning of Succoth. I obtained the necessary "Aryan" documents and struck out for the border of a neighboring country. I made two attempts to cross the border. The first attempt failed. After obtaining from me 20,000 zlotas, approximately $400, the first group of smugglers left me stranded in a forest. But I tried again. In February, 1943, I was finally taken across [the border.]

206

One Day in the Life of Ivan Denisovich by Alexander Solzhenitsyn—1962

Russian intellectual and writer Alexander Solzhenitsyn (1918–) served in the Red Army during World War II. In 1945, because of his criticism of Stalin, he was sentenced to life imprisonment in Siberia. He was released after Stalin's death 11 years later. He then began teaching high school and writing about his experiences in Siberia. During a period of political liberalization in the Soviet Union, One Day in the Life of Ivan Denisovich *was published and became an international success. However, after a reversal of Soviet policy, Solzhenitsyn was forbidden to publish any more of his work. Nevertheless, a number of his novels were smuggled out of the Soviet Union and received much critical commendation in the West; Solzhenitsyn received the Nobel Prize for Literature in 1970. However, he was accused of treason in 1973 and exiled from the Soviet Union. He recently returned to Russia from exile in the United States. The following excerpt provides a realistic portrayal of life in the labor camps of Siberia. Why*

From *One Day in the Life of Ivan Denisovich* by Alexander Solzhenitsyn, trans. by Ralph Parker. Translation copyright © 1963 by E.P. Dutton and Victor Gollancz, Ltd. Copyright © renewed 1991 by Penguin USA and Victor Gollancz Ltd. Used by permission of Penguin Group (USA), Inc.

was the job of cook favored in the camps? How did the prisoners try to obtain more food? How did the prisoners try to maintain their dignity and humanity in the camps?

Outside the moon shone brighter than ever. The lamps seemed to be paler now. The barracks cast deep shadows. The door to the mess hall lay beyond a broad porch with four steps. Now the porch too lay in shadows. But above it a small lamp was swaying, and creaking dismally in the cold. The light it cast was rainbow-hued, from the frost maybe, or the dirt on the glass.

The camp commandant had issued yet another strict order: the squads were to enter the mess hall in double file. To this he added: on reaching the steps they were to stay there and not climb onto the porch; they were to form up in fives and remain standing until the mess orderly gave them the go-ahead.

The post of mess orderly was firmly held by "the Limper." Because of his lameness he'd managed to get classed as disabled, but he was a hefty son-of-a-bitch. He'd got himself a birch club, and standing on the porch would hit anyone who came up the steps without his say-so. No, not anyone. He was smart, and could tell, even in the dark, when it was better to let a man alone—anyone who might give him as good as he got. He hit the down-and-outs. Once he hit Shukhov.

He was called an orderly. But, looking closer into it, he was a real prince—he palled around with the cooks.

Today all the squads may have turned up together or there may have been delay in getting things in order, but there was quite a crowd on the porch. Among them was the Limper, with his assistant. The mess chief himself was there too. They were handling the crowd without guards—the bruisers.

The mess chief was a fat pig with a head like a pumpkin and a broad pair of shoulders. He was bursting with energy and when he walked he seemed nothing but a lot of jerks, with springs for arms and legs. He wore a white lambskin hat without a number on it, finer than any civilian's. And his waistcoat was lambskin to match, with a number on it, true, but hardly bigger than a postage stamp. He bore no number at all on his back. He respected no one and all the zeks were afraid of him. He held the lives of thousands in his hands. Once they'd tried to beat him up but all the cooks—a prize bunch of thugs they were—had leaped to his defense.

Shukhov would be in hot water if the 104th had already gone in. The Limper knew everyone by sight and, with his chief present, wouldn't think of letting a man in with the wrong squad; he'd make a point of putting the finger on him.

Prisoners had been known to slip in behind the Limper's back by climbing over the porch railings. Shukhov had done it too. But tonight, under the chief's very nose, that was out of the question—he'd bust you so bad that you'd only just manage to drag yourself off to the doctor.

Get along to the porch and see whether, among all those identical black coats, the 104th was still there.

He got there just as the men began shoving (what could they do? it would soon be time to turn in) as though they were storming a stronghold—the first step, the second, the third, the fourth. Got there! They poured onto the porch.

"Stop, you fuckers," the Limper shouted and raised his stick at the men in front. "Get back or I'll bash your heads in."

"Form fives, blockheads," he shouted. "How many times have I told you I'll let you in when I'm ready?"

"Twenty-seventh," the Limper called, "go ahead."

The 27th bounded up and made a dash for the door, and the rest surged after them. Shukhov, among them, was shoving with all his might. The porch quivered, and the lamp overhead protested shrilly.

"What again, you shits?" the Limper shouted in rage. Down came his stick, on a shoulder, on a back, pushing the men off, toppling one after another.

Again he cleared the steps.

From below Shukhov saw Pavlo at the Limper's side. It was he who led the squad to the mess hall—Tiurin wouldn't lower himself by joining in the hullabaloo.

"Form fives, hundred and fourth," Pavlo called from the porch. "Make way for them, friends."

Friends—just see them, making way, fuck 'em.

"Let me through, you in front. That's my squad," Shukhov grunted, shoving against a back.

The man would gladly have done so but others were squeezing him from every side.

The crowd heaved, pushing away so that no one could breathe. To get its stew. Its lawful stew.

Shukhov tried something else. He grasped the porch rail on his left, got his arms around a pillar, and heaved himself up. He kicked someone's knee and caught a blow in the ribs; a few curses, but he was through. He planted a foot on the edge of the porch floor, close to the top step, and waited. Some of his pals who were already there give him a hand.

The mess chief walked to the door and looked back.

"Come on, Limper, send in two more squads."

"One hundred and fourth," shouted the Limper. "Where d'you think *you're* crawling, shit?"

He slammed a man from another squad on the back of the neck with his stick.

"One hundred and fourth," shouted Pavlo, leading in his men.

"Whew!" gasped Shukhov in the mess hall. And, without waiting for Pavlo's instructions, he started looking for free trays.

The mess hall seemed as usual, with clouds of steam curling in through the door and the men sitting shoulder to shoulder—like seeds in a sunflower. Others pushed their way through the tables, and others were carrying loaded trays. Shukhov had grown used to it all over the years and his sharp eyes had noticed that S 208 had only five bowls on the tray he was carrying. This meant that it was the last tray-load for his squad. Otherwise the tray would have been full.

He went up to the man and whispered in his ear: "After you with that tray."

"Someone's waiting for it at the counter. I promised. . . ."

"Let him wait, the lazy bastard."

They came to an understanding.

S 208 carried his tray to the table and unloaded the bowls. Shukhov immediately grabbed it. At that moment the man it had been promised to ran up and tried to grab it. But he was punier than Shukhov. Shukhov shoved him off with the tray—what the hell are you pulling for?—and threw him against a post. Then putting the tray under his arm, he trotted off to the serving window.

Pavlo was standing in the line there, worried because there was no empty tray. He was delighted to see Shukhov. He pushed the man ahead of him out of the way: "Why are you standing here? Can't you see I've got a tray?"

Look, there was Gopchik—with another tray.

"They were arguing," he said with a laugh, "and I grabbed it."

Gopchik will do well. Give him another three years—he has still to grow up—and he'll become nothing less than a breadcutter. He's fated for it.

Pavlo told him to hand over the second of the trays to Yermolayev, a hefty Siberian who was serving a ten-year stretch, like Shukhov, for being caught by the Germans; then sent him to keep an eye on any table where the men might be finishing. Shukhov put his tray down and waited.

"One hundred and fourth," announced Pavlo at the counter.

In all there were five of these counters: three for serving regular food, one for zeks on special diets (ulcer victims, and bookkeeping personnel, as a favor), and one for the return of dirty dishes (that's where the dish-lickers gathered, sparring with one another). The counters were low—about waist level. The cooks themselves were out of sight; only their hands, and the ladles, could be seen.

The cook's hands were white and well cared for, but huge and hairy: a boxer's hands, not a cook's. He took a pencil and made a note on the wall—he kept his list there.

The cook took an enormous ladle and stirred, stirred, stirred. The soup kettle had just been refilled, almost up to the brim, and steam poured from it. Replacing the huge ladle with a smaller one he began serving the stew in twenty-ounce portions. He didn't go deep.

"One, two, three, four . . ."

Some of the bowls had been filled while the stuff from the bottom of the kettle hadn't yet settled after the stirring, and some were duds—nothing but soup. Shukhov made a mental note of which was which. He put ten bowls on his tray and carried them off. Gopchik waved from the second row of posts.

"Over here, Ivan Denisovich, over here."

No horsing around with bowls of stew. Shukhov was careful not to stumble. He kept his throat busy too.

"Hey you, H 920. Gently, uncle. Out of the way, my boy."

It was hard enough, in a crowd like this, to carry a single bowl without slopping it. He was carrying ten. Just the same, he put the tray down safely, on the end of the table that Gopchik had cleared. No splashes. He managed, too, to maneuver the tray so that the two bowls with the thickest stew were just opposite the place he was about to sit down in.

Yermolayev brought another ten bowls. Gopchik ran off and came back with Pavlo, the last four in their hands.

Kilgas brought the bread tray. Tonight they were being fed in accordance with the work they had done. Some got six ounces, some nine, and Shukhov twelve. He took a piece with a crust for himself, and six ounces from the middle of the loaf for Tsezar.

Now from all over the mess hall Shukhov's squad began streaming up, to collect their supper and eat it where they could. As he handed out the bowls, there were two things he had to take care of: he had to remember whom he'd served, and he had to watch out for the tray—and for his own corner of it. (He put his spoon into a bowl—one of the "thick" ones. Reserved, that meant.) Fetiukov was among the first to arrive. But he soon walked off, figuring there was nothing to be scrounged that particular evening; better to wander around the mess, hunting for leftovers (if someone doesn't finish his stew and pushes his bowl back, there are always people hustling to pounce on it, like vultures).

The empty trays were handed in. Pavlo sat there with his double helping, Shukhov with his two bowls. And now they had nothing more to say to one another—the sacred moments had come.

Shukhov took off his hat and laid it on his knees. He tasted one bowl, he tasted the other. Not bad—there was some fish in it. Generally, the evening stew was much thinner than at breakfast: if they're to work, prisoners must be fed in the morning; in the evening they'll go to sleep anyway.

He dug in. First he only drank the broth, drank and drank. As it went down, filling his whole body with warmth, all his guts began to flutter inside him at their meeting with the stew. Goo-ood! There it comes, that brief moment for which a zek lives.

And now Shukhov complained about nothing: neither about the length of his stretch, nor about the length of the day, nor about their swiping another Sunday. This was all he thought about now: we'll survive. We'll stick it out, God willing, till it's over.

He drained the hot soup from both bowls, and then tipped what was left in the second into the first, scraping it clean with his spoon. That set his mind at ease. Now he didn't have to think about the second and keep an eye or a hand on it.

Now that he could look freely he glanced at his neighbors' bowls. The one on his left was little more than water. The dirty snakes. The tricks they play! And on their fellow zeks.

He began to eat the cabbage with what was left of the soup. A potato had found its way into one of the bowls. A medium-sized spud, frostbitten, hard and sweetish. There wasn't much fish, just a few stray bits of bare backbone. But you must chew every bone, every fin, to suck the juice out of them, for the juice is healthy. It takes time, of course, but he was in no hurry to go anywhere. Today was a red-letter day for him; two helpings for dinner, two helpings for supper. Everything else could wait.

Except, maybe, that visit to the Lett for tobacco. None might be left in the morning.

He ate his supper without bread. A double helping *and* bread—that was going too far. The belly is a demon. It doesn't remember how well you treated it yesterday; it'll cry out for more tomorrow.

He ate up his stew without taking much interest in what was happening around him. No need for that: he wasn't on the lookout for extras, he was eating his own lawful portions. All the same, he noticed that when the fellow opposite got up a tall old man—U 81—sat down in his place.

He'd been told that this old man had spent years without number in camps and prisons, and that he hadn't benefited from a single amnesty. Whenever one ten-year stretch had run out they shoved another onto him right away.

Now Shukhov looked closely at the man. He held himself straight—the other zeks sat all hunched up—and looked as if he'd put something extra on the bench to sit on. There was nothing left to crop on his head: his hair had dropped out long since—the result of high living, no doubt. His eyes didn't dart after everything going on in the mess hall. He kept them fixed in an unseeing gaze at some spot over Shukhov's head. His worn wooden spoon dipped rhythmically into the thin stew, but instead of lowering his head to the bowl like everybody else, he raised the spoon high to his lips. He'd lost all his teeth and chewed his bread with iron gums. All life had drained out of his face but it had been left, not sickly or feeble, but hard and dark like carved stone. And by his hands, big and cracked and blackened, you could see that he'd had little opportunity of doing soft jobs. But he wasn't going to give in, oh no! *He* wasn't going to put his nine ounces on the dirty, bespattered table—he put it on a well-washed bit of rag.

Shukhov came out with a full belly. He felt pleased with himself and decided that, although it was close to curfew, he'd run over to the Lett all the same. Instead of taking the bread to his barracks, he strode to Barracks 7.

The moon was high—clean and white, as if chiseled out of the sky. It was clear up there and there were some stars out—the brightest of them. But he had even less time for star-gazing than for watching people in the mess hall. One thing he realized—the frost was no milder. One of the civilians had said, and this had been passed on, that it was likely to drop to −25° in the night, and as low as −40° toward morning.